# THE TAO OF THE WEST

In this book, J.J. Clarke shows us how Taoist texts, ideas and practices have been assimilated within a whole range of Western interests and agendas. We see how Chinese thinkers such as Lao-tzu and Chuang tzu, along with practices such as *feng-shui* and *tai chi*, have been used as key Western inspirations in religion, philosophy, ethics, politics, ecology and health. *The Tao of the West* not only provides a fascinating introduction to Taoism, but it offers a timely insight into the history of the West's encounter with this ancient tradition and into the issues arising from inter-cultural dialogue. Anyone interested in understanding Taoism and the influence it has had on the West will welcome and embrace this book.

**J.J. Clarke** has taught philosophy at McGill University, Montreal, and at the University of Singapore, and is currently Reader in History of Ideas at Kingston University, UK. He is the author of *In Search of Jung, Jung and Eastern Thought* and *Oriental Enlightenment: The Encounter Between Asian and Western Thought*, all published by Routledge.

# THE TAO OF THE WEST

## Western transformations of Taoist thought

*J.J. Clarke*

London and New York

First published 2000
by Routledge
11 New Fetter Lane, London EC4P 4EE

Simultaneously published in the USA and Canada
by Routledge
29 West 35th Street, New York, NY 10001

*Routledge is an imprint of the Taylor & Francis Group*

© 2000 J.J. Clarke

Typeset in Times by Taylor & Francis Books Ltd
Printed and bound in Great Britain by TJ International Ltd, Padstow Cornwall

*British Library Cataloguing in Publication Data*
A catalogue record for this book is available from the British Library

*Library of Congress Cataloging in Publication Data*
A catalog record for this book has been requested

ISBN 0–415–20619–7 (hbk)
ISBN 0–415–20620–0 (pbk)

# CONTENTS

CONTENTS

# PREFACE

What is needed is...new philosophers. The moral earth, too, is round. The moral earth, too, has its antipodes. The antipodes, too, have the right to exist. There is another world to discover – and more than one! On board ship, philosophers!...the sea lies open again; perhaps there has never yet been such an 'open sea'.

(Nietzsche: *The Gay Science*)

Western scholars have in fact not needed much encouragement to explore this 'open sea'. Over the past five hundred years we have witnessed, not only a huge expansion of European power and culture across the whole face of the globe, but at the same time an intense effort of investigation, translation and analysis which has opened to the European mind the great intellectual and religious traditions of Asia, and which in all sorts of ways has entered into Western thought and imagination. This extraordinary expansion of horizons, perhaps unprecedented in human history, has in recent years begun to be the object of close and highly contested scrutiny in the shape of orientalist and postcolonial studies. These latter explorations have often perceived the 'open sea' as having been an arena for conquest, for the imposition of Nietzsche's 'will to power', and have interpreted the West's understanding of the East as a form of 'colonised' knowledge, an expropriation which has served to enhance the power of the West over Asia. While my own explorations have made use of this compass, I have charted a somewhat different course. Though taking full account of the fact of empire and colonial expropriation as the necessary underpinning of any such investigations, I have at the same time given much greater attention to the ways in which Western philosophical and religious thinking has been shaped by ideas emanating from the East. It has become almost a convention to see the West's understanding of the East – even this very distinction – as a European construct, and indeed the process of construction and reconstruction constitutes a central focus of this work, but what is not always given full attention is the pervasive impact of this on the Western tradition and on the multifarious ways in which the Orient, albeit often

PREFACE

gravely misrepresented, has become woven into and helped to shape the fabric of European thought and culture.

This study is an investigation within the field of history of ideas, specifically of Western ideas. It constitutes the third part of a trilogy of works. *Oriental Enlightenment* traced the history of orientalist ideas in broad terms and examined both their place within the Western intellectual tradition and the issues cast up by the encounter between East and West. In *Jung and Eastern Thought*, I focussed attention on the orientalist writings of one individual thinker whose work has been the source of much influence and controversy. In the present book I have concentrated on one single tradition, namely Daoism, in its relationship with Western thought. Here, as in other Asian traditions, the full extent of its impact on the West has not always been adequately acknowledged within the various disciplines, and as with Buddhism and Hinduism before it, its recent emergence into European consciousness has a history which demands fuller exploration. At the present time, Daoism is experiencing something of a renaissance in the West similar to that experienced earlier by Buddhism and Hinduism, an extraordinary burst of orientalist enthusiasm which ranges from the scholarly to the popular, from the close study of texts and traditions which have been half-hidden to the world outside China until recently, to the rapidly growing interest in Daoist meditation, health and sexual practices.

The chapter headings reflect, therefore, not so much the structure of Daoist thought as such but rather the areas of interest that spring from the West's own reflections on Daoism, built around such familiar categories as science, ethics, religion, mysticism and philosophy. Even Chapter 2, which includes a brief summary of the history of Daoism in China, raises the question 'what is Daoism?' from within a specifically European problematic. Chapter 3 offers a survey of the history of Western interpretations of Daoist teachings and texts. And the final chapter reflects back on the critical issues raised in the preceding text, and looks forward speculatively to Daoism's role in the global culture of the twenty-first century.

Although this book takes Western thought as the focus of its study, it also seeks to convey to the reader something of the nature and style of Daoism, its history and philosophy, its writings and spiritual practices. At the same time it does not seek to disguise my own admiration for this ancient Chinese philosophy of life. I have long been attracted by its attitude of oneness between the human and natural worlds, and its affirmation of life, good health and vitality, and have been drawn to its sense of stillness and silence, its sense of spontaneous simplicity and its gentle anarchism. I hope that readers will gain in understanding of and come to share my respect for this unique ancient tradition.

In the course of my research, I have also come to appreciate the extent to which Daoism has begun to penetrate different aspects of modern life, from lofty spiritual quest to everyday matters of health and diet, its relevance to contemporary concerns about the environment, peace and war, gender issues and life in modern societies. Whether it offers anything like a complete philosophy of life or a new religious cult for our spiritually hungry world I do not know, but increasingly in all sorts of ways it speaks to our world, while yet remaining obdurately and compellingly distinct.

I have approached the West's own enthusiasm for this tradition in a critical and scholarly spirit, laying before the reader a wide historical panorama of ideas and texts, and drawing out the serious debates and critical differences which this particular form of intercultural dialogue has inevitably spawned. There is no place in such a study as this for blissful adulation of the 'mystical Orient', therefore, although at the same time such orientalist attitudes will themselves be the objects of our attention. Like other oriental traditions, Daoism has been misunderstood and misappropriated in a variety of ways, and like China itself has been the object of both the best and worst kinds of free-ranging fantasy. The story of the emergence of 'The Tao of the West' is therefore one of enlightened encounter and creative symbiosis, while at the same time revealing Europe's insatiable appetite for antipodean plunder.

Nietzsche's 'other world' was in many ways more distant and alien than ours is to us, and the seas that separated his own European civilisation from its various antipodes have shrunk under the globalising impact of huge social, economic and technological transformations. The Other that in Nietzsche's day was still remote and enigmatic has in our own times become familiar and has established a presence in our midst, even within our very selves. Yet its otherness remains, and refuses the universalist demands of cultural uniformity. Daoism, I hope I will be able to show, still manages to retain that sense of otherness, a refusal to conform, confronting our complacent orthodoxies with its own self-evident 'right to exist'. In many ways both our academic and popular outlooks remain largely Eurocentric in spite of the seemingly inexorable march of globalisation and multiculturalism, and I hope that this book will be a contribution to a truly 'open sea' of learning, mutual understanding, and respect across cultural boundaries, and an encouragement to productive intercultural dialogue.

Respect for this Other world means, for a start, using China's own preferred method of romanising its language, and I have therefore adopted throughout the standard Pinyin method, rather than the older Wade–Giles system. Exceptions are: where the Wade–Giles and other earlier systems are used in direct quotation; the name 'Confucius', which is too deeply embedded in our language now to be transposed into 'Kongzi' or 'Kong Fuzi'; and the cover material where Wade–Giles is also preferred on account of its greater familiarity. An appendix has been included which will enable readers more conversant with the older system to transpose into Wade–Giles some of the Chinese terms used repeatedly in this book.

PREFACE

In my scholarly voyages, I have received guidance, encouragement and criticism from a number of friends and colleagues, and I owe especial thanks to Ray Billington, Chris Bloor, Jill Boezalt, Andrew Burniston, Jane Chamberlain, Bob Clarke, David Hall, Jean Hardy, John Hope-Mason, Stephen Karcher, Terry Sullivan and Gretl Wright. I also wish to thank Kingston University for giving me a semester's sabbatical leave in order to complete the work.

J.J. Clarke

# 1

# 'THE WAY THAT CAN BE TOLD'

## Introduction

### Orientations and disorientations

The Daoist philosopher Zhuangzi tells us in a famous passage how he dreamed that he was a butterfly but, on waking, was unable to decide whether he was Zhuangzi dreaming that he was a butterfly or a butterfly dreaming that he was Zhuangzi. Has he indeed awoken, he wonders, or is he still dreaming? Can he even tell the difference? 'There's no telling whether the man who speaks now is the waker or the dreamer', he muses. The sense of what is real or unreal, even the very distinction itself, becomes problematic for him. In the great transformation of things, dream and reality are endlessly confused (Graham 1981: 61, 91).

The West's encounters with the ancient civilisation of China have often betrayed this sort of confused ambivalence. Western images of the remote kingdom of Cathay have frequently exhibited a dreamlike quality, begetting mythical visions of the lands and the traditions of China that are half real, half fantasy, exotic displacements for unconscious needs, reveries at once both disturbing and enchanting, both threateningly obscure yet also compellingly seductive. This semi-dreamworld has often had the impossibly idealised character of a Shangri-La, a spiritual utopia that sets our own unsatisfactory reality in sharp relief and which furnishes us with a mirror in which to reflect on our own shortcomings. Yet at the same time, it is a world of darksome menace summed up in portentous phrases such as 'yellow peril' or 'oriental despotism', a land of eternal stagnation that points an instructive contrast to the dynamic, progressive West. In the European mind China has long been what Zhang Longxi has called 'the ultimate Other', a myth and symbol of cultural difference that in various contradictory ways has reflected the West's own inner tensions and contradictions, a dreamworld in which it has been able to enact 'all sorts of fantasies, philosophical speculations, and utopian idealizations' (1998: 20, 33). Even before Marco Polo's expedition in the thirteenth century, a mythical image of China had formed in the minds of Europeans, an archetype of the exotic

1

and fascinating. Such images were destined to be shaped and reshaped over the following centuries, and had a remarkably protean quality which, from the Renaissance onwards, not only served popular or literary needs but began to feed the West's political, religious and philosophical imagination.[1]

*Daoist* ideas and traditions have inevitably been caught up in this volatile phantasm of China, though its importance in Chinese thought and culture has often been obscured. The commanding presence of Confucianism and its identification with the ruling orthodoxy in China has meant that we often see Daoism through Confucian eyes. It is the latter that have tended to dominate Western consciousness of China, and the comparison between the West's perception of these two traditions is revealing. Whereas Confucianism has occupied an eminent, if frequently mythologised, place in the Western mind, in many respects the definitive symbol of Chineseness, Daoism has represented, as one scholar puts it, a 'censured chapter of Chinese history', or even, according to another, 'the least understood, the most commonly ignored and maligned, of all the major religions of the world', and according to yet another a tradition typically 'written off wholesale as superstition...interpreted as pure religious mysticism and poetry' (Lagerwey 1987: 274; Girardot in Schipper 1993: xvi; Needham 1956: 86).[2] Where Confucianism has at various periods been rated in the West as an enlightened form of humanism, Daoism has often been dismissed as, at best, a vague if harmless nature-loving mysticism, a form of quietism, characterised by the search for inner peace at the expense of serviceable social and political precept or practical moral guidance. As a set of religious teachings, it has been associated with a number of fanciful activities such as flying though the air, living on dew, indefinitely prolonged orgasm, and the search for the elixir of immortality. Even Chinese intelligentsia have in recent times looked upon Daoism as an embarrassment and as a mark of China's underdevelopment in relation to the West, a humiliating blemish on China's record which must be erased in the drive towards modernisation.

There are signs that in the West we have at last begun to awaken from these jaundiced reveries. A palpable change of attitude has taken place in recent decades, one which affects not only attitudes towards Daoism but also towards China as a whole and towards the other great civilisations and belief systems of Asia. In broad terms, we have witnessed a transformation in the past century from an imperial age in which Eurocentric attitudes and values enjoyed world ascendancy, to one of profound challenge to the dominance of Western power and ideas. In the recent past there has emerged a manifestly greater openness and an enhanced permeability between the traditions of East and West which has led to an intensively critical examination of traditional Western misconceptions of the East. Hegel's notorious pronouncement that 'The history of the world travels from East to West, for Europe is absolutely the end of history, Asia the beginning' (1944: 103), has certainly cast a long shadow over the West's understanding of Eastern thought in general, and the cultural and philosophical traditions of Asia continue to be viewed by many as locked in their past, objects of little more than historical interest. Nevertheless a counter-movement has been under way for some time which has drawn Eastern ideas and practices with ever-increasing intimacy into the orbit of contemporary culture and debate, and, following the earlier emergence into favour of Hinduism and Buddhism, Daoism has begun to penetrate Western consciousness.

Daoism's rising profile in the West is evident across a whole spectrum of domains ranging from the popular to the scholarly, from the spiritual to the philosophical. At one end of the spectrum can be observed the growing interest in such arts as *taijiqan* and *feng-shui*, and the way in which Daoist terms such as *dao* and *yin/yang* have begun to enter common vocabulary, and Daoist ideas such as 'going with the flow of nature' or 'unblocking one's energy' have acquired fashionable cachet. We have witnessed, too, a flood of books on Daoist and related matters, whether pertaining to health, sexuality, ecology or simply the arrangement of one's domestic furniture. Over the past few years, more than a hundred titles of the form '*The Tao of...*' have been published, covering an extraordinarily diverse range of topics including physics, psychology, leadership, business, diet, baseball, relationships, women, Jesus, Islam, and even Muhammad Ali. It is easy to ridicule this genre as so much rubbish, and one scholar has expressed his concern that the bizarre theories that this peculiarly Western obsession has given rise to are bound to render Daoism 'more obscure and unfathomable than before' (Palmer 1991: 110). But this new literary fashion, along with the burgeoning interest in Daoist health techniques, represents a cultural phenomenon which tells us much about our contemporary concerns and anxieties, and is undoubtedly an expression of a growing preoccupation with self-cultivation and the quest for alternative means of personal and spiritual fulfilment. A common thread running through many of these practices and writings is the search for a religious dimension to life that goes beyond traditional organised religions and doctrines, and for a form of spirituality which offers a sense of harmony and psychological wholeness by drawing together mental, emotional and physical aspects of life. Along with a number of other movements, Daoism is proving increasingly attractive to people who seek a form of spirituality and self-fulfilment which focuses on the experience of embodied existence within the living world rather than on a transcendent world beyond, and which offers a way of discovering meaning through reconnecting human life with its roots in nature.

At the opposite end of the spectrum, there has taken place a veritable revolution in Daoist scholarship over the past fifty years or so. Since the pioneering work of Marcel Granet, Henri Maspero and Joseph Needham in the middle decades of the twentieth century, a growing band of orientalists has been engaged in the labour of translating, interpreting and commenting on the large corpus of Daoist texts, and in the detailed analysis of the intellectual and cultural evolution of Daoist ideas and institutions. This in turn has had wide ramifications, for it is largely thanks to this scholarly revolution that philosophers have now begun to give serious attention to the implications of Daoist writings, and that students of comparative religion have started to investigate Daoism as a religion of world stature. Areas as diverse as cosmology and politics, alchemy and ethics, and teachings in such fields as mysticism and meditation have all been the subject of extensive investigation, and the practice, symbolic meaning and sociological significance of the Daoist liturgical tradition have been closely investigated for the first time. Moreover, the realisation of the central and pervasive role that Daoism has played in the evolution of Chinese society has immeasurably enriched our understanding of Chinese history and culture in general.

At various points in the middle of the spectrum that spans both popular and scholarly concerns, we can also identify a whole range of academic and intellectual interests which have begun to take aspects of Daoist thinking seriously in novel ways, parallel in many respects with earlier enthusiasms for Buddhism and Hinduism. Here the driving force is not so much the demands of historical scholarship but rather the exploitation of Eastern ideas as the means for confronting and illuminating certain key contemporary issues. A number of thinkers has sought quite explicitly to draw on Daoism in this way: Martin Buber, C.G. Jung and Martin Heidegger, to mention a few distinguished examples from earlier in the twentieth century, have all engaged with Daoist ideas as a way of confronting and clarifying issues of immediate concern to them. More recently, thinkers as disparate as Joseph Needham and Fritjof Capra have pressed Daoism into the service of their own science-related projects, and more recently still American philosophers such as David Hall and Chad Hansen have begun to weave Daoist ideas into the very latest postmodernist debates. Academic philosophy's reflection on these historical transformations has indeed been slow to materialise, and for the most part Chinese thought has been excluded from Western philosophical discourse. Nevertheless, there have been some promising signs of a widening of sympathies in the field of comparative philosophy over the past half-century, and, as we shall see, there is evidence of an increasing willingness to engage creatively with ideas from the Daoist tradition.

The aim of this book, then, is to give a broad historical and critical account of these emerging Western encounters with Daoism, tracing their historical genealogies and engaging with the range of contemporary debates that has arisen therefrom. It aims to give a picture of the overall shape of these intercultural engagements, one which is sufficiently detailed to provide a sense of their intellectual and cultural significance without burdening the reader with an exhaustive chronicle. In 'telling the story', I will need to examine the variety of ways in which this ancient tradition, apparently so alien and so 'other', has begun to enter into the spiritual and intellectual life of the West, and to become part of the complex ideological fabric of contemporary global culture. While, in the spirit of Daoism, I will avoid engaging in aggressive polemics, my aim is also to convey something of the intellectual vigour of this particular intercultural dialogue, and hence both to outline the debates that have surrounded Daoism's entry into Western culture and to engage with the philosophical spirit of the argument where this seems called for. The very process of intercultural communication itself raises important philosophical questions such as those concerning the universality of reason, values and experience, questions about cultural difference, and broad political issues relating to Western imperialist hegemony in Asia. These along with other issues will inevitably demand attention as our historical project unfolds.

This work is primarily, therefore, a study in the *history of ideas*, an investigation into the actual historical passage of ideas from East to West, and into the social and cultural processes that facilitated this passage. Thus, by examining a wide selection of Western writers and movements that have explicitly engaged with Daoist thought, and by placing these within appropriate historical contexts, the book will seek to uncover the ways in which Daoism has entered Western consciousness, and to examine the methods by which ideas and texts from this ancient Chinese tradition have been selected, translated, interpreted, reconstituted and assimilated within the framework of modern Western thought.

It is also largely a study in the history of *Western* ideas. The interest of this book in Daoist thought, whether as an intellectual system or as a cultural phenomenon, is therefore an indirect one. Some initiation will of course be needed into the historical origins and background of this ancient tradition in China itself and into some of the basic Daoist concepts and teachings, particularly in view of the fact that they are likely to be unfamiliar to many Western readers. To this end, a brief outline of Daoist history in China is offered in Chapter 2, and at appropriate points in subsequent chapters the various elements of Daoist teaching are explained. Thus, while this book is not designed as an introduction to Daoism, it will, in the course of examining the Western assimilation of Daoism, provide the reader with a broad understanding of its history and an initiation to its teachings.

This will entail taking a wide cultural perspective on Daoism in its native land. One of the important results of recent research is that we are only now beginning to appreciate the richness, originality and extent of the Daoist contribution to Chinese culture at all levels, to its religious practice, whether public or private, to the arts of painting, poetry and landscape gardening, to the birth and development of Chinese science, to the evolution of its medical ideas and practices, to its political thought and practice. In the words of a leading French sinologist, Isabelle Robinet, Daoism:

> has reabsorbed and digested, regathered and amalgamated, and preserved and organized various strands of Chinese culture...all without ever abandoning its own identity and coherence. It has thus become a constantly operating force coordinating and synthesizing Chinese traditions...[and] has impregnated all of Chinese civilization, penetrating ways of thinking in China in all kinds of ways.
>
> (Robinet 1997: 23)

And to this should be added the influence of Daoism over the centuries on China's neighbours – Cambodia, Korea, Japan and Vietnam – and more recently on the Chinese diaspora in Asia and beyond.[3]

The main target of this work, though, remains the Western appropriation of that tradition rather than Daoism in its Asian context, and this means that it must take into account recent critical debates concerning orientalist and postcolonial discourse in general. Through the writings of Edward Said and others, we have become acutely aware of the highly problematic nature of the dreamworld that Westerners have fallen into in their quest for 'Oriental enlightenment', and of the way in which Western knowledge of Asia, however scientific in intent, has often involved the construction of the 'Orient', not only as an imaginative distortion but as an ideology, as an expression and reinforcement of Western power over Asian peoples. Said has traced out important links between the discourse of orientalism in its various manifestations on the one side, and imperialism and colonial mastery on the other, making use of Foucault's discourse analysis whereby the strategies of orientalists are seen as embedded in the whole process of discipline and control by Western colonial power. Orientalism, in its affirmation of the ideological fiction of the 'West versus the rest', has, according to Said, played a role in creating a Western 'nexus of knowledge and power' whereby 'European culture gained in strength and identity by setting itself off against the Orient'. In broad terms, orientalism is 'a structure erected in the thick of imperial contest whose dominant wing is represented and elaborated not only as a scholarship but as partisan ideology...[which] hid the contest beneath its scholarly and aesthetic idioms' (Said 1985: 27, 3; Said 1989: 211).[4]

However, in spite of the importance of Said's critique in enabling us to unmask some of the hidden agendas beneath the seemingly benign exterior of Western investigation of the Orient, his approach has left us with many questions. Does it, for example, perpetuate an essentialist binarism, encouraging the long-held view that East and West are absolutely distinct cultural entities, each sealed inescapably behind what Ragavan Iyer has called a 'glass curtain' and locked into an eternal cold war? And does Said's argument rest too precariously on a reductive methodology which sees orientalism as explicable in the last analysis only in terms of the exigencies of colonial power? These are issues too wide-ranging to be dealt with here,[5] but we shall in fact find ourselves beating a path which, though starting from a common assumption that Western 'orienteering' must be understood against the background of the West's global expansion, moves in a different direction from that of Said.

This difference of direction is partly due to a recognition of the fact that, though the Western powers have wielded considerable imperial influence over China and much of the Western attitude towards that civilisation must be framed within that historical fact, the Western understanding and appropriation of Daoism cannot be theorised simply in these terms. In the first place, while it is true, as we shall see later, that the early attitudes towards Daoism were shaped in large measure by factors arising from a European missionary expansionism, Daoism featured only marginally within Western consciousness during the colonial epoch; the major thrust of Daoist studies occurred only subsequent to the main colonial period. By contrast with the Western 'discovery' of Hinduism, which helped both to reinforce European hegemony over India and at the same time to construct a nationalist Indian ideology, Daoism has played a much more neutral and insignificant role within the drama of imperial politics. It has neither helped to shape the mentality of colonial rulers nor been a focus of anti-imperialist struggle. The colonial mindset remains, of course, and attitudes towards Daoism still at times betray the stigma of our colonial history, but the recently emerging relationship with Daoism cannot be understood simply in terms of Western power over a passive and subjugated Orient.

Moreover, Daoism in particular and the Orient in general have often taken on the counter-hegemonic role of critic and even subverter of Western beliefs and values. By virtue of its very cultural remoteness and difference, the traditional East has often been seen to stand as an especially sharp contrast with indigenous Western traditions, in particular those that we have come to call 'modern', and as such it has constituted a mirror in which the West has been able to scrutinise itself in a revealing and critical light. Its role as external commentator, reminding us of the historical contingency of our own world-views, philosophical assumptions and social practices, is one which, as I suggested earlier, has a long history in orientalist discourse. One of the remarkable features associated with the West's imperialist expansion over the past few centuries has been the way in which Western thinkers have sought, not only to appropriate and control, but energetically to advocate and privilege non-European systems of thought. While Western missionaries have struggled for centuries with only limited success to convert Asian people to the Christian faith, the West has eagerly embraced Eastern ideas and practices and has, in a sense, carried out its own counter-missionary project. It is not simply that imperial expansion has brought about awareness of a greater sense of cultural plurality and susceptibility towards otherness, but that this in turn has given stimulus to bouts of both critical self-analysis and spiritual renewal on the part of the West. From this point of view, the 'clash of civilizations', to use Samuel Huntington's portentous phrase, which is often seen as a battleground of mutual animosity and incomprehension between East and West, or at worst of xenophobic and racist opprobrium, can become the building site for the creation both of an enhanced empathy and of a productive dialogue which encourages reflection on the adequacy of our own understanding and a stimulus to new thinking.

The West's engagement with Daoism itself, though driven by Western assumptions and preoccupations, has certainly not been unequivocally oppressive or manipulative. Nor has it been the exclusive domain of Westerners. As will become evident below, the growth of Daoist interest in the West has been the product of Asian as well as Western labour, and the Daoist renaissance in the West is in some respects parallel to a renewal of interest within Asia itself. With the increasing number of Chinese, Japanese and Korean scholars involved in this work, and with the revival of Daoist practices within Chinese cultural spheres, the Daoist renaissance has now taken on an international dimension where it is difficult to separate out Asian from European interests. Moreover, co-operation between Asian and Western scholars is now commonplace, a good example of which is the conference held in Xian in October 1995 at which sixty-five delegates from China and Germany exchanged ideas concerning the *Daodejing* (Hoster and Waedow 1995).

In the light of factors such as these, I find myself parting company with the more reductive versions of Said's orientalist critique. We will see that the relationship between Daoism and Western thought is too complex to be shoehorned into a simple model of Western power imposed on a passive East, or into the old binarism which constructs the East as wholly alien and other. In the course of the chapters which follow, it will be argued not only that Daoism has come to play an increasingly important facilitative role in prompting a rethinking of Western assumptions and a critical analysis of the formation and value of Western thought, but that as an agent of liberating challenge it intriguingly recapitulates its subversive role within ancient China itself, and that its newfound role within Western culture is in some respects a continuation of a hermeneutical drama that has long been enacted within China itself. It will also become evident that modern Daoist scholarship has yielded important insights into traditional Chinese religious and cultural institutions, and has opened up new areas of research which are of inestimable value to investigators from both sides of the globe. And whatever its motives, Western-driven scholarship has played a significant role in recovering and reinvigorating an ancient way of thinking which has, until recently, been all but obliterated in its country of origin. This too might be seen as a subtle version of imperialism, but equally it can be construed as an enlightened form of dialogue between cultures which are on the face of it distant and alien.

The orientalist critique associated with Said cannot indeed be dispensed with entirely. We will discover a variety of ways in which Daoism has undergone reconstruction and transformation in the hands of its Western commentators and interpreters, and has been reconstituted within the expansionist framework of Western thought, assumptions and agendas. Its mutating representations within modern Western culture will lead us to take note of the various interests, whether ideological or personal, whether political or religious, that lie behind them. Such considerations will be seen to form an important dimension of the complex transactions between Daoist and Western traditions that constitute the focus of this book.

## Ways and means

How, then, are we to understand these transactions? And by what ways and means has Daoism entered European consciousness? For the most part, Daoism has itself been for the West not so much a living tradition as a collection of writings – primary and secondary texts, translations, interpretations, commentaries – and our relationship with that ancient tradition has standardly taken the form of the reading of certain classic scriptures, in particular the *Daodejing* and the writings known as the *Zhuangzi*. But it would be a mistake to see the matter in quite so simple a way as this. In reading these individual texts we are engaged implicitly in the reading of a whole culture, and in reading the latter we locate ourselves in an historical relationship with a whole chain of intercalated readings and interpretations. This interpretative encounter is highly complex and multi-layered, an interwoven hermeneutical fabric in which readers and texts become multiplied and respond reiteratively to one another in sometimes bewilderingly convoluted ways. What we are engaged with here, then, is not the interpretation of a single cultural entity, or the reading of a single set of texts, but rather with an intertextual sequence of readings, a mosaic of citations, interpretations, translations and reconstructions which can be traced back over more than two millennia of cultural and intellectual history. We will discover that Daoism is not a single identifiable entity whose meaning is somehow hidden in a cleverly locked Chinese cupboard, but a tradition made of a multiple of inter-reflecting texts and schools, and that 'the various strands that make up the substance of Daoism interweave constantly and...each movement that appears retains the qualities of its predecessors and often contains seeds that will give rise to its successors' (Robinet 1997: xvi). China itself is an especially rich and complex culture which, perhaps pre-eminently amongst the world's civilisations, has almost obsessively created and recreated its self-image through readings of its own past, a trail of texts, commentaries and interpretations which leads back to foundational texts such as the *Daodejing* and beyond, and which in recent years has become enmeshed in the textual web of Europe's own cultural history.

This 'continuous chain of ever-new interpretations', in Nietzsche's phrase, is one which can usefully be illuminated by means of the philosophical hermeneutics of Hans-Georg Gadamer. Particularly relevant to our present study is his notion that all human understanding has to be construed, not as an impersonal interaction of disembodied ideas or passive recording of information, but as a kind of *dialogue*, an ongoing encounter in which a text or tradition is addressed and which answers questions, or itself questions the interpreter. It is a dialogue which involves 'the interplay of the movement of tradition and the movement of the interpreter' (1975: 261), a continuing exchange in which the sense of a text is sought by reiterative interplay or conversation between interpreter and interpreted, and in which meaning is a function of the interaction between the two, not a mystery that lies hidden beneath the text.

One of the consequences of this approach, according to Gadamer, is that we must avoid any supposition that by some kind of thought transfer we can enter into and fully recover the meanings and mentalities of past ages and their symbolic products. All knowing is historically grounded, which means that, though I may become critically aware of this fact, I can never escape the historical conditions in which I think and write. The prejudices which beset the interpretative process are thus inescapable, but far from seeing this as a block to communication, he regards it as a necessary condition thereof. The 'prejudice of the Enlightenment against prejudice itself', as he calls it, arose from the illusion that the quest for knowledge could aspire to a place beyond history where the world could be viewed with total objectivity (1975: 329–40). But once this is seen as an impossibility, we can come to terms with the fact that all knowledge is invested with what Heidegger called 'fore-understandings', and that without preconceptions and anticipations, knowledge would be impossible. Thus, attempts at understanding the past or another culture must involve, not an obliteration of difference, but a kind of rapprochement which Gadamer calls a 'fusion' of conceptual horizons. This does not mean a complete merger or Hegelian synthesis, Gadamer insists, but something more like a Socratic encounter, a dialogue involving the awareness of difference, the recognition of the otherness, even the alienness, of the other; for, as he puts it, the truth 'becomes visible to me only through the "Thou", and only by letting myself be told something by it' (1975: xxiii).

There are difficult philosophical questions here which we need to bring to the surface, while not pretending to resolve them. Talk of the East as a 'construct' and of ever self-reflecting interpretations has relativistic resonances, and may tempt us into the belief that Daoism is merely a creation of language, a linguistic carrousel that simply turns around itself. In contrast with this view, which is a version of the fashionable belief that language is an autonomous realm of signification, Gadamer reminds us that in our reading of the past its otherness always stands to challenge our fore-understandings and projections. Understanding begins, he insists, when something from beyond our wonted frame of reference addresses us. It is precisely this emphasis on the dialectical relationship between self and other, between interpreter and interpreted, which differentiates Gadamer's approach from the view that ancient texts are, in effect, purely modern constructs, mere pretexts for the creative activity of interpreters.

This may help to relieve us of – if not totally dispel – the fear that in emphasising difference and otherness, we place a distant culture, in this case the ancient Daoist tradition, into a realm of thought which is completely incommensurable with our own. On Gadamer's view, the very possibility, not only of dialogue but of understanding itself, presupposes distance, otherness, alterity. No desperate leap into the mind of an alien other is required, therefore, but rather a movement of thought based on the principle that 'the individual is never simply an individual, because he is always involved with others', and that therefore we are 'never utterly bound to any one standpoint, and hence can never have a truly closed horizon' (Gadamer 1975: 271). This view has been reiterated more recently by Chinese-American scholar Zhang Longxi, who points to the dangers of extreme cultural relativism which not only puts into question the very possibility of cross-cultural understanding, but also tends to resurrect the colonialist attitudes that it sought to transcend. The emphasis on difference, he argues, should not simply reduce China 'to a fantastic mirror image of Western desires, fantasies, and stereotypical notions', but can stimulate 'genuine efforts at understanding' (1998: 8–9, 14).

Moreover, this recognition of cultural difference not only enables us to see beyond ourselves to what is remote and different, but by the same token gives us the opportunity to reflect critically on ourselves. As Richard Bernstein put it at an East–West philosophy conference, 'it is only through an engaged encounter with the Other that one comes to a more informed, textured understanding of the traditions to which 'we' belong' (1991: 93). Thus, the fusion of horizons which Gadamer speaks of as central to the act of reading a text from a different time or tradition does not imply anything like a complete merger or synthesis, certainly not an act of transposing oneself into the place of another, nor yet a simple act of appropriation of another. Nor on the other hand does it imply an incommensurable difference, a mutual alienation of sympathy and understanding in which Kipling's 'twain' can 'never meet'. It is rather an agonistic encounter, an engagement in which we try to enter into and thrive on differences rather than seek to obliterate them, a potentially subversive engagement in which we are compelled to confront the assumptions, limitations and fractures in our own cultural traditions. It is thus a way of experiencing ourselves from the outside, as other; a point of departure which can lead to an enhancement of self-understanding. Hence, in the words of the German philosopher Hans Herbert Kögler, 'the hermeneutic experience of other meaning systems enables a substantive external stance towards one's own preunderstandings to be unfolded productively', engendering an 'illuminating contrast' which, while not guaranteeing the validity of one's premises, does at least testify to intellectual integrity (1996: 173–4).[6]

In relation to our present undertaking, this means that we must necessarily avoid any pretensions at rational closure while at the same time committing ourselves to the critical appraisal of all interpretative strategies, including our own. There is in an important sense no 'outside' to this process, no lofty peak to which we might hope to climb and from which we will be able to view Daoism with completely detached objectivity, and hence no separating out of some primordial and authentic Daoism into whose presence we may hope to be admitted by cutting through the layers of intervening interpretations. And of course the present study is no exception to this reflexive process but is itself just another mirror, one with its own peculiar camber and its own idiosyncratic refractions. It is not a 'view from nowhere', but the view of a white liberal, with pluralist and relativist inclinations, speaking from within the European academy, who nevertheless seeks to transcend its limitations by sighting it from a wider intellectual and cultural perspective. I make no attempt, therefore, to disguise my own partiality towards Daoism whether in its traditional forms or in its recent reincarnations in the Western, nor my belief in its importance for us at the present time. To echo a voice which will be heard later in this work, 'I stand in the chain of narratives, a link between links' (Buber 1956: i).

## The way to the West

What value might this study of intercultural encounter have for us? Zhuangzi tells the story of a frog who lives all its life at the bottom of a well, and is blissfully unaware of the wider world beyond. Then one day it is accosted by a wandering turtle who expatiates on the immense size and depth of the sea from which it has come. The frog is 'stunned with amazement to hear it, [and is] beside himself with bewilderment' (Graham 1981: 155).

Maybe from a Daoist point of view it would be best to leave the frog in its well, and indeed it is clear that from Zhuangzi's point of view the frog is far wiser than those who seek to understand the wide world with 'supremely subtle words', and is happy to remain in ignorance in its murky domain. Nevertheless, from a Western viewpoint the story might also stand as a warning to those who limit their outlook to the confines of their own culture, and who refuse to explore beyond their ancestral traditions. Improving our understanding of the relationship between Daoism and Western thought can add further to an already growing realisation that a purely Eurocentric approach to questions of a broadly philosophical nature is not only culturally impoverishing but also self-limiting. The creative potential of inter-cultural philosophy is beginning to be seen as a means to address a wide range of contemporary issues. In philosophy, for example, these issues include questions concerning language, meaning, morality, mind and knowledge, along with related questions about the nature of rationality itself. Another example is the field of religious experience. Here the quest for spiritual enlightenment has been greatly stimulated by encounter with non-Western traditions, and increasingly a dialogue of faiths has offered a way of revivifying indigenous belief systems and practices.

The study of Western encounters with non-European systems of thought can be seen, therefore, not just as an exercise in the history of ideas but also a contribution to the expansion of the philosophical and spiritual imagination. By challenging the self-imposed boundaries that are typically drawn around Western disciplines such as philosophy, the study of Daoism can provide us with the potential for unlearning our own conceptual habits and opens up the possibility of widening our range of sympathies and multiplying the conceptual tools at our disposal.

There are, of course, other ways of achieving this which are closer to home, but Daoism seems especially suited to such purposes and, as we shall discover below, seems to have special relevance for us today. On the face of it, Daoism offers a way of thinking which is alien and radically different from anything that normally comes within the Western purview, yet this very difference is such that it can jolt us out of our normal mindsets and encourage us to see the world through different eyes. The very strangeness of Daoist philosophy, therefore, may turn out to be, not a reason for dismissing it from our consideration or treating it as an historical curiosity, but rather an incentive for reflection on and criticism of the assumptions that lie beneath our own inured ways of thinking. The investigation of this tradition for its own sake is undoubtedly of great value, and the following chapters will pay tribute to the extraordinary expansion of our understanding which has been achieved by academic research. This has opened our eyes to a tradition which in many respects matches the scope and depth of those which have their origins in Europe. Nevertheless, some of the scholars involved in this endeavour have themselves been quick to grasp the wider significance of their work. A.C. Graham, for example, has no doubt that the study of Daoism 'constantly involves one in important contemporary issues in moral philosophy [and] the philosophy and history of science', in addition to its aptitude for 'the deconstruction of established conceptual schemes', and Randall Peerenboom insists that the investigation of Daoism is greatly enhanced if 'it can be made relevant to today's world and the contemporary philosophical scene'. Martin Palmer, while regretting the misappropriation of Daoist ideas by various groups 'who wouldn't know a Chinese character if it bit them', recognises that it 'has a great deal to say to our culture of individualism, of power, of dualistic thinking and of materialism', and Joseph Needham goes so far as to speculate that, though the Daoists' religion has atrophied in recent times, 'perhaps the future belongs to their philosophy' (Graham 1989: x; Peerenboom 1993: 265; Palmer 1991: 128; Needham 1956: 152).

In our struggle to leap beyond our Eurocentric confines, we might also learn to reflect carefully on the continuing ideological biases that beset the whole intercultural enterprise. We still need to remind ourselves of the danger that we may, like the frog, still be stuck in our own well in spite of our intention to escape, unreflectively projecting our narrow interests and theoretical assumptions onto other cultures and civilisations. Projective bias, as Gadamer has argued, is no doubt an inescapable component of all knowing, and it would seem to be impossible for any discourse to be free of ideological conditioning; here I agree with Lionel Jensen who, in his study of the Western 'manufacture' of Confucianism, acknowledges 'the ideological nature of all textual productions, Chinese no less than Western' (1997: 145). However, this does not exonerate us from the need for reflexive mistrust, and the deep-rooted nature of cultural biases in the East-West dialogue make an especially urgent demand on our capacity for critical self-awareness. The enthusiasm of Westerners for 'Oriental wisdom', and the desire to press it into useful service, must be tempered by the warnings of those who are troubled by what they see as the 'exploitation' of Daoism and by the continued annexation of East Asian ideas, purloined from their original context in order to be reshaped and reused for a variety of Western purposes. It is true that scholarly interest in Daoism has made significant contributions to the understanding and preservation of a tradition which was in danger of losing much of its past through neglect or wanton destruction, but scholarship itself is never pure or untainted by ideological bias, and this study may also contribute to sinology's own self-understanding by locating it within a wide historical and intellectual context. As Joanna Waley-Cohen points out, much of what we once thought we knew about China, even on well-informed authority, now seems little more than a set of stereotypes, and the process of laying to rest long-cherished myths is a difficult one, not only for Western commentators but for China itself (1999: 4–5).

But if, like the turtle, we have travelled all the way from distant seas, then we might feel entitled to expect a more affirmative outcome to our long journey. As the American political philosopher Fred Dallmayr has argued, we should have confidence that the new dialogical style of 'interhuman and cross-cultural entwinement will open up a hopeful vista for the future, one pointing beyond the (mutually reinforcing) dystopias of global bureaucracy and of xenophobic fragmentation or exclusivism' (1996: 59). Seen from this angle, the gulf that seems to separate us from ancient Chinese traditions is not merely an obdurate fact that we must stoically accept, nor an excuse to return to the defeatist binarism of East-versus-West, but can inspire us to engage in a creative dialogue and can help in combating some of the less desirable consequences of globalisation. The world we are now entering can no longer be seen as a purely Western world, even if in many respects it is still largely driven by Western assumptions and values, and the conservation of cultural diversity, the preservation of a rich gene pool of ideas, may to some extent compensate for the depredations wrought by Western-driven modernity on the traditional cultures of Asia. There are abundant examples going back many centuries of the ways in which Europe itself has been enriched by ideas, techniques and inventions that originated in China, and in recent times many scholars have pointed to the impact of oriental ideas on modern Western thought, an impact which has not always been adequately acknowledged by intellectual and cultural historians (Clarke 1997; Needham 1969). The study that follows is an attempt to give support to the ideal of a potentially global field of hermeneutical endeavour, one which does not lead back either to oppressive uniformity or to intractable antagonism, but towards productive and liberating exchange.

# 2

# 'THE MEANING IS NOT THE MEANING'

## On the nature of Daoism

### What is Daoism?

As Socrates discovered two and a half millennia ago, trying to define terms which play a key role in intellectual and cultural life can be a frustrating business. And for contemporary postmodern theorists, it smacks of the discredited quest for forbidden essences and impossible foundations. The case of Daoism proves especially troublesome. Almost any book on this subject begins by confessing that it is very difficult to say what Daoism is. Julia Ching, the historian of Chinese religions, concedes that it 'may designate anything and everything', that it is 'an umbrella term for everything from the practice of ch'i kung (breathing exercises) to religious beliefs in gods and spirits as well as religious rituals, sometimes including shamanic practices' (1993: 85; 1997: 108). Another writer laments that it is 'nothing more specific than a state of mind' (Sivin 1978: 304), and yet another that 'even among the philosophies commonly called 'mystical', there can hardly be one more resistant to an analytical approach than Daoism', and goes on to say that 'by mocking reason and delighting in the impossibility of putting his message into words, the Daoist seems to withdraw beyond the reach of discussion and criticism' (Graham 1983: 5). The sinologist Holmes Welch is more explicit but equally confusing when he tells us that Daoism is a very broad term which embraces 'the science of alchemy; maritime expeditions in the Isles of the Blest; an indigenous Chinese form of yoga; a cult of wine and poetry; collective sexual orgies; church armies defending a theocratic state; revolutionary secret societies; and the philosophy of Lao Tzu' (1957: 88). For some, 'a Daoist is by definition a man who seeks immortality in the present life, so that in death he or she may be "wafted up into the realms of the immortals in broad daylight" ', whereas for others Daoism is nothing more than 'a wise and merry philosophy of living' (Saso 1990: 3; Lin 1938: 6). It is certainly true to say that 'There is still no consensus of opinion amongst scholars specializing in Daoism as to what it really is', and hence that 'it is almost impossible to lay down a clear-cut definition' (Kimura 1974: iii).[1] This uncertainty is indeed indicative of the interpretative struggle that, as we shall see throughout this book, has characterised the West's encounter with this ancient Chinese tradition.

It has not helped Western or Chinese interpreters that over the past two thousand years Daoism has been linked with a bewildering variety of practices, including alchemical experiments, martial arts, medicine and callisthenics as well as a multiplicity of popular rituals and divinatory practices, yet seemingly without the need for overarching authority or canonical doctrines to bind them all together. It is like the *dao* itself which 'gave birth to the One; the One gave birth to two things, three things, up to ten thousand' (*Daodejing*: ch. 42). This inflationary tendency has inevitably led to differences of emphasis and focus. For some, the pursuit of longevity or immortality has been paramount, while for others this represents a pointless pursuit. In some cases the main emphasis is on 'external alchemy' with its refinement of pills and potions, while for others the emphasis is on 'internal alchemy', on self-cultivation and the practice of yoga techniques. There is on the one hand a strain of Daoism which has rejected the social and political life and sought salvation in solitude, while on the other hand there have been times when Daoists have played an active role in government and, more especially, in subversive and even revolutionary activity. There is a 'mystical' Daoism which emphasises the inexpressibility of the *dao* and the pointlessness of all rational knowledge, yet at the same time Daoists have been closely involved with many practical arts such as those of *feng-shui* (a method for achieving harmony between human activities and the rhythms and energies of nature) and *taijiqan* (a technique for attaining inner balance and harmony which combines the spiritual and the bodily dimensions). And there are Daoists who, according to Joseph Needham, have played a central role in the development of Chinese science and technology. In addition to this the canon of Daoist scriptures, an immense, diverse and often obscure collection of writings, offers no clear doctrinal framework, giving rise to a variety of sectarian disagreements and being subject to a bewildering range of interpretations. This sort of confusing prolixity prompted A.C. Graham to dismiss as 'pointless' the attempt 'to look for features common to everything called Daoism', and has often led to the word 'Daoist' being used 'as a convenient label to include everything to do with philosophy and religion that is not specifically Confucian or Buddhist' (Graham 1989: 172; Blofeld 1985: 19).

Perhaps the apparent paradoxical and elusive nature of Daoism is somehow intrinsic to it. Maybe it is 'the very absence of definition that constitutes the fundamental characteristic of Chinese religion' in general, and Lin Yutang is one of several writers who have identified the 'tricksterish' quality of Daoism, 'a certain roguish nonchalance, a confounded and devastating skepticism' on the part of Daoists who, with impish humour, deliberately thwart attempts to pin down their teachings (Schipper 1993: 3; Lin 1939: 34). As Graham notes, 'The denial that the Way is communicable in words is a familiar paradox of Daoism', which serves to 'remind us of the limitations of language' (1989: 199), for did not Laozi say that 'The Way is eternally nameless', and urge us to remember that 'Those who know do not speak; Those who speak do not know'? In brief, there seems to be in Daoism 'a boundless scepticism about the possibility of ever saying anything', a philosophical standpoint reinforced in practice by the fact that 'there has always been a certain shroud of secrecy surrounding Daoism...[which] has preferred anonymity and chosen to articulate its teachings in riddles' (Graham 1989: 199; Ching 1993: 85). All this is certainly very confusing for the Westerner who wants to know: is it philosophy? Or religion? Or a way of life? Or what?

The question, 'What is Daoism?', was first raised in an authoritative manner in a lecture given by the sinologist H.G. Creel in 1956, in which he attempted to break down the term 'Daoism' as an all-embracing category. In the West, it has not been uncommon to treat Daoism as if it were a single tradition, and indeed it has frequently been pointed out that across the whole range of orientalist interests there has been a tendency to construct Asian culture and its religious and philosophical ideas and institutions in overly simplistic ways in order to make them more in tune with Western categories, and hence more manageable and assimilable. Daoism is no exception. Creel himself was quick to insist that 'this term does not denote a school but a whole congeries of doctrines' and to point out that the major Daoist texts that have impinged on the West are in fact collections of writings drawn from sources which vary in origin and in time of composition (1970: 1). Moreover, he found in Daoism, in spite of its pervasive influence on Chinese culture and politics, no single definite moral philosophy or vision of life's purpose, but rather a variety of teachings which, though linked historically, are better seen as distinct traditions. The basis for this view, Creel tells us, is to be found in Chinese tradition itself which has long drawn a distinction between *Daojia* and *Daojiao*.[2] The former is identifiable as philosophical Daoism and is associated primarily with the writings of Laozi, Zhuangzi and Liezi, and with a form of mysticism which seeks ultimate unity with the *dao*. The latter is known as religious Daoism and is usually identified as an organised 'church', established in the late Han period, with teachings and rituals whose ultimate goal was physical immortality but whose day-to-day function was to cater for the religious needs of ordinary people. Creel elaborates on this by drawing a distinction between 'contemplative Taoism' and 'purposive Taoism', the former representing the Daoist philosophy 'in its original purity', and the latter pointing to the construction of a practical philosophy which was concerned with the pursuit of health and longevity, and which historically gave rise to a number of ritual practices and political attitudes (1970: 5). Moreover, he claims that there are irreconcilable differences between the former, which advocates retreat from the world, and the latter, which advocates a worldly philosophy of cultural and political engagement (1970: ch. 3).

The tendency to distinguish between at least two fundamentally different varieties of Daoism, though it has its origins in Chinese history and thought, runs deep in Western orientalist thinking and is in some respects a modern fiction, giving rise to a range of interpretative strategies. An extreme position is taken by the Confucianist historian of Chinese philosophy, Fung Yu-lan, who has argued that the 'two Taoisms' are not only different but mutually contradictory since 'Taoism as philosophy [in its acceptance of death] teaches the doctrine of following nature, while Taoism as religion [in search of techniques for avoiding death] teaches the doctrine of working against nature' (1948/1966: 3). Similarly, according to Welch, Daoism in its later form 'has almost nothing to do with the *Tao Te Ching*', and those who set up the Daoist church 'turned their backs on almost every precept' in it (1957: 87–8). The sinologist Michel Strickmann, in seeking to place Daoism more firmly in its historical and social context, goes even further by proposing to confine the term 'Daoism' to 'the Way of the Celestial Masters and the organization that grew out of it', a tradition which has long been dismissed as a corrupt descendant of a noble philosophical lineage. He thereby, untypically in Western commentaries, marginalises Daoist *philosophy* in relation to its 'degenerate' offspring by viewing it, not as a movement or tradition or even as a school of thought, but rather as a purely 'bibliographic classification', a loose collection of writings which are nothing more than 'a fictitious union under a single descriptive term' (Welch and Seidel 1979: 165–7; see also Strickmann 1980). In a similar way, Nathan Sivin sees in philosophical Daoism 'no sociological meaning beyond a scattering of texts through a long period of Chinese literary history', and Graham so despairs of the term 'Daoist' when applied to philosophy that he advocates replacing it in certain contexts with 'Laoist' and 'Chuangist' to indicate the differences between the ideas of Laozi and Zhuangzi (Sivin: 1978: 305; Graham 1990: 118, 124, 170–2). Some have taken a somewhat different path by offering further elaborations of Creel's distinctions. Chad Hansen, for example, divides contemplative Daoism into speculative (mystical–metaphysical) and critical (semantic–epistemological) compo-nents, and insists that the former comprises the 'core' of Daoism, rather than the metaphysical or mystical kind of Daoism which in the past, especially in the West, has been given a privileged status (1981: 321 and *passim*).

On the other hand, there are many who have found such distinctions unhelpful, either because they fail to do justice to the variety of the historical factors that enter into our understanding of Daoism, or because they fail to do justice to the mutual influences and connections between the two strands.[3] It is the latter viewpoint which has largely prevailed in recent decades. With the spectacular growth of Daoist scholarship, it has become evident that there are substantial historical and conceptual bridges between the 'two Daoisms'. Moreover, it is becoming increasingly evident that the old binary distinction is not only historically mistaken but, in the words of one critic, 'ultimately reflects specific cultural prejudices current among intellectuals in late imperial China and the modern West' (Kirkland 1992: 79; see also Kirkland 1997a). This has meant that, for reasons which we will examine later, from the time of the early Jesuit missionaries to modern secularist historians, we can see an almost concerted attempt to belittle Daoism by contrast with the supposedly more agnostic and philosophically respectable standpoint of orthodox Confucian thinking. This tendency has led generations of Western as well as some Chinese commentators to speak of *Daojiao* as a regrettable lapse from its classical origins in the pre-Han period, and by implication to place it in a poor light by comparison with Christianity. Many examples could be quoted. In his introduction to the first English translation of the *Daodejing* in 1868, John Chalmers referred to the 'superstition and blasphemy' of religious Daoism, contemptuously dismissing its 'endless absurd gibberish about the elixir of life', while towards the end of the century Édouard Chavannes similarly condemned religious Daoism as 'un mélange de superstitions grossières', and in 1915 the sinologist Herbert Giles distinguished sharply between 'the Taoism of superstition, with the grafts of Buddhism for the masses; and...the Taoism of speculation and paradox for the cultured' (Chalmers 1868: viii, xiv; Chavannes 1895–1915 1: xviii; Giles 1915: 178). More recently, Huston Smith's influential textbook, *The World's Religions: Our Great Wisdom Traditions* refers to religious Daoism as 'a murky affair' full of 'crude superstition', and Thomas Merton, almost equally influential in a more popular domain, has contrasted 'the degenerate amalgam of superstition, alchemy, magic, and health-culture which Taoism later became', with its original, 'pure' form of philosophical Daoism (Smith 1991: 205; Merton 1965: 15).[4]

Times are changing, however. It is now common to argue to the contrary that religious Daoism, far from being just a diseased branch grafted onto healthy philosophical stock, is a central trunk in the whole Daoist body and is heavily dependent on philosophical Daoism, retaining to this day important elements of the latter in its teachings and practices (Kaltenmark 1969: 107, 115; Kohn 1991a: Ch.10; Lagerwey 1987: 11–17; Saso 1983: 154; Schipper 1993: 192–5).[5] Thus, religious and philosophical elements are now seen to be deeply intertwined within Daoism. The *Daodejing* is recognised as an inspiration for both philosophical and religious interpretations, important in the formation of the popular Celestial Masters movement, yet also itself reflecting an amalgam of religious practices and philosophical speculation (Bokenkamp 1997: 2). According to Livia Kohn, the key to this convergence is to be found in the pursuit of perfection through identification with the *dao*, the One, a pursuit which, though central to the philosophical tradition, is also manifested in the varieties of religious Daoism. Thus the salvationist implications of teachings such as the *Daodejing* apply not only to hermits, sages and mystics, but also in the fields of moral conduct and religious practice in general and in the harmonious functioning of society at large. The quest for a higher purity and for harmonious oneness with the *dao* are aims to be found in different formulations both in the speculations of sages and in the practices of Daoist adepts, and in Kohn's view the history of religious Daoism, therefore, was not one of the decline and loss of some pristine doctrine, nor of a static structure of belief and practice, but rather a dynamic development of a powerful soteriological tradition, one which responded to historical changes and was manifested in a variety of writings and sects and at a variety of social levels (1991a: ch. 10). Hence on this view, in spite of the evident differences between *Daojia* and *Daojiao* as retrospectively constructed, and the diversity of sects and practices spawned by the latter, there are a number of features held in common by all forms of Daoism. Isabelle Robinet, for example, argues that while 'it is meaningless to speak of Taoism as a whole', Daoism represents a coherent, if diversified, tradition. Contrary to the kind of confusions voiced above which lead one to despair of identifying anything that could be called 'Daoism', she came to the conclusion that 'there is a single thread that runs through Taoism', a cumulative and integrative process in its evolution that can be discerned in such commonly held teachings as *yin/yang* cosmology, the five agents, reiterative correspondences in nature, a pantheon of functional spirits, and a concern with longevity and immortality (1997: 1–4).[6]

Alongside this integrative interpretation of Daoism there is also the recognition that it was a highly eclectic phenomenon, drawing into its 'single thread' not only the philosophical strands of Laozi and Zhuangzi but also shamanistic and magical traditions from an earlier period, as well as the Confucian classics and Buddhist ideas and practices. Indeed, as we shall see shortly, one of the difficulties in all this from a Western point of view is the way in which Daoism reveals a strong syncretistic tendency which draws inspiration from a seemingly incompatible variety of sources, and our Western inclination to classify and sharply differentiate the various sects and schools along the lines suggested by Creel is often frustrated by the sheer promiscuity of this tradition. As Kohn points out, Daoism 'does not exclude any particular practice or method from its repertoire. As long as it serves the purpose of leading people closer to oneness with the Tao, anything will do', a syncretistic tendency which embraces not only a variety of religious and philosophical teachings but also draws on the methods of dietetics, medicine, gymnastics, breathing exercises and meditation techniques (Kohn: 1991a: 223). This tendency is compounded by the fact that, in spite of the underlying themes that give it a recognisable identity,

Daoism not only absorbed an assortment of cultural sources but also begat a variety of schools and traditions of thought in its long history, and inevitably took on different characteristics at different times and places.

The difficulties that Western commentators have experienced in their attempts to classify and define Daoism have not been helped by the linguistic remoteness of Daoist writings. There is always difficulty in translating words, ideas and institutions from one linguistic tradition or culture to another, and the fundamental differences between Chinese and European languages present us with more than the usual problems. The difficulties we have just noted in defining Daoism are compounded by the fact that the word 'religion' itself has no precise equivalent in Chinese, and hence there is the danger that in defining Daoism we will simply be forcing it into inappropriate Western categories; indeed it is arguable that the very notion of religion as conceived in the West is an obstacle to our understanding of Daoism. Thus for example, the *Daojia/Daojiao* distinction which we have just encountered is by no means isomorphic with the Western distinction between philosophy and religion, and further, as the historian of religions Jordan Paper points out, the tendency in European studies to mark out a separation between religion and culture, terms familiar enough in the West, proves to be artificial and misleading in the Chinese context (Lin *et al.* 1995: 745; Paper 1995: 2; Schipper 1993: 2).

## The 'Three Teachings'

Some of the confusion which Westerners experience in trying to understand or explain the nature of Daoism arises from attempts to distinguish it clearly from the other central Chinese traditions, Confucianism and Buddhism. This perplexity is exacerbated by oft-quoted sayings such as 'Every Chinese wears a Confucian cap, a Daoist robe and Buddhist sandals', and by the puzzling fact that Chinese appear to be able to follow all three teachings at the same time, so that 'a man could be a Confucian in his active life...a philosophical Taoist in his leisure hours...and frequent the Buddhist temple to offer prayers for special intentions' (Ching 1993: 223). From a Western viewpoint it would only be natural to ascribe separate identity to these traditions, nevertheless it has become firmly established that these three traditions do not in fact constitute three distinct religions but interact and overlap in many complex ways. Moreover, it is increasingly accepted that the 'Three Teachings' have a place in Chinese culture which bears little comparison with the history of the relationships between the religious traditions that have flourished in the West, and hence talk of 'being' a Daoist or of 'belonging' to one religion to the exclusion of others is a locution that needs to be used with great caution in the Chinese context.

It will be useful in this context to identify two myths which have blossomed in the contentious hermeneutical ground between Chinese and

Western traditions. The first of these can be called the 'classical' myth. According to this story, the three schools are seen as three quite distinct religions with distinct doctrines, each competing with the others for the allegiance of the Chinese people. Secondly, there is the 'romantic' myth. This perspective, capitalising on recent scholarship which has sought to demolish the classical myth, has gone in the opposite direction and portrayed Chinese intellectual life as a milk-and-water tradition in which harmony and togetherness precluded any real debate or philosophical tension between different schools of thought.

The classical myth initially became enshrined in Western thinking in the seventeenth century through the agency of the Jesuit missionaries, and remained until recently the unchallenged assumption behind Western perceptions of Chinese religious life. It was almost inevitable that the Jesuits, whose very creation had come about in response to the violent sundering of religious unity in Europe, viewed the Chinese situation through the lens of European religious factionalism, and when in 1913 W.E. Soothill opened his work on *The Three Religions of China* with the words 'There are three recognized religions in China', he was simply appealing to an assumption about the nature of religious differences that had for long been deeply embedded in Western consciousness. Nevertheless, the classical myth is now very much in retreat in the minds of scholars, even though the neat division between 'the three recognized religions of China' remains a tempting cliché. This cliché is not a purely Western invention, it must be added, and has roots that go far back in the cultural and intellectual history of China itself. The threefold division was first referred to in the sixth century by a scholar named Li Shiqian who wrote that 'Buddhism is the sun, Daoism the moon, and Confucianism the five planets', and was commonplace amongst the Neo-Confucianists of the Song period (Teiser 1996: 3). Nevertheless, the boundaries between the Three Teachings – the *san-chiao* – have never been as sharply drawn in China as those between different religions and religious sects in the West, and even prior to the arrival in China of Buddhism in the first century CE there were signs of syncretistic accommodation between Confucianism and Daoism (Le Blanc 1985). As one sinologist puts it: '[China is] a culture where no religion claims *extra ecclesiam nulla salus* (no salvation outside the Church) and where the urge to unify and syncretise beliefs has always been stronger than the urge to find exclusive formulations of universal truth' (Seidel 1989–90: 246). And for Jacques Gernet, the key lies in the absence of transcendent, eternal truths or sacrosanct dogmas in the Chinese religious traditions (1985: 66). The tendency on the part of some Western commentators to distinguish sharply between the teachings of Confucianism and Daoism, therefore, misconstrues their mutually complementary nature, and as Jordan Paper observes, it is 'still difficult for most Western historians of religion to understand that religion in China is a single complex' (1995:

11–12; see also Hall and Ames 1998: 150–56; Yearley 1980). It is true that each of the Three Teachings has emphasised a distinctive attitude to life, morality, society and nature, leaving aside for the moment the historical complexities of their interactions. Thus the Confucians have always had a central concern with ethico-political matters, in contrast with the Daoist focus on harmony with nature, or the Buddhist concern with karma and reincarnation. But at the same time, there is a recognisable tendency towards the harmonisation of these schools, and a philosophical and cultural cross-fertilisation which has little parallel with Western religious institutions.

Moreover, the problem here has not merely been the projection of inter-religious conflict or doctrinal purism which are peculiar to the Abrahamic traditions onto Chinese traditions, but also the negative connotations usually attached to the very idea of syncretism. In the Western context, this label has usually conveyed a somewhat jaundiced attitude, suggesting equivocation and unprincipled thinking rather than an uncompromising pursuit of truth, a fact which has helped to confirm in Western minds the second-rate nature of Chinese thinking and the debased quality of their religious traditions. This attitude has been present in Western attitudes towards Chinese religions right from the time of Matteo Ricci, who wrote that the tendency towards syncretism in China created 'the greatest confusion' and represented a lack of commitment to the truth (Gernet 1985: 64). It is true that in recent times this tendency in Chinese thought has increasingly been seen to contrast in productive ways with the 'either–or' mentality that has predominated in the West, but in spite of the move on the part of some scholars towards a more multivalent, de-essentialised conception of religious phenomena, there are still those who find it difficult not to conceptualise Daoism in the light of Christian notions of doctrinal orthodoxy and exclusivity.

It will be useful to give some examples of the syncretistic proclivity within the Chinese tradition. One of the most striking of these can be seen in the Neo-Confucian attempts in the Song dynasty to construct a more inclusive philosophy, a bold intellectual movement which combined elements of cosmology from Daoism and metaphysics from Buddhism with the moral teachings of Confucianism. Another is to be observed in the formation of the self-styled 'Three Teachings' sect by the religious leader Lin Chao-en (1517–98) who sought to integrate Confucianism, Daoism and Buddhism into a new sect, a movement which received wide support in Daoist circles, and which still survives as a living tradition in Taiwan and amongst overseas Chinese in Singapore and Malaysia.[7] Although the more explicitly formalised projects to integrate the different schools into a single *Weltan-schauung* or into an organised movement occurred only from the Song onwards, there were tendencies toward syncretism much earlier. Even as far back as the early Han period there was an attempt to forge an intellectual synthesis, albeit under Confucian hegemony, which aimed explicitly at giving stability to the new régime (Graham 1989: 370–82). Moreover, in the early days of their formation in China, religious Daoism and Buddhism both borrowed heavily from each other, the former providing a convenient instrument for the transplantation of the latter into China by furnishing it with terminological and conceptual anchorage in Chinese waters, the latter helping the former to broaden its metaphysical range and to deepen its spiritual practice. Indeed, from their followers' point of view the two traditions were often in practice indistinguishable, and so close did they come, both in terms of teachings and of spiritual practice, that Chan (Zen) Buddhism was sometimes described as 'Taoism in Buddhist dress' (Bodde 1953: 56). Erik Zürcher comments that, in the light of extensive terminological, conceptual and practical borrowings, 'we can almost speak of 'Buddho-Taoist hybrids' (1980: 85),[8] and Henri Maspero, one of the earliest scholars to challenge the view that Daoism and Buddhism were two distinct religions, pointed out that 'over a rather long period [there was] a confusion of doctrines' between the two (1981: 412).[9] It should be added that the work of such scholars suggests that this feature of Chinese religious life was by no means an isolated factor that can be confined exclusively to the religious sphere, but rather a deep and pervasive quality in Chinese cultural life in general. Thus, the sinologist Derk Bodde speaks of 'the Chinese mind, with its strong preference for working compromise in place of unworkable absolutes', and sees as 'basic among Chinese thought patterns...the desire to merge seemingly conflicting elements into a unified harmony' (1953: 51, 54).[10] Moreover, this syncretic tendency is evident not only at the level of the educated élite who found it possible to follow all three teachings by drawing on texts, ideas and attitudes from each, but also at a popular level where ordinary people could participate in the rites and festivals of all three 'religions' without the necessity to make an exclusive commitment to any one of them.[11]

Nevertheless, in unmasking Western projections concerning the Three Teachings we are sometimes in danger of falling into other, opposite ways of constructing Chinese cultural life. These may take the form of our second, 'romantic' myth, namely the over-idealisation of harmony and of the quest for agreement and compromise. It is perfectly true that these latter virtues are ideals that can be identified, in various forms, at all levels of Chinese culture, but at the same time this should not disguise from us the level of debate and argument, not to mention sheer bad-tempered bickering and vituperation and even outright persecution, that have at various times beset the relationships between Confucianism, Daoism and Buddhism. To be sure, from at least the second century BCE onwards we can detect a strong desire for unity in Chinese intellectual life, encouraged by the emperor as a means towards achieving greater social and political harmony, but the very urgency of this demand meant that the stakes were high and that consequently the resolution of philosophical difficulties was more than a matter of genteel dilettantism or of disinterested academic speculation.[12]

Religious wars, heresy trials and excommunications of the kind familiar in Europe are largely absent from Chinese history, but there was greater intolerance and more in the way of religious oppression than is often supposed. It is true that the persecutions, such as the suppression of Buddhism in 845 CE and the burning of Daoist books in 1282 CE, were carried out on imperial orders, but in such cases the instigation often originated with the Daoist or Buddhist schools themselves, which were frequently locked in unbecoming rivalry and sought to win the Emperor's favour in order to enhance their power and influence. There is no evidence in early Daoist or Buddhist texts of charges of heresy, but verbal insults and acrimonious polemics were often exchanged between the two schools, especially in the fifth and the twelfth centuries when rivalry was at its most intense, and Confucians and Daoists maintained a running battle over the interpretation of classic texts such as the *Yijing*. And while there was little serious internecine strife between the various branches of Daoism, there was active conflict between Daoists and popular religious cults, and Robinet speaks of a 'battle' between the two in which Daoism sought to expose and suppress 'wrong paths' and 'extremist cults' in sometimes violent ways.[13]

But at the same time, it is also important to emphasise that the rivalries between the Three Teachings frequently took the form of civilised argument and debate. It has often been assumed in the West that Chinese intellectual life has for the most part lacked the vibrant culture of controversy and disputation which is seen as having characterised the Western intellectual tradition from the Ancient Greeks onwards. Certainly there was nothing in China like the liberal public sphere – in Habermas's phrase – which developed in nineteenth-century Europe and which provided a permissive social framework for collective argument. Nevertheless, recent studies have begun to dispel the myth of bland intellectual conformity, and, while often emphasising the subordination of contentious argument to overall social values of harmony and accommodation, they have enabled us to see that there is 'much more rational debate in the literature than used to be supposed' (Graham 1989: ix).[14] Central teachings such as those concerned with correlative cosmology, the pursuit of immortality or the Daoist Immortals (sages who have overcome death) were subject to vigorous debate at various times, and, as the historian Wang Gungwu has argued, the independence and autonomy of Chinese intellectuals has been consistently underestimated in the West where the supposed docility and conformism of the latter have almost routinely been contrasted with the free-thinking independence of European intellectuals (1991: ch. 15).[15]

Several examples of this spirit of debate are worth citing in a little detail. The most famous of these occurred in the period of Warring States prior to the unification of China under Qin Shi Huangdi in 221 BCE, which witnessed vexatious and long-enduring disputes amongst the 'hundred schools', including Confucianism, (proto-)Daoism, Mohism and Legalism. According to the historian Heiner Roetz, this amounted to nothing less than a revolutionary breakthrough towards what he has called 'postconventional thinking...[a] reflective dissociation from everything hitherto valid'. It bore the marks of a deep crisis in Chinese political and cultural life, a collision of values and world-views that, as with contemporaneous philosophical debate in Greece, was crucial in shaping the intellectual agenda of China for the following millennia (1993: 5–6; see also Cua 1985; Graham 1989). A further period of intellectual agitation followed the decline and fall of the Han dynasty, the arrival of Buddhism on the scene and the emergence of Daoism as a significant cultural force. It was in this period that a unique kind of disputation arose in the shape of a movement entitled 'Pure Talk' (qingdan). Though not allied to any formal school, this movement (which could more properly be called an intellectual fashion) was part of the so-called Neo-Daoist current of thought (or 'Dark Learning') that flourished at that time amongst dispossessed and out-of-office literati, and which engaged in informal and convivial discussion of metaphysical and literary topics.[16] Movements such as this acquired a reputation for anti-Confucian and even for what might be called nihilistic views, and provided an important stimulant to philosophical debate. The most famous exponents of Pure Talk were undoubtedly 'The Seven Sages of the Bamboo Grove', whose conversations were aided by wine and natural surroundings, and who have left a mark on Chinese culture as exemplars of self-expression and non-conformity (Balazs 1964; Chan 1991; Ching 1993; Fung 1966; Henricks 1983).[17] Another example of philosophical disputation can be seen in the remarkable series of formal debates between the rival Daoist and Buddhist sects that took place from the fourth century CE onwards. These were often held under the patronage and even in the presence of the Emperor, and while they were often in effect 'power struggles disguised as doctrinal disputes', their aim of demonstrating the usefulness of a doctrine to peace and social order led not only to a further stimulation of syncretising tendencies, but also to a sharp probing of underlying assumptions and arguments, and to a discussion of philosophical issues such as the creation of the world, the nature of time and the survival of death (Kohn 1995: 7).[18] These debates, which continued until the Yuan dynasty when the Mongol emperor finally pronounced Buddhism as the victor, were clearly confrontational and had a strong political impetus behind them.

Such debates must, however, be seen in the wider environment of an attitude of toleration and pluralism that has long been endemic at certain levels of Chinese cultural life, a cultural attitude which has not until relatively recently become acceptable in the West.[19] Inevitably it has led to tension between the Chinese and Western viewpoints. As we noted above, from a Western viewpoint a tolerant, liberal syncretism has often been seen in negative terms, a recipe for sloppy, inconsequential and even dangerous thinking, for if 'each of the three traditions borrowed so much from each other that, except for terminology, there was little that was unique in any one of them', then we might infer that none of them has anything clear or distinctive to say about anything (Welch and Seidel 1979: 1). It is all very well to say 'I am a Confucian by family tradition; a Taoist by temperament; a Buddhist by religion and inspiration' (Fang 1981: 525), but how can such a blithesome medley help us to confront the important religious, moral and political issues of life? It is hardly surprising that the syncretistic tendencies of the Chinese were viewed with scorn by the Jesuit missionaries who saw in them a scandalous lack of firm belief or conviction (Gernet 1985: 64–7).[20] But it is also unsurprising that this tendency sits well with contemporary open-minded pluralism and has a growing appeal in our relativistic, postmodern age. Hall and Ames have argued that the Chinese tendency towards intellectual accommodation, which 'de-emphasizes dialectical debate in the quest for rational standards is quite likely based upon an implicit recognition of the problems of incommensurability', which in the case of the Daoists is probably based on their experience that 'efforts at rational adjudication continually break down' (Hall and Ames 1995: 154; see also Hall and Ames 1998: part 2, *passim*). We will return to these issues in Chapter 8.

## Historical origins

The difficulties which face the Westerner in trying to understand Daoism are in part due to its history, or rather to the way in which its history has been constructed. Nietzsche once remarked that philosophers suffer from a lack of historical sense and tend to construe concepts in a timeless and unchanging way. This has often been the case with Western understanding of Daoism, where not only has there been a tendency to simplify it conceptually, but also to see it – and indeed Chinese history generally – as lacking in any real developmental dynamic. The teachings of Laozi and Zhuangzi have enjoyed increasing appeal in the West, but their ideas have been placed in an historical vacuum, their historical context and development often ignored and the differences between them frequently overlooked, and, as we noted above, the investigation of the history of the Daoist religion and its relationship with philosophical Daoism has only recently been undertaken in any depth. Another difficulty arises from the portrayal of Daoism within Chinese historiography itself, where hard historical data are in short supply, and where even the meagre historical sources are liable to offer divergent and even mutually contradictory pictures. Such accounts tend at one level to be suffused with fanciful mythologies of origins and with colourful hagiographies of the Immortals, and at another level to be refracted through the official and usually unsympathetic accounts of Confucian scholar-officials, or through the polemical lenses of rival Buddhist treatises (Bokenkamp 1997: 32; Schipper 1993: 5).[21]

Daoist scriptures themselves are of little help here, for this huge corpus of writings carries little in the way of explicit historical information which would enable them to be dated or their authorship or provenance clarified. Corresponding to and in some ways mirroring this are the often highly questionable attempts on the part of Western historians to delineate Chinese history in general and Daoism in particular in terms which have been forged in the furnace of Western historiography but which are not necessarily appropriate in non-Western contexts. One such assumption, to which we have already drawn attention, concerns the assumed coherence and distinctive identity of Daoism, a term only invented in the nineteenth century. In recent years, the reach and boundaries of Daoism in relation to Chinese society as a whole have come to be seen as both broader and less clearly defined than they used to be, and the pervasiveness and embeddedness of Daoism within Chinese culture has led to some uncertainty as to what is specifically Daoist and what is more generally Chinese.[22]

Another such assumption concerns the very origins of Daoism. In the West we have tended to assume that religions have identifiable founders and foundational utterances or texts. This view, sometimes dubbed the 'arborescent' model, imagines that from an original single trunk later schools branch off, a model which clearly derives from Judaeo-Christian-Islamic archetypes. Standardly, Laozi has been nominated as fount and origin of Daoism, and the *Daodejing* as its foundational scripture, and while it may be as harmless to identify Laozi as the founder of Daoism as it is to identify Kierkegaard as the founder of existentialism, we need to recognise that the historical origins of Daoism – as of existentialism – cannot be constructed quite so simply as this. In the light of recent scholarship, Daoism must be seen as the product of a wide spectrum of factors which, while including the textual tradition associated primarily with Laozi and Zhuangzi, constitute a much richer cultural mix, one which reaches out to popular religious cults on the one side as well as to the literate traditions of scholars and officials on the other. No identifiable Daoist school or sect can be found prior to the Han period, but rather there is a loosely connected set of traditions concerned largely with self-cultivation, longevity and magical powers. In later times the figure of Laozi came to be accorded a foundational, and even at times a divine, status. However, in accordance with the standard Chinese practice of appealing to the authority of ancient sage rulers, the ultimate origins of Daoist teachings were located even further back in the third millennium BCE. It was the legendary Yellow Emperor, Huangdi (*c.* 2697–2597 BCE), who was reputed not only to have been the creator of the arts and sciences, but also to have first discovered the secret 'Way of the True One', the process of preserving one's vital forces in order to achieve immortality. This foundational role ascribed to the Yellow Emperor was, of course, an essentially legitimating one, for as Peerenboom notes, '[in China] to trace an innovative concept back to legendary figures of personal and cultural achievement constitutes an argument', and in the case of Daoism it was a useful gambit in the continuing contest with the Confucian establishment (1993: 85; see also Le Blanc 1985–6).

Leaving aside these mythological accounts, it is more plausible to trace Daoism's origins to ancient shamanic practices and beliefs which show many traces of themes that in more developed and articulated form became characteristic features of Daoism. This influence is now recognised as present not only in the popular religious forms of Daoism but also in the philosophies of both Laozi and Zhuangzi, though the sharp distinction between philosophical and religious Daoism has inevitably rendered otiose the linking of these revered figures with 'primitive superstitions' (Paper 1995: ch. 3). Shamanism itself predates Daoism by several thousand years. It probably originated in Siberia, spreading from there to China, Japan and eventually to the Americas where it survives to this day. The shaman, to speak in general terms, was reputed to have the power of communicating with and entering into the spirit world by means of trance-like states, and thereby to practise the arts of healing and divination on behalf of the community. It is in this shamanic tradition that we find the origins of a number of typically Daoist ideas such as the ecstatic journey, physical immortality, sexual yoga, and in particular the aspiration to harmonise human life with the way of nature.[23] Shamanic practices have remained a feature of Chinese cultural life up to modern times, and towards the end of the first millennium BCE became associated with the distinctive and increasingly respectable class of persons known as the *fangshi* (men of secret arts), who were specialists in astrology, magic, medicine, divination and geomancy, and who as healers developed drugs, talismans and breathing exercises aimed at the prolongation of life.

The period in which the *fangshi* emerged as a significant factor in Chinese life also saw the emergence of a tradition of philosophical speculation which was destined to play an equally important part in the subsequent shaping of Daoism. This speculation, which was concentrated mainly during the period known as the Warring States, a period of political chaos and social distress, was also one of intense intellectual activity and begat a whole variety of opinions and doctrines.

Contrary to the Hegelian view of China as stuck immovably in tradition, this was a period which saw, not only dramatic political upheaval, but, as we noted above, a momentous collision of worldviews that took Chinese intellectual life beyond the conformities of convention and tradition (Roetz 1993: ch. 1). The ideas we now associate with the names Laozi and Zhuangzi were part of this 'axial age' transformation, as Karl Jaspers called it, and were the outcome of a much wider controversy concerning the ordering of the state and the conduct of personal life. From the Daoist point of view, the most significant product of this intellectual ferment was the mystical politics of Laozi. This sought the harmonisation of political and social order, not through reliance on the ritual prescriptions of the Confucians, but on spontaneous adaptation to the *dao* which is ultimately inexpressible in words. The ideal state is one in which the usual apparatus of government has been reduced to a minimum, and the sage ruler governs with minimal interference in accordance with the *dao*; in the words of the *Laozi*, 'So long as I do nothing the people will of themselves be transformed' (ch. 57).

The non-interventionist approach of the *Laozi*, which relies heavily on the cultivation of certain desirable states of mind and which is probably common to a number of quietistic schools that existed in China in the fourth and third centuries BCE, can also be related to other features of this period. The first of these was an emerging idealisation of the virtues of living in small communities, and the utopian-anarchistic ideal of a social order based on mutual trust and simple living. The second was the growing emphasis on subjectivity and self-cultivation, the emergence of what Arthur Waley called 'the gradual inward-turning of Chinese thought, its preoccupation with the self and the perfection of the self' (1977: 43). This is particularly evident in the writings associated with the names of Zhuangzi and Mengzi, in which there is a palpable shift of emphasis from external behaviour patterns towards the 'heart–mind', and in the case of Zhuangzi a valuing and cultivation of the personal life above service to the state. This self-cultivation took a variety of forms, including the growing interest in this period in retreating into private life, in solitary living in the mountains and, along with these, the development of techniques of meditation. The ideal of self-cultivation could also be linked with the so-called cult of egoism associated with the name of Yangzhu. Under the influence of the victorious Confucianists, Yangzhu has been condemned as a pure egoist, but more recent scholarship has revealed a much more interesting thinker who anticipated and perhaps influenced later Daoist thinking in his advocacy of a kind of existentialist ideal of authenticity and a Stoical simplicity of life.[24] The third feature of this period was the emergence of cosmological speculation which helped to construct a lasting framework in which the fundamental components of the world were conceptualised as a unified, organic whole. All things were seen as manifestations of a universal energy, *qi*, impelled by the tension between the opposing yet complementary forces of *yin* and *yang*, and structured through a complex system of correlations whereby five basic elements or processes – water, fire, wood, metal and earth – provide a matrix in which human and natural phenomena cohere in meaningful patterns.[25]

The Han dynasty which, following the unification of China in 221 BCE, has generally been thought to represent a period of Confucian consolidation and of intellectual retrenchment following the political and philosophical agitation of the preceding period. It was also a period in which we can begin to discern the distinctive lineaments of Daoism as we have come to know it. Here, if not earlier, we can observe a remarkable confluence of the ideas and practices that we have just outlined, and the emergence of a recognisable, if still disparate and variegated, stream of thought that can arguably be called Daoist. In this period we see its emergence as a set of teachings which brought together the shamanism and the quest for immortality of the *fangshi*, the cosmological ideas of the *Yin–Yang* school, and the anti-conventionalist teachings of Laozi and Zhuangzi, and their formation into an identifiable network of ideas and practices. This is more than just modern historical hindsight. The second-century BCE historiographer Simadan in his famous classification of the Six Schools identified for the first time the *Daojia* (School of the Way) as a distinct school of thought alongside other schools. Not content with giving it a separate identity, he went even further and praised its vision as the most comprehensive and inclusive of all the schools, drawing on the best elements of its rivals and exhibiting a simplicity and flexibility which rendered it capable of adaptation to varying circumstances (Graham 1989: 377–8). Moreover, in recent years there has come to light evidence of the formation in the early Han period of a school called *Huanglao*, which took its name from the Yellow Emperor, Huangdi, and from Laozi. Though incorporating some elements from the Legalist school (*Fajia*), it preached recognisably Daoist values such as the renunciation of wealth, practised sexual yoga and the cult of longevity, and advocated government by non-intervention (Peerenboom 1993: 4; Robinet 1997: 46; Schwartz 1985: 237–54).

The *Huanglao* movement satisfied for a while the desire for some kind of syncretistic accommodation following the unification of China under the Jin and Han rulers, but it became eclipsed by the installation of Confucianism in the early Han period as the official state cult. The political settlement under the Han certainly brought a period of stability and order, but at the same time it would appear to have opened up a social and spiritual vacuum in the country, especially away from the centres of power, and paved the way for new forms of Daoism that were to have important long-term consequences in the history of Daoism.

First there were the Yellow Turbans, a messianic movement not unlike those which appeared in England during the Puritan revolutionary period of the seventeenth century. Under the leadership of Zhang Jue, they created a religious organisation based on cures through the confession of sins and meditational retreats, and preached the idea of the Great Peace (*Taiping*), a Daoist-inspired ideal of an era of harmony, wisdom and social equality which was believed to have existed before the birth of civilisation and which was destined to return. The revolt they instigated in 182 CE failed and the movement was destroyed, but the Han dynasty was mortally wounded in the process, and the decline of the Han power helped to facilitate the emergence of a number of autonomous theocratic structures, anarcho-messianic movements and even some semblance of local democracy, inspired *inter alia* by broadly Daoist philosophical principles.

Among the most successful of these new movements was the Celestial Masters sect, founded in the second century CE by Zhang Daoling who claimed to have received a revelation from Laozi. Its characteristic features were a nation-wide organisation (though mainly in the Western provinces), comprising a network of loosely related village parishes, clergy and popular ritual practices that have survived into modern times. It provided a mixture of moral precept, spiritual guidance and the arts of divination, geomancy, astrology, exorcism and healing which served the needs of the populace at large in ways that the official Confucian rites and teachings could not. This development has caused some difficulties for Western commentators. In the first place, there has been a tendency to characterise this movement as the 'Daoist *church*', and while at one level this is a matter of linguistic expediency, the implicit analogy with the Christian church is misleading, particularly in view of the lack in the Daoist case of any centralised institutional or doctrinal authority. There were indeed many Daoist religious sects which emerged and flourished in the period following the foundation of the Celestial Masters sect which bear obvious analogies with Christian sectarianism, but these Daoist movements constituted a loose collectivity which lacked any tendency towards strong doctrinal coherence or institutional hierarchy.

The second problem concerns the customary identification of the foundation of religious Daoism with Zhang Daoling, and beyond this, as we saw earlier, to see this foundation as a profoundly regrettable departure from the pristine teachings of Laozi, Zhuangzi and Liezi. This view, however, not only underestimates the long-lasting and pervasive cultural role that Daoism played in the life of the mass of Chinese people, but also fails to recognise the extent to which the Celestial Masters movement was a continuation and amplification of social movements, religious practices and philosophical ideas that had been forged over the preceding centuries. The *Daodejing* itself was a prime canonical text of the movement, a central focus of Daoist practice, and as Francesco Verellen points out, the arrival on the scene of Zhang Daoling was by no means a 'signal for the creation *ex nihilo* of "religious Taoism"', as has frequently been assumed, for it absorbed many teachings and practices from earlier traditions, especially those relating to alchemy and the prolongation of life (1995: 322; see also Girardot 1983: 276–8; Kohn 1998).

The Celestial Masters movement was only one of a number of similar messianic movements which emerged at the beginning of the Common Era, and according to Henri Maspero, Daoism was already widespread amongst all classes in China by the second century BCE (1981: 416–30). Furthermore, rituals such as that of Cosmic Renewal, performed by Daoist priests, though certainly in many ways a new departure, at the same time carried within them traces of teachings and attitudes that were recognisably drawn from the earlier Daoist traditions. The extraordinarily rich liturgies of the Daoists, practised right up to the present day in Taiwan, have remained largely ignored by the West, and it is only in recent years that the overall aim of these liturgies, namely to ensure balance and harmony between Heaven, Earth and humanity, have begun to be understood and this aim linked to the earlier Daoist philosophical writings as well as to the lone quest of the sage for unity with the *dao* (Lagerwey 1987; Schipper 1993).[26]

The period following the fall of the Han in 220 CE, the so-called Weijin period, was one of continuing social and political instability, while at the same time leading to the further evolution and proliferation of Daoism. Freed from the repressive Confucian ordinances of the Han period, this was 'a truly refreshing moment of intellectual emancipation in Chinese history' (Zhang 1992: 53). Renewed Daoist speculation flourished, many new schools sprang up and a whole body of scriptures was created. In addition to schools like the Celestial Masters which catered to the needs of town and village communities, there were several closely connected movements or sects of a more esoteric kind which served the needs of a more narrowly defined group, usually educated, and often appealing to disillusioned, unemployed or exiled scholar-officials. Of these schools the best known is the *Maoshan* (or *Shangqing*) school dating from the fourth century CE, to which the term 'mystical' is often applied. At the heart of the teachings of such schools was the search for immortality and for unity with the *dao*, in pursuit of which they developed a variety of breathing and meditation techniques and often followed a reclusive lifestyle. Set within the broad cosmological framework of the well-established correlative system, the human person was seen as a microcosm of the universe, and the circulation of the breath and the visualising of internal organs were seen as a means towards the harmonisation and unification of the microcosmic with the macrocosmic world, and thereby as a key to physical immortality. An important aspect of esoteric or mystical Daoism was the practice of alchemy. This drew on an earlier tradition which sought health and longevity by means of drugs and herbs, later giving rise to a form of 'internal' alchemy which concentrated on breathing, meditational, dietary and sexual techniques in order to conserve and enhance the life forces within the body.[27] Monasticism, influenced in part by Buddhist practices and including women as well as men, emerged as a result of the spiritual aspirations of such schools and became an important dimension of both Daoist life and the cultural life of China as a whole.

At about the same time as the development of these religious and spiritual aspects of Daoism, there emerged an intellectual/literary movement sometimes entitled 'Neo-Daoism', though in view of its debt to the earlier philosophical writings of Laozi and Zhuangzi it is more appropriately termed the 'Lao–Zhuang' tradition. The period of dynastic disintegration and social upheaval from the second century CE onwards witnessed not only the proliferation of recluses and hermits, but also a renaissance of philosophical Daoism amongst the disillusioned literati and aristocratic élite which combined elements of both Daoism and Confucianism. This development was not entirely distinct from the Daoist religious movements of the time, but its orientation was primarily intellectual and artistic rather than devotional, and was concerned more with metaphysical problems than with political or soteriological questions. It was associated with appellations such as the 'Dark Learning' and 'Pure Talk', and its most characteristic view was the identification of *dao* with nothingness/emptiness (*wu*), a notion identified with its leading exponent, Wangbi (226–249 CE). Its followers cultivated natural living and self-expression, and were often intentionally eccentric and anti-establishment in both attitude and lifestyle. Here the teachings of Zhuangzi clearly come into their own, and their best-known exponents were the 'Seven Sages of the Bamboo Grove' who reputedly found solace and inspiration in wine, poetry, music and good conversation, and who, as we saw above, are often seen as an important inspiration for subsequent developments in painting and poetry as well as on the formation of Chan Buddhism in China. Julia Ching is not the only commentator to find their romantic spirit of spontaneity and whimsical non-conformity 'evocative of the "hippie" movement of the 1960s', and a reason why 'Taoism is attractive to many young people in the West', though this modern perception may do less than justice to the philosophical and political seriousness lying behind the unorthodox behaviour of this group (1993: 99, 101).[28]

By the time of the Tang dynasty Daoism had come to enjoy semi-official status. Daoist texts were included in the state examination curriculum, and Laozi was worshipped not only as an imperial ancestor but as a divine personification of the *dao* itself.[29] This period, followed by that of the Song, represented in effect the peak of Daoist power and influence, when many Daoist monasteries were created and the first complete printing of the Daoist scriptural canon was carried out under imperial orders. The Song period, however, also witnessed the re-emergence of Confucianism as a dominant ideological force. In this epoch of unsurpassed cultural efflorescence, Confucianism saw a revival both of its philosophical formulation as well as its institutional status, and while Daoist as well as Buddhist ideas were brought into the construction of new syntheses by such thinkers as Zhuxi (1130–1200), Daoism ceased to play an important role at the centre of imperial power. As we have emphasised on several occasions, the teachings we have come to identify separately, and even in opposition, as Confucian and Daoist flowed into each other across many conceptual and institutional channels, and with the development in the Song dynasty of the movement that became known as Neo-Confucianism, the traditional ideas of Daoist and Buddhist thinkers were to some extent ingested and re-defined. As public and intellectual life came to be dominated by the Confucians, Daoism came to be looked upon with increasing disfavour, and thereafter began a long period of slow decline, a process which in the nineteenth century was assisted by the irruption of aggressive and proselytising powers from the West (Schipper 1993: 16–19). New Daoist sects emerged, however, and Daoist influence remained, in particular amongst the general populace through the local parish clergy and also through the network of monasteries to which even orthodox Confucian scholars and bureaucrats might go for spiritual retreat or medical treatment. Unlike institutional Confucianism, Daoism has survived to this day as a living tradition, not only in the Chinese diaspora but also in the People's Republic where, following its near-destruction in the Cultural Revolution, something of a Daoist renaissance has occurred since the end of the Cultural Revolution (Dean 1993: 3–4). It remains to be seen whether this development will lead to a true resurgence of Daoism in mainland China or remain a marginal phenomenon under strict government control, though its association with anarchism and rebellion points towards the latter fate.[30]

# 3

# 'CRAMPED SCHOLARS'

## Western interpretations of Daoism

### Daoism under Western gaze

The long slow decline of Daoism in China is synchronous with its long slow rise in Western consciousness. When Europeans first acquired detailed knowledge of the Chinese civilisation in the sixteenth and seventeenth centuries, however, it was Confucianism rather than Daoism that attracted their notice and which they came to identify as that nation's heart and soul. Daoism was accordingly largely ignored or, at best, refracted through the reducing lenses of the Confucian literati, the official custodians of the Chinese cultural legacy. As the historian Lionel Jensen observes, for the Jesuit missionaries and their European readers 'Confucius was, in effect, China', and not only did this lead to an optical occlusion of Daoism in Western eyes, but more broadly has long prevented commentators on China from fully appreciating the rich and dialectical diversity of Chinese intellectual and religious culture (1997: 123, 267).[1] Indeed this Confucian-saturated construction has been perpetuated by the Chinese themselves, and even up to recent times Chinese intellectuals have tended to portray Daoism as an embarrassing throwback to a superstitious and reactionary past. As late as 1961 C.K. Yang wrote that to include Daoism in an account of Chinese religious history was a 'humiliation', for 'its activities have not benefited the nation at all [but] have repeatedly misled the people by their pagan magic' (1961: 5; see also Zhang 1998: ch. 6). The modern fate of Daoism is undergoing some interesting transformations within the Chinese world itself, and reports of its demise, circulated equally in China and in the West, can now be seen to have been exaggerated. But our main task here is with its fate in the West, and the aim of this chapter will be to recount in outline the ways in which, from the Enlightenment period onwards, Daoism has been digested and redigested within the insatiable maw of modern Western thought. What will become apparent is the sheer complexity of this hermeneutical phenomenon, parallel in this respect too to its career in its ancestral land, a cultural odyssey which is still unfolding beneath our inquisitive gaze.

By the time the Renaissance had run its course and the first outlines of what we now think of as the modern world were emerging in Europe, the image of China as a place of marvel and mystery had already imprinted itself on the European mind through the writings of Marco Polo and Sir John Mandeville, as well as from the reports of European traders (Mackerras 1989: ch. 2). But it was the Jesuits who, having for two centuries enjoyed privileged access to the political and cultural heart of China, brought that civilisation clearly into the field of European vision for the first time. The detailed reports they sent back to their superiors in Rome concerning the peoples, institutions and belief systems of China were widely disseminated in Europe and helped to form a seductive image of Chinese thought and culture which has produced palpable reverberations down to the present day.

The outlines of this story are well known. The first Jesuit missionary to reach Beijing, Matteo Ricci, initially allied himself with the Buddhists whose rituals and way of life bore some superficial resemblances to those of his own religion, but he soon abandoned this tactic and associated himself with Confucianism and with the scholar–bureaucrat class, the *ru*. Confucian teaching, with its supposedly rationalistic outlook and deistic frame of mind, appeared in its Jesuit-constructed version to be at least not incompatible with Catholic doctrine, and opened up the possibility of some sort of accommodation. Though at one level it was clear that Daoism and Buddhism resembled Christianity more closely than Confucianism, at any rate in their overt practices, it was this very similarity which made them dangerous rivals and drove Ricci and his followers to align themselves with Confucian teachings and practices which, represented as being free of superstitious religiosity, were therefore more open to the revelation of the Christian Gospel. Ricci's overriding aim, then, was to find some sort of common ground with Confucianism and on this basis to attempt to replace the degenerate spiritual elements of both Daoism and Buddhism with the far superior spiritual ideals of Christianity (Mungello 1989: 64).[2] Daoism was accordingly branded as an idolatrous superstition and, by contrast with the enlightened deism of the state religion, dismissed as a 'false sect' whose teachings were inspired by the devil and whose practices gave rise to ravings and delirium. In the course of the seventeenth century the Jesuits did indeed gain some understanding of the history of Daoism and formed an admiration for the *Daodejing*, two Latin translations of which were made by members of the order around 1700. However, with encouragement from Chinese intellectuals, they continued to propagate the view that, with its spells, talismans and exorcisms, Daoism betokened a form of perverted paganism, and in its modern religious embodiment represented a sorry lapse from the purity of its original philosophical teachings.

This was a portentous beginning to the encounter between Daoism and the West, and bears the seeds of a number of long-lasting misunderstandings about Chinese culture, including the acceptance of a sharp division between the different 'religions' of China, a clear distinction between 'pure' Daoist philosophy and its 'degenerate' offspring, and an underestimation of the role of religion both in the Confucian establishment and in Chinese cultural life as a whole (Paper 1995: 4–10). The generally negative attitude towards Daoism that was formed in these early days remained fairly constant throughout the seventeenth and eighteenth centuries, and the judgements of Ricci were repeated and elaborated in most European writings on the subject of China. Thus Athanasius Kircher's *China Illustrata* of 1667, an important disseminator of information about China, characterised Daoism as full of 'abominable falsehoods', and portrayed it as a form of idolatry originating in Egypt. China, according to Kircher, was crammed with idols and Daoism, a religion of the common people, practised repulsive rituals associated with exorcism, geomancy and longevity. Another influential work was *De Conversione Indorum* & *Gentilium* (1669) which drew on all the available Jesuit literature on China to draw a vivid picture of that civilisation. The author, Johann Hoornbeck, was in general highly laudatory of China, as were most other Jesuit commentators of the time, praising its government, society, manners, morals, learning and laws, and arguing that Christians could well emulate that country's love of learning. On the other hand, Daoists were sharply distinguished from Confucianists, and the teachings and practices of the former were dismissed as so much superstition. This kind of judgement was repeated a few years later by Charles le Gobien in a more thorough and extended appraisal of Daoism in his *Histoire de l'édit de l'Empereur de la Chine* (1698), in which he accused Daoists of 'poisoning' the Chinese way of life with a stream of 'magicians, enchanters, and professional crooks', and pronounced their search for longevity by alchemical means as 'ridiculous' (Mungello 1989: 350–3).[3]

It was in ways such as these, therefore, that Daoism was constructed and schematised in a manner that could conveniently be read in accordance with the expansionist demands of the Counter-Reformation Church: enlightened Confucianism demonstrated that the Chinese mind was open to conversion, while benighted Daoism justified the urgency of this project. The most important group of people to inherit and propagate this Jesuit-inspired picture were the philosophical thinkers of the seventeenth and eighteenth centuries. They relied largely on Jesuit sources for their information about China, and wove these sources with considerable alacrity and skill into their own radical programme. Naturally they approached matters with a different agenda from the Catholic missionaries. For them the enemy was not Protestantism or paganism, but rather the Leviathan of state and church, the *Ancien Régime* and the Catholic Church, *l'infâme*, in Voltaire's memorable characterisation. The leading sinophile of his day, Voltaire seized on what he saw as the secular and rationalistic nature of Confucianism and held it up as a model political philosophy that was based on reason rather than superstition and which provided the foundation for what was believed to be an enlightened and harmonious political order. The Jesuit representation of Confucianism allowed him to see in it the ideal of a tolerant, deistic religion that was free from dogmas, miracles and priests, an image which contrasted sharply with the hated Catholic Church.[4] Inevitably Daoism, which with Buddhism gets only a passing reference in his writings, was cast as the villain which conveniently mirrored the perfidy and corruption of the Catholic Church.

Leibniz, who from an early age had taken a great interest in China and who engaged in a long correspondence with the Jesuits on this matter, had a yet different agenda. His main concern was not the corruption of the old régime or the infamous superstitions of the Catholic Church, but rather the need for principles of harmony whereby the warring religious factions of Europe could be reconciled. In the pursuit of this objective China was adopted as an ally. Through his Jesuit friend Joachim Bouvet, he acquired a deep respect for Confucian philosophy and was especially drawn to the idea that the Confucian classics contained a near complete system of the true religion which underlay all creeds, a universal lost knowledge – the *philosophia perennis* – that had been preserved in China in embryonic form (Mungello 1977: ch. 3).[5] He showed no interest in Daoism as such, which in its contemporary form would no doubt have represented for him a tragic departure from the fundamental principles of the perennial philosophy, but nevertheless he was quick to notice resemblances between his own metaphysics and Chinese organicist thinking which, as we saw earlier, had integrated elements of Daoist naturalism within the Neo-Confucian synthesis.

This opens up the intriguing possibility that a certain strand of modern Western metaphysics may have had a significant Chinese input, and scholars have long disputed whether this was indeed a case of influence or merely one of corroboration. Joseph Needham has taken the view that Leibniz's monadology was indeed given an important stimulus by Neo-Confucian metaphysics, and that this way of thinking in its turn led to a counter-cultural organicist tradition in the West, one associated in his judgement with a line of thinkers from Schelling through Bergson to Whitehead and beyond. Hence, 'since the [Western] philosophy of organism owes a great deal to Leibniz', it owes something to Chinese scientific thinking as well, and since, according to Needham, an organicist model has begun to replace the Newtonian mechanistic model in recent times, the organic outlook of the Chinese thinkers 'may turn out to have been a necessary element in the formation of a perfected world-view of natural science' (1956: 292, 339). There were, Needham concedes, other, Western influences at work in

Leibniz's thinking, such as that of the Cambridge Platonists – and he could also have mentioned a long tradition of organicist thought in Europe stretching back as far as the ancient Greek cosmologists – but it was Chinese philosophy that provided him with the most complete model of an organic universe with which to combat the mechanistic and materialist thinking of his day (Needham 1956: 496–505).

This view has been disputed by a number of scholars; David Mungello, for example, argues that Leibniz had already formulated his organicist thinking prior to his acquaintance with Chinese philosophy, and that 'the Chinese influence on Leibniz was more corroborative than germinal' (1977: 15).[6] Be that as it may, this whole debate reinforces the thesis that is central to the present study, and highlights the manner in which Chinese ideas were beginning in this period to be transformed and transposed in Europe through a series of textual readings which in turn were patterned by local interpretative interests. In Leibniz's case there was his concern with rediscovering the perennial philosophy on which to found political and religious accord, and in Needham's reading there was the desire to champion an organicist alternative to Newtonian mechanism.

The decline of Confucianism in Europe's affections which began in the late eighteenth century did little in the short term to improve Europe's understanding of Daoism, and indeed some of the obloquy that Daoism attracted in the West became attached to Chinese culture and society as a whole. Kant took only cursory notice of Chinese thought, and was venturing little beyond common stereotypes when he referred to 'the monster system' of Laozi who, according to him, taught that nothingness was the highest good and who advocated a kind of perpetual tranquillity in which all distinctions are annihilated; indeed, according to Kant 'philosophy was not to be found in the orient' (Ching and Oxtoby 1992: 222–3; see also Glasenapp 1954: 104). Hegel, though no more sympathetic to Chinese thought than Kant, was better informed historically and succeeded in finding a place for Daoism in his historical dialectic. Where Kant placed Eastern thought in a timeless realm of exclusion from philosophical discourse, Hegel incorporated it into his historicised account of the maturation of human freedom and into his narration of the dialectical life-trajectory of Spirit. While he was prepared to take Daoist philosophy seriously, even drawing tentative parallels with Pre-Socratic philosophy, he showed somewhat less sympathy for Eastern systems of thought than many of his contemporaries, and his views have been a baneful influence on the West's perception both of Daoism in particular and of the cultures of Asia in general.

The Romantic period, it will be recalled, was one of growing orientalist enthusiasm, no longer for China but for the philosophies, myths and poetry of India, and while Hegel's thinking was certainly affected by this trend, he by no means shared its rhapsodic extremes. Indeed, he was in many ways critical of the Romantic outlook as a whole, even while being powerfully influenced by it. His historicist account of the growth of consciousness and freedom of Spirit, with its apotheosis in Western Christian culture, led him to detest the 'wild excesses of fantasy' and the 'unrestrained frenzy' which he found in the Orient, and he came to regard the civilisations of the East as stagnant, frozen in their past and incapable of regeneration. Certainly in his reading of their history, these ancient traditions were not destroyed but were rather preserved and carried forward into the higher synthesis of later times, but the East itself is now petrified, a stagnant culture bound to a past which of itself it cannot overcome or transcend. Consistent with this overall view, Hegel consigned Daoism to the infancy of philosophy, stuck 'in its most elementary stage' as he put it (Hegel 1995: 125), and, following Kant's reduction of Daoism to a form of nihilism, he portrayed it as representing the initial stages of philosophical thinking where Spirit is viewed in purely abstract and unreflective terms and where the ideas of subjectivity and freedom are not yet known, a condition wherein 'the origin of things is nothing, emptiness, the altogether undetermined, the abstract universal' (1995: 124–5; see also Halbfass 1988; Hulin 1979; Kim 1978).

Something of this attitude was reflected a hundred or so years later in the work of Max Weber. Like Hegel, his outlook was eclectic and global, and his sociological studies of China represent a landmark in cross-cultural studies. However, his overriding aim remained firmly Eurocentric, and while he offered the first major systematic analysis of Chinese society, his studies of its religious culture were intended as support for his key thesis concerning the rise of bourgeois capitalism in Europe. Weber's conclusion was that the rational transformation of the world, driven in the main by Protestant theology in Europe, was impeded in China by the sense of passive adjustment to the world conveyed by its major religious systems. In brief, Chinese religions lacked the radical sense of transcendence that in Europe provided a decisive innovatory potential. Even more than Confucianism, Daoism was deficient in the drive of individual religious inspiration that characterised the Puritans in Europe and America. Thus, in spite of its intra-worldly orientation, Daoism was a serious obstacle to social and economic progress. It was devoid of that 'tension with the world' that characterised the Protestant ethic, and hence was incapable of exercising 'the leverage for influencing conduct through inner force freed of tradition and convention' (Weber 1951: 236). As with Hegel, he attempted a sympathetic portrayal of the spiritual qualities of Daoism, but in the final analysis saw it as backward-looking, unable to divest itself of its magical orientation towards an 'enchanted' world or of its pious adjustment to the way of nature. It thus lacked the power of rational mastery over nature that made possible the creation of the modern world, and thereby served as a contrasting foil to Western rationalism (Roetz 1993: 3–4).

Hegel's understanding of Chinese philosophy reflected a stage of transition in Western understanding of the ancient culture of China and gave expression to, and indeed in some senses gave a powerful impetus to, the growing ambivalence towards the East which we reflected upon earlier. On the one hand, we can see an enhanced aspiration towards a more scholarly approach towards Asian cultures from the early nineteenth century onwards, and while Daoism remained for a long while yet in the shadow of Buddhism and Hinduism, its ideas began to flow gently, if barely perceptibly, into the mind of the West. Yet at the same time this was a period in which there was significant reaction in the West against Chinese culture in general and in which China as a whole became a byword for decadence and corruption. The Chinese were typically dismissed as adapters of the traditions of others, lacking in originality and creative thought of their own. The nineteenth century was, of course, a period of rapid imperial expansion, and the campaign to conquer the languages, traditions and literatures of the Orient marched side by side with the expansion of European commercial and political power. This whole development was given vigorous expression and justification by the emergence in the second half of the century of the evolutionist anthropology of Herbert Spencer and Edward Tylor. According to this approach, savage cultures yielded in time to barbarian cultures and finally to civilisation, nobler religions blossoming on the remains of 'baser' faiths, and thus the ossified religions of China could conveniently be allotted a place on the evolutionary ladder well below that of the Christian West. Not only was Hegel's dialectical philosophy thereby given empirical validation, but a scientific foundation was laid for a policy of enforced modernisation and the imposition of superior Western cultural norms and values on the inferior nations of the East.

Nevertheless, in spite of the tarnishing of China's image in Western eyes in the nineteenth century, the expansion of Western political and military power in the East gave fresh impetus to the growth of scholarly interest in China in that period, and contributed towards a recognition of the philosophical significance of the *Daodejing*. An important event was the appointment in 1815 of Abel Rémusat (1788–1832) to the first European Chair of Chinese language and Literature at the Collège de France, followed by the founding of the Société Asiatique in 1822 and the endowment of chairs in Chinese studies in Russia in 1838 and in Britain in 1876. The work of interpretation and translation of Chinese texts was subsequently carried on by a number of figures including Stanislas Julien, who translated the *Daodejing* into French in 1841, Édouard Chavannes (1865–1918), one of the first to study Chinese religious traditions, and J.J.M. de Groot (1854–1921), the author of a six-volume study of the religious systems of China published between 1892 and 1910. Rémusat followed Hegel in giving certain proto-philosophical credentials to Daoism, while at the same time reinforcing the earlier view that popular or religious Daoism represented a sad decline into a degraded form of superstition. This view became almost a dogma from the nineteenth century onwards, repeated and elaborated by a number of writers and typified in Chavannes's dismissal of Daoist religion as 'a jumble of vulgar superstitions' (1895–1915, 1: xviii).[7] It was through thinkers such as these, therefore, that a European-constructed Daoism – the very word itself was invented in France in 1839 – began to take shape in Western consciousness. In this way an essential and original Daoism came to be defined, a teaching associated with certain classic texts, which was seen as reflecting a certain timeless spiritual quality: 'words of wisdom for all time', as R.K. Douglas expressed it (1911: 202). Yet it also served to marginalise and demean contemporary Chinese religious culture by depicting it as a degraded tradition, the latter-day product of a long decline from original purity, thereby again reinforcing the condescending attitudes that helped to justify imperial policies towards a stagnant and degenerate China.

These attitudes, shaped largely in Catholic France and amplifying earlier Jesuit-inspired archetypes, were matched in the nineteenth century in certain respects by the work of Protestant missionaries from Europe and America, who nevertheless made significant contributions towards the opening up of Chinese language and literature to Western minds. One of the most influential of these was the Scottish Congregationalist missionary James Legge (1815–97). He played a leading role in defining Daoism for the West, creating a vocabulary and a way of speaking about it which remained authoritative for many decades to come, and on his return from China he assumed the first British chair in Chinese studies at Oxford in 1876. For Norman Girardot he was 'The single most important figure contributing to the late Victorian invention of "Taoism" as a reified entity' (1992: 188). He was a prolific translator, and rendered into English five volumes of Chinese classics from 1861 to 1885 which became standard editions well into the twentieth century. In view of Legge's long-held eminence as a translator, his emphasis on the classic texts, though of inestimable importance in awakening the West to the rich traditions of China, has inevitably led to the identification of Daoism with certain ancient texts and doctrines and to the consequent underestimation of the doctrinal diversity, the textual diversification and the institutional proliferation that have more recently come to be recognised as important facets of Daoism. Of course much of this is simply the result of the limitations of the scholarly tools available in his day, and it would be perverse to criticise Legge for lacking knowledge which was only available to later generations. At the same time, however, it is important to recognise the often unconscious factors that worked their way through his work into common understanding. Like his predecessors and contemporaries in this field, Legge tended to dismiss popular and religious Daoism as 'superstitious', 'unreasonable', 'fantastic' and 'grotesque' by comparison with the philosophical depth of the teachings of Laozi and Zhuangzi (1881:

ch. 3), and while he did not attempt to disguise his admiration for Chinese culture, he made it quite clear that the negative assessment of popular religion in China pointed unmistakably to the need for the Christian Gospel (1881: 308). There was an interesting corollary to this, for Legge's negative assessment of the Daoist religion did not prevent him from detecting in it certain anticipations of Christianity, a figuration which for a while became popular within orientalist discourse in general, echoing similar speculations about Hinduism. Thus, for example, he claimed to discern in the Daoist concept of the Three Pure Ones a foreshadowing of the Christian Trinity, and repeated Rémusat's belief that the name of Jehovah was encoded in the *Daodejing* (1881: 210–11; see also Welch 1957: 5–7).

The same period produced several studies which adopted a similar perspective. In 1881 the British scholar F.H. Balfour spoke of the 'sublime doctrines' of Daoism as becoming 'obscured in a mist of hocus-pocus and imposture...a system of superstitious folly' (1881: vi), and in 1905 Edward Parker, while likening traditional philosophical Daoism to the Stoicism of Marcus Aurelius, dismissed contemporary Daoism as 'degraded' and the whole Chinese race as sunk in 'degeneration and universal corruption' (1905: 48–9). Even where grudging admiration for the philosophy of the *Laozi* was allowed, its genius, incomprehensible in the context of the 'unimaginative' and 'stagnant' nature of Chinese culture, was at times ascribed to influences from India or the Middle East rather than to those of China itself (Edkins 1889; Girardot 1999: ch. 6). However, more emollient sentiments were being expressed in that period on the other side of the Atlantic. A growing public and academic interest in Oriental religions became evident in America in the latter part of the century, a development which received a boost at the time of the World's Parliament of Religions held in Chicago in 1893 when the Daoist representative was awarded a prize (Seager 1995). Of considerable importance in this respect was Samuel Johnson's popular work on Oriental religions of 1877, which devoted considerable space and sensitive analysis to Daoism. Johnson was a member of the transcendentalist circle, and, like Emerson and Thoreau, he sought in the East the inspiration for a universal spirituality independent of creed and sectarian allegiance, which, unlike Christianity, did not rest on a radical separation of the natural from the supernatural. It is not surprising, therefore, that Daoism won his approval. He contrasted it favourably with Buddhism since, unlike the latter, it did not deny the reality of the material world and was in his view much more closely tied to the practicalities of life and society. The writings of Laozi, 'this Chinese non-conformist' as he called him, represented in his view 'a voice of universal truth, appealing to all ages', a wonderful ethical teaching of spiritual simplicity which 'is neither ascetic nor pessimistic [and] does not despise the body', a teaching which advocated 'the love and service of mankind...spontaneity and simplicity of life...[and] non-interference with the freedom of others' (1877: 862–72). This remarkably sympathetic portrayal, however, is almost predictably cancelled out in Johnson's final judgement of Daoist religion as 'a perversion of the highest fruits of spirituality', and in his lament that these enlightened teachings were transformed over time into a mythology by the infection of superstitions such as astrology and alchemy (1877: 882–3).[8]

In spite of these final and at the time almost obligatory reservations, Johnson's treatment of Daoism as a profound ethical teaching with a sublime yet naturalistic conception of the human condition represented a move towards a more serious engagement with Daoism. From the late nineteenth century into the early decades of the twentieth we find Daoist ideals, concepts and values entering increasingly, if still marginally, into Western discourse. In 1906 the British orientalist Lionel Giles characterised the *Daodejing* as 'a great system of transcendental ethical philosophy...[a] magnificent scheme of thought' (1906b: 11), and in similarly enthusiastic tones the historian Adolf Reichwein, writing a few years later, described Laozi as 'a great luminary...for the present generation', pointing to the increasing number of translations of the *Daodejing* that had appeared over the past few decades which gave evidence of the 'demands of our time for inwardness of life' (1925: 4–5).

This burgeoning interest in Daoism was in part a consequence of a growing scepticism in Germany towards the ideal of progress and towards the alarming growth of industrial capitalism. A number of thinkers in the late nineteenth and early twentieth centuries had given voice to deep concern over the moral and spiritual vacuum that modern Western civilisation seemed to have engendered, and many people turned to alternative non-orthodox pathways for salvation, for example, to various pre-Christian pagan cults, to occultism and to nature worship. In Germany this mood was closely connected with the *völkisch* movement, a cultural phenomenon that expressed restless nationalist sentiments and sought political and cultural assuagement through a return to an idealised age in the past. The sense of spiritual and cultural disenchantment also helped to stimulate a strong growth in orientalist interest in the years around the turn of the century. Hinduism and Buddhism had by that time already become firmly established in the European imagination, but the *fin de siècle* mood just described, allied to a significant increase in the number of popular orientalist publications, helped to give Eastern wisdom an ever more attractive image in the West. Reichwein characterised this mood as nothing less than an 'Asiatic fever' which was 'destined to reveal to the West its own decadence', and to bring about a spiritual transformation (1925: 4).

The turning towards the East in this period was also accompanied by a spirit of neo-Renaissance syncretism which sought a new universal outlook with the help of, *inter alia*, oriental religions. This was, of course, a time of the rapid expansion of European overseas empires, a process anointed at the Congress of Berlin in 1878 which confirmed Europe's right to colonise the world. Yet paradoxically this aggressive expansionism was an important factor in helping to engender not only an atmosphere of European suprematism, but also of openness to non-European traditions. This was especially evident in the emergence at that time of various 'universal wisdom' movements such as the Theosophical Society with its championing of the ideal of a *philosophia perennis* that embraced the world's major religions, as well as in the ecumenical impetus of the World's Parliament of Religions, and in the huge success of writings such as Edwin Arnold's *The Light of Asia*, first published in 1879. Such factors gave expression to a growing sense of the limitations of the traditional Western outlook in general and a more critical approach towards Christian teaching in particular.

Daoism still lagged behind its Asian counterparts in the strength of its appeal, but its teachings were beginning to be brought to the public's attention through a growing body of writings. It was even touted as a possible model for a universal religion, in view of its supposed lack of doctrinal content (Reichwein 1925: 9). A leading exponent in America of the new universalism was the German-born Paul Carus. He believed passionately in religious toleration and in drawing the Asian and Western traditions into dialogue, and saw the publication of his version of the *Daodejing* in 1913 as an important contribution to the ideal of a universal brotherhood, claiming to discover in that work some significant analogies with Christian teaching. Echoes of this kind of attitude were also to be found in G.G. Alexander's edition the *Laozi*, in which the classic Daoist text was presented as a manifestation of a universal wisdom tradition, and also in the version by I.W. Heysinger, entitled *The Light of China* as an echo to the more famous work of Edwin Arnold, which boldly placed the *Daodejing* and the Bible on equal moral footing (Alexander 1895; Heysinger 1903).[9]

The influence of these more encouraging approaches to Daoism was by no means confined to scholars and orientalist specialists, but became evident in the broader cultural scene and in the modernist revolution that was taking place in European culture in the early decades of the twentieth century. The list of literary figures from that period who took an interest in Daoism includes Hesse, Brecht, Kafka, Lowry and Claudel, and the popular novels of writers such as Pearl Buck and Edgar Snow were important in bringing China in general to the attention of the public at large. Of even wider intellectual significance are the names of Tolstoy, Buber, Heidegger and Jung, all of whom, as we shall see later, were drawn in various ways to Daoist ideas, and who saw in Daoism an important confirmation of their own particular visions. Indeed the first three on this list embarked, with varying degrees of success, on plans to translate Daoist classics, though only Buber completed the task, a translation with commentary of the *Zhuangzi* published in 1910, which had a significant impact amongst German thinkers of his generation (Herman 1996).[10] A little later, the missionary Richard Wilhelm helped to advance European interest in Daoism even further through his translations in the 1920s of the *Yijing* and *The Secret of the Golden Flower* (a Daoist alchemical text). These editions were widely read and re-translated, and had a seminal influence on, amongst others, C.G. Jung, for whom they were important in helping to confront what he saw as a spiritual crisis at the heart of European culture.

Another significant transformative factor in the Western encounter with Daoism came with the work of the French sinologist, Henri Maspero (1883–1945). Building on the earlier work of J.J.M. de Groot, Alfred Forke and Marcel Granet, and thereby helping to broaden sinological studies from their hitherto narrowly textual base, Maspero embarked on the first full-scale study of Daoist religion in its social as well as its doctrinal aspects, and thereby established definitively its importance within a total picture of Chinese history and culture. This work moved decisively away from earlier negative appraisals, and sought to draw out the continuities and interactions between philosophical and religious Daoism rather than to depict the latter as simply a debased version of the former. Thus his rejection of the entrenched view of Daoist religion as 'only a corrupted and degenerate descendant of the doctrines of the ancient masters' (1965: 265) represented an important shift of opinion, as too did his challenge to the long-held view that China was an essentially Confucian culture, a mindset which, as we have already noted, was as much the product of Chinese as of Western scholarship.

The work of Maspero was carried on and developed by a growing band of scholars in Europe, America, Asia and Australasia, helped by the establishment of specialist journals and, since 1968, by regular international conferences, and marked by such projects as the editing and translation of the Daoist canon.[11] A notable factor here, witnessing to the transcultural nature of this scholarly endeavour, has been the work of Western-based Chinese scholars such as Wing-tsit Chan and Fung Yu-lan, as well as the growing band of Chinese and Japanese scholars working within more strictly Asian academic environments. In broad terms, this kind of work has made it possible for the first time to integrate the Daoist tradition into the comparative history of world religions in which it has often been allowed only a condescendingly marginal status.[12] They have also entered in all sorts of ways into wider academic and cultural domains in recent times, led in part by scholars such as Kaltenmark, Creel and Welch who have sought to make their findings available to non-specialist audiences, and who have drawn attention to the moral, spiritual and therapeutic potential that Daoism holds for the West.

The explosion of popular interest has also been the work of many amateurs, specialists from other disciplines, and enthusiasts of all sorts who have drawn Daoism, both in its theoretical and practical aspects, into their own spheres of interest, and reinterpreted and reshaped it accordingly. In the years following the Second World War many Eastern traditions, from Zen and Tibetan Buddhism to Yoga to Hari Krishna, have penetrated Western consciousness, the texts and practices of Asian religions threatening at times to supplant indigenous spiritual traditions. Daoism has played a significant, if not always prominent, part in this. Writers such as Alan Watts have seen in Daoism an eloquent response to the liberationist demands of his time, and have drawn it in close alliance with the cultural preoccupations of that epoch (1973, 1979). More recently this sort of interest has been carried forward on the wave of New Age enthusiasm which has greatly contributed to Western involvement with Daoism, albeit often as a form of watered-down perennial wisdom, and we have witnessed an extraordinary growth in the popularity of Daoism in recent years even after the decline of the 'counter-culture'. The classic texts of Daoism have been widely read and various facets of Daoism have been enticed into a whole range of contemporary concerns, stretching from spiritual development and personal growth to the world of business and politics. Buddhism has long been a model for those seeking alternatives to supposedly discredited Western ideas and practices, and now it is the turn of Daoism to be drawn into and reinterpreted for this purpose.[13]

The academic world beyond that of Chinese specialists has, it is true, been a little less eager to take Daoism seriously. However, over the past half-century and more it has increasingly entered the field of comparative religious and philosophical studies. A fascinating example of this sort of enterprise can be found in the series of *Eranos* seminars which took place annually between 1933 and 1951 at a villa overlooking Lake Maggiore, at which a number of celebrated scholars including Martin Buber, Mircea Eliade, C.G. Jung and Rudolf Otto sought common ground between the religious traditions of Asia and Europe. The comparativist movement has found an especially welcome home in the USA, where oriental studies in general have expanded well beyond the borders of specialist orientalist departments. As we noted earlier, a number of thinkers in philosophy and related fields has come to take an interest in Daoism, not as an example of benighted superstition or of ineffable mysticism, but as a serious partner in dialogue across a whole range of issues from relativism to eco-philosophy. The details of recent encounters of this sort will occupy us in subsequent chapters, but it is worth emphasising here the extent to which Daoism has, in the context of Western orientalist discourse, undergone a profound transformation. While with the Jesuit missionaries it was regarded as a primitive superstition ripe for replacement by the truths of Christianity, and in Hegel as part of the yet unformed, embryonic stage in the formation of Spirit, it is now being welcomed as an active ingredient in certain central aspects of contemporary thought, as a key to spiritual and physical health, and by some even as a blueprint for the earth's very survival.

## Reading Daoism

The long historical disclosure of Daoism to Western gaze has until lately been marked by a concentration on a remarkably narrow range of sources, and more than any other Eastern religion Daoism has impinged on Western consciousness as a mainly *textual* object rather than as a living tradition. In spite of the earlier sinological endeavours of Christian missionaries such as Legge and Wilhelm, and leaving aside the anthropological work of de Groot, only recently has the West acquired systematic access to first-hand experience of this ancient tradition. And until the last few decades there have been no Asian missionaries of the stripe of Vivekananda or Suzuki to bring 'pure' native Daoism to Western shores.[14] Thus, while the development of Daoist scholarship from Henri Maspero onwards has enabled us to understand that tradition within the wider context of the religious and social history of China, there has been a marked tendency in the West to construct Daoism almost exclusively through a narrowly selected range of ancient texts, and to see it as a predominantly philosophical/mystical tradition. Moreover, according to certain critics this 'textual reification' is not merely a consequence of historical accident but, in the words of Richard King, of the 'clear literary bias within modern Western conceptions of religion' which has tended to portray religions as originating primarily in the written word of sacred scripture (Almond 1988: 25; King 1999: 62; see also Wright 1960b: 242). From their earliest days, sinological studies have tended to assume that certain key texts reveal the timeless essence of Chinese thought, a view supported by the fact that schools and literary traditions within China itself have constituted a continuous hermeneutical fabric. Within that tradition scholars have tended to treat such ancient writings, and even the act of writing itself, with a quasi-religious veneration, and to consider certain classic works as containing the fundamental principles on which the political and social order rested (Schwartz 1985: 407–9).[15] The *Daodejing* was undoubtedly one of the most important of these texts in the Western mind, and for a long period it represented the unique summation of Daoist teaching, tending on account of its elusive nature to confirm the mystical character of this philosophy while at the same time holding it at a convenient distance from popular religious practices in China. This attitude was expressed most vividly at the turn of the century by R.K. Douglas, who saw the whole of Daoist teaching arising from this one work like an inverted pyramid standing on a single point (1911: 186).

Recent scholarship, in China and Japan as well as in the West, has shaken this rather simplistic and convenient piece of mythology, helping to paint a much fuller picture of the Daoist tradition. As we shall see shortly, these foundational texts turn out to be internally very complex, not the heroic inventions of a single originating author but redactions created over periods of time out of a variety of sources, shaped by a mixture of influences and interpreted in widely different ways. The *Daodejing* itself is now seen to be a multi-layered, polysemic text that has been continuously reinterpreted throughout Chinese history, and has been subject to no less than seven hundred Chinese commentaries (Robinet 1998: 119). Another major contribution to this shift in perspective has been the discovery in the West of the Daoist canon, the *Daozang*, which contains a variety of kinds of text ranging from philosophical expansions of and commentaries on the Daoist classics to writings on health, ritual and meditation. It offers a textual resource considerably more variegated and more extensive than had hitherto – at least in the West – been conceived. Produced and extended over many centuries, the first known compilation of the *Daozang* was made in 471 CE, comprising over 1,200 separate pieces, and at various times since then further and more extensive compilations were made, including the first printed version in about 1100 CE, ordered by the emperor. The final printed edition, comprising over 5,000 separate texts, was produced in about 1445.[16] Though a copy was acquired by Édouard Chavannes and deposited in the Bibl<sup></sup>Bibliotèque Nationale in 1911, it has only recently been subject to careful study, and through the skills and diligence of a number of Daoist scholars a growing body of texts from this rich source has been translated and is being made available for the first time to Western readers.

This compendium of writings, carrying no information about authorship or dates of composition, written for a select group whose cultural environment has completely vanished, and often using common expressions in obscure and sometimes deliberately coded ways, has proved difficult to translate and interpret. The kind of hermeneutical perplexity this gives rise to has indeed been present from the outset of Daoist studies in the West. Right from the time of the Jesuit missionaries in the seventeenth century it has been recognised that rendering classical Chinese texts into European languages, or vice versa, confronts us with more than the standard translational headaches, and with philosophical issues that go well beyond what the philosopher W.V.O. Quine called the 'indeterminacy of translation'. The difficulties which the Jesuits encountered in translating terms like 'God' or 'grace' into Chinese are matched by more recent dilemmas over the rendering words like '*ren*', '*qi*' or '*wu-wei*' into European terms; the word *dao* itself has been variously translated as 'way', 'nature', 'mind', 'reason', 'law', 'logos', 'God', 'meaning', 'guiding discourse' and even as 'the ongoing process of the real' and 'the undifferentiated aesthetic continuum'; and in a 1915 Chinese-German dictionary, no fewer than forty-six meanings were offered for this one word (Walf 1997: 15). Key concepts within traditional European culture like 'religion' and 'philosophy' have, as we have seen, no exact equivalents in classical Chinese, and literary styles and genres defy easy matching with Western categories. The supposed 'mystical' or 'poetic' styles of Laozi and Zhuangzi respectively, for example, have proved especially obdurate and controversial, giving rise to a wide range of differing renderings of the text, provoking broad issues about whether

Zhuangzi was 'really' a poet or a philosopher, and more specific questions about the appropriate style to be adopted in the European version. Some versions, particularly those from earlier generations of translators, have been deliberately biblical in tone while others have adopted a more lyrical style. Related to this are oft-repeated questions about whether the translator should endeavour to return to the 'authentic' voice of the author, and about whether a translation should take account of the commentarial tradition which has often been the means through which the classic works have been mediated for their Chinese readership (Chan and Pollard 1995; Fleming 1998; Lin *et al.* 1995: 750–2).

There are major structural issues, too. It is not just that Chinese is a non-alphabetic language, based on ideographs or pictographs rather than composed out of a short array of abstract symbols, though this certainly poses interesting questions of principle (as we shall see in Chapter 8), but that its whole grammatical structure differs fundamentally from that of Western languages. Thus, it has frequently been pointed out that where the latter are built around a fairly strict set of rules which define circumscribed roles to different classes of words, and which specify without too much ambiguity variables such as case, tense, number and (in most instances) gender, Chinese characters, being able to function as any part of speech, person or tense, are much more open-ended, equivocal and allusive, so that context rather than inflexion provides the appropriate semantic clues. It must be emphasised that this does not present a problem exclusively for Western interpreters. As Homes Welch points out, the huge commentarial industry which has gown up in China is in large measure the result of the compressed and cryptic nature of classical Chinese writing with its lack of grammatical devices and inviolable rules, a factor which leads him to the interestingly postmodern conclusion that, 'To read is an act of creation' (1957: 12).

We need also to be aware of some of the ideological factors that enter into this hermeneutical process, stemming from the almost complete separate historical development of Western and Chinese civilisations. This is especially true in the case of religion and philosophy, where there is an almost inevitable mismatch between conceptual frameworks of the Chinese and European traditions. As David Hall and Roger Ames point out, 'The entire vocabulary of Western religious life – God, creation, sin, grace, eternity, soul, and so on – proves inappropriate for describing the non-theistic spirituality at the core of Chinese religion'. And in similar vein Benjamin Schwartz observes that 'Words such as nature, reason, science, religion, and freedom, which are deeply encrusted with countless layers of meaning in our own past, meet Chinese terms such as *tao*, *li*, and *ch'i* which have a complex history of their own within the Chinese tradition' (Hall and Ames 1995: 280; Schwartz 1985: 12).[17] Injustice is inevitably going to be done in the process of translation, and A.C. Graham, in the introduction to his translation of the *Zhuangzi*, speaks with resignation of the 'battering which a text may suffer between being written in one language and being transferred to another at the other end of the world some two thousand years later' (1981: 27).

The 'battering' which Graham refers to here is, of course, by no means value-neutral, and reminds us that all translations are inevitably affected by some sort of cultural or religious or philosophical bias. This is especially so in the present case where the West's intellectual encounter with China is located within the wider context of its global political and religious strategies, and it is hardly surprising that early translations of the *Daodejing* gave it a theistic spin, and that 'Dao' became rendered as 'God' in a number of versions (Alexander 1895; Strauss 1870).[18] In more recent times the idea that translation, like any other activity of scholarship, is both a work of interpretation and the product of a particular historical and ideological perspective that has become commonplace, and has helped to dispel the hope that, with the assiduous application of technical skills on the part of the translator, ancient authors may some day be empowered to 'speak for themselves'.[19] Nevertheless, in spite of a growing hermeneutical self-consciousness amongst scholars, there remain serious differences in approach and methodology. Thus, some translators, applying the best of historical and linguistic techniques, have set themselves the task of getting back to the authentic voice of Daoism, hopefully returning to the 'true' meaning of the original text beyond centuries of 'distorting' commentarial accretions. On the other hand, there are those who treat Daoist texts as part of an on-going, still-living tradition that has relevance today, and who therefore have no difficulty in drawing Daoist ideas into the orbit of contemporary problematics. Some versions of Daoist classics have indeed been quite openly populist or explicitly shaped by interests and enthusiasms which go well beyond those of pure scholarship, and in some cases, such as those of Martin Buber, Witter Bynner and Thomas Merton, the 'translator' was almost completely lacking in knowledge of Chinese and made use of other Western language versions and Chinese-speaking assistants.[20] No doubt Duyvendak had versions such as these in mind when he commented that 'The *Tao Te Ching* has become the victim of the worst dilettantism' (1953: 1).[21]

Whatever the problematic nature of the translations, European readers now have available a rapidly growing list of Daoist writings to choose from, including a number of new texts from the *Daozang*. In spite of this, it is still the *Laozi* and the *Zhuangzi* that attract most interest and which continue to shape Western attitudes towards Daoism, but before we turn to look at these in more detail we should note that several other Daoist texts have been available for some time in the West (Chan 1963a; Legge 1891), amongst which the *Liezi* is the most important. This work is a collection of stories and philosophical reflections dating from around the fourth century BCE.

Though first translated by Ernst Faber as long ago as 1877, the *Liezi* has been relatively neglected in the West, in spite of the fact that it represents a highly readable and entertaining presentation of Daoist ideas. In the introduction to his 1960 translation of the text, Graham comments that 'it has the merit of being by far the most easily intelligible of the classics of Taoism. For the Westerner it is perhaps the best introduction to this strange and elusive philosophy of life' (1960: 1).[22]

It was, however, the *Daodejing* which from early times until relatively recently has attracted most Western attention. Though mainly interested in Confucian ideas and writings, the Jesuits came to the view, albeit late in their Chinese sojourn, that this was the one Daoist text worthy of their attention, and several translations into Latin were made by members of the order during the eighteenth century.[23] The first European scholars of any standing to take a close interest in the *Daodejing*, however, were the French orientalists Abel Rémusat, who while pronouncing the work 'full of obscurity' likened its supposed author to Plato, and Stanislas Julien who produced the first complete French translation in 1841. This was followed in 1868 by the first complete English edition by John Chalmers, in which the text was treated for the first time as a serious contribution to metaphysics (and which, incidentally, provided inspiration for Tennyson's poem 'The Ancient Sage' (Benton 1962)). Several more versions appeared during the course of the nineteenth and early twentieth centuries, including one by Legge in 1891, and by 1925 the historian Adolf Reichwein could claim that the *Daodejing* had 'become for the present generation a bridge between East and West' (1925: 4–5). The passage across the bridge was largely one-way, however, and each edition of the work tended to draw it firmly onto Western cultural soil. Thus Victor von Strauss's first German edition of 1870 treated it as a theosophical work, an example of the kind of ancient esoteric wisdom tradition currently in vogue, and as Julia Hardy argues, 'explicit comparisons with Christianity were the norm' in most translations in that period (1998: 166). By the time of Arthur Waley's translation of 1934, an edition still widely used, the work had definitively acquired the epithet 'mystical' along with associated notions such as 'nihilist', 'quietist' and 'passivity', words which were to continue to cling to it for a long time to come. In the same period Aleister Crowley produced a translation in which he sought to encompass the Daoist text within the occultist and Kabalistic traditions, and from a completely different viewpoint the highly popular edition produced by Witter Bynner in 1943 was inspired by an ecumenical and libertarian ethic derived primarily from Emerson and Thoreau, a translation dismissed by one recent critic as 'a patchwork of Yankee transcendentalism' (Bradbury 1992 :34).[24] In recent years there has been a tendency towards a much more self-critical approach to the art of transla-tion, and Michel LaFargue, for example, aimed 'to see the world as the [Daoists] saw it', and to return the text's original historical context rather than construing it as an example of some perennial mystical philosophy which might be 'meaningful for us', or as a treatise on cosmology on the model of Plato's *Timaeus* (1992: 195, 208, 189; 1998).

Being 'meaningful for us' is indeed from any perspective a problem for a work which appears at times almost perversely elusive, and which even the eminent sinologist Marcel Granet declared impossible to translate (1934: 502–3). This is not merely a problem for Western scholars, however, for the difficulties that they have experienced in translating and interpreting the *Daodejing* reflect in some ways the learned debates over its meaning in the country of its origin. Thus in China the text has been subject over the centuries to many hundreds of separate commentaries, has been published in a number of different versions, and has been interpreted 'according to all sorts of belief patterns' (Robinet 1997: 29).[25] Moreover, classic Daoist texts such as the *Daodejing* were frequently interpreted in a variety of different ways at different levels of discourse, often making use of coded formulae whose meanings have long been forgotten, so that for example a treatise on high-flown metaphysics could equally be construed as an esoteric sexual manual.[26] According to Holmes Welch, the famous opening lines of the *Daodejing*, which have usually been taken to convey the most exalted mystical sentiments, were once glossed as 'Eat good things in the morning, and have a bowel movement in the evening', so it is hardly surprising that, after wrestling with the problems of translating this work, he concluded that 'The Chinese classics are deep waters indeed, and I think that we must recognize at the outset that of all of them the *Tao Te Ching* is the one least susceptible of a definitive translation. We cannot be certain of what it means' (1957: 119 and 13). Legge confessed he found the work 'extraordinarily obscure', its author dismissed as 'only a dreamer', and another distinguished translator was moved to ask in exasperation: 'What is all this about?' (Welch 1957: 13–14; Duyvendak 1953: 131).

Welch was resigned to taking a somewhat distant view of these matters, preferring to concentrate on the important ideas contained in the book, though it is difficult to know how you can be sure about the identity of these ideas given the uncertainties he points to in the text and in its translations. Even in the last century when Daoist scholarship was in its infancy, Herbert Giles, in the spirit of German biblical criticism, rejected the traditionalist/classicist views of Legge and others by arguing both that there was no historical evidence for the existence of Laozi, the conjectured author of the *Daodejing*, and that the text itself was a late Han forgery, or at any rate a palimpsest of textual fragments (Giles 1886; see also Girardot 1992: 190–1; Legge 1883). Since then much work has been done on such questions, and the prevailing consensus is that, whether or not Laozi actually existed, the *Daodejing* is certainly not the work of his hand, and must be seen rather as a collection of sayings, maxims or proverbs from various sources and times, originating between 650 and 350 BCE and assembled into its roughly present form in around 250 BCE. There are various shades of scholarly opinion on this issue, but all tend to reject an earlier habit of viewing it as the work of a single inspired individual who, by analogy with Christianity (not to mention Confucianism), was assumed to be the founder of Daoism; indeed, Daoism was itself once called 'Laoism' for precisely this reason.[27] Such factors as these must inevitably disappoint the expectations of the European reader who will tend to want to read it not only as a single-authored 'book', but also by analogy with classic home-grown models as a logically coherent and closely reasoned discourse (Mair 1990: 124). The translator D.C. Lau has called it an anthology, and even its standard categorisation as a work of philosophy is questionable in the light of its probable origin as a collection of aphorisms reflecting the work of diviners and astrologers (Lau 1963: 14; Schipper 1993: 185).

Debate on these matters has been further complicated by the discovery in 1973 of two silk versions of the *Daodejing* dating from the beginning of the Han dynasty, along with a number of other Daoist-inclined texts. Though there are no radical differences between these and subsequent versions, the new findings throw much fresh light on the origins and composition of the *Daodejing*, including some detailed variations in particular words and in syntax, and indications of a link between Daoism and the Legalist school. There is also an intriguing inversion of the standard order of the text, placing the later '*De*' section before the opening '*Dao*' portion, possibly reflecting the original order and at the same time imparting a somewhat different emphasis to the text by giving the politically oriented chapters priority over those with more clearly philosophical import (Graham 1989: 374; Henricks 1979, 1990; Jan 1977; Mair 1990).[28]

In the light of these difficulties, it is surprising the degree of popularity the text has attained in the West, for the *Daodejing* is one of the most frequently translated of all the world's classic texts, with over two hundred versions in seventeen different languages (Walf 1997).[29] There are various possible reasons for its wide appeal. One is the protean quality of the text, namely its readiness, as one writer puts it somewhat cynically, to 'furnish whatever the reader needs', a factor which gives it 'an immense advantage over books written so clearly that they have only one meaning' (Welch 1957: 13). It is certainly a text which, as Isabelle Robinet observes, 'is open to many interpretations and even demands them' (1997: 29). At various times it has been seen as a book of moral guidance, a treatise on mystical philosophy, advice on political or military strategy, a utopian tract and an advocate of scientific naturalism (Schwartz 1985: 192).[30] Mair even points to a materialist proto-Marxist construal (1990: 128).[31] Certainly its pithy and suggestive paradoxes command our immediate attention, and its promptings towards a more simple and more natural existence have a major appeal to those living anxiety-prone and unfulfilled lives in the modern world. It is often said too that its apparent lack of mythological, historical and personal references, its freedom from any obvious cultural or theological baggage, makes it a universal text which transcends all local particularities. As early as 1855 the Protestant missionary J. Edkins had noted the absence of myths and legends in the *Daodejing* and had concluded that the work 'belongs to the history of philosophy rather than that of superstition' (1855: 83). However, this kind of judgement may be purchased at the price of overlooking some of the more hidden, esoteric aspects of the text which are conveniently ignored in the desire to recruit it for Western-originating purposes. Whatever the differences of approach to the text, however, many would agree with Lin Yutang's judgement that the *Daodejing* is simply 'one of the profoundest books in the world's philosophy', one which provides 'a therapeutic alternative to Western thought', and perhaps even a solution to its endemic problems (Lin 1963: 25; Hardy 1998: 171).[32]

Far more accessible, in some respects at least, and growing in popularity, are the writings of Zhuangzi. What place do these have in relation to Daoism? And are they any more than a lightweight appendage to the *Daodejing*? From the end of the Han dynasty they have been included within the canon of foundational Daoist classics, and since that time in both China and the West both the *Zhuangzi* and the *Daodejing* have been seen as offering complementary accounts of the fundamental tenets of Daoist philosophy. However, while the basic outlook of these two works is largely compatible, there are some significant points of difference, ones which should help to deter us from affirming too univocal an account of the Daoist tradition *tout court*. For example, the *Zhuangzi* emphasises individual development rather than political effectiveness, and exhorts us to float along freely with life in the present rather than harking back to a golden age (Kohn 1992: 57). Though on the face of it a collection of witty reflections, the *Zhuangzi* itself turns out to be a much more complex and challenging text than was at one time supposed, offering a perplexing variety of often divergent opinions, a 'confusing collage' as one Chinese scholar calls it, and in the words of an American critic, a 'pot-pourri of anecdotes, symbols, ironies, paradoxes, metaphors and bits of narrative' (Wu 1990: 363; Burneko 1986: 393). This multivocity is emphasised by Burton Watson, who in the introduction to his translation of the text comments that 'The *Chuang-tzu* allows [the translator] to assume a dozen different roles, to be solemn or quizzical, rhapsodic or paradoxical by turns, to speak in the voice of a madman or a millipede, a long-winded sea god, or a ruminative skull' (Watson 1968: xi).[33] The text has variously been described as a work of mysticism, philosophy, anarchic individualism, linguistic analysis, epistemological scepticism, serious literature or just plain fun. For some Western commentators, it has a strong philosophical significance, Robert Allinson describing it as 'a masterpiece of the first philosophical order', and Hansen as 'like philosophical honey' in spite of its maddening elusiveness (Allinson 1989a; Hansen 1992: 265), while for others

57

it is a work of ironical wit and of literary play (Wu 1990). As Jonathan Herman ruefully observes, the various renderings into English are so diverse as to indicate that at times they 'hardly appear to be addressing the same text' (1996: 3).[34]

In China itself, the work has penetrated deeply into many aspects of cultural life, and has had an influence on Chan Buddhism as well as on landscape painting and poetry and on certain pervasive attitudes and lifestyles classically associated with the Seven Sages of the Bamboo Grove. Many of the stories contained in the work are to this day familiar to Chinese children, and Michael Saso has found the work still used in Taiwanese monasteries as a manual for meditation instruction (Shaw 1988; Chang 1975a: 169–238; Saso 1983: 140–57).[35] As with the *Daodejing*, the *Zhuangzi* has been subject to a considerable range of interpretation and commentary over the centuries, as well as textual variation, and though it was largely ignored in the Han period it became popular during the period of Daoist renaissance that accompanied the decline and fall of the Han dynasty. It is now generally accepted that it is not the work of a single author, but the product of several writers who represent different schools and streams of Daoist thought, though the so-called 'Inner Chapters' are now judged to be the work of Zhuangzi himself, who lived from *c*.370 to 320 BCE during the period of Warring States. The remainder was added, in all probability, by disciples or later commentators and the complete work, more or less as we now know it, was compiled at the beginning of the Han dynasty (Graham 1979, 1981).[36]

It is hardly surprising that the playful style and overtly lightweight content of the *Zhuangzi* held no appeal for the stern minds of the Jesuit missionaries or the French *philosophes*, who in both cases ignored it. However, there were several translations made in the late nineteenth century, the first complete German edition being published by von Strauss in 1870 and the first in English by Frederick Balfour in 1881, with another by James Legge in 1891. Though not reaching out as widely to Western readers as the *Daodejing*, these editions evoked resonances at various cultural levels. For example, an 1889 edition produced by Herbert Giles was greeted enthusiastically by Oscar Wilde as 'the most caustic criticism of modern life I have met with for some time which could have the effect of putting some check in our national habit of self-glorification'.[37] This judgement anticipated by about a hundred years some of the assessments of this work, whose popularity has grown considerably in recent years, and while it has not yet achieved the status of the *Daodejing* in the Western mind, it has increasingly provoked interested responses and has stimulated much philosophical as well as philological debate. As we shall see in a later chapter, this collection of writings, hitherto often consigned to the category of 'mere' literature and afforded little attention even as such, has begun to be taken seriously by philosophers who see in it an example of a way of philosophising quite distinct from, and hence a challenge to, that which has been traditionally practised in the West. It is not just, as Chad Hansen remarks, that Zhuangzi's masterpiece 'blends image and argument as no other work in philosophy, East or West, has done' (1989: 116), but that it is a thought-provokingly different way of doing philosophy from the one practised in the West since Plato. The philosopher Wu Kuang-ming has been especially critical of the way in which the *Zhuangzi* has been treated – by Chinese intellectuals no less than European ones – as a minor appendage to Laozi, with Zhuangzi himself being depicted in recent times as a kind of hippie recluse, little more than an amusing curiosity. He is critical too of the way in which certain sinologists have sought to constrain this work, and indeed of Chinese philosophy in general, within Western modes of thought. Graham, for example, is taken to task for adopting an excessively scholastic approach to the *Zhuangzi* and seeking to transpose it into the language of modern analytical philosophy, and in similar vein Creel is criticised for arguing that the work stands in need of being 'properly systematised'. The problem with such versions is that they lapse into a kind of 'cognitive literalism' and close off interpretations rather than recognising and exploiting the wide possibilities of meanings offered by the text. For Wu, Zhuangzi is a major philosopher in his own right, and the challenge of his thought, in its capacity to be 'a satirical stab in the back of our convention and common sense', is 'vital' and 'universal' (1982: 1–14; 1990: 12).[38]

Finally, a few words must be said about the *Yijing*. It is a work which is not strictly or exclusively a Daoist text, for it has enjoyed a pre-eminent position in the whole of Chinese intellectual and cultural life. Nevertheless it has been closely associated with the Daoist tradition, both in China and in the West, and its ancient origins are inextricably linked to the cultural ethos that gave rise to Daoism. In many ways it expresses a philosophy which is completely in tune with Daoism, and in the context of popular religious practices it has long been used by Daoist priests for purposes of divination. While the core text of the *Yijing* considerably predates both Confucius and the early Daoist writings, recent scholarship suggests that some of the later commentaries, the so-called 'Appended Statements' or 'Ten Wings', that were subsequently integrated into the text, display a distinctively Daoist outlook. These supplementary texts were traditionally attributed to Confucius, but their Daoist origins, first recognised by Legge as long ago as 1882, was confirmed a hundred years later by the sinologist Willard Peterson. Stephen Karcher argues that the text, though originally closely associated in both its spirit and its practice with the tradition that was later to become Daoism, was subsequently appropriated by the Confucians for their own purposes (Peterson 1982; 310; Karcher 1999; see also Cleary 1986; Shaughnessy 1996). For Karcher, the *Yijing* was indeed 'a hermeneutical battle ground' on which the two great indigenous Chinese traditions fought for the soul of China, a contest which has been echoed in certain twentieth-century disputes over its meaning (1999: 8, 17).

The attachment of these Commentaries to the *ur*-text, probably in the early Han period, underlines the fact that the *Yijing* has been considerably expanded and elaborated during the course of its long life, a process of evolution and amplification which stretches back to the second millennium BCE when it was probably a set of omens used for the purpose of divination. Though continuing to be widely used as a book of oracles, over the centuries it became transformed and systematised into a complex, multi-layered work of symbolic, philosophical and cosmological significance, and at the time of the Han dynasty when it was nominated the first of the 'Five Classics', it had not only been used by thinkers of all Chinese schools as a foundational text, but had had an important influence on the early development of Daoist thought itself (Cheng 1989: Robinet 1997: 15).[39] This influence can be detected for example in the *yin/yang* polarity which undergirds the text, in the central notion of change or transformation and in the sense of the underlying unity that binds the human world to the cosmic process.

Though in recent times the *Yijing* has been the subject of increasingly intense interest, attracting a vast range of scholarly and philosophical exegesis, and acquiring almost a cult status in the West, its early career in Europe was fragmentary. The Jesuit missionaries were both baffled and intrigued by what they gleaned of the *Yijing*, and though it is merely referred to in passing in the *Confucius Sinarum Philosophus*, a selection of translations of Chinese classics published in 1687, a partial Latin translation by Fr Régis appeared for limited circulation around 1710. With such a complex and multifaceted work, it is hardly surprising that it provoked a variety of diverse responses, and we can see right from these early explorations how the text was drawn into and interpreted in terms of various European projects. Some saw it as a cryptic anticipation of Christian doctrine, for others it was essentially a work of metaphysics or cosmology, while for most it has until recently remained little more than a book of oracles and divination. One early Western commentator, Paul Carus, placed it in the category of 'occultism' and considered it 'one of the most mysterious documents in the world', while at the same time 'based upon a rational, nay philosophical, or even mathematical conception of existence' (1907: 25–6). More recently, other commentators have seen it variously as a collection of proverbs, a dictionary, a filing system, a phallic cosmogony, a textbook of logic and a historical chronicle (Shchutskii 1979: 55).[40] For Leibniz, the first European philosopher to take the work seriously, the rendering of Régis came as something of a revelation, leading him to speculate that the *Yijing* was an historical antecedent to his experiments in binary arithmetic and that it offered support as well for his own distinctive form of organicist philosophy (Mungello 1977; Cook and Rosemont 1981, 1994).[41]

The difficulty of the text was almost as notorious as that of the *Daode-jing*, and Maspero pronounced the work 'almost untranslatable' (1965: 444). However, in spite of its seemingly intractable obscurities, several translations were made in the nineteenth century, including a German version by Ernst Faber in 1877, a French version by Charles de Harlez in 1889 and an English version by James Legge, first published in 1882 and included in 1899 with a lengthy introduction in the *Sacred Books of the East* series. Legge confessed to having little understanding of the text he had worked on, characterising much of it as 'grotesque', and according to the Russian sinologist J. Shchutskii the work continued for some time to be viewed in the West as 'childish' and 'nonsensical'. It was not until the translation of Richard Wilhelm in 1924 that the work was given the status due to it and that the intellectual significance of the work began to impinge on European minds (Shchutskii 1979: 35). Following its English translation in 1950 it achieved considerable popular success, with sales of more than half a million copies and with further translations into over forty languages. Wilhelm himself deemed the work to be 'a unique manifestation of the human mind...one of the most important books in the world's literature' (1989: xvi–xvii, xlvii).[42] C.G. Jung concurred with this judgement, dismissing the claims of a Chinese acquaintance that it was 'nothing but an old collection of magic spells' (1995: 121). For many years Jung had made use of the book both personally and with his patients, and his foreword to the 1950 English translation of Wilhelm's version undoubtedly gave a considerable boost to its popularity in the West and helped to give it an enduring place in the counter-culture movement in the West. For Jung, the text represented not a work of divination, but rather a therapeutic tool 'of uncommon significance as a method of exploring the unconscious' (1995: 122), and also provided the outlines of a serious holistic theoretical alternative to the prevailing mechanistic paradigm. He saw its central conception as virtually synonymous with his own idea of synchronicity, and believed that its focus on the chance connections between simultaneous events rather than on linear causality anticipated his speculations concerning meaningful coincidences between events which are not causally related. This conjunction was itself for Jung a matter of considerable significance, for he saw the idea of synchronicity as a key to breaking out of the mechanistic paradigm that had characterised Western thought from the time of the Scientific Revolution, and the foundation for an alternative understanding of nature and human nature in terms of meaningful patterns of events (1995: 120–36; see also Clarke 1994: 89–102).

Other commentators have been less enthusiastic. Needham, while offering an extended and largely sympathetic discussion of the *Yijing*'s links with natural philosophy, was inclined in the end to dismiss it as a 'pseudo-explanation' of events based, not on observation of the natural world but on a fantastic mirror image of Chinese bureaucratic society. In the long run its influence was baneful, a 'mischievous handicap' to the development of Chinese scientific thinking (1956: 336). And in the view of Michael Nylan and Nathan Sivin, 'The Book of Changes is an assorted and jumbled compilation of omens, rhymed proverbs, riddles, and paradoxes' (1987: 43). Nevertheless the work has in recent years received much serious attention from translators and commentators, who have in various ways sought to rethink its significance and to recover its original meaning and context beneath both Western and Chinese sediments that have overlain the ancient text.[43] The perception of the *Yijing* as full of dangerous superstitions still prevails in China, though, where its use (though not its academic study) is banned by law.

# 4

# 'THE GREAT CLOD'
## Daoist natural philosophy

### Order out of chaos

The cosmological thinking embodied in the *Yijing*, as we saw at the end of the last chapter, often seems remote from modern ways of thinking. Nevertheless, in recent years Chinese speculation about the natural world has evoked some serious and productive responses in various fields of Western thought. To put this in wider perspective, Western cosmological and metaphysical thinking has at various times in its history displayed an inclination to draw on earlier traditions, sometimes of non-European origin, as a way of reflecting on and challenging prevailing ways of thought and of helping to stimulate radical changes. Thus, early Christianity drew on Plato, mediaeval philosophy drew on Aristotle, the Renaissance thinkers turned to the Hermetic tradition and the Jewish Kabbala, early modern science revisited Greek atomism and Hellenistic thought and the Romantics returned to earlier esoteric and gnostic traditions. In recent times Daoism has begun to play a similar, if more modest, role in attempts to rationalise and make acceptable fundamental changes in ways of thinking about nature, the cosmos and the place of human life within it. Certainly, as a notorious philosophy of detachment and mystical reflection, Daoism seems an unlikely contender for such a role, yet it has proved a strange attractor for certain contemporary thinkers seeking to move beyond older mechanistic paradigms and to forge new alliances between recent developments in science and some alternative metaphysical ways of thinking.

The phrase 'strange attractor' derives, of course, from chaos theory, which has become a fashionable topic in recent years and at the same time has been identified as a significant point of contact between the apparently remote worlds of Daoism and contemporary natural science. Looking back beyond modern science, the notion of chaos has played a problematical role in the Western philosophical tradition. Right back as far as the world of Ancient Greece this idea has been treated with caution rising to fear and contempt, often seen as a metaphysical, moral and social threat to

63

harmonious order and the rule of *Logos*, and opposed to the very notion of divinity. In the words of two contemporary critics, it represents the 'nonrational, unprincipled, anarchic; it is the indefinite in need of definition; it is the lawless, the anomic; it is the unlimited begging limitation' (Hall and Ames 1995: 10). Nietzsche was one of the first modern thinkers to challenge this mindset. In a famous aphorism he wrote that 'One must have chaos in oneself if one is to give birth to a dancing star', and it is precisely here, in what the historian of religions Norman Girardot has called the 'hidden order of chaos', rather than in any transcendent ordering principle, *Logos* or Reason, that Daoism and modern cosmological thinking are seen strangely to attract each other. Girardot has been a thoughtful, if cautious, exponent of this particular cross-cultural connection, and has helped to demonstrate the key role of the theme of chaos in both Daoist thinking and Chinese cosmology and religious thinking at large. While rejecting anything more precise than 'a very simple rhetorical symmetry' between chaos theory and Daoist cosmological ideas, Girardot nevertheless suggests that 'chaos theory of contemporary science has rediscovered part of the traditional Chinese meaning of the Tao', namely the complex and ever-changing flux and flow of nature which, out of its very unpredictable spontaneity, gives birth to a harmonious universe (1983: xi–xii). The connection has also been made from the scientific side, with Mitchell Waldrop of the Santa Fe Institute describing chaos theory as 'total Taoist' and pointing to broad structural similarities between the two (1993: 330).

A few brief words must be said about chaos theory itself by way of background. Recent speculations in this field, and in the related field of self-organising systems, have helped to push us further away from earlier ways of thinking in which the world was seen as evidence for some underlying principle of order, an order which is eternal and is somehow embedded in the very nature of things, and has nudged us towards the view that order is emergent and that orderly structures have arisen spontaneously.[1] In the science of complexity, for example, behaviour which is complex and apparently chaotic is seen to give rise to orderly structures which, in Stuart Kauffman's phrase, stand precariously 'on the edge of chaos', where the world, ranging from complex living things to subatomic processes, seems poised between disintegration and frozen rigidity. As Kauffman puts it, speaking of the application of these ideas to the evolution of life, 'The best exploration of an evolutionary space occurs at a kind of phase transition between order and disorder' (1995: 27). In such a world there is no need to postulate either a transcendent watchmaker or a principle of blind chance, and hence it is a world in which we can begin to feel 'at home...in ways not imagined since Darwin' (1995: 86, 92, 26). The idea of self-organising systems – 'autopoeisis' as it has been called[2] – has important implications not only for evolution theory but also in the wider field of physics and cosmology where, for example in the physicist Ilya Prigogine's study of 'dissipative structures', it maps out a theoretical terrain in which the self-organising structures, both living and non-living, can be seen as achieving order and stability within a context of dynamic flux and dis-equilibrium (Prigogine and Stengers 1984). More recently, cosmologists have speculated that at the 'big bang' the universe was almost literally generated out of nothing, or rather out of what is called the 'quantum vacuum' state. Related to this is the conjecture that particles of matter and quanta of energy are vibrations of quantum fields whose lowest state, or vacuum state, is equivalent to a condition of virtual emptiness. On this view, the entire universe can be viewed as a tiny fluctuation on an immense ground of nothingness.[3]

Chaos theory is, though, only the most recently evolved species of thinking about the natural world and must be seen in the context of a veritable revolution that has been taking place in this century. This revolution has witnessed a decisive shift of attitude in a number of scientific disciplines away from the mechanistic/deterministic models which came to full realisation in the nineteenth century, to conceptions which revolve round such notions as holism, organicism and self-organising systems. These changes can usefully be described in terms of a shift from a bottom-up to a top-down mentality, one which alters our perception from a reductive, atomistic, mechanistic view of the world to one which is holistic, organismic and ecological. Alternatively, it can be seen as a move away from a 'block universe' in which everything is ordained by eternal laws, to an open universe in which radical novelty and creativity become possible. This transformation is evident in a variety of fields from quantum physics to ecology, and involves a growing emphasis on the interconnectedness of phenomena, and a corresponding move away from seeing the world in terms of discrete entities and away from a methodology which seeks to analyse every process into its constituent elements. Moreover, this shift can also be viewed as part of a much wider mutation in which the whole evolution of Western philosophical speculation has been altered and transposed from its long-standing emphasis on being and substance to one which privileges becoming and process, and a shift away from thinking in terms of individual units that act according to universal laws towards structures which are formed spontaneously and which are replicated across many levels within a system (Gare 1995a; Griffin 1988).

The sense of an orderly and harmonious structure emerging precariously and unpredictably out of seeming disorder and confusion, the idea that 'the universe possesses in itself its own organisational principle and its own creative energy', is one which has increasingly been emphasised in studies of Daoism (Gernet 1985: 210).[4] According to Hall and Ames, 'Daoism is not a vision grounded upon order in the usual sense, but upon the spontaneity of the unordered', and for Girardot it evinces a 'strange solicitude for chaos' and a 'mystically austere passion for confusion' (Hall and Ames 1995: 230;

Girardot 1983: 2). Whether from a philosophical or a religious perspective, the universe is seen by Daoists to arise out of the matrix of primal chaos (*hun-dun*), which, by a ceaseless and spontaneous movement of transformation, gives rise to matter/energy (*qi*), which in turn separates out through the polarising agency of the *yang* and *yin* principles into 'the ten thousand beings'.[5] This is seen as a cyclical rather than as a linear process, one of emanation and return, of emergence out of chaos and return to the primeval condition, a continual rhythm of beginning and return, a 'many universe' conception, indeed, in which the cosmos is viewed not as a single, uniquely ordered totality, but rather as a multiplicity of world orders (Girardot 1983: ch. 2; Yu 1981).[6] Moreover, the originating source of this ever-burgeoning universe was seen as equivalent to emptiness (*wu*), for according to the *Daodejing* 'Being is the product of Not-being', and hence the unnameable *dao* is not to be identified with some eternal, ineffable reality but strictly speaking with non-being (ch. 40).[7] Daoism offers an image of nature, therefore, in which 'Universal harmony comes about, not through the celestial fiat of some King of Kings, but by the spontaneous co-operation of all beings in the universe brought about by their following the internal necessities of their own natures' (Needham 1969: 323). 'The Way gave birth to the One; the One gave birth to two things, three things, up to ten thousand' (*Daodejing*: ch. 42).

This conception of the cosmos as engaged in the process of self-creation, a *creatio continua* in which 'Being comes into being from Non-being...by itself' (Fung 1966: 221) has led some commentators to align Daoist cosmology with modern *process* thinking, and even to compare it with modern evolutionary thought (Graham 1981: 183; Legge 1883: 107).[8] In process philosophy, a way of thinking associated chiefly with A.N. Whitehead, emphasis is placed on universal flux and on the idea of an open, creative universe in which order is seen as 'emergent', arising out of the mutual adjustment of natural processes within a synergistic whole, an 'aesthetic' rather than a 'logical' or 'transcendent' order, as some have termed it (Hall and Ames 1987: 131–8).[9] In comparing Daoism with Whitehead's process philosophy, David Hall draws a sharp contrast between traditional Western thought, with its stress on 'the overcoming of chaos through rationalization', and the Chinese emphasis on spontaneity, on creation-without-a-creator and on a 'presumed positive harmonious chaos with which one must co-operate rather than against which one must struggle'. On this view, nature, though manifesting order and harmony overall, is not governed by necessary or eternal laws or by an act of divine will, but by the process of self-creation and self-actualising. Nature in this Daoist/Whiteheadian view is therefore 'an inexhaustible field of creative potential' (Hall 1982a: 186, 255; see also Hall 1978; Hartshorne 1979).

One of the important consequences of this autopoeic way of thinking about Daoist cosmology, then, is that, contrary to one commonly held view, *dao* does not in any way represent a predetermined order. In transposing this central Chinese concept into European terms it was almost inevitable that it should be interpreted in the language of traditional Western notions of a transcendent order of things – God, *Logos*, Forms, natural law, laws of nature and so on – in which the emergence of the pattern and variety of things can be explained by reference to a pre-existent and predetermining ordering principle. Recent interpretations, emerging almost parallel with the appearance of post-mechanistic thinking in the West, have sought to alter this view. For Peerenboom, for example, the Daoist universe is open and creative and its order is emergent and unpredictable, not pre-established; a view which, as we shall see later, tallies with the Daoist rejection of rule-ethics and of moral absolutes, and with its attitude of tolerance and open-mindedness (1993: 191–6). This point has also been emphasised by Needham. He was acutely aware of the dangers, originating with the efforts of the early Jesuit missionaries, of assimilating Chinese metaphysical concepts into Christian theology and Western philosophy, and was concerned to stress the distinctiveness of Daoist cosmology which is 'profoundly incompatible with the conception of a celestial lawgiver'; heaven does not command the processes of nature, but rather acts in accordance with the principle of *wu wei*, non-action or unforced action. It is also at odds with the metaphysical assumptions of Newton, Descartes *et al.* who believed that, in uncovering the laws governing natural phenomena they were 'revealing to the human mind...the edicts that had been issued by a supra-personal supra-rational being' (Needham 1956: 562–4).

Nevertheless, it is important to remember that there are also significant differences in overall conception between the thinking of China and the West which warn us to be circumspect when drawing comparisons between ancient Chinese and modern Western cosmological thinking. This latter point is well illustrated if we look a little more closely at the place of the transcendent or divine principle within cosmological thinking. As we saw in the previous chapter, the Jesuit missionaries in their eagerness to assimilate Chinese thought to their own Christianising discourse were too quick to identify Chinese terms with those of Christian theology. In our own eagerness to draw Daoism into contemporary cosmological debates, there has at times been a tendency to demythologise it, and to ignore the range and complexity of Chinese thinking. The simple assertion, often made nowadays, that the Chinese in general have had in their history no notion of a creator god and that Daoism itself is a non-transcendental philosophy, needs to be qualified by the recognition that there are indeed traces of transcendence and of creationism not only in both popular religious contexts but also amongst intellectual traditions.[10] As far as the former are concerned, the idea of a creator god is certainly present, even widespread, in religious Daoism, and indeed Laozi was himself sometimes depicted as creator of the cosmos after his divinisation in the late Han period. To be sure, amongst the educated classes in China the concept of a supreme creator deity was for the most part of little consequence and, as Graham notes, there is no equivalent in Chinese thought of the 'argument from design' or the 'doctrine of signatures' so dear to Christian mediaeval and Renaissance thinkers (1960: 178–9).[11]

But though for Zhuangzi the world has no origin but creates itself spontaneously and perpetually, there are some Daoist texts which suggest that the cosmos was created by a 'fashioner', and there are even hints of theistic/creationist ideas in Zhuangzi himself, who is usually depicted as indifferent to common religious and mythical matters (Robinet 1994).[12] Moreover, the spirit world has always played a central role in religious Daoist traditions, as in Chinese religious practice as a whole, and governing all – though not creating all – was the Jade Emperor, the second of the Three Pure Ones who stood at the summit of the Daoist pantheon. Such a world is inhabited by myriads of invisible beings who, modelled on and providing legitimation for the bureaucratic system of imperial rule, held sway over all aspects of life in a system which cuts right across the dualist divisions of matter and spirit. They wielded authority over natural phenomena such as fire, wind, water and thunder, and also over the human world of war, wealth and literature, and occupied and directed various aspects of the individual's internal economy as well where, as we shall see later, they played an important role in Daoist spiritual practice (Maspero 1981). As the sinologist Stephen Bokenkamp insists, 'There is no...easy division between the here-and-now and the divine', and the spirit world 'is both as distant as the stars and as near as your nose' (1996: 268).

This close integration of the spiritual and the natural world is a central feature of Daoist thinking, both in its philosophical and its religious forms, and serves to remind us that Daoist cosmological thinking is not an exercise in pure scientific speculation. As with Chinese thought in general, it is concerned primarily with placing human life firmly within the wider domain of nature and cosmos, and 'seeks to recapture a sense of the cosmic context of human life – that man's well-being is primarily related to and defined by nature even while he lives within the cultural order' (Girardot 1983: 258). Whether in terms of the mystical verses of the *Daodejing* or of popular Daoist ritual procedures, the whole purpose is liberating and redemptive, concerned 'to bring humans, with their mundane concerns, into harmony with unseen and all-pervasive forces of order', and ultimately to 'reconnect humanity with the primordial Dao' (Bokenkamp 1996: 268–9). Even the emphasis on chaos within Daoist thinking, which otherwise might appear just intellectually diverting, has profound soteriological significance in so far as it conjoins human redemptive aspirations with cosmic transformation, spiritual with natural alchemy. We will examine these practical implications in subsequent chapters.

## Cosmology: the standard picture

The placing of the microcosm of human endeavour within the macrocosm is part of a wider cosmological conception known as 'correlative' thinking, and has given rise to a number of interesting interpretative reflections and controversies in the West.[13] At the centre of this cosmological picture is the conception of nature as a series of interlocking correspondences, of different levels of reality brought into symmetry with each other by means of complex and detailed analogical correlations. Its specifically human significance lies in the postulation of homologies between the human, the social, and the natural worlds, a metaphysical picture which helps to make sense of human and political life within the cycles, rhythms, and patterns of the wider cosmic order. Thus the human body itself is portrayed as corresponding in detail to the forces of the cosmos, and even Daoist ritual practice, whose ultimate objective was union with the *dao*, was constructed as a representation of the cosmos at large (Lagerwey 1987: ch. 3; Kohn 1993: ch. 6). This model, brought to a high level of detailed sophistication in the Han period and linked closely with astrological theory, was supported by two further influential ideas: first, the belief that the world is composed of five elements or processes (*wuxing*) – wood, fire, earth, metal and water – and second, that the transformations in the world are energised by two opposing yet complementary forces – *yin* and *yang*.

For certain Western thinkers this model, even leaving aside the profusion of spirit-beings referred to in the previous section, was proof that Chinese thinking about the natural world was essentially primitive. This view fitted in well with anthropological theories that were widely supported earlier this century and which sought to identify a common category of 'primitive' thinking supposedly characteristic of all early societies. Émile Durkheim and Marcel Mauss, for example, argued that the Chinese cosmological system was a particular manifestation of primitive classification schemes, and they compared Chinese systems of correspondence with, *inter alia*, those of Australian aborigines. This view was echoed by the anthropologist Lévy-Bruhl, who described Chinese correlative cosmology as an example of 'arrested development', or 'pre-logical thinking', even as 'balderdash' (Durkheim and Mauss 1963: 73–4).[14] This portrayal of Chinese correlative thinking accorded happily with Eurocentric theories about progress and social evolution, and confirmed in people's minds the belief that the Chinese world-picture was little more than a superstitious relic from the past which deserved to be swept away by the forces of enlightened progress.

This kind of assumption has been challenged in recent years from several quarters, all seeking to bring into focus the historical parallels and continuities between Chinese and Western thought. Several authors have pointed out that Chinese correlative thinking displays strong similarities with Western mediaeval and Renaissance cosmologies, particularly in regard to the latter's key idea of the Great Chain of Being in which microcosmic and macrocosmic levels of reality mirror each other. Graham goes further to suggest that the sort of correlative thinking which is common to the traditional Chinese and European traditions is broadly speaking a universal characteristic that underlies the operations of language itself, and is a formalised expression of the way in which sets of terms gain their meaning through their correlation with other sets of terms (1989: 318–25; see also Henderson 1984: 41).[15]

It is in the writings of Needham, however, that this line of argument is most fully articulated. In studying the development of Chinese cosmological speculation, he was struck by the parallels between correlative thinking and the continuing strain of organicist thought which prevailed in Europe alongside the dominant mechanistic paradigm from Galileo onwards. Moreover, the writings of Norbert Wiener, which drew an early link between biological and computing systems, encouraged him to see Chinese cosmological thinking in cybernetic terms whereby the elements of a system, whether natural or artificial, are understood in the language of synchronic mutuality and balance rather than of diachronic causality (1956: 289, 344). The most significant point of East–West contact for Needham, however, was the monad theory of Leibniz. This theory construed the world to be not a machine but a living being, whose parts – the monads – were also living beings, each of which mirrored the universe and acted in harmony with other monads. All of this 'irresistibly reminded' him of the Chinese correlative system in which the various parts and levels of the universe co-operate harmoniously with each other. He also drew attention to the way in which Leibniz's theory concerning the uninterrupted flow of the universe, ever-unfolding but without sharp beginnings or endings, corresponded with the Daoist idea that there is no creation or destruction but 'only densification and rarefaction' (1956: 499–500). This represented for Needham not merely a curious parallel but a significant point of influence, a gateway through which Chinese thought could be seen to have entered not only the thinking of Leibniz but a significant, albeit largely unorthodox, stream of modern Western thought. Needham points out that Leibniz, drawing on Jesuit informants, had more than a superficial acquaintance with Chinese correlative cosmology, and he argues that the closeness – in overall spirit rather than in precise detail – between the Chinese cosmology and Leibniz's monadology suggests that he was at least partly influenced by Chinese metaphysical thinking. Moreover, in view of Leibniz's importance in modern Western philosophy, if not in science (leaving aside his invention of the calculus, of course), this influence might well be seen as extending beyond him to the line of organicist thinkers that extends from Herder, Hegel, Schelling and Coleridge to Smuts, Alexander and Whitehead. Furthermore, he argues, if we trace the organicist way of thinking back from Whitehead it leads to Leibniz but then seems to disappear, a puzzle which is eased, if not definitively solved, if we allow the thread of influence to go Eastwards at this point.[16]

Needham was also concerned to explore the relevance – though not in this case the influence – to Western thought of the five-element theory of Chinese cosmology. It is now accepted that these are not strictly speaking elements but rather processes, not five sorts of fundamental material stuff but five sorts of process or energy which are characterised by constant activity and change and which merge and flow into one another, constantly condensing and dissolving in an ever-flowing cyclical current.[17] Like the related principles of *yin* and *yang*, they are therefore dynamic principles and, in so far as they provide the matrix out of which the cosmic correlations are constructed, they indicate a cosmic system which, like a living organism, is both in balance and yet in constant interactive transformation; 'on the edge of chaos', to quote Kauffman again. In this sense, Needham points out, they are radically different in basic conception both from the four-element theory of Empedocles and the atomic particles of the pre-quantum era, and much closer in spirit to more recent thinking. Where until recently Western philosophical and scientific thought has tended to see the fundamental constituents of the material world as impenetrable and indivisible particles of stuff which, in classical Newtonian physics, are entirely passive and inert, there is now a palpable move towards a much more dynamic and even organic conception of the natural world within mainstream science which has moved beyond the increasingly disputed mechanistic materialism associated with Descartes and Newton. Needham concludes his discussion with the conjecture that 'Perhaps the theoretical foundations of the most modern "European" natural science owe more to [Chinese thinkers] than the world has yet realised', though he is also careful to point out that this is only 'a hypotheses for further research' (1956: 505, 292).

In spite of this and other reservations, however, it is possible that Needham, in his desire to associate correlative thinking with Western organicist philosophy and thereby to legitimise his own organicist view of the world, has overlooked a crucial difference between Daoist and Western thinking in this matter. He states that the five processes constitute 'the most ultimate principles of which the ancient Chinese could conceive' (1956: 232), but this may be a misleading way of putting it, for it suggests a kind of foundationalism which, though appropriate in terms of pre-Socratic and subsequent Western cosmology, may not be appropriate in the Chinese case. Though the quest for the fundamental ingredients of nature has typified Western thought from the Pre-Socratics to modern physics, the notion of basic building blocks of matter is not found in Chinese thought. As Benjamin Schwartz points out, there is a danger here of assuming that the Chinese were asking the same question as the earlier Greek thinkers, namely, what is the 'stuff' of which the world is made? Hence, their five elements or processes functioned in the same way as the Greek elements, namely as the final residue of a reductionist analysis of the ultimate constituents of the material world.[18] According to Schwartz, the Chinese were not interested in reducing the manifold universe of experience to five fundamental components, nor in seeking to penetrate beyond the world of 'appearance' to an ultimate 'reality' beyond. Rather, he argues, they were concerned with the more 'holistic' enterprise of interrelating the manifold world of experience into a meaningful and patterned whole, one which sought to correlate the realities of ordinary experience and hence 'to accept the world of "appearance" as they find it' (1985: 358–60).[19] This 'anti-foundationist', 'acosmic' view certainly appears to fit well with the ideas of Laozi and Zhuangzi, who tend to avoid any attempt to uncover an ultimate rational explanation of things, whether in terms of transcendent principles or immanent substances. It also resonates with chaos theory and recent ideas about complex systems which are more concerned with the dynamic patterning of events rather than with their ultimate constituents.

This resonance is enhanced when we turn to the final set of cosmological concepts, the famous *yin/yang* polarity. Originally related to the contrast between darkness and light, and the dark and light side of a valley, these terms came into philosophical use in about the fourth century BCE. They not only played a central role in Chinese culture and thinking as a whole, but had an especially crucial role in the cosmological thinking of the *Yijing* and in Daoist philosophy itself, as well as in the correlative thinking we have just been discussing. Indeed, the principle of polarity had a significance in Chinese thought which runs through the whole range of phenomena from the macrocosmos to the microcosmos, indicating the mutuality and balance of complementary forces within nature at large, and the need for corresponding harmony within human and social life in order to attain happiness, health and good political order. It is often pointed out nowadays that this binary distinction is not one of absolute mutual opposition and exclusion but rather of interdependence, and that, by way of contrast with the Western tendency (with a few exceptions such as Heraclitus, Blake and Schelling) to see pairs of opposites as mutually exclusive, the Chinese *yin/yang* concept represents a complementary pairing of terms which stand in a relationship, not of mutual opposition or competition, but of creative tension and mutuality. It is a process whereby, in the words of the *Zhuangzi*, 'Yin and Yang [are] the greatest of energies', and in which 'when *yin* reaches its apex, it changes into *yang*, and vice-versa' (Graham 1981: 151; Schipper 1993: 35).

Perhaps because of its perceived contrast with traditional European modes of thinking, the *yin/yang* theory has proved very attractive to Western minds and has been pressed into various kinds of polemical service. Most notoriously, the theory has been seen as offering some kind of solution to the gender imbalance believed to be endemic in the West, the Daoist cultivation of certain feminine qualities being seen to counterbalance the West's excessive masculinity. Needham, for example, has frequently reiterated his claim that, by contrast with the unsatisfactory Christian reliance on an overpoweringly *yang*, masculine, monarchical image of God, the Daoist *yin* motifs of water and the feminine spirit are ones which have much to teach the modern Western world (1979).[20] From yet another perspective there has been an inclination to link *yin/yang* theory with the Romantic idea of polarity, evident in the work of Goethe, Schelling and Coleridge, and to associate it with an organicist/holistic outlook in which elements in dynamic interplay are seen as inseparable both from each other and from the process as a whole.

This approach proved especially attractive to C.G. Jung. Like his Romantic predecessors (his thinking was influenced by Goethe and Schelling amongst others), he used the idea of polarity as a way of countering what he saw as the mechanist/materialist paradigm that had dominated Western thought in the modern period, and in formulating his theory of psychological types he used *yin/yang* binarism as a way of explicating his theory of the psyche as a process in which opposite forces seek mutual accommodation and balance. It was thus an important influence on his theory of individuation, and on his idea of the self as a kind of homeostatic system which seeks balance through the compensatory interaction between conscious and unconscious levels. It also played a part in his later conjectures concerning synchronicity – meaningful coincidences – and in his speculations about the possibility of a holistic alternative to the prevailing mechanistic/materialistic world picture. One of the major characteristics of Chinese thought, in his view, was its intuitive sense of grasping the whole of a situation, by contrast with the more analytical and reductive Western approach. 'Unlike the Greek-trained Western mind', he wrote, 'the Chinese mind does not aim at grasping the details for their own sake, but at a view which sees the detail as part of the whole...and thus placing the details against a cosmic background – the interplay of Yin and Yang' (1985: 49).

These speculations of Jung have received little encouragement from the scientific community, even though they were forged with the help of the eminent quantum physicist Wolfgang Pauli and have enjoyed wide appeal in New Age and counter-cultural circles. Nevertheless they, along with Needham's conjectures, do point to the impact that Daoism was beginning to have on Western thinking in a period when its own understanding of the universe has been undergoing transformation. This impact, and the interweaving of Daoist with Western thought, becomes even more conspicuous when we take a broader perspective on the relationship between Daoism and modern science.

## Science: a new paradigm?

Daoism and science have not always enjoyed an amicable relationship in Western eyes. Writing in 1956 before the wave of recent speculation, Needham lamented that 'Taoist thought has been almost completely misunderstood by most European translators and writers', that it has been 'interpreted as pure religious mysticism and superstition...[with its] scientific or "proto"-scientific side...very largely overlooked' (1956: 34). It has seemed scandalous to many commentators that scientific thought is absent, not only from Daoism but from Chinese civilisation as a whole. At the turn of the century the Dutch scholar J.J.M. de Groot expressed deep puzzlement as to how 'so large a portion of the human race...has grown up to manhood without arriving at even an elementary knowledge of the true laws of nature', insisting that 'the Chinese never built up anything better than a speculative system based on ancient formulae and mystic diagrams', a system 'so unscientific, so puerile, that it can only move us to a smile' (1892–1910, Vol. 3: 1050). This view was echoed in Whitehead's influential book, *Science and the Modern World*, first published in 1925, which, while dismissing any suggestion that the Chinese were intrinsically incapable of the pursuit of science, pronounced that 'Chinese science is practically negligible', and that left to itself China would never 'have produced any progress in science' (1925: 8–9).

Some eloquent voices have been raised against this view in the second half of the twentieth century and have helped to bring about a remarkable change of attitude towards Daoism, even to the point where it could be described as 'the Chinese counterpart of Western science' (Welch 1957: 134).[21] One of the earliest Western commentators to appreciate the sophistication of Chinese science was the German sinologist Alfred Forke, who in the 1920s offered the first full account of Chinese cosmology. While expressing the need to systematise the 'hopelessly mixed-up' jumble of Daoist ideas in a more rigorous and scientific way, he recognised the central importance of the idea of chaos 'in which the future world was already contained...[and] from which at the same time heaven and earth were produced' without the need to resort to a mythological cosmogony (1925: 40). Holmes Welch, also writing before the main wave of Daoist enthusiasm, pointed to certain factors which he saw as having attracted Western interest to Daoism: its focus on impersonal, non-teleological laws rather than gods or mythical beings, its use of experimentation, and its applicability to fields such as medicine and to the production of things like porcelain and gunpowder, the latter in the face of Confucian distaste for practical accomplishments (1957: 134–5). And, writing in 1960, Graham commented on the broad coincidence of Daoism with the modern scientific outlook in its insistence on the littleness of man in a vast universe; the inhuman Tao which all things follow, without purpose and indifferent to human needs; the transience of life; the impossibility of knowing what comes after death; the unending change in which the possibility of progress is not even conceived; the relativity of values; a fatalism close to determinism, even a suggestion that the human organism operates like a machine.

(Graham 1960: 13)

If these views were somewhat too expansive and unspecific, Jung made a more detailed attempt to bring Daoism within the orbit of twentieth-century debates about scientific methodology and suggested that in broad philosophical terms, if not in methodological detail, Chinese science could be placed in some kind of dialogue with speculations about post-mechanistic science. He was once asked how it was that so highly cultivated a people as the Chinese had produced no science, to which he replied that this was an optical illusion, since the Chinese did indeed have a science whose standard textbook was the *Yijing*, and which, as we noted above, could be exploited as a way of correcting what he saw as the 'bias' of mechanistic causal explanations (1995: 74).

A more detailed case along these lines has been made out by Fritjof Capra in his book, *The Tao of Physics* (1976). It is a work which has attained an extraordinary level of popularity and has helped to initiate a fashion, not only for the cult of Daoism in certain circles, but also for speculations concerning the wider religious and metaphysical significance of contemporary science. In spite of the Daoist mistrust of the analytical methods appropriate for the development of scientific thinking, Capra saw in their philosophy an attitude which was nevertheless 'essentially scientific', one which bore clear intimations of modern scientific theories with their leanings towards a dynamic view of nature and in the underlying interrelatedness of phenomena. In modern physics, he argued, the universe is experienced as 'a dynamic, inseparable whole which includes the observer in an essential way' and in which 'traditional concepts of time and space, of isolated objects and of cause and effect, lose their meaning', such a conception being 'internally consistent and in perfect harmony with the views of Eastern mysticism' (1976: 86 and 321).[22] In brief, Daoism, with its dynamic conception of nature as movement, flow and change, its emphasis on energy (*qi*) rather than substance, its grasp of the web of interconnections that bind together all phenomena both human and cosmic, and its rejection of rigid laws and absolute boundaries, is especially close in spirit to modern physics, in spite of differences in empirical detail, methodology and overall aims.

Capra's objective was to establish Eastern mysticism, which embraced Hindu and Buddhist ideas as well as those of Daoism, as a 'philosophical framework which can accommodate our most advanced theories of the physical world' (1976: 11), and thereby to promote the idea of a 'new paradigm', an alternative framework of thought to replace the mechanistic/atomistic paradigm that had prevailed since the time of Galileo and Descartes. He was concerned, moreover, to combat the perceived shortcomings of traditional Western philosophy with its dualist and rationalist assumptions and to meet the demand for a new spiritual/religious outlook which, with its syncretistic and universal appeal, could reunite the sundered traditions of religion and science. This approach has had a wide following amongst certain groups of people who, disillusioned with orthodox Christianity and scientific rationalism, yearn for new redemptive pathways which do not simply reject science. It is a move which has helped to place Daoism and Eastern thought in general at the centre of New Age thinking where it has a wide following.[23]

This approach has also provoked much critical discussion. It has been pointed out that there lies a huge chasm between the cultural contexts of Daoist sages and modern physicists, and that their aims and methodologies are not in any useful sense comparable. It is argued that while there are certain vague analogies between the two traditions, the two systems of thought when examined in any detail are not only more internally complex and diffuse than Capra allowed, but diverge from each other in a significant number of ways; there is no advantage in trying to demonstrate close parallels between them, or in using one to support or validate the other. This kind of criticism is important in alerting us to the hermeneutical questions that arise when comparing ideas from traditions widely divergent in place and time. There are clearly dangers in applying ideas like 'holism' and 'participatory universe' in an indiscriminate way to the fields of quantum mechanics and mysticism. Nevertheless, it might be said in Capra's defence that the wide scope and philosophical implications of contemporary physical theories, as well as the eclectic speculations of some leading figures in this field, make broad intercultural comparisons understandable, and in spite of the well-publicised shortcomings in Capra's account of both mystical and scientific traditions his work is important in its insistence on the need to look beyond the limited visions of current orthodoxies. In this context, it is worth recalling that the use of analogies has led to the development of new models and theories, and that mystical and even occultist elements have sometimes played a catalytic role in the evolution of modern physics (Scerri 1989: 690).[24]

Capra's view that Daoism is in some sense commensurable with modern science was anticipated in certain respects by Needham, who later signalled his broad agreement with Capra's approach (1979: 12). They begin, though, from widely different premises and assumptions. By contrast with Capra, who could be described as a 'green physicist', Needham was a biochemist whose thinking on cultural matters started out from an explicitly Marxist premise, and was driven by political motives as much as by purely scientific ones. This orientation is clearly in evidence in the Introduction to *Science and Civilisation in China*, where he looks forward to 'the dawn of a new universalism which...will unite the working peoples of all races in a community both catholic and co-operative' (1954: 9).[25] At the same time his thinking was also, in ways that we have already noted, shaped by the organicist philosophy of Whitehead, which he not only saw as compatible with the dialectical approach of Marx and Engels but also as the philosophical basis for a post-mechanistic paradigm (1969: 129).

In pursuit of this overall strategic aim, Needham set about constructing a history of Chinese science in such a way that its development could be placed on a comparative footing with the history of science in the West, a goal which contrasted sharply with standard attitudes of the time, which usually deemed the two traditions to be fundamentally incommensurable. Though his investigations range over the whole spectrum of Chinese intellectual and cultural life, Daoism played a central role in this study. Contrary to stereotypical images of Daoism in the West, where it has largely been viewed as a form of mystical esotericism, he argued that in fact it was 'among the Daoists that we have to look for most of the roots of Chinese scientific thought' (1956: 57). With its fundamental openness to the natural world and its involvement with alchemical processes, Daoism could be seen to be responsible, not only for materially assisting in the development of a range of technological developments, but also for the articulation of a consistent set of what, according to Needham, must be described as scientific theories. To be sure, these theories differ from those of modern science in that they are based on organic rather than mechanistic thinking, and lack the analytical, mathematical and experimental tools of modern science. And because of their mistrust of the powers of reason and logic, they failed to develop anything resembling the ideas of laws of nature. Nevertheless, far-reaching comparisons could be drawn with the history of Western science for, with 'their appreciation of relativism and the subtlety and immensity of the universe, [the Daoists] were groping after an Einsteinian world-picture without having laid the foundations for a Newtonian one' (1969: 311; see also Needham 1956: 291; 1969: 328). Moreover, Needham argued, the influence of Daoism extends, however remotely, to a number of crucial recent developments in field physics, biology, psychology and political sciences, and Daoist contributions to scientific thought, though they lack the essential ingredients of modern scientific method, do constitute an original and historically significant formulation. In the course of its long evolution, Daoism 'developed many of the most important features of the scientific attitude'; we owe to it 'the beginnings of chemistry, mineralogy, botany, zoology and pharmaceutics...[and they] show many parallels with the scientific pre-Socratic and Epicurean philosophers of Greece' (1956: 161). In brief, under the chief influence of Daoism the Chinese developed 'an extremely and precisely ordered picture of the universe', an organic model based on 'associative or coordinative thinking [which] was essentially something different from that of European causal and "legal" or nomothetic thinking'. Yet it was a picture that was by no means primitive, one which anticipated in interesting ways recent scientific developments, and could thus be counted as a 'proto-scientific naturalism' (1956: 286, 164).[26]

One of the intriguing questions which Needham raises in the pursuit of this bold thesis is whether a systematic and modern organicist science could have arisen without the intermediary step of atomism/mechanism; in other words, could Chinese science have led directly into post-Newtonian science? Could it be that 'the Chinese shot an arrow close to the spot where Rutherford and Bohr were later to stand without ever attaining to the position of Newton'? (1956: 467). In view of the parallel yet different path of development of Chinese science, is it necessary to postulate a unique global line of development for science, or could it have evolved along a radically different path, through an organicist/holistic paradigm without passing through a mechanistic phase as in the West? It is easy to assume that the path taken by the development of science in the West from the Greeks, through Galileo and Newton to Darwin, Einstein and beyond, represents a non-contingent line of evolution – it could *only* have happened in this way – but if we pursue Needham's line of thinking, we may question with Hideki Yukawa, a Nobel Laureate in physics, whether 'Greek thought is the only system of ideas that can serve as a basis for the development of science' (Yukawa 1983: 58–9; see also Needham 1956: 582–3).[27]

This issue, which Needham put to one side as merely an interesting conjecture, is related to another question which runs as a *leitmotiv* through all his writings, one which echoes Max Weber's key question mentioned in the last chapter,[28] namely: 'Why has modern science not developed in Chinese civilisation but only in Europe?' This question arose as a result of many years of research into the development of science and technology in China, in the course of which he came to the conclusion that China had achieved a substantial lead over Europe in the period just prior to the scientific revolution and indeed had contributed a number of crucial discoveries thereto, including Francis Bacon's famous trio – gunpowder, printing, and the compass – as well as a long list of less well-publicised discoveries. Why then was it that Europe alone underwent the transfiguration of the scientific revolution, and took an historically decisive lead in a field in which China had long excelled (1969: 190)?[29] His reply to this question came in various forms, but predominantly he favoured a sociological explanation which is summed up in the following sentence:

differences in social and economic pattern between China and Western Europe will in the end illuminate...both the earlier pre-dominance of Chinese science and technology and also the later rise of modern science in Europe alone.

(Needham 1969: 217)[30]

Thus the endemic conservative bureaucratism of the Confucian-dominated society, in which individual initiative at the top social level was severely limited and in which direct dealings with the material world were often looked upon with distaste by the ruling élite, meant that opportunities for new and revolutionary developments in scientific thought and practice were severely curtailed, by contrast with a Europe in which the restrictions of the old feudal order were giving way in the Renaissance period to conditions favourable to individual endeavour in all fields.

This 'externalist' approach, by contrast with one which concentrates on factors internal to an intellectual discourse, has certainly become more widely – though by no means exclusively – accepted in general methodologi-cal terms by historians of science in the days since Needham began his investigations. Nevertheless, objections have been raised about the manner in which he posed the question, 'Why did modern science first develop in Europe and not in China?' Graham is one of several scholars who believe that this question represents a 'pseudo-problem'. After all, he argues, in historical studies we normally ask why events *do* happen, not why they do not, and it would be odd to ask, for example, why the Egyptian civilisation 'failed' to survive into the modern age as the Chinese has done (1989: 317).[31] In spite of Needham's insistence to the contrary, the very raising of this question might be seen to imply that the culture of Europe represents an archetype of cultural evolution. Needham was indeed insistent that no privileged status could be accorded to Europe in historical or cultural terms, and preferred to speak of 'modern universal science' rather than 'Western science', a viewpoint which certainly helps to combat 'that intellectual pride which boasts that "we are the people, and wisdom was born with us"' (1969: 54). Nevertheless, in the view of some of his critics his work might be seen as an attempt to measure Chinese culture by Western standards, an exercise which is accompanied by the largely unexamined assumption that 'modern universal science' is in some sense culture-free (Lin *et al.* 1995: 748). The Australian philosopher Arran Gare goes even further and suggests that on these grounds Needham 'seems to have all the failings Said identified with Orientalism...[for we] find him setting up a conception of China that is then used to define the West'; in other words the West's 'superiority' is demon-strated by showing that China failed to measure up to a standard defined in Western terms (1995b: 312).[32]

A further question arises here: what do we mean by 'science' anyway? Needham finds no difficulty in speaking of a Daoist 'proto-science', and many have followed him by repeating the mantra 'the Taoists were scientists'. Nevertheless there are those who argue that, while Daoists certainly experimented with alchemical techniques and showed a much closer interest in natural processes than the Confucianists, the whole thrust of their endeavour was directed by methods and towards goals which were totally at variance with modern science, an objection we have already noted in the case of Capra. Schwartz, for example, points out that, while the careful observation of nature did indeed flourish in China, 'there is very little ground for assuming that it had anything to do with the vision which we find in the Lao-tzu' (1985: 205).[33] The central role often attributed to intuition rather than observation, the rejection of conceptual knowledge and analytical thinking on the part of many Daoists, and the acceptance by some of the authority of revelation, all point to fundamental differences in methodology.[34] Furthermore, the Daoist concern with meanings rather than causes, which we have already noted in relation to Chinese correlative cosmology, surely makes it totally unsuited for confronting the complexities of natural phenomena; and moreover the fundamental goal of Daoism, namely self-transformation, is completely different from that of the quest for objective knowledge of the natural world. It is for this sort of reason that Derk Bodde maintains that the Chinese approach to nature is 'incompatible with science', and that for the Daoists 'any attempt at rational analysis would destroy the vision of the universal Tao' (1991: 329–30).[35]

Needham's use of the terms 'organic' and 'organicism' has also caused some problems. Such notions have played an important part in recent debates about new models and paradigms in science, as well as in issues relating to eco-philosophy. Needham himself used them, as we have seen, in order to demonstrate the commensurability, and even a line of influence, between traditional Chinese and modern scientific thought. But is the Daoist concept of nature an organic one in any useful sense? It is true that its thinking was rooted in the language and metaphors of nature, and that its sense of the transformative and interrelational properties of phenomena display a biologically-inclined way of thinking (Bodde 1991: 123; Robinet 1993: 156), but it is still questionable whether Daoism contains anything like a consistently articulated organicist philosophy, or one which bears anything more than a tenuous resemblance to the sort of organicist thinking that emerged in Europe from Leibniz onwards (Bodde 1991: 345–55). Indeed, it is arguable that once again Needham has drawn historical and conceptual links between Chinese and Western intellectual history that are unjustifiably close, and that his use of the term 'organicism' is inseparably tied to models peculiar to the Western philosophical tradition. In this vein, Hall and Ames argue that the Daoist cosmos 'bears little resemblance to anything like the organismic theories as we in the West have developed them'. In fact, they argue, the model the Chinese cosmologists employ is much more closely analogous to the state bureaucracy of traditional China than to a living organism, a view anticipated long ago by Marcel Granet who observed that 'the structure of society [was] the model upon which [the Chinese] conceived the general structure of the world' (Hall and Ames 1995: 270–71; Granet 1975: 48).[36]

Furthermore, Needham's commitment to the concept of organicism also led him to deny that the Chinese developed any clear notion of 'laws of nature', a significant factor, he believed, in preventing the Chinese from developing mechanistic science. The Graeco-Christian idea of laws of nature which, according to Needham, provided a vital foundation for the development of Western science had no parallel in China, largely due to the absence of the idea of a supreme lawmaker. The model of the cosmos as an organism meant that nature was viewed as self-activating, needing no exogenous principle to explain its workings, and hence the idea of a superimposed order was out of place in the Chinese philosophy of nature (Needham 1956: ch. 18). Once again, though, Needham has been criticised for pushing his case too far. His argument is correct when applied to the dominant Chinese viewpoint where the concept of an external law-giver/maker is largely absent, but evidence suggests that there are indeed some Daoist thinkers who have subscribed to some notion of laws of nature which they see as grounded in the natural order (Bodde 1979, 1991: 332–45; Peerenboom: 1990b: 80; 1993: 81–4).

These points are not made to diminish the importance of Needham's contributions to our understanding of Chinese culture, but they do indicate the extent to which Chinese and Daoist ideas get refracted through specific Western ideological lenses, and the way in which Chinese studies can become a medium for Europe's own self-reflection. On the other hand, this process clearly has a positive aspect as well. It can be a powerful stimulus to further debate within a field which is increasingly contentious at the present time, and can provoke us into rethinking some of the assumptions underlying Western intellectual history.

## Environmentalism: new ways?

This self-reflexive potential is, on the face of it, more plausible in the case of environmental thinking than in the fields of physics or cosmology. The holistic qualities of Daoism, with its rejection of any absolute division between the physical and the spiritual, its emphasis on harmony with nature, its closeness with all living creatures and its perception of the interlocking fittingness of natural phenomena, have a distinctively ecological quality and have in recent years begun to feature in discussions about the environment and the relationship between the human and the natural worlds. Moreover, even though some Western commentators have been inclined to project certain traditional European metaphysical assumptions onto the concept of the *dao*, seeing it as a transcendental reality, others have emphasised its earthy quality. Creel, for example, draws attention to the fact that the *dao* is identified not with 'infinite mind' or with 'absolute reason', but with 'ordure and urine' *inter alia*, and is characterised as 'The Great Clod' (1970: 31, 36). Even before the counter-culture period proper, when environmentalist ideas came into prominence, writers such as Allan Watts and the American beat poet Gary Snyder allied themselves with Zhuangzi and other Chinese thinkers in order to confront Western aggressiveness and destructive attitudes towards nature. Such themes as these, in which Daoist and other Oriental philosophies were employed to administer to the diseased body of the modern West, became almost commonplace in both academic and popular writings concerning the environment from the 1960s onwards, and in a celebrated classic of environmental history Roderick Nash wrote that, by contrast with the West, in ancient Chinese thinking 'the man–nature relationship was marked by respect, bordering on love...[and] Taoists postulated an infinite and benign force in the natural world' (1967: 192–3). More recently, Martin Palmer has expressed the belief that 'the cosmic renewal liturgies and the cosmological models of Taoism can perhaps offer us a new way of appraising our place in nature in the light of the current environmental crisis', and Peter Marshall in his history of ecological thinking argues that Daoism 'provides the philosophical foundations for a genuinely ecological society and a way to resolve the ancient antagonism between humanity and nature which continues to bedevil the world' (Palmer 1991: 128; Marshall 1992b: 23; see also Ip 1983; Smith 1972).

On a more down-to-earth plane, nothing underlines the contemporary interest in the ecological potential of Daoism more than the extraordinary growth of interest in *feng-shui* (literally 'wind-water'). As a geomantic art it has been closely associated with ancient divinatory practices, with correlative thinking, and with the quest for healthy and harmonious living, and though not exclusively identified with Daoism, *feng-shui* has strong historical and philosophical associations with that school. Though Needham refers to it as a 'pseudo-science', he sees it as one which is in tune with Daoist scientific thinking and which made an important contribution to Chinese natural philosophy, especially in its invention of the magnetic compass (1956: 359–63). Often scorned by high-minded Confucians (Feuchtwang 1974: 5), and long derided in the West as a 'chaos of childish absurdities...a ridiculous caricature of science...a farrago of absurdities' (de Groot 1892–1910, vol. 2: 15–16), it has nevertheless become for an increasing number of people – in Asia as well as in the West – a key to harmonising modern urban life with the primal energies of nature. Some of its wider applications are tendentious, to say the least; writings on the subject range from concerns with romance and fame to children and education, as well as with more traditional topics such as the alignment and layout of buildings, and it is true that questions of wealth and happiness rather than green issues predominate in the burgeoning *feng-shui* literature. Nevertheless this ancient practice, which was originally concerned with the siting of graves, has helped to draw attention to the closeness of our relationship with the natural world and the need to connect our activities with the natural elements. Moreover, its concern with rocks, water and wind in the context of highly urbanised environments suggests a nostalgia for a more natural mode of living, and reflects current anxieties about the alienation of the city from our roots in nature. No doubt some would agree with the negative assessment of early investigators of this tradition, such as Ernest Eitel of the London Missionary Society who, after a surprisingly sympathetic account, went on to dismiss it as an amalgam of superstition and primitive science (1984: 69). But the emergence of environmental concerns in recent times has enabled many to see *feng-shui* not just as a relic of an outdated science, but, in Eva Wong's words, as a way to 'rediscover our sensitivity towards the world...[one which] reveals the hidden mysteries of the universe and provides us with a way of living harmoniously with them' (1996: 255; see also Pennick 1979; Walters 1989).

This kind of language points to the way in which Daoism in general has begun to prove a handy conceptual tool with which to address issues concerning our problematic relationship with the natural environment. Our home-grown world-view has failed, some would have it, and an alternative source of philosophical inspiration is needed, one which goes beyond the endemic anthropocentrism and the will-to-dominate that has been so characteristic a feature of the Western Enlightenment tradition. Daoism, with its non-hierarchical cosmology, its ideals of self-creativity and spontaneity, and its avoidance of matter/spirit dualities, is seen as an admirable candidate for such a role. As a philosophy which focuses on the values of balance and co-operation with nature rather than of human achievement and domination over nature, it appears to offer 'an alternative set of categories for rethinking some of the issues of environment ethics', and might even provide a key to the reconstruction of the West's world-view. Daoism's very remoteness from the modern world is seen as important here for, by travelling mentally to China, it becomes possible to position ourselves 'outside of the Western philosophic tradition and [thus to view] it from relatively neutral ground', a point of view 'from which the West can more clearly discern the deeper substrata of its inherited intellectual biases and assumptions' (Callicott and Ames 1989: 113, 115, 288).

This critical deployment of Daoism is evident in the writings of some ecofeminists. They point out that the *dao* can be construed as a feminine reality, a maternal life-producing energy, and that Daoism along with other Asian systems represents an enlightened alternative to Western patriarchal attitudes or to its antagonistic dualisms. It is a philosophy, they argue, which helps to reconceptualise the human self and human relationships in ways which honour 'holistic integration, interrelatedness, embodement, caring, and love' (Tucker and Grim 1994: 187). Yet another group of thinkers who look upon Daoism as a 'conceptual resource' for purposes of philosophical reconstruction are the advocates of Deep Ecology who, from its originator founder Arne Naess onwards, have been especially keen to draw on Daoist ideas in elaborating their own system of thought. Advocates of this view, such as the philosophers Richard Sylvan and David Bennett, point to 'the remarkable, and remarked convergence of themes between...Deep Ecology and Taoism', arguing that 'the older wisdom of Taoism can profitably be drawn upon to elaborate and enrich' its modern counterpart (1988: 148; see also Callicott 1994: 86; Tucker and Grim 1994: 150–6; Zimmerman 1994: 51–2).

A key Daoist idea that has attracted the interest of ecologically minded people is that of *wu-wei*. It means literally 'not-doing', but as a philosophical concept it is used to characterise spontaneity and naturalness of action devoid of conscious premeditation, and implies non-intervention in the natural flow of things. In the *Daodejing* it has a clear political significance which is summed up in the following lines: 'Tao never does; yet through it all things are done. If the barons and kings would but possess themselves of it, the ten thousand creatures would at once be transformed' (ch. 37). Once dismissed in the West for promoting a typically oriental attitude of apathetic indifference to the demands of the world, it is now increasingly seen as a counterbalance to the West's inclination to dominate and control nature, and as a support for currently favoured ecological ideas such as 'sustainability' and 'limits to growth'. The philosopher Russell Goodman, in seeking to apply Daoist principles to contemporary ecological questions, argues that *wu-wei*, far from implying an eccentric quietism, has wide-ranging practical implications for us. After all, the *Zhuangzi* itself tells us that 'in doing nothing there is nothing it [the *dao*] does not do' (Graham 1981: 151, also 185–7, 204, 209), a dictum that could be interpreted as recommending a more natural way of living rather than merely accepting the status quo. As an ideal, Goodman insists, it encourages the very practical task of recycling waste by helping us to realise that the natural cycles of nature should be co-operated with rather than mastered. It supports the practice of organic farming by advocating respect for the forces and creatures in the natural world rather than constantly seeking to intervene and control them. And it points to the advantages of small-scale, local, alternative energy projects such as passive solar power systems which interfere minimally with the environment. In corroboration, he quotes the second century BCE Daoist writer Huainanzi: 'The sages, in all their methods of action, follow the Nature of Things' (Goodman 1980: 80).

Following the 'Nature of Things' carries with it the ideal of plain living, the celebration of the artisan and of craftsmanship, and the emphasis on the simple and the small-scale. Daoism teaches us that modernity, and even the project of civilisation itself, has taken us too far in the direction of bigness and complexity, and that we need to 'turn back to recover important things lost in the progress of civilisation, the things that [Daoists] were trying to protect' (LaFargue 1992: 189). This implies a simplicity of life in which, as with Buddhism, the demands of the ego which lead to envy, aggressiveness and conflict are viewed as self-defeating. It advocates an alternative way of life 'based on love, respect and compassion for all things, attuned to what is essential, shedding what is unnecessary, where simplicity and frugality are sought, and excess avoided', all ideas which controvert the 'Western drives to power, fame, competition, possessions, excess commodities, [and] useless knowledge' (Sylvan and Bennett 1988: 152).[37] At the socio-political level, this implies the shifting of power from the large-scale to the small, from the centralised to the local. As Roger Ames insists, the ideal of *wu-wei* means not merely adjusting our personal relationship towards the natural world but also thinking afresh about institutions in which authoritarian domination holds sway and in which creative self-realisation is diminished (1986: 342–7).

How useful or appropriate are these borrowings? Can the standard Western interpretation of Daoism as a form of naturalism really have any relevance to contemporary environmental issues? As in other cases that we have looked at, the tactic of drawing into contemporary ecological discourse ancient ideas from a totally different background, while helping to stimulate and clarify important methodological as well as substantive issues, has proved problematic. It is worth noting for a start that in traditional China itself there has been some debate about the desirability of following the way of nature. The ancient Confucian philosopher Xunzi, for example, who held a somewhat pessimistic view of human nature and espoused a quasi-utilitarian outlook on moral questions, scoffed at the Daoist inclination to glorify nature and advocated the need to dominate and control the natural world rather than to follow its way. Peerenboom, seeking to rebut Xunzi, believes that this view, and contemporary opinion which sees Daoism as a form of *pure* naturalism, involves a mistaken interpretation of the *Daodejing* and the *Zhuangzi*, arguing that these works stand for balance and harmony between the human and the natural worlds, not a privileging of the latter over the former (1993: 219, 224). Issues of a similar kind are to be found in contemporary environmental debates, and are part of the wider controversy concerning the relationship between the human and the natural worlds. The admonition to live in accordance with the ways of nature certainly has great appeal in an age when we have not only cocooned ourselves in all kinds of prosthetic contrivances, but where these very contrivances, so promising of happiness and liberation, have begun to be a cause of harm and subjugation to their makers. Arguably, one of the great myths of modernity is that we can and should use all means in our power to control nature for the sake of human welfare, but we are now beginning to question whether the benefits of this new power outweigh the disadvantages.

Does this mean that we should reverse the motor of modernity and seek to return to a pre-civilised state where we might regain a symbiotic unity with nature? Is not the Daoist image of a rural arcadia simply an impossible dream, a romantic image of an illusory Golden Age? In the last analysis, can its seductive ideal of *wu-wei* do anything more than distract us from the urgent problems and tasks that face us? Moreover, is there not something contradictory about the very notion of 'returning to nature' or seeking to recover our oneness with the *dao*? After all, Daoism teaches that we are part of nature, so how is it possible for us to act *un*-naturally, let alone seek to regain our lost naturalness? The *Zhuangzi* claims that 'Wherever we walk, how can the Way be absent' (Graham 1981: 52), and hence, Ames asks, 'if all is *tao*, and *tao* is natural, what is the source, the nature, and the ontological status of unnatural activity?' (1986: 342). And if the *dao* is a ultimate reality such that nothing can depart from it, how is it possible for there to be unspontaneous actions?[38]

One possible answer to such questions is that the problem only arises within the context of Western philosophical discourse where it is assumed that ethical principles, indeed any principle whatsoever, must rest ultimately on metaphysical foundations which are themselves supported by the application of the appropriate rational method. This approach has been elaborated by Peerenboom in an interesting way. He takes to task such thinkers as Needham and Fung Yu-lan, who maintain that Daoist philosophy is a form of naturalism premised on a belief about how the universe works, and which therefore enjoins 'acting in accordance with nature' as its fundamental ethical principle; such a view inevitably leads to the paradox we have just outlined. Peerenboom argues, to the contrary, that Daoist ideas about the right way to live do not rest on absolute epistemological foundations for, quite to the contrary, they precisely put in question whether one can know what is natural and what is human, and hence put in doubt the possibility of digging down to a firm philosophical bedrock on which to build a secure ethical edifice. He proposes instead an alternative interpretation of Daoist naturalism which abandons the specious certainty sought within foundational metaphysics and opts instead for a 'value-relative', pragmatic interpretation. On this view, the *dao* is not to be viewed as a predetermined order to which one must align oneself but as a spontaneously emergent order, so that there are no fixed patterns, no categorical imperatives or ethical absolutes, but rather a heuristic image of harmony to which we and the rest of nature aspire. This interpretation avoids any grandiose assumption, sometimes voiced in Western writings, that Daoism can provide us with a complete philosophy, a panacea for the environmental ills facing the modern world, and replaces it with a vision of harmonious living which encourages us to approach problems in an intelligent, sensitive and case-by-case way (Peerenboom 1991).[39] It is unclear whether this argument resolves the paradox at the heart of Daoism which sees all things as manifesting the *dao* yet sees our lives as in some sense lapsing from this condition, or whether it clarifies the problematic use of the word 'nature' in this context. Nevertheless, Peerenboom's argument does point to the essentially pragmatic role of Daoism in accordance with which we are invited to re-examine the way in which we act in relation to the natural world.

This rethinking by means of a Daoist-inspired environmentalism further leads one to wonder just how compatible this ancient philosophy is with modern environmental ideas. Is it as pro-nature as some would have it? In a later chapter we shall see that Daoist techniques demand a discipline and self-control which, from a contemporary standpoint, might appear decidedly artificial and even anti-nature; for example, Daoist sexual techniques, often vaunted in the West as more in tune with nature's way than the supposedly more repressed Western attitudes, appear on closer examination to require a blocking off rather than a release of the flow of natural sexual energy; and as we shall discover in Chapter 6, the Daoist pursuit of immortality or longevity might seem to demand an overcoming of natural processes rather than a flowing with them. Then there is the contentious matter of China's own record in dealing with its natural environment. It is all very well to quote from Zhuangzi or to point to Chinese landscape paintings as ecological utopias, but history often shows us a different face and suggests either that the Chinese were not very good at putting their ideals into practice, or even that these ideals are not as benignly disposed towards nature as is sometimes thought. According to one authority, China's reputation for environmental conservation is a poor one. An abundance of evidence is cited of deforestation, soil erosion, loss of arable land, industrial and urban pollution, and water shortages which are not merely products of China's twentieth-century modernising programme but go far back into its past. There may well be 'a reverence for nature [which] runs unmistakably through the long span of China's history…a view of man as part of the natural order of things', but at the same time there has been 'a clearly discernable current of destruction and subjugation' of the natural world (Smil 1977: 6–8). This inevitably leads back to the question whether, assuming ideas have any impact on practice in general – an issue which itself is brought into focus here – Daoist ideas, whatever their intrinsic qualities, have any value for us in helping to combat environmentally destructive ideas and practices. Western ideas, including those of Christianity and of rationalist and scientific origin, have at various times been blamed for the modern ecological crisis, but the example of China suggests that the link between how people live and what they think is more tenuous than we sometime suppose.[40]

Another conclusion that might be drawn from this is that if we are to make use of Daoist ideas then they will need to be radically transformed. Perhaps Daoism contains appropriate recommendations for dealing with life in a rural, pre-modern culture, but, as the environmental philosopher Holmes Rolston has insisted, it can do little more than set a mood or tone to counterbalance the ethic of consumption and growth. To achieve more than this in the modern world 'it needs to be demythologized (or remythologized) to test whether it contains contemporary wisdom', and 'the East needs considerable reformulation of its sources before it can preach much to the West' (Rolston 1987: 181, 189).[41] On the other hand, perhaps this whole way of thinking, which treats Daoism as a 'resource' that can be manipulated and reconstituted in accordance with our will, is mired in precisely those exploitative and masculinist attitudes for which Daoism has been billed as the cure. The philosopher Gerald Larson, for example, sees this enterprise as simply an extrapolation of the exploitation of Asian material resources that took place in the colonial period for the benefit of Western economies. He does not object to comparing Eastern and Western ideas in order to illuminate contemporary issues, nor to gaining thereby a greater degree of critical understanding of our own deep-rooted assumptions, but he believes that we need to emancipate ourselves from the mindset which allows us to believe, not only that Asia is a 'resource' for us to 'exploit' but also that philosophy can stand outside all conceptual schemes and manipulate them towards some rationally contrived purpose (Larson 1987).

Larson's argument is a useful reminder that the sins of orientalism can be recommitted even in the most apparently benign contexts, and that colonial attitudes survive even into our supposedly post-colonial period. But it does not fully recognise the extent to which in such a period the ideas as well as the economic benefits that have flowed from an earlier exploitative period are now, inevitably, constitutive of contemporary global life and not merely exotic imports from alien and faraway lands. The rapidly changing nature of the ecological crisis which we face means that, whether we approach it with Eastern or Western conceptual tools, these tools will inevitably require the 'considerable reformulation' that Rolston speaks of. It would be idle to expect ancient Daoist philosophy to match precisely our current needs, but this Chinese way of thinking does seem to have the potential to inspire us to rethink our attitude towards nature in ways which our own cultural inheritance does not always appear able to do. The complete rejection of civilisation is hardly a realistic option for most, but its advocacy in Daoist terms may at least help us examine our current ways of living in a new light. The recapturing of a sense of the cosmic context of human life at one extreme, and at the other the cultivation of a non-aggressive attitude to life may, as contributions to a changing attitude of mind, be the key to a more ecologically benign way of life than one

88

which is driven by the ideal of 'progress' and which is strenuously busy trying to change the world. Exactly what that 'way of life' is for the Daoist, we will examine in the next chapter.

# 5

# 'GOING RAMBLING WITHOUT DESTINATION'

## Moral explorations

### Daoist moral vision

Daoism is not noted in the West for its moral vision. Frequently perceived as a doctrine of detachment and withdrawal rather than of moral commitment and engagement, it was summed up by Richard Wilhelm as 'a philosophy of inaction, escape from the burdens of office, and retirement into a leisured way of life in the countryside' (1931: 140), and Max Weber labelled it an ethic of 'indifference' which minimised the importance of worldly action (1951: 187).[1] In ancient China itself, Daoists were often accused of teaching a doctrine of quietism and of retreat from social responsibilities, a criticism popular amongst Confucianists for whom the social dimension of human life, along with all its obligations and rituals, was paramount. The philosopher Yangzhu, a contemporary of Zhuangzi who had Daoist leanings, was notorious for his remark that he would not sacrifice a single hair of his head even if thereby he could save the whole world, and Zhuangzi himself was often seen as a representative of a selfish, hedonist philosophy which ignored the demands of society.[2]

On the other hand the Daoist outlook has been conspicuously romanticised at various times. The exotic image of groups of like-minded companions drinking wine amongst the bamboo, reciting poetry, playing the zither and creating artworks with brush and ink has, as we noted earlier, played an archetypal role in the Chinese psyche, and Daoism thus portrayed has certainly triggered a favourable response in certain quarters in the West in recent times. Lin Yutang's 'scamp' who enjoys lolling about and refuses to take life too seriously, the genial rebel who is indifferent to convention, or the 'wild man' or 'holy fool' who turns all such convention on its head, such images have provided a welcome antidote to moral earnestness, whether Chinese or European, and have encouraged Westerners to believe that Daoism offers a way of undemanding insouciance, going with the flow, and dwelling childlike in an eternally present oblivion (Lin 1938; Watts 1979).[3]

These romanticised images have inevitably drawn the fire of modern counterparts of Confucian moralists. According to Arthur Danto, writing at a time when Daoism was beginning to be associated with the counter-culture movement of the 1960s, the follower of the *dao* was 'necessarily a loner', and Daoism was a philosophy which offered a narrowly individualistic ethic, giving little moral guidance beyond the injunction to 'do your own thing' (1976: 118). Murray Bookchin, a social ecologist with strong anarchist leanings, echoes earlier worries of Arthur Koestler when he speaks of the lamentable 'rhetorical recycling of Taoism...into vulgar Californian spiritualism', linked dangerously to the occult and the cultic (1995: 100).[4] It is a philosophy which, he believes, gives support to a 'biocentric monism' which, as with its modern version of Deep Ecology, reduces the human 'to merely one life-form among many, the poor and the impoverished either becoming fair game for outright extermination...or brutal exploitation' (Bookchin 1989: 12). Thomas Merton, usually an admirer of Eastern philosophies, wonders in similar vein whether Daoist quietism leads inevitably to totalitarianism through its discouragement of political and social activism (1961: 50).

Lying behind such views is the suspicion that Daoism advocates a dangerously relativistic viewpoint, one which has the effect of inhibiting any move towards moral judgement. Herrlee Creel insists that Daoism not only fails to offer any basis for positive action in the world, but teaches that 'All things are relative. "Right" and "wrong" are just words we apply to the same thing depending upon which partial point of view we see it from' (1970: 3). The *Zhuangzi* in particular is often held up as a notorious example of the belief that all ethical claims are equally valid, an attitude of mind which has been strongly resisted by most Western philosophers and held by many to be a social menace; 'a new spectre haunting Europe', as Ernest Gellner portentously described it.

What puzzles Westerners, and also offended many Confucians, was the apparent rejection by Daoists of ethical norms, or at least their indifference to them. For the Confucians, *li*, principles of proper interpersonal conduct, represented the bedrock on which human fulfilment and social harmony rested. *Li* originally meant 'religious ritual', but under Confucius and his followers it came to express not only ritualised and ceremonial behaviour which linked the cosmic with the social order, but also, as Creel puts it, 'the whole complex of conventional and social usage which he endowed with a *moral* connotation', and as such the cement which binds society together (1954: 32).[5] Now while the collection of ideas underlying the notion of *li*, in particular those concerned with harmonious living and self-cultivation, is not explicitly rejected by Daoists – indeed as we shall see, there is much common ground here – there are nonetheless important differences between Confucianists and Daoists. This is especially so with regard to the rules concerning etiquette or propriety, which the Daoists considered to be largely irrelevant both to personal conduct and to social harmony. Such rules represented for them an artificial imposition, laid onto and distorting the natural functioning of human life, 'disrupting man's nature' as Zhuangzi puts it, and as such harmful to the goal of life which is to live in accordance with the *dao* (Graham 1981: 128, also 174–5, 188, 205). While the ritual side of Confucianism has had little appeal in the West, its emphasis on guiding moral principles and on the cultivation of human and civilised forms of behaviour has at times proved more attractive to Western thinkers than the alarmingly anarchic Daoist way. In the Enlightenment period in particular, when Chinese ideas became fashionable in Europe, the Confucian moral teachings, with their common-sense reasonableness, their explicit commitment to practical humanistic values, and above all their seeming avoidance of metaphysical or mystical warrant, had considerable appeal in the salons of the *philosophes* and offered an attractive alternative to moral teachings based on religious foundations.

In view of all this, it is hardly surprising that Daoist thinking concerning morality has been ignored in the West, or simply marginalised as insignificant. Recent research, however, has led to a review of these kinds of attitude and, along with developments in the field of moral philosophy in general, the Daoist approach to human conduct has begun to be viewed in a different and more positive light. Critics have begun to realise that Daoism is engaged in combating a particular form of ethical theory which gives priority to rules and names rather than in attacking morality as such, and is therefore a way of thinking about human conduct which, while running counter to certain central strands of Western thinking on the subject, offers an intriguing and fertile alternative. There is no conflict here with the Confucians concerning the belief that all should aim at harmony and contentment, but rather a conviction that this harmony is likely to be achieved, not by socially promulgated regulations, reinforced by ritual formalities, but by an inner transformation and a recovery of the naïve spontaneity that is usually associated with childhood. For the Daoists, harmony emerges contextually in the realm of human praxis, rather than through pre-determined laws or rules, and comes about by following the *dao* of nature rather than the *dao* of convention. There is indeed plenty of 'moralising' talk in the *Daodejing*, but it is concerned with the cultivation of virtues such as softness, stillness, emptiness, yielding and femininity rather than more conventional ones such as honesty and fairness, and is directed towards the encouragement of inner and outer harmony rather than of precise patterns of behaviour. There is indeed a recognition in Confucian teaching of the need to cultivate right motivation and attitude rather than mere mechanical compliance with rules, but in practice this teaching has tended to be seen in the West, rightly or wrongly, as encouraging social conformity rather than personal authenticity.

The accentuation of this perceived difference between Confucian and Daoist approaches to morality has suited some Western commentators, especially those who have sought to use it in order to subvert what they see as the overly masculinist tendencies in modern Western culture, with its emphasis on rules and laws rather than on feeling and compassion. Needham, for example, in pursuit of his own organicist agenda draws an exaggeratedly sharp contrast between Confucian and Daoist moral teachings. He maintains that the Daoist way of thinking about ethical questions involves 'a receptive passivity in contrast to a commanding activity, and a freedom from all preconceived theories in contrast to an attachment to a set of social conventions', and that contrary to Confucian and Legalist teachings which were 'masculine, managing, hard, dominating, aggressive, [and] rational', the Daoists emphasised instead 'all that was feminine, tolerant, yielding, permissive, withdrawing, mystical and receptive' (1956: 59).[6]

The deployment of such language, however, might simply reinforce the conviction that what we are encountering here is in the final analysis a morally defective system which, while liberal and tolerant, lacks any clear guide to action. This worry has led to some interesting deliberations in recent times. The philosopher David Wong, for example, argues that indifference to moral rules or absolutes does not in any way imply that Daoist ideas are an ineffective basis for the moral life, since a change of heart can be a more potent factor in transforming human behaviour than the adoption of abstract, impersonal rules. Furthermore, he claims, the abandonment of the attempt to ground ethics in some rational scheme leads to an increase in compassion and toleration, not to amorality, and will help us to recognise the equal worth of all individuals (1984: 175–98; see also Ivanhoe 1996b: 202–11). Conversely an axiological ethics, one based on rules, might encourage a rigid and unemotional attitude which could lead to uncaring and even brutal conduct. Kant's uncompromising distinction between the universal, rationally grounded rules of morality and the contingent inclinations of the human heart, though consonant with long-held philosophical and theological assumptions in Europe, is hardly uncontroversial in a period in which the very notions of universality and objective rationality are in question and affairs of the human heart are given an almost unprecedented importance. According to the modern Chinese scholar Chang Chung-yuan, it was 'because of the artificiality and coldness [of the Confucian ideal of *jen*, benevolence] that the Taoists often declared that they would banish *Jen* so that the people could once again love one another', and Zhuangzi went so far as to claim that it was necessary to get rid of *jen* so that virtue might flourish (1975a: 23).

This sort of argument points to a fundamental conflict between traditional Western and Daoist understanding of ethical discourse. Daoism is sometimes seen as undermining the very notion of a prescriptive moral code founded on logocentric principles, and as a rejection of the emphasis on outward conformity to rules rather than self-knowledge and self-cultivation. Anthony Cua, for example, speaks of the 'primacy of practical reason' in Chinese ethical thinking in general, and Robert Eno goes even further by speaking of the rejection in early Chinese thought 'of reason as privileged and the identification of practical knowledge as the principal means of obtaining certain understanding of the world' (Cua 1989: 209; Eno 1996: 128). As we noted earlier, in the writings of Zhuangzi we find no clearly stated moral prescriptions and no search for foundational principles, but rather a serious, if mordantly ironic, questioning of traditional moral language and categories, leading to a 'transformation in how one thinks and feels about the world' (Kupperman 1996: 188). At best he seems to offer a moral vision based, not on rules or conceptual knowledge, nor on the teaching of abstract principles, but on the cultivation of naturally arising human skills. Hence it would seem that Daoist ethics is best understood, not in terms of theoretical knowledge but, by analogy with the mastering of certain practical techniques such as engraving, archery or swimming, as skills aimed at the cultivation of equanimity, spontaneity and a sense of being in harmony with the world (Ivanhoe 1993a; Kjellberg and Ivanhoe 1996: chaps 6–7; Graham 1981: 135–42).

In a similar vein the writings of Zhuangzi and other Daoists are some-times seen as aiming to shock us, not out of behaving morally but out of the strenuous pursuit of absolute, rigid, universal principles. They encourage us to return to a spontaneous feeling of affinity with others and with the natural world, and incline us towards those 'feminine, tolerant, yielding, receptive' qualities that Needham so eloquently advocates. As Graham puts it, the Daoist 'loosens the grip of categories made habitual by naming, [and] frees the current of thought for more fluid differentiations and assimilations' (1989: 235). There are those who argue that, contrary to the standard view, Zhuangzi did not teach moral scepticism or relativism at all but rather a kind of Nietzschean stratagem of unravelling the closely woven fabric of delusions and deceptions that clothe our standard values, exemplified graphically in Zhuangzi's vivid deployment of the images of madmen, monsters, criminals, deformities, mutilations and all kinds of unconven-tional behaviour. Moreover, his was a Nietzschean method of genealogy whereby the hidden historical roots of conventional morality are revealed: moral principles were invented at an historical moment for purely utilitarian purposes which, as the breakdown of the feudal order demonstrates, had proved inefficient at attaining these goals (Roetz 1993: 252). As the Chinese philosopher Chen Guying notes, there is about both Nietzsche and Zhuangzi a profound eccentricity and individualism which leads both to become severe critics of the respective historical traditions and values that they have inherited: 'Nietzsche initiates his own transvaluation of values in the face of Christian and traditional Western values, while Zhuang Zi initiates his transvaluation of values against the values of the vulgar world of traditional Confucian morality' (Chen 1991: 126; see also Cooper 1990: 22–3). Even if this is unfair to the Confucian teaching, it does point to the alluring absence in Daoist moral philosophy of the ideas of evil and sin, and of questionable Christian concepts such as guilt, pity or humility. In a similar vein, Roger Ames draws a direct comparison between the Nietzschean idea of *Übermensch* or self-overcoming and the Daoist idea of *de* or virtuality, both of which he sees as giving expression to an ethic of self-transformation rather than of conformity to moral law, and of creative expression rather than repressed resentment (1991b: 147).

## The ethics of self-cultivation

Critics might wonder if there is anything more in this than a cynical contempt of convention. Certainly the · Daoist writers were skilled at subverting long-established habits of thought and mocking the language of Confucian ethics. Nevertheless, there emerges out of this the outlines of a constructive moral point of view. In the words of Frederic Bender, it is becoming apparent that, 'Instead of teaching a doctrine of virtue or obligation, Taoism teaches an "ethics" of self-cultivation', a teaching which Daoists themselves contrasted (perhaps unjustly) with 'a Confucian ethics of generating unnatural guidelines of human conduct' (1983: 16).[7] By contrast with the Western religious and philosophical traditions, Daoism is understood to offer no absolute set of objective ideals nor any morally transcendent grounding upon which eternal moral principles, rights and duties could be established, but rather to recommend a way of self-transformation and self-actualisation. The *Zhuangzi* has proved a particularly fruitful source for this alternative conception. It is a book whose general objective is described by the philosopher Robert Allinson as 'the self-transformation of the reader', and whose underlying theme is that of a spiritual metamorphosis, or change in the level of consciousness, which 'does not depend upon the belief in any system of putative truths' but rather on the silencing of analytical thinking, and which leads to an alteration of personality and perspective rather than of beliefs (1989a: 24, 7–8). At the heart of this is the idea of the sage who, through mirroring and cultivating in himself the way of nature, the *dao*, exemplifies but does not specify in law-like terms the way for others; like an artist, his self-creative activity should inspire rather than be imitated.

This emphasis in Daoism on self-cultivation rather than rule-following has led to some interesting convergences with contemporary Western thought. The background to this is the perceptible shift of interest amongst certain Western philosophers in recent years from the Kantian/liberal characterisation of morality in terms of rules, justice, rights and autonomy towards a discourse of character-formation, self-fulfilment and the fostering of human excellence. This is not tantamount to a rejection of the relevance of moral principles to human behaviour, but rather an insistence that in the moral choices we make we are, to a certain extent at least, engaged in expressing and creating the kind of person we wish to be or to become; thus a soldier may avoid a cowardly action, not only in the light of what he sees as his moral duty, but also because he wishes to avoid *being* a coward. As Alasdair MacIntyre points out, in making moral decisions we have recourse, not only to abstract principles but also to a perception of the kind of person we think we are and to a narrative sense of what we see our lives to be about, especially in relation to the kind of social roles and virtues with which we tend to identify. In brief, he argues that what Enlightenment moral theory, with its concern with rules, failed to address adequately was the question 'what sort of person am I to become?' (1981: 112). A similar trend is to be found in the writings of the Canadian philosopher Charles Taylor, who defends the intrinsic moral worth of 'authenticity', the ideal of being true to one's own individual identity in one's own unique way. This ideal, which he refers to also as 'self-truth' or 'self-wholeness', may indeed be in conflict at times with conventional moral norms which can frustrate a person's desire to be responsible for the formation of their own life. Modern English-speaking philosophy, he believes, has tended to focus too narrowly 'on what it is right to do rather than on what it is good to be', and needs to re-anchor itself in 'the ontology of the human' (1989: 3, 5).[8] Feminist philosophers have also been active in promoting ideas such as these. For Carol Gilligan, to take one example, the crucial elements of morality are virtues such as responsibility for self and others, care and harmony, and moral development is more a matter of personal and emotional maturity than the ability to apply abstract, universal principles (1982).[9]

Accompanying this shift has been a growing suspicion of the relevance of ethical *theory*, and a move towards a view of ethics which gives emphasis to collective historical narratives and to the promotion of appropriate psychological attitudes, rather than to the search for foundational and validating principles of action (Furrow 1995). In a wider context, embracing various movements in humanistic psychology and holistic health, there has been a conspicuous surge of interest towards the ideals of self-realisation, personal growth and individuation as fundamental moral objectives. Popular ideas such as Abraham Maslow's 'self-actualisation' have inevitably led to dialogue with much longer-established traditions in the East, and thinkers with an interest in transpersonal states of being, namely those which seek to go beyond purely ego-consciousness, have often felt it useful to look to Eastern thought as a source of theoretical models and practical guidance.[10] Daoism is certainly not alone in the pre-modern period in encouraging the articulation of what Philip Ivanhoe has called 'a pluralistic ethic of human flourishing' (Ivanhoe 1996b: 211; see also Ivanhoe 1996a). It is widely accepted now that all major schools in Chinese philosophy are programs of self-cultivation, and the Confucian ideal of sagehood rests as much on the development of personal qualities and on the cultivation of a particular way of being human, as on the devotion to ritual performance (see Ames 1985; Ivanhoe 1993a; Munro 1985). Moreover, while it is often argued that the goal of self-cultivation has for the most part been neglected in traditional Western religious and philosophical thinking, there are obvious precedents amongst thinkers of the Romantic period, for example, where self-cultivation was often pursued with quasi-religious fervour.[11] Nevertheless, Daoism, with its long-held ideals of inner and outer harmony and its promotion of yogic disciplines that have been fashioned over many centuries, has provided a distinctive and readily usable model for this kind of human flourishing.

This insistence on the development of the person rather than on the regulation of social conduct might seem paradoxical in the Chinese context, for the Chinese culture as a whole has often appeared in Western eyes to encourage a faceless collectivism. Daniel Defoe's characterisation of the Chinese people as 'slavish' has embedded itself deeply in Western minds. Individual Chinese, historically inured in a despotic political culture, are often thought to be 'cogs in the machine', and to lack that prized Western value, individuality, while the demands of social solidarity and political cohesion are seen to be paramount. This common prejudice has been reinforced by sociologists such as Marcel Mauss who, in a lecture delivered in 1938, insisted that China as a nation and as a traditional culture was, by contrast with the more highly advanced West, deficient in the quality of individual autonomy and had failed to conceive of the human person as 'a complete entity, independent of others' (Carrithers et al. 1985: 13–14).

However, while it would be an historical misrepresentation to claim that modern Western-style individualism had any place in traditional China, the Daoists did develop a distinctive form of subjectivism and inwardness that provides an interesting counterpart to typically Western ethical ideals, one which plots a middle way between the extremes of individualism and collectivism, and which is relevant to contemporary doubts about Enlightenment conceptions of the individual. Historically, a robust conception of selfhood as such can be traced back to the classical period of Chinese thought, not only to Zhuangzi who in many ways initiated the idea of the pursuit of wisdom by private individuals, or to eccentric figures like Yangzhu, but also to Confucians such as Mengzi who, in the third century BCE, espoused the ideal of self-cultivation and encouraged self-reflection. Moreover, the ideal of spiritual transformation is evident in the 'Ten Wings' of the Yijing, probably composed by a Daoist master in about 400 BCE, and it is arguable that the emergence of the ideal of self-cultivation marked a veritable transvaluation of values in that period, one that parallels the shift in ancient Greek thought from an emphasis on warrior values to a cultivation of the moral and rational self. Moreover a specifically Daoist concept of selfhood and individuality came to maturity with the Neo-Daoist movement some six hundred years later, emerging at a time of social disruption and disillusionment following the collapse of the Han dynasty. This was a period of violence and anarchy which witnessed a growing concern about the value of human life unsupported by established social constraints, bringing into play the ideas of naturalness and spontaneity (*ziran*), and leading to a search for inner authenticity and meaning in a world that for many was perched on the edge of chaos (Mather 1969–70; Yü 1985). This was also the period which saw the emergence of formalised Daoist groups such as the Celestial Masters sect which encouraged quiet-sitting and self-examination, practices which were later incorporated into the Neo-Confucian movement.

Cultivation of the self, it must be emphasised, did not necessarily imply a Yangzhu-like self-sufficiency to be pursued in isolation from social reality, for it was implicit in Daoist thinking that the human subject was not an isolated, self-constituting entity, but rather a dynamic process, an 'ecological self', in Arne Naess's phrase, which seeks harmony within itself by pursuing harmony with the wider whole. As with the earlier cosmologists, the human individual is seen as a microcosm in whom the macrocosm is mirrored. There is therefore little warrant in Daoist thinking, or for that matter in Confucian thinking, for the idea of the autonomous subject which formulates and pursues its goals prior to or independently of the wider context. As Zhuangzi himself says, 'Without an Other is no Self' (Graham 1981: 51), a conception which seems remarkably similar to certain contemporary contextualist, decentered models of selfhood. Neither was it seen as a purely mental affair, for the cultivation the self implied the cultivation of the body, an aspect of Daoist thinking which has proved especially attractive to the West. The physical dimension of the moral life as a factor in human knowledge has been given only marginal treatment in traditional Western philosophical speculations. However, a palpable change of attitude begins to be evident under the influence of Nietzsche and more recently in the writings of Maurice Merleau-Ponty, and the body has begun to play an increasingly important role in areas such as epistemology, phenomenology and ethics. This change reflects not only the rejection of Cartesian dualism but a growing understanding of the role of bodily processes, of sexuality and the emotions in human behaviour as a whole. The Daoist prescriptions for living a more healthy and balanced life are seen to resonate well with the shift in the contemporary West to a more positive evaluation of the body and its role in the quest for psychological well-being and spiritual growth. With its pursuit of such things as gymnastics, breathing exercises, dietetics and sexual yoga, Daoism contrasts sharply with the earlier Christian distrust of the body, and is virtually unique amongst world religions in holding physical health and longevity to be crucial components of the spiritual path (Kohn 1991a: 8; Schipper 1993: ch. 6).[12]

It is true that the Daoists valued the body not so much for its own sake but more because it was the dwelling place of gods, and by dint of that a projection or manifestation of the cosmos at large (Robinet 1997: 110–13). Nevertheless, they were insistent that the spiritual and physical dimensions of human existence formed parts of the same ontological continuum, and offered no hint of the kind of radical spirit/body dualism which in the West has sometimes led to the neglect or even disparagement of the physical dimension. This does not mean that they encouraged sensuality or physical indulgence, for there remains a strong element of self-discipline and restraint in most Daoist traditions, including those concerned with sexual methods, but at the same time it does imply a clear affirmation of the inherent value of human life and the rejection of the kind of religious pessimism or existentialist angst that have often bedevilled Western thought. For the Daoist, the body/spirit is 'at home' in the universe, and its cultivation, even to the point of the indefinite prolongation of life, is affirmed in all kinds of ways. It is an ideal which, by contrast with religions such as Christianity and Buddhism with their emphasis on the suffering and transience of human existence, has inevitably caught the attention of Westerners through its celebration of the value of a long and healthy life and its practical guidance on how to achieve this (Wu 1990: 81).

The attractiveness to the West of this aspect of Daoist teaching is amplified by its related teaching concerning spontaneity. As we have seen, self-cultivation means acting in accordance with nature rather than in accordance with artificially imposed rules. To quote David Hall again, 'Taoist ethics is in fact a sort of aesthetics in which we are "enjoined" to be spontaneous (*tzu-jan*) – that is to act…in harmony with things', an ethic which eschews antecedent principles or norms (1987: 170). This means that the person who aspires to live in accordance with the *dao* needs to cultivate *wu-wei*, a concept which, as we noted in the last chapter, means literally 'not-doing', although it has the connotation of 'doing without conscious effort' rather than of complete inaction. We have already seen that this Daoist notion has caused some problems with Western interpreters, who were at one time inclined to view it as an invitation to idle quiescence or even resignation in the face of the dictates of fate. More recently, however, the idea of *wu-wei* has been construed in a much more positive light, seen as a commitment to an ideal of fullness and living and expressive selfhood which is more in tune with nature than the limiting constraints of conventional morality. This ideal is well captured by Norman Girardot when he writes that

Part of the perverse genius of the early Taoists was to question the cosmological determinism of the ordinary Chinese cultural grid imposed by an emperor's glance, Confucian ethics, or the Chinese language. The early Taoist vision sought to return to an experience of a deeper and more primitive life-order hidden by conventional language and culture and yet 'waiting in silence for the moment of its expression'.

(Girardot 1983: 2)

And on a more spiritual plane, Stephen Karcher sees in *wu-wei* 'a practice whereby the ego is emptied so that the *tao* may fill the soul', an emptying of self which encourages the values of freedom, imagination and unconventionality (1999: 8). Jung speaks of it as 'the art of letting things happen', a key to inner freedom that circumvents the mistrusting and interfering habits of rational consciousness (1995: 89).

Certain practical implications were seen to flow from this notion. It meant adopting the simple life which rejects the conventional trappings of wealth and power, and advocated living modestly and selflessly in harmony with the processes of nature. It also encouraged attitudes of non-resistance and non-violence, and cultivated 'feminine' virtues of yielding and compassion summed up in the injunction 'Practice Non-Action, practice gentleness, keep your femininity; never take the initiative'.[13] At a deeper level, it meant living in such a way that the busy, activist, striving demands of the ego are transcended, and developing the kind of emptiness or voidness which is of the essence of the *dao* itself. It was a matter of giving or emptying out rather than of self-empowerment, for 'To fill the self with glory, power, success, or wealth is to run contrary to the *Tao*, of *Lao-tzu* and *Chuang-tzu*', an idea which some have compared with Heidegger's notion of 'releasement' (Saso 1990: 117).[14]

This way of thinking about ethics has inspired a positive response amongst those who are critical of what they see as the oppressively masculine ethos of traditional Judaeo-Christian morality, or those who seek a way beyond the supposed moral imperialism of modernist thinking. But it has also provoked doubt and debate. To echo the parallel discussion from the last chapter, it might well be asked whether the injunction to act spontaneously in accordance with nature has any useful moral content, or can provide any guidance as to which is the right course of action. Nature itself appears to be amoral; after all, in the *Laozi* itself, the *dao* treats humans as 'straw dogs', and offers little in the way of moral guidance. And if all things arise out of the *dao*, as Daoists assert, then how could one possibly *not* act in accordance with its dictates? There is evidently an issue here of free will versus determinism or fatalism which, from the standpoint of Western philosophy, seems to be unresolved in Daoist thinking.[15] And even if we leave the thorny issue of free will on one side, the very notion of spontaneity seems ungrounded, and appears to derive its validity from a questionable contrast with actions which are grounded in socially constructed dispositions such as language.[16] Moreover, does not the talk of spontaneity and self-cultivation inevitably lead to an ethic of blatant egoism? Is this not the implication of Zhuangzi's statement that 'Emptiness and stillness, calm and indifference, quiescence, Doing Nothing, are the even level of heaven and earth, the utmost reach of the Way and Potency', not to mention Yangzhu's selfish refusal to sacrifice a single hair for the sake of helping another person (Graham 1981: 259)?

Furthermore, the admonition to act spontaneously seems dangerously open-ended, for it appears to be compatible with the committing of evil acts as much as virtuous ones; indeed, it is arguable that virtuous acts require a greater degree of confrontation with one's natural inclinations than evil ones. After all, from earliest times Daoists have tended to avoid speaking about the need for such virtues as benevolence, filial piety, righteousness and compassion, and the *Daodejing* positively discourages us from making moral judgements. The open-endedness and unregulated nature of the Daoist way, which prescribes no clear, single, universal path for us to follow, certainly has an allure for late modern sensibilities, echoing Nietzsche's remark, '*The* way does not exist'; but this road can lead to nihilism, as Nietzsche himself warned. Creel speaks of the enlightened Daoist as 'beyond good and evil', cautioning us that this philosophy has 'truly terrifying consequences' (1954: 124), and in his popular work on the history of civilisations Will Durant insisted that the person who follows the Daoist injunction to act in accordance with nature is 'much more likely to murder and eat his enemies than to practice philosophy' (1942: 657).

On the other hand, the promulgation of moral rules has not always resulted in an outbreak of virtue, and an ethic of self-cultivation could well be seen as rooting itself more deeply in the human personality than abstract principles of conduct. Some argue that any true follower of the *dao*, a person who has engaged in the process of self-cultivation outlined above, 'will by definition be a stranger to anger, cupidity and sefishness...[and] that causing harm to others is the very negation of *wu wei*' (Blofeld 1985: 187).[17] The practice of pursuing inner harmony is likewise seen as implying harmony with others, and the circulation of energy (*qi*) within oneself implies its circulation towards others in a spirit of openness and a transcendence of egoistical desires; to live long, says Kaltenmark, 'is necessarily to live morally' (1979: 41). It is an approach to human conduct which, according to the philosopher F.S.C. Northrop, far from engendering an amoral attitude, 'gives...Taoist man his compassionate fellow-feeling for all men' (1946: 332). In other words, the encouragement of an ontological rather than an axiological attitude towards morality tends to diminish selfish egoic tendencies by helping to break down dualist-inspired distinctions between self and others. Daoism has sometimes been compared with existentialism, but the emphasis in Daoist teaching on the integration of the narrow self within the wider context of the rhythms of nature contrasts significantly with the existentialist idea – at least in its Sartrean formulation – of personal authenticity that is pursued independently, indeed even in the teeth, of the circumambient world of people and things. It has also been compared with what has recently come to be called 'therapeutic individualism', namely the obsessional pursuit of personal health; but here again we need to emphasise the Daoist concept of selfhood which, with its ecological implications, implies a notion of subjectivity which is necessarily tied to a wider contextual framework. This wider sense of the self means that 'The Taoist sage is unselfish, neither by acting out his nature nor by obeying moral principles, but by seeing through all dichotomies including self and other' (Graham 1989: 193). Moreover, for the Daoist a morally pure life is not only a consequence but also a necessary precondition of the pursuit of oneness with the *dao*. From its early days there was a strong emphasis in Daoist sects such as the Celestial Masters on good works, and an insistence on such activities as feeding orphans, maintaining public roads, caring for the sick and giving one's fortune to the poor, all of which were seen as essential prerequisites to embarking on the path of spiritual cultivation (Boehmer 1977: 73; Kleeman 1991: 163; Maspero 1981: 273, 323–4).[18]

Moreover, in spite of its reputation for nonconformity and eccentric reclusiveness, Daoism has in practice played an important social role in Chinese history. The romantic image of Daoism, whether inspired by accounts of the bibulous and poetic activities of the Seven Sages of the Bamboo Grove or by images of hermits contemplating remote mountain scenery, undoubtedly conveys an important aspect of Daoism, but it is far from being the full picture. The political aspects of Daoism will be dealt with in the next section, but here we need to draw attention to the hitherto often neglected social role of Daoism which provided a practical moral and soteriological framework for millions of people in China, an aspect which has been neglected in the West until relatively recently. Even with regard to its more esoteric dimensions, we need to be wary of certain ingrained views about Daoism's supposed anti-social stance, or its supposed encouragement of an aesthetic, drop-out lifestyle, views which were first voiced by Confucian critics but which became clichés in the West. Amoury de Riencourt typifies this sort of attitude in his comment that while 'Confucius wrote for social and political man who is history-conscious and devotes his life to action...[Laozi] wrote for the world-weary individualist who seeks refuge in solitude and yearns to obliterate history' (1965: 32). For Livia Kohn, on the contrary, the ecstatic flights leading to oneness with the *dao* do not imply that the sage avoids life in the world, but rather that 'he remains faithful to inner nature in whatever situation he finds himself...The true sage is one with heaven, yet active in the world' (1991a: 159–60; see also Kohn 1992: 172–6). And Mark Berkson argues that the ultimate goal of the

Daoist sage is to be 'in the world, but not of it', and to live wisely and skilfully in the world rather than to escape from it (1996: 119). In similar vein, some have suggested that, contrary to the standard view, Daoists do not advocate a reversion to a primitive, pre-civilisational condition but rather a recovery of primitiveness within the fullness of civilised life itself, and that it does not necessarily encourage withdrawal from society as such but rather the adoption of a more sceptical attitude towards its conventions and the reversal of some of its ingrained exploitative values (Neville 1989: 63, 70; Hansen 1992: 211–14). It is worth noting, too, that Daoist monas-teries were often not simply places of escape and exclusion from the world but performed important social functions as hostels for travellers, medical dispensaries, advice and welfare centres, and places of retreat and refresh-ment for scholar officials.[19]

## The politics of anarchism

There has, then, been a perceptible shift in our understanding of the ethical and social dimensions of Daoism, and of the degree to which Daoist values have penetrated the whole fabric of Chinese life. In recent years scholars such as Kristofer Schipper have argued compellingly for Daoism's inseparability from the traditional practices and activities of everyday life in China, while at the same time showing how to this day Daoism remains in touch with its ancient philosophical roots (Ching 1993: 217–23; Schipper 1993). The stereotypical picture of Daoism as essentially apolitical, to be identified with an individualistic reaction against Confucian social practice, a way of 'dropping out' from social and political obligation, is one that is increasingly being questioned. We must remind ourselves, of course, that Daoists and Confucians have often been at loggerheads with one another over attitudes towards the political and social worlds, but Daoist and Confucian concerns have historically intersected and complemented each other at a number of points, even while competing for imperial patronage. On the one side, Confucians were often much less conservative and more critical of the status quo than they are usually made out to be.[20] On the other side, Daoists, despite their reputation for refusing to go to the imperial court even when urgently summoned, have frequently been participants in the processes of government, have given advice to emperors and have constituted a significant factor in political argument in China for over two thousand years.[21] The *Daodejing* itself has long been recognised as expressing a distinctive political philosophy, albeit one which stands in marked contrast with Confucian teachings. And even subsequent to the classical era of Chinese thought in the period of 'Warring States', when philosophical thinking in general was largely orientated towards social and political ends, Daoism continued periodically to play a significant role in political debates.[22]

What species of politics, then, can we discern in the Daoist tradition? In spite of the fact that at various times over its long history Daoists and Daoist principles have penetrated the inner sanctum of imperial power, its origins betray a distinctly recalcitrant, even subversive, quality. It often stood apart from and in opposition to the state, displaying a model of knowing and behaving which was centred outside the main sites of metropolitan power, distrusted by the Confucian establishment as a religion of rebels, visionaries and protest movements. As one historian of Chinese political thought puts it, the early Daoist philosophers 'adduced an ideal of a free society of a kind that had never existed in history', and hence one which was a major inspiration of insurgency (Hsiao 1979: 20).[23] It was not just that its reclusive inclinations encouraged eccentricity and an attitude of indifference towards the state, but that its dream of a return to a primitive condition free from state interference posed a constant if implicit threat to the interests of the established political order. As with Rousseau, who spoke out against the iniquity and unnaturalness of civilised urban life, Daoism represented a focus of social discontent that was feared or at least mistrusted by those in power. From the fourth century BCE onwards, Daoists were closely associated with opposition to feudal society, and later to the bureaucratic and economic centrism which followed the unification of the empire. They harked back to an earlier mythical society of frugal simplicity, social equality and spontaneous collectivism, a characteristic which continued to cling to the Daoists all through Chinese history. And while the *Daodejing* may have been addressed to the concerns of rulers and their advisors, the writings of Zhuangzi, which have often in the West been seen as those of a lonely, defeatist recluse, 'have constantly been favourites of rebels, social outcasts, and those whose worldly ambitions were failed' (Graham 1960: 10).[24] The same is true of other more recently translated Daoist texts such as the *Scripture of Salvation*, which was widely read by people from all classes of society and which taught salvation for all, rich and poor alike (Bokenkamp 1997: 376).

The philosophical attitude of the early Daoists became politically activated with the rise of the Daoist 'church' in the second century CE, a movement which not only installed the Daoist religion as a popular movement beyond the privileged sphere of the literati, but which helped, then and subsequently, to articulate the voices of the disempowered masses and to make the somewhat esoteric statements of the *Laozi* relevant to the lives of ordinary people. There was also present in Daoism as an organised religion a messianic/millenarian element which helped to instigate popular uprisings against authority and, as Girardot comments, Daoism served 'essentially as the "official" legitimation of the "non-official" world of the people of the land, those who were traditionally the flesh and blood of the "real country" of China' (Schipper 1993: xv; see also Bokenkamp 1994; Seidel 1969b). This observation is especially relevant to the period up to the fifth century CE when several Daoist-inspired rebellions erupted with the aim of establishing the reign of the 'Way of Great Peace', a dream of a return to a society free from oppressive state interference and economic exploitation, recreating a condition believed to have prevailed before the coming of civilisation. Its connection with philosophical Daoism is not a simple one, but can be discerned in the latter's suspicion of the restrictive and manipulative force of language and social convention, and in its belief in the possibility of personal transformation as a way towards a more harmonious life. Amongst these insurrectionist eruptions, the most important was the Yellow Turban rebellion of 182 CE, discussed above in Chapter 2, which had a wide appeal among all classes. It was suppressed after spreading through many provinces of China, but it helped to weaken the Han dynasty and established a number of autonomous, self-governing, quasi-democratic communities.[25]

It would be a mistake, however, to identify Daoism as a perennial force for liberation and emancipation by contrast with prevailing Confucian-inspired despotism. In the first place, Confucianism itself advocated benign rulership based on the principle of the Mandate of Heaven, and whatever the actual practice of individual rulers, it was generally held as a theoretical premise that the welfare of the people constituted the *raison d'être* of the state, a view which is at odds with the standard Western picture of China as founded on absolute and unconstrained totalitarianism (Peerenboom 1993: 98–102; Turner 1990; Yan 1994). Second, in the centuries that followed the Yellow Turban rebellion, right up to the tumultuous final years of the Celestial Empire, Daoists for the most part sought accommodation with official centres of power, supporting a largely conformist moral outlook and advocating responsibilities towards family, community, state and gods, for, as Terry Kleeman observes, 'as we would expect of any major world religion, the establishment of ethical standards and their justification and enforcement were a central element of Taoism from its inception' (1991: 163). Nevertheless, at various times Daoist ideas also inspired dissent and were often associated with the forces of opposition, protest and rebellion in Chinese society. Thus in the Mongol Yüan dynasty, Daoists provided a nucleus of passive resistance against foreign occupation, and in the fourteenth century peasant revolts were linked to the Daoist-inspired Sect of the White Lotus. In more recent centuries groups with Daoist leanings engaged in seditious activities directed against the Manchus, another foreign dynasty, and in the Boxer Rebellion (1900–01) the Daoist image of perfect government, Daoist-inspired secret societies, martial arts and 'magical' techniques of invulnerability all played a part in encouraging radical ideas and anti-imperial insurgency (Liu 1979: 53–65; Schipper 1993: 14; Welch 1957: 157).[26]

In the light of all this, it is not surprising that Daoism has been drawn into the orbit of Western *anarchist* discourse. Ever since Laozi became known in the West, anarchists 'have claimed [him] as one of themselves' (Graham 1989: 299), and indeed it has become almost a commonplace to identify the two; as one writer puts it, the *Daodejing* 'is one of the great anarchist classics', and according to another, Daoism as a purely secular and social vision 'anticipated [Western] anarchism in many ways' (Clark 1983: 65; Zarrow 1990: 11; see also Ames 1983a, 1983b; Bahm 1958; Marshall 1992a).[27] Nevertheless, this comparison has proved contentious and has given rise to some interesting debates, the distancing between the Daoist and Western notions providing a useful means for examining the underlying assumptions of Western anarchist thinking, as well as uncovering some of the pitfalls of intercultural comparisons. Some recent studies suggest that the close association between Daoism and anarchist theory, while indicating some specific convergences, involves an uncritical projection of Western libertarian ideas without sufficient regard for certain fundamental differences between them, and especially for the philosophical basis on which Daoist thinking rests.[28] The latter, according to Roger Ames, involves a distinctively organistic conception of human existence in which the individual is understood as 'a matrix of relationships which can only be fully expressed by reference to the organismic whole'. By contrast, Western anarchism has usually conceived the person as an 'autonomous, discrete, and discontinuous "atomistic" individual', a viewpoint which implies 'tension between individual liberty and the collective will' (Ames 1983b: 32). This has important implications for the notion of freedom in the two traditions, for, it is argued, while Western anarchism has often (in the cases of Bakunin and Stirner, for example) been premised on the ideas of rational self-determination and freedom of action, the Daoist notion entails a non-egoistic conception of self-actualisation through harmony with the community and with nature.[29] Views such as this are evidently of more than antiquarian interest at a time when Enlightenment humanistic assumptions are under question, and when the relationship between the human and the natural worlds has come to a prominent place in the political agenda. Such considerations enter into the thinking of David Hall, who argues that in devising its own form of anarchism in the context of a distinctively organismic cosmology, Daoism offers a view which is not anthropocentric but 'polycentric' in that it gives no privileged status to humans, let alone to any specific class of humans. It presupposes a sense of cosmic harmony which arises spontaneously, a 'harmony of self-creative events' which is quite at variance with the Western tradition, going back to Plato, of a harmony imposed from outside (Hall 1983: 51, 62).

There are further suggestive differences, ones which concern the relationship between government and citizen. The ideal society for Western anarchists is one in which the role of government is reduced to a minimum or abolished altogether, whereas a Daoist is concerned more with removing supposedly artificial hindrances to the spontaneous and natural workings of the state than with abolishing it completely. It is often pointed out that the *Daodejing* itself is, at least in part, a treatise on statecraft and even on military strategy, and 'abounds in advice and exhortations directed to rulers' (Schwartz 1985: 210). Some scholars argue that the starting point of Daoist political theory is the transformation of self at the level of the ruler rather than, primarily, the level of society, giving rise to the idea that in a properly ordered state the ruler should do nothing except set an example and rely on sound advice and an effective bureaucracy (Bender 1983: 9–10; Creel 1970: ch. 4). Contrary, then, to the conception of abstract citizens' rights in the Western Enlightenment tradition which could be enlisted to challenge state power and legitimacy, Daoist thinkers stressed a more conservative approach to statecraft which encouraged the refinement of harmonious attitudes, whether in rulers or ruled, and which saw political authority, not in terms of power and manipulation, but rather of example. Such a radically different approach to politics not only amplifies our understanding of anarchism, but also 'helps us understand that there are many kinds of authority, and that some imply neither membership of a special office-holding group possessing power nor even "authoritarianism" in any sense' (Clark 1983: 83).[30]

One of the consequences of this attitude towards the state was that, while rebellions were frequently inspired by Daoist ideals, revolutions in the European sense were not. It has been pointed out that early Daoist uprisings rarely took an ideological stance in opposition to the imperial remit as such, or sought to overthrow the oppressive institutions of family, tribe or state, but that they might turn against a particular emperor if he was seen to have forfeited his mandate through misrule. Indeed, some have gone so far as to claim historical collusion between Daoism and the quasi-totalitarian ideals of the Legalist school (*Fajia*) which insisted on the fundamental requirement of conformity to social/legal rules. Though Daoists emphasised the image of the ruler whose rule was perfectly adapted to the natural order, in opposition to the privileges and ritual practices of the feudal aristocracy, both schools idealised the political order in which people obeyed absolutely yet spontaneously. Indeed, according to Heiner Roetz, its very naïvety and lack of substantive moral principles left Daoism open to exploitation by unscrupulous legalists (1993: 268).[31] Nevertheless, for the Daoists this spontaneous order implied the absence of the need for force and coercive state action which, in their view, was the cause of and not the remedy for social disorder: 'To impose order by force only results in disorder' (Graham 1989: 308).

While therefore Daoist thinking could be said to encourage a *laissez-faire* attitude towards politics – indeed, this term was an eighteenth-century translation of the Daoist concept of *wu-wei* – it was one which encouraged self-cultivation and self-fulfilment rather than a libertarian ideal of unfettered rational agency. Moreover, the idea of individual human rights which could be used as a platform from which to criticise or even overthrow the state cannot easily be inferred from this way of thinking which always sees self-cultivation as embedded in wider considerations of harmony and balance. The distinctive characteristic that emerges from Western discussions of Daoism, therefore, is not that of 'the absolute value of the individual which underlies Western anarchism', or indeed Western liberal thinking in general, but a kind of 'paternalistic anarchism' (Graham 1989: 303)[32] which advocates an ideal of self-realisation within the compass of a harmonious and natural whole. This 'whole' embraces, as we have noted, the cosmos at large, and the idea of 'chaos' which we identified earlier as a key concept in Daoist cosmology is clearly reflected in its political thinking and is seen as having implications for the ideal role of the individual within the social order.[33] The Daoist model, therefore is not a predetermined order, nor out-and-out individualism, but rather the kind of order which, as in the case of the self-organising system of the cosmos of which we spoke earlier, achieves its order out of its own inner unfettered agency 'from the edge of chaos'.

According to J.P. Clark (1978: 23), one of the richest veins of modern anarchism is communitarianism, and it is in this context that Daoism is sometimes seen to make its most important contribution to anarchist theory. Civilisation is typically perceived by Daoism as artificial and stultifying, reducing the capacity for self-realisation, and the aim is therefore not simply the abolition of constraints on freedom but rather the encouragement of a more simple society with reduced wants, small human groupings, and a central government which interferes little and encourages local autonomy. Julia Ching is one of a number of thinkers who see Daoism as advocating the need to recover important values and ways of life lost in our departure from the *dao*, a 'back to nature romanticism' which envisages 'a small, pacifist village state with minimal government' (1993: 89–90).[34] In all of this there is a conscious isomorphism between individual and political transformation, between the aim of self-cultivation which leads ultimately to union with the *dao*, and return to the primitive unity that purportedly once prevailed in the realm of social intercourse, an isomorphism which emphasises once again the continuity between the philosophical and religious traditions. Other critics have emphasised this primitivist proclivity of Daoism with its antipathy towards the inflationary and centralising tendencies of civilisation, and its overtones of a lost paradisal state. Needham, for example, who prefers the phrase 'primitive collectivism' to 'anarchism', tends to see the Daoist utopia through the lens of Marxist primitive communism rather than the libertarian individualism of certain nineteenth-century anarchists. In his view, the Daoist political ideal is a kind of pre-feudal agrarian collectivism whose organic unity reflects the natural condition of life prior to the institution of private property and the development of social classes. Furthermore, in line with certain anthropological theories that emerged in the early part of the century, such as those of Margaret Mead, he sees it as an egalitarian, non-aggressive, co-operative society, a reaction against both Confucianism and Legalism, whose 'social-ethical thought-complex was masculine, managing, hard, dominating, aggressive' (1956: 59, also 104–5). Girardot too, though his guiding interpretative model is primal chaos rather than organicism, sees in Daoism a 'mystical primitivism' which carries with it the idea of an original state of 'perfect harmony in the distant past', a paradise which was lost but to which we still aspire individually and collectively, and to which we must return as a prelude to a new life (1983: 68).[35]

The pacifist tendency in Daoism, underlined in Needham's commentaries (1956: 105, 126–7) has attracted much interest, not least because of Daoist dislike of egocentric individualism and anthropocentric metaphysics and its encouragement of an ecological rather than an atomistic sense of the self. Peace and anti-war sentiments are recurrent in Daoist writings, and the great messianic text of early religious Daoism, the *Taipingjing*, looks forward to a future epoch of 'The Great Peace' which will re-establish the reign of peace thought to have prevailed before the advent of civilisation. Certainly Chinese Daoism has little in common with the nihilist-inspired terrorism or the aggressive confrontationalism associated with certain strands of nineteenth-century European anarchism or twentieth-century revolutionary politics, and early Daoist scriptures tended to echo Buddhist interdictions against the harming of sentient beings. As Isabelle Robinet points out, periodic rebellions inspired by Daoist precepts were always carried out in the name The Great Peace and aimed at restoring an order which had been compromised by a failing dynasty (1997: 185). Nevertheless, the adumbration of military strategies in the *Daodejing*, and the develop-ment of martial arts within Daoist circles over the past millennium, might seem to run counter to this claim. It would certainly be false to maintain that Daoists have never been involved in warfare, or even that they were pacifists in principle, but it is important to note that their concern with military and pugilistic methods was based on a recognition of the inevitabil-ity of violence rather than its desirability, and was associated with the attempt to formulate means of dealing with conflict in the least destructive of ways and on the refinement of defensive techniques which minimise the use of force. Here once again the doctrine of *wu-wei* is relevant, for in this context it implies, not simply avoiding all active conflict, but rather the adoption of the Fabian tactic of allowing one's enemies or opponents to defeat themselves. This view was typically expressed in epithets such as 'weapons of war are wont to rebound', and 'the softest thing in the world [i.e., water] overcomes the hardest' (*Daodejing*: ch. 43). The glorification of war, of fighting, of military prowess and combat plays no part in Daoist thinking and practice, and indeed in Chinese culture generally the warrior virtues have ranked far less eminently than in European traditions. It must be emphasised that this attitude, and the concomitant rejection by Daoists of capital punishment, was not based on any absolute precept of non-violence or on any principle concerning the inherent right to or sacredness of life, but rather on the belief that violence has a way of producing more violence, and so never achieves the end intended. Hence, 'To impose order by force only results in disorder' (Graham 1989: 308).[36] Furthermore, the privileging of non-violent activities and attitudes in Daoist traditions is not based on a high estimation of the virtues of meekness and humility, but rather on a belief that violence is a form of weakness, not of strength, and that the '*yin* power of passivity is more enduring than the *yang* force of direct action' (Cooper 1990: 40; see also Liu 1979: ch. 5; Peerenboom 1993: 63).[37]

Does any of this have practical relevance for us today? James Legge, the earliest commentator on the political thinking of the *Laozi*, set the tone by dismissing its ideas as 'impracticable', and was baffled as to how its attack on Confucian principles of benevolence could help bring about a return to social and political order (1883: 91–4). Many would still agree, seeing this work as an amusing distillation of an unworkable anarchist ideal and concurring with Girardot's reference to 'the wistful impracticality of the early Daoist political ideal of primitivism', or with Thomas Merton's dismissal of Daoist philosophy as an evasion of the real world which 'would have worked very well in the Garden of Eden' (Girardot 1983: 280; Merton 1961: 50). And would we even want to return to a Daoist Garden of Eden in which we lived in a state of agrarian simplicity, with limited needs and in timeless accord with each other and with nature? Looked at from our modern perspective, would this not frustrate our evident need for tension, variety, perpetual advance? After the 'fall' into civilisation, could we ever become reconciled to the boredom of universal harmony?

In the face of such objections it is worth remembering that a state based on Daoist ideals was in fact established by the Celestial Masters movement for a short time in the late Han period, and that, even though within the wider political context of China it proved to be unsustainable, it merited imperial interest and patronage at various times (Robinet 1997: 56–8). Perhaps, though, these political ideas are important for us today, not as a utopian blueprint or systematic political programme but rather as a reminder of alternatives, as a way of 'expanding the range of creative possibilities open to us', as Hall puts it (1983: 62). They can be a way of encouraging us to re-examine some of the assumptions that underlie our political thought and practice, for example attitudes towards competition, power, aggression, individualism and our relationship with the natural environment. They may help us in the process of unmasking networks of domination which are built into the political order, and of disrupting some of our unexamined beliefs and attitudes in the field of social values. At a more personal level, the anarchist yearnings in Daoist writings may be read as allegorical rather than as literal, more ontological than political in intent. In this vein Girardot argues that the early Daoists were not seeking 'to dissolve man and society permanently back into the seamless unconsciousness of nature', or to escape into a mythical Golden Age, but to provide a medicine or therapy that addressed the sickness and entropy of ordinary life. In this way, the return to the anarchist primal chaos before the advent of civilisation is not necessarily to be construed as a realisable political goal, but as the rediscovery of the original (mythic) balanced wholeness within the actual life of human beings and society in the present (Girardot 1983: 40–42).

## Women and gender

Daoism's questioning of such factors as power and domination, and its corresponding partiality to yielding and permissiveness has unsurprisingly drawn the attention of feminist theorists, and the 'wistful impracticality' of Daoist ideas has proved surprisingly effective in helping to challenge long-established gender attitudes. The association of Daoism with certain strands of feminist discourse is not yet as firmly established as that of Buddhism (Gross 1993), but increasingly it is being seen not only as a potential critique of institutionalised and socially embedded power structures, but also of the symbolic systems which have traditionally enshrined and privileged masculine-biased values. The complementarity of the *yang* and *yin* principles seems to offer the possibility of a less divisive way of thinking about gender issues, and Daoism itself represents an image of human connectedness and non-aggressive harmony that contrasts with the masculine values of assertive independence and competitiveness that have typified modern Western cultural attitudes. The issue here is seen to be not only between Daoism and the West, for the 'feminine' voice of Daoism has also been contrasted with the 'masculine' voice of Confucianism, the latter once again playing the role of *yang* to the Daoist *yin*. It is frequently asserted that in both its religious and philosophical forms, the special place that Daoism has given to 'the feminine' contrasts with the endemic masculinism of Confucianism with its emphasis on rule and discipline (Ching 1993: 95; Kaltenmark 1969: 37, 58–60).[38] There is a parallel here too with ecological matters, and ecofeminists have been especially attracted to what can be described as the *relational* sense of the self in Daoism where the focus of individual human life is on the wider social and natural environment rather than on the 'skin-encapsulated ego', in Alan Watts' phrase. The Daoist adumbration of an ecological notion of the self is seen to contrast with the notion of the self as atomistic and as tending towards manipulation and control rather than towards care and co-operation (Olds 1991: 20–1; Zimmerman 1994: 304). Moreover, in a wider context some feminists have seen the subjugation of nature – of the land, of animals, and of matter and energy in general – as directly parallel to the subjugation of women, and have contrasted the masculine reduction of nature to abstract scientific categories as contrasting with a more feminine mode of understanding which gives prominence to immediate and sensual appreciation of the natural world, a view which broadly speaking matches the outlook of Daoist philosophy (Griffin 1978).

It would be a mistake, however, to infer from this that Daoism offers us a systematic critique of patriarchal attitudes; that would be a completely anachronistic interpretation, for the very idea of liberating women is totally absent not only from Daoism but from China's history as a whole. Pre-modern Chinese society in general has been strictly patriarchal and patrilineal, and women have typically occupied a low status compared with men, a status institutionally enframed within the rigid stratification of Chinese society from the emperor downwards, and by Confucian teaching where loyalty to one's husband was portrayed as directly parallel to loyalty to the dynastic government. In spite of this, the *yin-yang* paradigm does seem to express a surprisingly balanced conception of gender meanings and roles. Several writers have emphasised the ways in which in Daoist thinking masculine and feminine gender traits are integrated in a harmonious and balanced relationship, seeing it as transcending 'agonistic dualisms' and 'sharp divisions and separations' typical of the West, and endorsing by contrast the values of caring and love (Tucker and Grim 1994: 187). Some have gone further and claimed that Daoism privileges the feminine over the masculine, quoting such passages as 'Woman is superior to man in the same way that water is superior to fire'.[39] Graham, for example, points out that, just as the familiar ranking of strength and hardness above passivity and yielding is reversed in Daoist thought, so too in the case of the male/female polarity where Daoist texts typically give precedence to the latter over the former (1989: 224).

Needless to say, this whole way of talking is highly questionable. Reference to a 'balanced relationship' between 'feminine' and 'masculine' characteristics – the 'marriage of East and West' – and indeed to their rebalancing in favour of the former, will be seen by many feminists as perpetuating an uncritical binarism where genders are stereotyped and reified by means of paired lists of personality traits. And the notion that there are but two fundamental sites of gender identity around which the infinite variety of individual identities must revolve will offend many. Moreover, the identification of Daoism with femininity will recall the way in which orientalism in general has been seen to manifest a complicity between colonial and patriarchal oppression; the radical otherness of the East which assures us of its subordination to the West is reinforced by attaching to it the contrast between feminine weakness and masculine strength.

112

Nevertheless, Daoist thinking does seem to open up the possibility of a different way of conceptualising gender identity and difference, offering us a resource with which to reflect on our own experience. As Hall and Ames point out, the Chinese conception of a 'realized person' gives expression to 'the full range of human traits and dispositions', and the interweaving complementarity of *yin* and *yang* principles suggests a conception of the self which transcends the traditional Western tendency to polarise the sexes into mutually exclusive categories. They believe that in the Chinese way of thinking, gender is 'more fluid and lacks the exclusivity' of Western approaches, pointing to a 'polyandrogynous' range of possibilities for self-cultivation (1998: 81, 95).

Amongst the earliest commentators to recognise the importance of the feminine in Daoist thought and practice was Robert van Gulik who, in his study of sexual life in ancient China, noted that 'Taoism has on the whole been much more considerate to women, and given much more thought to her physical and emotional needs than Confucianism ever did' (1961: 84). At about the same time the French sinologist Max Kaltenmark drew attention to what he described as the 'primacy of the feminine' in the *Daodejing*, and argued that its 'exaltation of the femininity went dead against all conventional thinking' (1969: 59; see also Chen 1969; Duyvendak 1947; Waley 1977: 57). Since that time the pervasive symbolic role of 'the feminine' and 'the mother' in the *Daodejing* has frequently been emphasised. Attention is frequently drawn to such passages as 'Know the male, but keep to the role of the female' (ch. 28), and to the use of the image of childbirth and nurturing as a way of comprehending the creative power of the *dao*. This latter aspect is stressed by Benjamin Schwartz, who observes that while the feminine role in sex is ostensibly passive, by her very 'non-acting' the female plays the leading role in procreation and conquers the male by stillness. In this way the woman

> represents the nonassertive, the uncalculating, the nondeliberative, nonpurposive process of generation and growth – the process by which the 'empty' gives rise to the full; the quiet gives rise to the active, and the 'one' gives rise to the many. The female is [thus] the epitome of *wu-wei*.
>
> (Schwartz 1985: 200–1)

And in the words of Kristofer Schipper, 'the body of the Tao is a woman's body. The female body, the body of the pregnant mother...the only one able to accomplish...the work of the Tao' (1993: 129).[40]

While some writers have given prominence to the cosmological significance of the feminine principle, others have drawn attention to the way in which it operates at the more popular level of Daoist religious belief and practice. In the Daoist pantheon, for example, a key role is played by figures such as the Queen Mother of the West and the Mother of the Bushell, as well as by the myriad of lesser goddesses, river nymphs, dragon ladies and rain maidens who make their appearance in Daoist mythology (Cahill 1993; Sangren 1983; Schafer 1973). Furthermore, in the context of Daoist institutional practice it is now recognised that there has been an unusual degree of parity between men and women. Thus the Celestial Masters sect was organised in a way that established virtual equality between men and women, mastership being accessible to both, and in the Tang period there is evidence of the way in which Daoism opened up the possibility for a fulfilling life for women beyond their restricted domestic roles, providing opportunities for them to engage in the sorts of spiritual practice that have usually been associated exclusively with men. In that period, many royal princesses were ordained to the Daoist priesthood, and female practitioners of internal alchemy followed a spiritual path similar to that of men. In revealing this dimension of Daoism for the first time, historical research has provided a means whereby women's voices can at last be heard, and an account of their life in China extricated from its traditionally exclusive male narrative (Benn 1991; Cahill 1990, 1993; Mann 1997: 66–75; Schipper 1993: 58, 128).[41]

It has been particularly difficult for Western scholars to come to terms with this gender equality in Daoism. As Jordan Paper points out, from the Western point of view the Chinese religious outlook in general has been dominated by the belief in the supremacy of a masculine deity, and there has been a corresponding difficulty in accepting the idea that in the Chinese tradition male and female spirits may be of equal importance and power. The roots of this Eurocentric perspective, he argues, can be traced back to Matteo Ricci and his fellow missionaries. As members of a celibate religious order and as loyal upholders of monotheistic orthodoxy, they inevitably worked on the assumption that 'female subservience to the male was part of God's plan and the mark of a civilized society' (Paper 1995: 219). Thus, in their attempt to forge some kind of accommodation with Confucianism, the Jesuits chose to read into China their own patriarchal assumptions, a misunderstanding which had baneful long-term consequences for Western perceptions of China in general and of Daoism in particular (Paper 1995: ch. 8).

There has indeed been a reaction against the sort of historically endemic cultural misogyny that Paper has identified here. As we noted above, this reaction has sometimes led to the idealisation of the Daoist view of women by contrast with traditional Western attitudes, seeing it as advocating the primacy of 'feminine' over 'masculine' qualities in individual, social and political spheres. This tendency is especially evident in some of the growing popular literature on Daoist sexual yoga, which we will examine in the next chapter. In the meantime, we can cite Needham as a more scholarly example of this tendency. In many of his writings he has shown a strong partiality for what he takes to be a feminist viewpoint, one which he links closely with his favoured organicist paradigm and, by contrast with the 'masculine' and 'managing' tendencies of Confucianism, he portrays the Daoist way as feminine and receptive, one which could arise 'only as the fruit of a passive and yielding attitude in the observance of nature' (1956: 152, 59, 33). He argues that in ancient times Chinese society 'was in all probability matriarchal', from which source arose a Daoist tradition which gave primacy 'to all that was feminine, tolerant, yielding, permissive, withdrawing, mystical and receptive', a philosophy of life which preferred a passive rather than a commanding attitude (1956: 105, 59). Water, a central Daoist symbol, is essentially feminine for it 'is yielding and assumes the shape of whatever vessel it is placed in', and epitomises the Daoist concept of leadership which, in marked contrast to the Confucians and Legalists, achieves order without imposing it from above. Thus in Needham's view, not only was the Daoist conception of nature inextricably connected with feminine spontaneity and yieldingness, but it was also a principle that should inform human and social relations where its pre-eminence was a recipe for harmony and a harbinger of 'a cooperative collectivist society' (1956: 57–8).

Leaving aside questions about the vocabulary employed here by Needham, how adequate is the foregoing as an understanding of Daoist views? Taking his stand from almost the opposite end of the spectrum from Needham, Creel sees the *Laozi*'s 'feminist' passages in a rather different light. For him, the text is primarily one of political strategy, and it exploits feminine symbolism and proto-feminist sentiments not as an assertion of their importance in the order of nature or of society, but purely as a cunning device for achieving political aims. By using such rhetorical devices, the ambitious ruler can impose his will by encouraging passive acceptance on the part of his people, an argument which is sometimes echoed in contemporary feminist debates where a similar suspicion hangs over attempts to characterise a distinctive femininity in terms of passivity and yieldingness (Creel 1970).[42]

Between the two extremes represented by Needham and Creel, there lies a middle way. For Roger Ames, Creel's interpretation reduces the *Laozi* to little more than a cynical political stratagem, and violates the spirit of the text. The central teaching of Daoism, in Ames's view, is that human persons can fulfil their highest goal by achieving integration with nature, thereby becoming one with the *dao* and contributing to cosmic harmony. Now this harmony and integration, whether at the human or cosmic level, is necessarily one of balance between forces that are in tension yet mutually complementary, and from this point of view it would clearly be a mistake to value one side over the other, the *yin* over the *yang*, the female over the male. The *Laozi*, he argues, is certainly a politically driven text; but its aim is not to substitute the feminine for the masculine, as Needham suggests, but to restore the equilibrium which is the natural way of the *dao*, or in other words simply as a way of emphasising what Susan Cahill has called 'the essential importance of the *yin* side of humanity' (1986: 168). Therefore the text is clearly 'not advocating the substitution of a feminine-oriented set of values for the prevailing masculine values...[but pursuing] both a personal and a political ideal that reconciles the tension of opposites in sustained equilibrium and harmony' (Ames 1981: 33; see also Hall and Ames 1998: 90–100). The orientation of the text is *androgynous* rather than feminine, one in which both masculine and feminine qualities are embraced and reconciled (Ames 1981).[43] Furthermore, for Ames the importance of this argument lies not simply in the rebuttal of what he sees as a misunderstanding of Daoist thought, but rather in a more general misreading of Daoism in the West, namely its persistent characterisation as negative, escapist and quietistic, and our converse failure fully to recognise its positive values and ideals. These, and the values of reconciliation and integration, are aspects of Daoism which offer us, not the life-avoiding features of some still-persistent interpretations of Daoism (though certainly not Needham's), but 'some positive ideals of the consummate human being, an ideal which although consistent with nature does represent a peculiarly *human* realization' (Ames 1981: 23). This positive, naturalistic basis to the Daoist ethical vision will become even more evident in the discussion of alchemy, to which we turn in the next chapter.

# 6

# 'THE TRANSFORMATION OF THINGS'

## The alchemy of life, sex and health

### The Way of immortality

The question of how to cope with the fact of mortality and the passing of life, on how to make sense of the apparent absurdity of an existence that ends in arbitrary extinction, is central to all religions and is a key to Daoism as well. However, like so much else in Daoism, its idiosyncratic answer to this key question has caused much unease for Western interpreters and provoked ambivalent reactions. While most religions including Christianity are concerned with life beyond death and find life's ultimate meaning in its apotheosis beyond the grave, Daoism, with its concern with *physical* immortality, with the conferring of eternal youth and with the indefinite prolongation of life, is almost unique in focussing its attention almost completely on finite, embodied existence on earth. This focus, it must be insisted, is not a peripheral aim, a means towards another higher end, but is 'part of [its] very definition...the Taoist science of all sciences' (Lagerwey 1987: 272). Such a preoccupation, with its emphasis on physiological processes, fits awkwardly with our traditional preconceptions about the nature of religion and the aspirations of the spiritual life, and even if orthodox beliefs about our eternal destiny have begun to fade in many people's minds, the association of physical fitness and longevity with the religious quest will inevitably seem eccentric to many people whose roots lie in the Christian, Jewish or Muslim traditions.

In spite of these reservations, the discovery that for ordinary people in China the Daoist religion offered health, long life, happiness and offspring, as well as an open and constructive attitude towards sexual practice, has certainly encouraged Westerners to look with growing interest at this ancient tradition. Livia Kohn's assertion that 'Taoist practice begins by becoming physically healthy' seems a refreshing novelty to many in a culture where religion has often been seen to be indifferent and even hostile to bodily needs (1991a: 8). The allure of this teaching to orthodox Christian believers is probably marginal,[1] but it harmonises well with recent attempts

117

to formulate a secular, post-Christian spirituality in which the body becomes a vehicle for rather than an impediment to spiritual growth, and where cultivation of physical and of mental health are seen as going hand in hand. Nevertheless, the pursuit of physical immortality itself has inevitably proved somewhat problematic in European minds. It is true that the recently developed science of cryogenics has opened up the enticing possibility of bodily resurrection, and biotechnology offers the prospect of extending our average life expectancy, but the notion of indefinitely prolonging life through the ingestion of pills and elixirs may seem to most people nowadays unappealing and even dangerous. While the promotion of a long and healthy life, especially one in which sexuality is given a prominent place, has obvious attractions, the quest for an imperishable body through the imbibing of mixtures and compounds derived from such substances as gold, mercury, sulphur, lead and jade is easily dismissed as quackery. Even a sympathetic scholar such as Henri Maspero thought that the Daoist concern with immortality betrayed a lack of spiritual imagination, and spoke with irritation of the 'innumerable, meticulous, wearisome practices' of bodily conservation, which in the end 'repelled the better minds' amongst the educated Chinese and pushed them in the direction of Confucianism and Buddhism (1981: 256, 298).

This sort of ambivalence has also been evident within the Chinese tradition itself, where there have been differences of opinion about the nature and role of alchemy within Daoist philosophy. One such issue arises from the fact that the alchemical methods just alluded to seem to imply a transcendence, not only of death but of nature itself, and the attempt, as one early Daoist put it, to 'steal the secret of Heaven and Earth' seems to run counter to certain fundamental Daoist principles.[2] The almost obsessional concern with physical immortality, which dates back at least as far as the Qin dynasty, employing a whole range of highly sophisticated macrobiotic techniques, seems to imply a desire to wrest from nature the mystery of life itself, and to conflict with the ideal of *wu-wei*, of going along with the natural flow of things rather than attempting to manipulate and control them. Furthermore, if we look at the *Zhuangzi* we see there a quite different ideal, a 'lyrical acceptance of death' rather than the overcoming of it, a resigned, even joyful acceptance of our mortality which views death as simply one of the phases in the continuing cycle of nature.[3] And in the *Liezi* too, we discover not the busy search for elixirs, but rather the exhortation quietly to make the most of the passing moments of life and to be unconcerned with what comes after death: 'Birth and death are part of the natural cycle of things...In the natural order of things, life and death are not something we can control' (Wong 1995: 32, 172).

This difference of emphasis tells us several interesting things about Daoism which have not always been clear to Western minds. In the first place, it points once again to the fact that within the Daoist tradition there is variety of opinion and tradition even on so central a matter as the attitude towards death. When we look more closely at its history, we find that the pursuit of physical immortality was not maintained consistently as a dominant aim. Due to the costliness and the sophistication of its techniques, the alchemical quest was always a minority concern, and over the centuries, with the lack of any convincing evidence that the elixirs of immortality actually worked, it fell somewhat into the background and was replaced by an emphasis on longevity and good health. Certainly by the tenth century CE the dream of discovering the secret of immortality through the compounding of mineral substances seemed to be at an end. Furthermore, there were always Daoist adepts who were indifferent to and even hostile towards certain aspects of the cult of immortality and its attendant alchemical practices; Max Kaltenmark goes so far as to say that 'the Taoist philosophers had nothing but scorn for the majority of the physiological techniques for prolonging life indefinitely', and contrary to the standard Western view which has tended to see the history of Chinese culture in homogenised terms, there were plenty of sceptics in China throughout its history who were ready to challenge such widely held beliefs (1969: 94–5).

To make matters even more complicated, recent scholarship has suggested that at a philosophical level the ambivalence outlined in the previous paragraph is apparent rather than real. Some earlier critics, in their efforts to draw a sharp distinction between philosophical and religious Daoism, emphasised what they saw as the chasm between the 'degenerate' cult of immortality characteristic of the latter and the more sophisticated philosophical approach to death to be found in classical Daoist writings (Creel 1970: ch. 1). Fung Yu-lan likewise contrasted Zhuangzi's philosophy of 'going with nature' with the alchemical tradition by means of which we 'gain our end though gaining control over the forces of nature', the stress on power here being 'essentially scientific in spirit' (1952–3, vol. 2: 432). It is now increasingly recognised, however, that the pursuit of immortality is not to be understood simply as the literal prolongation of individual existence or the indefinite protraction of life's span, and certainly not as a kind of Promethean or Frankensteinian conquest of the forces of nature, but rather as part of the search for unity with the *dao*. Immortality, though exceptional, was seen as perfectly natural, and to live in accordance with nature (*xing*) was to live out the full term of life with all one's faculties in sound order. Ageing and dying, both involving the loss and dissipation of the three principles of life – *qi* (vital energy), *jing* (sexual essence) and *shen* (spirit) – were seen by contrast as unnatural.

In order to understand this, we need to place the Daoist concern with macrobiotics within the wider context of the correlative cosmology which, as we saw in an earlier chapter, became dominant in Chinese thought from the Han period onwards. It will be recalled that in that system the human body/spirit (the Chinese did not make any absolute distinction between these two terms) is a microcosmic reflection of the cosmos at large, from which it was deduced that the prolongation of life is an affirmation of the correspondence between human existence and the continuing life of nature. Taking care of one's body/spirit, and conserving the energies which give it life and which give rise to a healthy and full lifespan, means therefore co-operating with the processes of the universe; hence, 'Because the physical body itself embodies the cosmological forces responsible for the natural processes, one can therefore control the very processes of nature, including death, by controlling one's own body and the cosmological forces within one's body'. At a deeper level this meant that for the Daoist the concern with prolonging life was in some sense 'a reenaction of the cosmic processes and a return to the undifferentiated ground' (Peerenboom 1993: 259; Boehmer 1977: 62; see also Bertschinger 1994; Liu 1979: 130; Robinet 1997: 4, 87–8; Schipper 1993: ch. 6). Indeed, the very term 'immortality', carrying as it does in the West the notion of disembodied survival of the individual person, may fail to do justice to the Daoist goal of ultimate absorption in the *dao*, for strictly speaking only the *dao* itself is immortal, all individuals being subject ultimately to change and transfiguration. As we saw in an earlier chapter, Daoism offers us a radically transformative paradigm which sees change as an ultimate property of nature, and as such stands in sharp contrast to typical yearnings in the Western religious and philosophical traditions for ultimate permanence and stasis (Bokenkamp 1997: 22).[4] It must be emphasised too that the Western/Christian notion of immortality as disembodied existence has no purchase either in Daoist alchemy or in Chinese thought in general, for it will be evident from what has just been said about 'body/spirit' that there is no conception in either of the latter that the spiritual element in us can leave the body and survive independently. Moreover, the English translation of the term 'immortality' is misleading, for in Chinese *xian* does not connote attainment of an infinite lifespan in the Christian theological sense but rather the protraction of life for an unusually long period.

Alchemy itself, though not synonymous with Daoism, had in Girardot's phrase, 'a particular coincidence with the religious concerns of Taoism', and, particularly in view of its somewhat questionable connotations in the modern Western mind, we need to be clear about its role in Chinese culture (Girardot 1983: 291).[5] The first historical references to alchemy in China date from the second century BCE, but its origins can be traced back beyond that to the long-established arts of metalworking, to traditional herbal medicine, and to ancient shamanistic and magical practices. Its primary focus became in time the quest for immortality by the formulation of chemical-based elixirs, health-giving plants and dietary prescriptions, supplemented in time by breathing and meditation exercises. The primary tool of the alchemist was the furnace, and the chief substances employed were gold and cinnabar,[6] and it was through the refinement of these substances and others in the alchemical furnace that the pill of immortality was to be concocted. Again it is important to appreciate the link between these practices and the theories of correlative cosmology. The imbibing of apparently poisonous substances was, as we have seen, based on the belief that the human body corresponded to and was a replica of the macrocosm, and hence that it was proper and natural to use certain properties of the latter – in this case the property of incorruptibility – in order to enhance and perfect the former. The aim of alchemy therefore was to refine certain elements from the macrocosmic world in order to render them suitable for nourishing the microcosm of the human body/spirit, a principle familiar to the West in the shape of homeopathy. Moreover it was a process which for the Chinese had as much symbolic as practical significance, 'a great play of metaphors', as Schipper puts it, for as in European alchemy the manipulation of chemical substances implied a spiritual as much as a physical transformation and, as we shall see shortly, could be carried out ritually and inwardly as much as in the alchemical furnace (1993: 178).[7]

A more sympathetic understanding of Chinese alchemy has undoubtedly been helped by the revolution in alchemical studies that has taken place in the West in the course of the twentieth century. Through the efforts of such figures as Titus Burckhardt, Mircea Eliade and C.G. Jung, mediaeval alchemical practices have come to be viewed not as some bizarre and muddled form of proto-chemistry, but rather as a manifestation of a refined spiritual tradition in which the transformation and ultimate unity of matter and spirit are sought and celebrated. Although Chinese alchemy differs in a number of important detailed respects from its European cousin, there is a sufficient overall affinity of purpose and process to allow for fruitful dialogue between the two (Girardot 1983: 294–8).

Jung was one of the first thinkers to engage in this dialogue, an involvement triggered in 1928 by an invitation to write a psychological commentary on the alchemical text *The Secret of the Golden Flower* by its translator, Richard Wilhelm. The text itself, which is a fascinating syncretic amalgam of alchemical ideas, tantric yoga, Daoist philosophy and Buddhist meditation practices, had a powerful impact on Jung and provided him with confirmation concerning his own ideas about the human psyche and the archetypes which, following his traumatic break with Freud, he was in the process of shaping into his own distinctive psychology. In his reading of *The Secret of the Golden Flower*, Jung sought to dispel those Western prejudices which tended to dismiss such a text as the 'overwrought mystical intuitions of pathological cranks', and drew attention to significant parallels, both theoretical and practical, between Daoist alchemy and his own burgeoning psychological speculations. Through his reading of the text he came to believe that in his own consulting room he had been 'unconsciously following that secret way which for centuries had been the preoccupation of the best minds of the East', and was led to conclude that 'the human psyche possesses a common substratum transcending all differences in culture and consciousness' (1995: 83, 85–6). A crucial aspect of the text for Jung was the idea of the joining of the opposite elements of *yang* and *yin* in the alchemical process, which he saw as corresponding both to the Western mediaeval notion of the *coniunctio*, the sacred marriage of unlike but complementary substances, and to his own idea of the complementarity of polarised elements within the human psyche, especially the conscious and unconscious factors, through which a more balanced psychological condition is attained. Unfortunately for Jung, it transpires that the text from which he was working was inadequate in a number of respects, and in his introduction to a new translation of the work Thomas Cleary remarks that, while Jung credited *The Secret of the Golden Flower* with having clarified his work on the unconscious, 'what he did not know was that the text he was reading was in fact a garbled translation of a truncated version of a corrupted recension of the original work' (1991: 3). This may not have mattered too much to Jung, who claimed that his ultimate concern was with human suffering rather than with historical reconstruction, but it does provide a salutary reminder that attempts to 'build a bridge of understanding between East and West' (Jung 1995: 117) require more than moral effort.

## The Way of inner cultivation

If, in spite of Jung's hermeneutical efforts, the image of Chinese alchemists concocting elixirs in order to promote longevity remains alien to the Western mind, the practices of *internal* alchemy have come to be seen as its more acceptable face. There has long been a distinction in China between two forms of alchemy, on the one hand 'external alchemy' (*waidan*), the kind we have just been examining, which pursues immortality through the ingestion of minerals and herbs, and on the other 'internal alchemy' (*neidan*), which seeks transformation through the cultivation of energies within the body without the help of externally derived substances. The latter kind has attracted increasingly close attention in recent years, and as Max Kaltenmark remarked, 'the real interest of Taoism for us today lies in the psychological value of [its yoga techniques] and, above all, in its spiritual content' (1969: 148). Daoist techniques of meditation, callisthenics, massage and of sexual sublimation have all in various ways and degrees attained acceptability in the West, and have come to be seen as offering realistic and desirable aspirations. On the whole they appear to place no undue strain on metaphysical credulity in a secular age, and fit well both with a post-Christian, postmodern ethos, and with contemporary concerns with health and psychological well-being. In many ways Daoism could be described as a religion of healing, and for Norman Girardot, as for Jung with whom he allies himself, 'the whole thrust of Taoism has always been in terms of healing methods that seek to reestablish the original balanced wholeness of human nature and society'. From this point of view, the alchemical paraphernalia, symbolic as well as tangible, is by no means a mere distraction and diversion from spiritual pursuits, but represents a functional component in an art which seeks 'healing reidentification of man with the greater life of the universe', and is 'more a matter of the healing of man to the fullness of cosmic life than it is a saving from the world' (Girardot 1983: 42, 298).

The distinction between external and internal alchemy only became common after the Tang dynasty, and it was towards the end of this period that confidence in external alchemy began to decline significantly, largely as a consequence of the many deaths from poisoning. Emperors were especially vulnerable as they more than anyone had the resources and the incentives to seek indefinite prolongation of their lives through alchemical means. Longevity, if not immortality, continued to be held up as a desirable goal, but the means towards its attainment were seen to lie increasingly in the techniques of *neidan*, though still supplemented by the 'external' methods of diet and herbs. However, it is important to realise that from ancient times there was no conflict in principle between these two forms of alchemy, for they shared roots in a common cosmological system and employed a common symbolical vocabulary. The central point of confluence lay in the belief that both methods were concerned with the preservation and enhancement of vital processes occurring within the body. Just as with external alchemy, the overall aim of *neidan* was an inner transformation, the production of an inner elixir, directed at reversing the processes which, through a wasting of vital energies, normally end in death. It was to all intents and purposes a sublimated and interiorised version of external alchemical procedures in which the material processes of the latter were simulated through the concentration and circulation of vital energies within the body. Much of the language associated with both types was identical, and the technical vocabulary of furnaces and chemical processes, and talk of the refinement and transmutation of elements, could be interpreted in both external and internal terms. Indeed, the two were in an important sense identical, for in the context of internal alchemy it was believed that the experimental processes that were taking place within the body exactly paralleled those taking place in the alchemist's laboratory, and that within the body itself there resided the equipment with which to practise the refinement of those substances necessary for the sustaining of vital processes. As Girardot puts it, 'Both types of alchemical pursuit are constantly and ambiguously intermingled in the history of Taoism', so that 'the distinction between an inner and outer alchemy is finally moot' (1983: 292).

Meditation and breathing techniques were at the heart of internal alchemy. As aids to health and well-being, they were known even earlier than the period of the composition of the *Daodejing*, though the earliest Daoist text on such techniques dates from the late Han period.[8] There were inputs too from Buddhist sources, though some of the central Daoist concerns, such as the conservation and refinement of energy as a way of returning to the original cosmic unity, were not shared with the Buddhists. The practice of meditation has often provoked negative attitudes in the West, where it has been characterised as 'escapist' or even 'narcissistic', and indeed as early as the mid-eighteenth century when these oriental methods first became known in the West, meditation was condemned as a form of Stoic apathy or indifference. Nevertheless, it is important to emphasise that in pursuing such practices Daoist adepts were engaging and identifying with the wider processes of nature rather than retreating from them. Whatever may be said about other forms of meditation, the Daoist tradition cannot simply be dismissed as escapist and life-denying, for it was a quest for the recreation of life rather than a 'refuge in a sterile void' (Robinet 1997: 219). It was a method which in general terms demanded a symbiosis of both mental and material faculties rather than the denial of one in favour of the other, and involved practices in which the standard distinction between the mental and the physical is often difficult to draw. Matters such as diet, exercise and physical well-being are as important as, and intimately associated with, purely mental cultivation, and while Daoist monks and sages were renowned for their feats of ascetic endurance and self-control, they did not deem it necessary to deny the physical dimension of life in their pursuit of the spiritual (Eskildsen 1998).

It is important, moreover, not to think of Daoist meditation as a single, univocal form of practice, nor to see it as confined to a few hermits living on mountain tops. It entered into Daoist religious life at all levels. Across the whole complex range of Daoist traditions there are many different techniques and systems of meditation, involving different methods and orders of spiritual attainment, bringing into play a variety of aspects and emphases within the whole body/spirit structure.[9] Methods known as 'quiet sitting' or 'sitting in oblivion', combined with a cultivation of a life of harmony and simplicity, were widely used in China. They were not at all exclusive to Daoists but were practised by Confucians as well, and in some respects filtered through to the population at large. More specifically Daoist were methods which taught a progressive movement from simple inner repose, aimed at garnering and conserving energy, to complete absorption in the *dao*. In the early stages of this path of spiritual development the prescribed techniques were concerned with cleansing the mind of distractions and desires, moving on from there to methods of internal observation in which the practitioner fixes attention on the rise and fall of thoughts, emotions, and sensations. From there the adept progresses to methods known as 'Focusing on the Centre' and 'Holding to the One', whereby the mind becomes concentrated on the psychic centre and aspires to identification with the *dao*. The method which was pivotal to all these practices, and which harmonises most closely with broad alchemical principles, was the attention to the breath (*qi*) and its circulation in a very precise manner throughout the various parts of the body. This practice was unique to the Daoists, who attempted through slow 'embryonic breathing' to imitate the respiration of the foetus in the womb and thereby to return to origins. Here we can see again a direct reflection of Daoist cosmological theory and of the way in which human activity reflects the wider activity of nature, for in this process the cosmic flow from *yang* to *yin* and back again is reflected in the practitioner's inhalation and exhalation of breath, and the circulation of breath throughout the body brings it into harmony with the flow of *qi* through the world at large. This cosmically related process is evident too in the method known as 'Gathering and Circulating the Light' where again the aim is not just to contemplate light and to reflect on its regenerative significance, but actually to visualise and experience it circulating through the body/spirit and thereby participate directly in the work of cosmic transformation.[10]

Daoist meditation methods have only recently begun to be available in the West, lagging behind Buddhist and Hindu importations which have flourished there for some time. Instruction in some of the simpler forms of Daoist yoga (as it may be called) is now available in both America and Europe, though usually well sieved to render it palatable to Western tastes. Basic techniques such as relaxation, breathing and mental concentration are better known in their Buddhist forms, from which in any case Daoist methods are to some extent derived, and some of its more esoteric techniques along with its ultimate goal of union with the *dao* remain largely a closed book. Westerners engaging with Daoist practices are not normally admitted to a Daoist sect or initiated into the ancient secrets of internal alchemy, and many aspects of advanced stages of *weidan*, such as abstaining from solid food in order to facilitate the circulation of breath or holding one's breath for one thousand heartbeats in order to prolong life, will have little appeal today.

In one area, though, there are some interesting cross-currents, namely in regard to the method which has come to be known in the West under the generic term of 'visualisation', or what Daoists called 'Inner Vision'. This form of yoga is a crucial component of Daoist internal alchemy, one which appears to open up avenues of inner exploration which are not part of the traditional Western spiritual repertoire. It typically involves the method, just alluded to, of 'circulating' the breath or the light within the body through an active process of inner 'seeing' or 'imaging'. By this means adepts are taught to enter into an inner space, and to contemplate the inner bodily organs and the myriad spirits or gods who are thought to permeate the whole body. Thus by turning their gaze inwards and following the motion of the breath, adepts are able to 'fix distinctly and sensibly the gods in his body', 'visualizing them as a kind of procession that leads them through the inner world', and so to marshal and conserve life's energies and to attain unity with the *dao* (Kroll 1996: 149; Schipper 1993: 134).[11] This is clearly more than narcissistic introspection. As we saw in an earlier chapter, Daoists believe that the inner world – the microcosm – contained and was animated by a great multitude of spirits who were identical with their counterparts who dwelt in and animated the natural world at large, and it was these beings who were to be contacted and cultivated through the practice of inner vision. Such visualisation techniques became progressively refined throughout the history of Daoism, but they probably had their origin in ancient shamanistic practices, and were not the exclusive province of monks and hermits but were often employed by local Daoist priests as a way of communicating with spirits in order to gain favours on behalf of their parishioners.

Jung is once again an important go-between, and his hermeneutical efforts afford us some interesting insights. In his commentary on *The Secret of the Golden Flower*, he was the first Western thinker to acclaim the importance of such techniques for an understanding of the human psyche. He was not the first to enter into a psychological investigation of the inner world of images, but he was a major pioneer in this field, and one of the earliest to argue for the central place in psychological understanding and therapeutic practice of the imaginal function and of inner exploration in a culture which had often distrusted such activities.[12] Visualisation practices have indeed sometimes been viewed in the West as schizoid, and Jung himself feared that without proper supervision the use of visualisation techniques could in some cases lead to psychotic episodes. Indeed, in view of the fact that such visionary experiences have at times been described by adepts as flying through the air or as becoming detached from one's body, it is not surprising that they have been seen as a form of magic, or simply as hallucinations.[13] As we saw earlier, Jung's encounter with *The Secret of the Golden Flower* helped to confirm for him a number of ideas that he had been formulating, including his belief that the healthy human psyche is one in which its disparate elements are developed in a full and balanced way, and that, in the overdevelopment of the conscious intellect – the 'monotheism of consciousness', as he called it – modern Western culture has allowed itself to be cut off from its instinctual roots in the unconscious. The use of visualisation techniques, and in particular his own version of this called 'active imagination', represented for him an effective way of countering this tendency by opening up the psyche to its suppressed unconscious layers, a lowering of the threshold of consciousness to permit the upwelling of archetypal fantasies and mythic images. The key notion for him here was the concept of *wu-wei*, the Daoist 'art of letting things happen' in which 'the light circulates according to its own law', and which encourages us to trust the psyche to achieve wholeness and balance through its own 'natural' momentum, by contrast with the ever-interfering activity of consciousness

126

(1995: 89).[14] In Jung's view, therefore, the imaginal flights and ecstatic journeys of the Daoist mystics were not to be seen literally as magical, but viewed symbolically as journeys of self-discovery and transformation, an exploration of the *mundus imaginalis*, an idea which became the kernel of his notion of self-realisation or 'individuation'.[15]

Many have welcomed Jung's engagement between Daoist yoga and Western psychology. Chang Chung-yuan, for example, warmly appreciates his achievement in explaining Daoism 'in the light of modern psychology' (1975a: 5), and in demystifying ancient ideas in a way which is relevant today. Building on Jung's earlier insights, some schools of psychology, especially the humanistic and transpersonal varieties, have found in Eastern philosophies in general an important source of theoretical approach and practical technique. However, he has been easy prey for postmodern orientalist-hunters, who have detected in him a colonialist frame of mind and have seen him as propagating an essentialist East–West binarism that continues to give privileged status to the latter. More specifically, some have questioned whether a project such as Jung's simply appropriates Daoist ideas for its own foreign purposes and thereby radically distorts them. One critic, while not seeking to deny the legitimacy of transposing terms from one tradition to another – how could one avoid doing so? – challenges Jung's strategy of substituting his own theoretical constructs from analytical psychology for Eastern religious concepts. Jung's own concept of individuation, for example, involves a purely psychological process, whereas the Daoist alchemical quest is tied, as we have seen, to a patently cosmological paradigm in which the myriad spirits of the cosmos are reflected in a similarly populated inner world (Jones 1979). Jung certainly disclaimed sinological expertise, and was careful to disavow any privileged insight into the meaning of *The Secret of the Golden Flower*, which he found strange and alien to Western ways of thinking, and he warned against an over-simple assimilation of Daoist ideas and practices by enthusiastic Western imitators. But in spite of this cautious approach, he was also inclined to ascribe to the authors of the Daoist text the view that its teachings were not intended to be taken literally or to carry any metaphysical implications, but should be understood in purely symbolic or psychological terms: 'I suspect them of being symbolical psychologists, to whom no greater wrong could be done than to treat them literally' (1995: 113). This interpretation fits all too evidently not only with his own theoretical assumptions but with a standard Western approach which, embarrassed by some of the metaphysical speculations that accompany Eastern ideas, tends to strip them of these in order to make them psychologically acceptable. It is one thing for Jung to say that he is solely concerned with the study of the psychological dimension of religious experience, yet quite another to suggest that this dimension offers the exclusively correct way to understand that experience. Moreover it points to a parallel issue that haunts much Western speculation in this field, namely the question of whether it is right to make an easy transition from the spiritual to the psychological, and whether an approach such as Jung's is a form of reductionism – known as psychologism – whereby spiritual and religious experiences are seen in the final analysis as purely psychological phenomena.

These are difficult issues that cannot be dealt with in detail here, but they do alert us once again to some of the wider problems that we encounter in the field of intercultural hermeneutics.[16] In Jung's approach, there is clearly a danger of implying that the 'mysterious orient' can only make sense to us in so far as it is transposed into contemporary theoretical language. On the other hand, we need to recall that frequently, as in Jung's case, Daoist ideas, transposed into Western terms, have been important catalysts for Western thinking, and that paradoxically thinkers like Jung, as one critic puts it, have 'in fact empowered Asian religious traditions generally, the inaccuracy of his generalizations turning into a blanket blessing' (Gómez 1995: 232). These are questions to which we will return on several occasions below.

## The Way of sexuality

Internal alchemy is not confined to meditation, for this is only one of the many methods whereby Daoist adepts sought health, well-being, longevity and oneness with the *dao*. Perhaps even better known in the West than the techniques just discussed are those of Daoist sexual yoga and callisthenic arts such as *taijiqan*. Chinese traditions relating to sex, health, exercise and macrobiotic diet have all had a significant impact on the West in recent years, giving rise to a considerable literature and tapping into a number of prominent contemporary cultural issues and concerns. They have also, inevitably, given rise to a high level of projection, idealisation and distortion. Sexual matters are of considerable importance in any culture, including our own, of course; but as is often pointed out, in the traditional Western world-view, dominated by Judaeo-Christian values, issues concerning sex and health and their disciplined cultivation have not been central concerns. In China it has been otherwise. No civilisation has paid such systematic attention to matters of sex, health and diet as the Chinese; ideas on such matters have deep roots in both intellectual and folk traditions, and are reflected in all levels of Chinese culture from rulers to peasants. The contrast with the West is illuminating for both.

We begin with sex. The reader hardly needs to be reminded that in the twentieth century, sex, along with the body and physicality, has after long relegation to the margins of serious discourse and overt cultural attention become promoted to a central pre-occupation within Western societies, and it is not surprising therefore that ancient sexual ideas and methods from Asia have caught the Western imagination. These methods were initially associated in the Western mind with Tantric yoga and the teachings of the

*Kama Sutra*, although Daoist sexology, again a latecomer as far as the West is concerned, has in recent years gained a reputation in the West. Many books have been published on the subject, and associated practices are taught in a variety of educational and therapeutic contexts. The reasons for this development are not hard to conjecture. The dominant tendency in Western religious traditions has been to treat sex in largely functional or even negative terms, as necessary for procreation but as sinful if not confined within strictly defined social limits. Even to think about sex, at any rate in lustful ways, has been deemed to be wicked. Moreover, there has long been a sharp distinction drawn between sacred and profane love, between *agape* and *eros*, which has not only tended towards an exaltation of the former over the latter but has even been associated amongst certain heterodox groups with a wholesale condemnation of the physical body and its sexual functions as irredeemably evil. There have of course been counter-traditions, such as those associated with romantic or courtly love, or with eccentrics such as William Blake, but in general the religious and cultural environment in the West has until recently relegated sexuality to a marginal and clandestine sphere, and has offered limited opportunities for either an open and healthy discussion of sex or practical instruction in sexual techniques. In our own secular age, which attaches much greater importance to sex than previous generations, and which places much emphasis on physical pleasure, on the need for sexual satisfaction and on the psychological importance of love and sex, people have often turned to the East to find the conceptual and practical resources which have been lacking within the Western tradition. Paradoxically, since the emancipatory movements of the 1960s and 1970s, which saw a revolutionary release from traditional inhibitions and an unprecedented celebration of the orgasm as a key to happiness, there has been something of a retreat, not necessarily into traditional ways but into a state of uncertainty and even disillusionment. At a more basic level, the interest in Daoist sexology may simply be a manifestation of the Westerners' obsession with sex, and an indulgence in the pleasures of talking about it more freely and openly than has hitherto been possible. In the light of all this, it is hardly surprising that Daoism, with its rejection of celibacy and continence as supreme values and its guilt-free treatment of sex as natural, wholesome and life-enhancing, has been drawn into the orbit of Western thinking and transposed for the West's own specific uses.

What, then, are the Daoist views on sex? In the first place, we must be clear that its teachings on this subject, which date back at least to the second century BCE (Harper 1987; Wile 1992: 19) were closely integrated into its overall cosmology, and that the sexual act was viewed primarily not in terms of pleasure, or even of production of offspring, but rather as an active participation in the life-enhancing processes of nature and an integral part of the process of self-cultivation. As the sinologist Douglas Wile puts it,

'The followers of the sexual school of Taoism encouraged the development of a sexual sensibility that invested every act of coition...with an indelible metaphysical significance' (1992: 11). This implied that the immediate aim of sexual techniques was 'to increase the amount of life-giving *jing* [sexual essence] as much as possible by sexual stimulus, but at the same time to avoid as far as possible the loss of it' (Needham 1956: 149). This means that, while the activation of sexual potency was deemed to be life-enhancing, ejaculation implied loss of vital energy, and much of Daoist thinking on this matter was concerned with the development of a sexual yoga or discipline which both enhanced and yet at the same time conserved this energy. One outcome of this was the promotion of the technique of *coitus reservatus*, whereby ejaculation was forestalled by means of mental and muscular control, and also the method of intromission whereby the semen was directed into the bladder by putting pressure on the lower part of the penis at the moment of ejaculation. The female orgasm, by contrast with the male, was not seen as depleting the woman's vital essence but was deemed to strengthen her own as well as her male partner's powers. Hence it was considered desirable for a man to have intercourse with many partners in order thereby to absorb as much as possible of the vital essence released by the woman in orgasm.

Such practices had a public, ritual dimension as well as a private one. In the early days of the Daoist religion, following the fall of the Han, sexual practices were sometimes incorporated into public rituals as well as within ordinary conjugal life. These rituals, which were common around 400 CE, consisted of formal dancing and concluded with union of members of the assembly in chambers alongside the temple courtyard. Not surprisingly these liturgies sometimes turned into sexual orgies, and, following condemnation from Confucians and Buddhists as well as reaction within the Daoist community, they largely disappeared after the seventh century.[17] They were replaced either by private practice or by ritualised versions that became indistinguishable from Daoist liturgical practice in general, and a certain veil of disapproval was thereby drawn over public displays of sexuality. In some periods this disapproval extended to its practice in private, and the general attitude towards this aspect of Daoism remained ambivalent and sometimes even hostile.

Though the basic belief in the fundamental importance of sexual energy remained central to Daoist thinking, there was considerable debate and difference of opinion over the centuries about precisely what practices were implied by this belief. Many Daoist monks believed it necessary to remain entirely celibate and to sublimate sexual activity by other 'purer' practices of internal alchemy, yet in other contexts it remained permissible for Daoist monks and nuns to marry and have sexual relations, though not usually with each other. The sinologist Suzanne Cahill tells us that, though sexuality since the Song dynasty has in monastic contexts usually expressed itself in spiritual rather than physical terms, sexual union with a Daoist nun was not entirely *outré*, and that 'a love affair with one of them provided a delightful path to immortality' (1993: 3, 231). Aside from the practices of some sects, therefore, and taking account of the fact that even the private performance of these practices, particularly in monastic contexts, was at times condemned and even subject to persecution, the general view was that abstinence from intercourse was harmful and that the drawing together of the *yin* and *yang* elements produced health, harmony and long life. The link with internal alchemy in general is important, for the broader aim of such activities was nothing less than the extension of life, possibly even immortality, and ultimate unity with the *dao*. These goals were of course central to the whole Daoist enterprise, and for this reason it becomes evident that Daoist sexual teaching is closely integrated into Daoist philosophy in general, indeed pivotal to its ideas and practices.[18]

As far as the West is concerned, detailed knowledge of Daoist sexual ideas and practices first came to attention in the middle years of this century through the writings of Henri Maspero, Robert van Gulik and Joseph Needham. Following their pioneering efforts, a number of other sinologists and anthropologists have studied this intriguing aspect of Chinese culture, and in the wake of all of these has come a whole regiment of explorers, theorists and popularisers who have sought to mediate Daoist sexual lore for eager Western neophytes. Not all writers on this subject have been completely enthusiastic about their subject matter. Van Gulik was somewhat inhibited when it came to the technique of injaculation, and, in his earlier study at any rate, was inclined to see Daoist sexual practices as perversions or even black magic (Gulik 1961; Wile 1992: 58). Needham, who claims to have helped convert Gulik from his earlier prudish view, portrayed Daoist sexual yoga in a largely favourable light. He was however critical of the physiological theories that underlay Daoist practices, which he described as 'primitive and fanciful', and was dismissive of the value of certain of their techniques aimed at retaining seminal fluid which simply diverted the all-important *jing* into the bladder rather than directing it up into the brain as was commonly believed (1956: 152, 149). He nevertheless commended what he saw as a number of enlightened aspects of Daoist sexual yoga. He regarded the acceptance of sex as a natural and inherently healthy process, one to be cultivated as an integral part of the process of self-transformation rather than seen as guilt-laden and sinful, and in general lauded the Daoist approach as inherently superior to the 'paternal-repressive austerity of Confucians' and the 'chilling other-worldliness of Buddhism', as well as to Western Christian traditions (1956: 151–2). There is an urgent need, he believed, for 'a new theology of sexuality' which would transcend some of the Manichaean ideas which have bedevilled the Christian Church, and which might lead towards a condition of 'cosmic libido' in which, following

131

the inspiration of the Daoists, the principles of *eros* and *agape* would be reconciled.[19]

Kristofer Schipper, by contrast, was somewhat critical of the tendency in the West to idealise Chinese sexual practices and to portray them as natural, spontaneous and non-problematic. It is simply not true, he argued, that the Chinese were (at any rate, prior to the Jing period) sexually liberated, a view which had been advanced by van Gulik. He pointed out that Chinese sexual practices, both Daoist and non-Daoist, had always been closely hedged around with inhibitory rules and restrictions. The 'Art of the Bedroom' literature, therefore, has to be understood not in terms of modern attitudes of sexual freedom and emancipation, but rather 'in the context of conceal- ment and suppression', and the supposed Daoist bias in favour of the feminine cannot simply be transposed into terms of sexual practice, which in fact remained heavily biased in favour of the male (Schipper 1993: 147).[20] In the light of these comments, it is interesting to note that from the late nineteenth century onwards, progressive Chinese intellectuals looked to the *West* for inspiration and models in their search for sexual and women's liberation (Wile 1992: 51).

Popular literature in this field has proliferated in recent years, extolling the virtues of Daoist sexology and recommending it to Westerners as part of a whole new approach to life. A common feature of such writings is the construction of a great divide between traditional Chinese and Western approaches to sexuality, the one claimed to be healthy and open-minded, the other repressive and guilt-laden, and a commitment to a new and productive synthesis between the two. Daniel Reid, for example, an American who lives in Taiwan and writes on Chinese medical and health matters, is not only keen to advocate the Daoist approach as a way of encouraging the West's newfound openness and affirmativeness towards sexual activity, but also crusades for a new and deeply transformative attitude towards both the male and female orgasm, and as a result of this a renewed and heightened sensitivity in love-making. The evident differences between the male and the female sexual experience are exacerbated in a tradition where the male orgasm and the desirability of ejaculation are stressed, whereas Daoist methods are in his view a 'two-way street' in which harmony between the sexes, not competition and conflict, is cultivated and male chauvinism curtailed. Thus, while admitting that the emphasis in this tradition was not on romantic love in the modern Western sense but rather on correct technique and the cultivation of vital energies, and gave what from our modern point of view is undue attention to the male orgasm at the expense of the female, he believed that the Chinese methods could now be used to encourage the enhancement of satisfaction for both partners (1989: Part 2).

A similar emphasis on the importance of balance between the sexes and mutually induced satisfaction, and beyond that on the possibility of ecstatic experiences that surpass those of ordinary love-making, are found in the writings of Mantak Chia. Born in Thailand to Chinese parents and now teaching Daoist practices in America, his work covers the whole range of Daoist spiritual and healing practices which are interpreted for modern use. Like those of Reid, his writings on sexual matters have a strong proselytising thrust behind them, and are equally insistent on the need to draw Daoist ideas and practices into the Western orbit, not just for the enhancement of health or heightened physical sensation but also as a vehicle for a new spiritual awakening. The West is in a state of crisis – an opinion which is almost *de rigueur* in such writings – and he sees the modern Western profligacy in the use and wanton disposal of its natural resources as a direct parallel with its failure to develop means of conserving its (male) sexual energy. The latter form of energy, like its ecological analogue, should be conserved and recycled if we are to attain a way of living which is more balanced and more in harmony with the ways of nature (Chia 1984; see also Wile 1992: 63–5).

Some writers on this subject make strong claims about the compatibility of Daoist principles and the views of modern Western sexologists. Jolan Chang, writing in the mid-1970s, is typical in his insistence that these principles, including regulation of ejaculation, the importance of female satisfaction and the understanding that male orgasm and ejaculation are not necessarily one and the same thing, are now central to contemporary sexological thinking and have become keynotes in the women's movement and in the scientific studies of Kinsey, Masters and Johnson, and the rest (Chang 1995: 17).[21] Mantak Chia's writings show a similar inclination to weave traditional Chinese and modern scientific theories together. The link with modern scientific attitudes is particularly interesting in the light of Capra's parallel claims about the compatibility of the world outlooks of Daoism and the new physics.

But once again we must ask whether it is appropriate to draw together two traditions whose historical background, language and theoretical assumptions are so diverse. Such a question arises in the case of Stephen Chang's writings on various aspects of Daoist health techniques including dietetics, herbology and acupuncture. According to Wile, there is an all too easy transition in writings such as this from the language of ancient Daoism to that of modern biology, a tendency which in his view amounts to a superficial 'packaging of Chinese pills in Western bottles', and a 'facile homogenization, which blurs many distinctions in the two systems' (1992: 65–5; see also Chang 1986).

A more sympathetic reading of Chang's books might characterise them as an attempt at a new syncretism in the spirit of traditional Chinese cultural practice. Nevertheless, when we look more closely at Daoist sexology, some of the more idealised Western attitudes appear misplaced. After all, the fundamental direction of Daoist thinking on such matters, by contrast with more widely disseminated sexual wisdom, was not towards romantic love, which is more a Western notion, nor towards sensual satisfaction in our modern sense, but towards ends which we might now consider strange or even laughable. As John Lagerwey succinctly puts it, 'Early Taoism taught the art of the bedchamber not to enhance the joys of sex but to become immortal' (1987: 272), and indeed the word 'love' occurs very infrequently in Chinese writings on such matters. Moreover, the close association between sexual practice and spiritual progress, which in the traditional literature sometimes appear to be indistinguishable, is a matter which would elicit little enthusiasm in the modern West. And as Schipper suggests, the exalted status and even sacredness accorded to sexuality meant that it was not practised with the kind of personal freedom which we have come to value in the modern world (1993: 146).[22] There is also the question of the extent to which the Daoist obsession – for that is how it might appear to us – with retaining semen is in fact energising over the long term; Freudians and Reichians, *inter alia*, might well consider such practices as *coitus reservatus* as downright dangerous if practised over an extended period. We have already noted Needham's scepticism on the question of injaculation, and Michael Saso also argues that this practice is 'based on the false notion that losing semen causes early death and saving semen promotes long life', going on to condemn the 'grossly male chauvinist act of having sex an endless number of times with many women or maintaining prolonged erection' as having 'no known health benefit in medicine, other than bolstering the male ego' (1995: 171). There are indeed those, including Saso, who have worried that, in spite of its seemingly feminine-oriented approach which led some Daoists to express the view that woman is superior to man, Daoist sexology with its emphasis on the male orgasm is decidedly phalocentric. Furthermore, contrary to the views of contemporary writers such as Jolan Chang and Mantak Chia, who see mutual sensitivity and love as inseparable from the basic Daoist principles concerning sexual experience and the sexual needs of women as of equal importance to those of men, Daoist sexual teachings do not explicitly encourage mutual love and respect, or indeed carry any ethical implications of any kind; rather they seem to depersonalise sexual relations, making them a vehicle for largely abstract goals (Wile 1992: 71). Daoist sexual teachings are even condemned by some as exploitative of women, and Wile conjectures that the method of *coitus reservatus* was the means whereby in China the male achieved 'mastery' over the female libido in a way which parallels the method of clitorectomy favoured by other societies (Wile 1992: 15).[23]

Such criticisms might point to an impassable gulf between ancient Daoist and modern Western concerns. However, it is important to remember that the ideas and practices we have been discussing did not constitute a single monolithic teaching but, like other aspects of Chinese intellectual and cultural life, underwent considerable change, diversification and proliferation over time. As Needham observes, 'No sharp line of distinction can be drawn between [sexual] arts specific to the Taoists and the general techniques of the lay bedchamber' (1956: 147), and while self-transformation and the mastery of sexual energy may have been the goal of Daoist adepts, the wider dissemination of these teachings had less demanding and more prosaic implications for many ordinary practitioners of the sexual arts. There is what one might call a 'loose fit' between the refined and esoteric theories espoused by Daoist adepts and the sexual practice of both educated and uneducated people to whom these ideas had filtered through in various ways. Thus, Daoist-inspired techniques which might have been employed in lay households were not necessarily directed to higher spiritual goals but were most often seen as simply adjuncts of a healthy and satisfying life, manifestations of cultural attitudes and habits which were not specifically or consciously tied to Daoist philosophy. But at whatever level, it is evident that we are looking at a tradition which, in its conviction that sexuality is part of the natural order of things, and indeed a key to a healthy life, must in these terms at least find a harmonious resonance with some aspects of contemporary culture.

There is clearly much that is attractive about a tradition which was 'aware of the central position of sexuality in life and nature and accords it this same prominence at every level of its thought and practice', and where, contrary to the Jewish and Christian association with original sin, sexual intercourse 'imitates the harmony of Heaven and Earth', and represents an idea which 'certainly seems beautiful, good for the health, and right' (Schipper 1993: 144–5). Furthermore, in view of the absence of any sexual yoga tradition in the West, there is much that can be gained at a purely practical level, leaving aside the more esoteric aspects of Daoist theory. At the very least, Chinese techniques for enhancing female satisfaction by postponing the male ejaculation and experimentation with a variety of copulatory positions anticipate and reinforce attitudes that are now becoming more widely accepted in the West. Amongst others, they might help to challenge the modern Western preoccupation with the orgasm as the *summum bonum* of sexual activity. On a wider plane, the modern confusions concerning sex and sexuality, arising both from the earlier movements towards emancipation and from the more recent anxieties concerning AIDS and transgender realignment, might be assuaged to some extent by an encounter with a sexual tradition which is wholly different from the Judaeo-Christian-Enlightenment inheritance and which locates sexuality within a comprehensive and coherent world-view that has some obvious attractions for the modern mind. Some might go further and argue with Wile that the Chinese teachings contribute to a veritable paradigm shift, and 'to the forging of a truly egalitarian sexual covenant, offering…enhanced sensitivity and control, and providing a greatly enriched vocabulary for sensual communication' (1992: 73).

## The Way of good health

Daoist sexual yoga is, as we have seen, intimately connected with concerns about health and well-being, and with effecting a sense of inner and outer harmony. Like all aspects of Chinese yoga, it also presupposes the unity of the mental and the physical. Indeed the very foundation of health in general, and hence the therapeutic power of sexual intercourse, implies a harmonising of the mind and the body and precludes any attempt to treat sex in purely physical terms. It is this sort of holistic approach which has proved so appealing, not only with regard to sexual yoga but even more compellingly in relation to the various callisthenic (or gymnastic) and martial arts which have become so popular in the West in recent years. Where some of the sexual methods just outlined may continue to alienate Western sensibilities, meditative-gymnastic methods such as *taijiqan* ('boxing of the highest ultimate') and the related breathing and bodily movement techniques of *qigong* ('working the energy') have become readily adapted to Western taste. They have begun to establish a recognisable identity within Western cultural traditions, and to fit easily within the growing culture of health and fitness where there is a palpable demand for holistic methods of personal development.[24]

There has also been a considerable growth of interest in recent years in traditional Chinese medicine. The latter shares much common philosophical ground with the ideas discussed in this chapter, for example in its holistic conception of physical health and in its sense of symbiotic unity between the human and the natural worlds, and while Chinese medicine must be understood in the wider context of Chinese culture in general, it owes much to Daoism (Unschild 1985: 101). The attraction of these ancient systems is obviously due in part to their perceived healing powers, and to the apparent efficacy of such techniques as acupuncture, but it is also linked with the fact that they appear to offer a completely different way of looking at health and are thereby seen to challenge some of the already questioned assumptions of Western medicine. In the classic work on medicine, the *Neijing*, attributed to the legendary Emperor Huangdi, the key to health is rhythmic harmony and balance and the co-ordination of the spiritual and the physical elements, ideas which are in various forms enjoying growing appeal in the West. There is an interesting reversal of fortune here, for where once Western medicine was used to marginalise and to demonstrate the inadequacy of non-Western varieties, Chinese medical systems are now seen by some in the West as superior in certain respects to modern medical methods.[25] These broad issues, however, take us into fields that are beyond the scope of this book, and we will concentrate on those aspects of health which are not explicitly medical in nature.

Historically, Chinese callisthenics have had a close but by no means exclusive relationship with Daoism. As with sexual yoga there is a loose fit between the two, and breathing and gymnastic exercises were not specifically Daoist but were also practised by Confucians and others who were not explicitly associated with Daoism. It is easy, however, to make sense of them within overall Daoist philosophy, for, although their roots predate Daoism, their aim is the familiar one of cultivating health and longevity through the internal circulation of energy, *qi*. Their origins probably lie in magical practices, especially those associated with shamanism where dancing was a means of stimulating the vital energies and of inducing ecstatic states.[26] Such origins have long been left behind, however, and their therapeutic qualities in due course led to their integration into Daoism. The origins of *taijiqan* itself, which is only one of a number of similar techniques, are usually ascribed to a Daoist patriarch called Zhang Sanfeng who lived in the Song dynasty, but there is probably an element of mythology in this (Zhang was reputed to have lived for over 200 years and to have become an immortal); there is no doubt that the underlying patterns and thinking behind this method are much older. The chief aims of *taijiqan*, a practice which combined mental and physical discipline through slow movements modelled on those of certain animals, were the circulation of *qi*, the balancing of the forces of *yin* and *yang*, and the attainment of inner strength. It was not only used as a means towards explicitly spiritual ends, however, but also as a form of self-defence in which an opponent was defeated, not by aggressive confrontation but by a strategy of going with the flow of one's opponent's movements and thereby allowing him to defeat himself, in effect a practical manifestation of the philosophical ideal of *wu-wei*.

This combination of the martial and the spiritual might seem paradoxical from the Western standpoint where the two are typically seen as mutually exclusive categories, but for the Daoist the security and defence of the body were, like good health, necessary conditions for the pursuit of higher goals; as Schipper puts it 'This wonderful method of harmony and well-being is a martial art for the defence of the inner world' (1993: 138). Indeed, from the Daoist standpoint callisthenics were considered inferior to or simply a means towards the more meditative practices of internal alchemy, but from the time of Zhuangzi right up to the present they have, along with related practices such as *qigong* and self-massage, continued to play an important role in Chinese therapeutic culture. For this reason, and in spite of philosophical as well as historical links with the practice of Daoist adepts, we must beware of viewing them as purely and simply techniques of internal alchemy. You do not have to be a Daoist to practise *taijiqan* or *qigong*, a fact that is evident to any visitor to contemporary China where it has a wide following amongst people who have no interest in traditional religions.

Nevertheless, Schipper is surely right when he remarks that *taijiqan* is 'an excellent initiation into the very essentials of Taoism' (1993: 138), and this leads us to ask how it is that these techniques, deeply embedded in Chinese culture, have become so popular in the West. By contrast with the case of sexual yoga, the West is certainly not without its own well-developed indigenous traditions in these fields, whether in the category of gymnastics or of martial arts. I believe that part of the answer lies in the typically competitive and even aggressive nature of the Western gymnastic methods. The Greek Olympic tradition is essentially one of competition in which the development of physical prowess is firmly linked with strenuous exercises which lead to the enhancement of personal power and superiority, and where the aim is usually to go longer, faster or further than anyone else. These are goals which, as the French sinologist Catherine Despeux points out, are currently being called into question and Chinese callisthenic methods, in spite of their connections with the martial arts, are seen as essentially non-competitive, more 'feminine' in spirit, and linked more integrally to the goals of general health and well-being than comparable Western practices (Despeux 1989: 258 and *passim*). They are also viewed as more holistic, in that they fuse both psychological and physiological processes and aim at an integrated sense of well-being that makes no absolute distinction between the mental and the physical or between the spiritual and the worldly.

There is undoubtedly something modish about the concept of holism. The very word is relatively new (it was invented by the South African philosopher-statesman Jan Smuts in the 1920s), and in recent years it has come to imply, almost uncritically, everything that is good, wise and beneficial in a whole range of fields. It is also seen by some thinkers as a key to a fundamental break, or paradigm shift, between an older, flawed way of thinking about the world and human life, characterised by atomism in the physical sciences and mind–body dualism in philosophy. This is not the place to enter into a critical discussion of this concept, but, whether or not it is capable of bearing the intellectual and cultural weight that is increasingly being put upon it, it certainly represents for many people a desirable icon. Such a concept, which suggests a more harmonious way of living, points to a quasi-religious dimension in the Western attitude to Chinese callisthenic practices. This is not to suggest that *taijiqan* has become a substitute for religion, or that its practice is incompatible with orthodox creeds in the West. Nevertheless, its integration of mind and body, along with its emphasis on mental concentration and its meditational quality, are designed to produce a sense of inner harmony and well-being along with a heightened state of consciousness, both of which have traditionally been associated with religious experience and have been seen as at least the accompaniments, if not the goals, of the religious quest. From this point of view, Chinese callisthenics might be seen as part of a tendency, albeit a minority one, towards a religiosity without gods or beliefs, a cultivation of a sense of well-being and self-transcendence that implies no credal commitment or institutional identification, and which sees no clear break between the cultivation of physical and spiritual excellence.

This sense of a wider, deeper significance that goes beyond yet embraces the pursuit of purely physical health has been emphasised in a number of recent writings on *taijiqan* and *qigong*. Both families of techniques are frequently taught in a simplified form appropriate for modern Western culture, but equally they are also often presented in connection with fundamental Daoist principles of balance and harmony with nature and offered as means towards spiritual goals as well as promoting general health and well-being. The field is undoubtedly open to abuse by self-styled masters with doubtful lineages who sometimes make misleading and exaggerated claims, a hazard augmented by the fact that these arts were traditionally handed down by secret transmission and the few classical texts which remain were written in an obscure coded language which is difficult to decipher. Nevertheless, a number of recent books on these subjects represent a serious attempt to place the techniques taught within a broader philosophy of life. Daniel Reid, for example, in his book on *qigong* emphasises its role within a complete system of life in which 'your body, energy and mind work together as a team to achieve your goals and keep them firmly on the path of Tao', and, before proceeding to outline the *qigong* in detail, he shows how these exercises are components within an ancient system of self-cultivation 'patterned on the eternal ways of nature and the transcendent laws of the universe' (1998: 281, 25). It is inevitable that in their transposition to the West these ancient arts, along with their theoretical presuppositions, should have undergone a degree of metamorphosis, but certain basic elements – the integration of physical and mental therapies, or internal and external energies, the emphasis on meditation, harmony and balance, and perhaps above all their sense of being close to the rhythms of nature – mean that these techniques will enjoy continuing appeal in the West.

# 7

# 'THE WAY IS INCOMMUNICABLE'

## Transcendence

### Mysticism

'Self-delusion or dreamy confusion of thought'; we have moved a long way from this earlier *Oxford English Dictionary* definition of mysticism, but it remains a term which is notoriously difficult to pin down, and we are still often inclined to consign it to the margins of our everyday consciousness or to deploy it as a synonym for 'irrationalism', 'superstition' or 'occultism'. The term 'mysticism' has proved especially contentious when applied within Eastern contexts, where it often appears as an orientalist platitude, and as a means of canonising the belief that there is something inherently irrational about the Asian mind. The stereotyping of the 'mystical Orient' by contrast with the 'rational West' has often been elevated to archetypal status, and stands symmetrically alongside other binary contrasts which serve to set East and West at a comfortable distance from each other, whether to secure the latter in a position of authority over the former or to exalt the East to a status of transcendental supremacy over the West. Thus, on the one hand the cliché of the 'mystical Orient' is exploited in order to confirm the 'rational' West's hegemonic role in relation to the East, or on the other to romanticise the East as the transcendent source of a profound and eternal wisdom.

As far as Daoism itself is concerned, the term 'mystical' has become its inseparable partner, the phrase 'Daoist mysticism' representing almost as familiar a twosome as 'the mystical Orient'. This coupling has a long intellectual ancestry, one that can be traced back to the Jesuits' attempt to marginalise and denigrate Daoism: for them, Confucianism, suitably reconstructed, represented an enlightened philosophy that could be manoeuvred into a productive relationship with Christian theology, Daoism, though not at that stage meriting the title 'mystical', represented for the Jesuits a form of cultural experience which was irredeemably alien to their own way of thinking. Hegel did not explicitly characterise Daoism as 'mystical' either, but his insistence on its pre-rational inwardness and lack of universality helped to underwrite the mystical–rational/East–West binarisms that came into favour in the nineteenth century. And when in 1906 the sinologist Lionel Giles spoke of 'the rather fantastic vagaries of [Daoist] mysticism', he was doing little more than confirming what was already a well-established habit of mind (1906a: 36). Twentieth-century writings have often continued to subscribe to this way of classifying Daoism. Perhaps the most influential was Max Weber, who characterised Daoist teaching as 'world-denying mysticism' (1951: 178–90). Herrlee Creel, whose publications have had an impact well beyond scholarly confines, calls on the authority of Henri Maspero to assure us that 'Taoism is...a mystical philosophy', and more recently Benjamin Schwartz has insisted (though with reservations) that Daoism 'is as mystical as any orientation to which that term has been applied in any other culture' (Creel 1954: 101; Schwartz 1985: 193; see also Robinet 1997: 33). Moreover, in China itself attitudes towards Daoism's supposed mystical bent were almost as equivocal as they have often been in the West, and stretch back into ancient history. Mysticism in China probably had its roots in shamanic practices, and the trance-like states that were ritually induced were commonly frowned upon and given a wide berth by the educated élite. As far as so-called philosophical Daoism was concerned, its classic writings were in effect viewed from the third century CE onwards as key works in a mystical tradition and were often dismissed as obscure and incomprehensible; for example, the 'dark profundity' of the *Daodejing*, characterised as such in the writings of the second-first century BCE historian Simaqian, was often contrasted with the clarity and practical good sense of the Confucians. As Stephen Karcher notes, the *Yijing* itself was suitably cleansed of Daoist mystical intimations in the Han period in order to render it compatible with the new Confucian-based political order (1999: 8).

What can we learn, then, from attempts to apply the term 'mysticism' in the case of Daoism? Is it a help or a hindrance in cross-cultural studies? One of the important issues arising out of recent discussions of mysticism revolves round the question whether this term refers to a pure unmediated experience and can properly be applied cross-culturally without equivocation, or whether it can only be understood within distinct cultural contexts. In broad terms, this debate is between on the one hand the 'universalists' who take the view that mysticism represents a common and perennial human experience that can be identified in many different cultures and religious traditions, and on the other hand the 'particularists' or 'contextualists', who claim that experiences grouped under this term are culturally specific phenomena, shaped differentially by distinct languages, values and belief systems. This latter position is sometimes underpinned by the claim that the term 'mysticism' itself is a social construct, representing an experience which is not 'pure' but rather is fabricated through specific cultural beliefs and expectations.[1] The universalist paradigm has been in the ascendant until recent decades, and classic studies of mysticism in the twentieth century by such figures as William James, Evelyn Underhill, W.T. Stace and F.C. Happold have tended to identify a number of essential, and hence universally applicable, characteristics of mysticism, which have often been deployed as a methodological framework for studies in this field. The list of such universal characteristics has typically included: an ineffable quality that goes beyond language, a sense of timelessness and of the sacredness of things, a conviction of the oneness of all things and of the unity of the self with this oneness, and an overwhelming experience of certitude and intuitive insight.

For some Daoist scholars, this list of criteria has proved acceptable and has made it possible to draw Daoism into the universalist paradigm. Maspero, following the universalist inclination of his time, saw the Daoism of Laozi, Zhuangzi and Liezi as having all the characteristics of mysticism stipulated by William James in his ground-breaking work *The Varieties of Religious Experience*, and maintained that the Daoist experience was identical in all essential respects with that of Christian, Jewish and Islamic mystics, even though the way in which the ultimate goal of the mystical path was apprehended differed from one culture to another (1981: 413–26). Schwartz is less precise but also sees in Daoist mysticism some of the assumptions lying behind the mystical philosophies of the West, in particular 'the assumption that finite humans...can achieve oneness or some kind of mystical union with the ultimate ground of reality'. Moreover, as he points out, the theme of the inaccessibility of the ultimate reality to language, which is typical of the classic, perennialist conception of mysticism, is a basic theme in Laozi and Zhuangzi as well (1985: 193, 197). Another theme which is sometimes perceived as drawing Daoist mysticism into a more universalist paradigm is that of 'emanation and return'. Thus, the idea of the recovery of unity with the *dao*, a goal which reverses the cosmic 'fall' whereby the phenomenal world in all its unsatisfactory multiplicity originated from the *dao*, seems to echo in some respects the Neoplatonic mystical tradition in which the soul carries within it a knowledge of the divinity from which it has originated and with which it will be reunited.[2]

There are several Western thinkers who have gone somewhat further than this in linking together Daoist and Western mystical traditions and in drawing the Daoist mystical tradition into their own special concerns. One of these was the Cistercian monk Thomas Merton. He clearly felt a strong personal bond with Zhuangzi – 'my own kind of person', he called him – seeing him not only as the greatest and most spiritual of the Chinese philosophers, but as representing a form of contemplative practice which resonated with his own preference for a mysticism of simplicity rather than of ecstatic visions. He felt at ease with Daoism's lack of concern with 'words and formulas' and its 'direct existential grasp of reality', with its sense of being at home both at the level of 'the divine and invisible Tao that has no name, and that of ordinary, simple, everyday existence'. Merton professed no interest in eliciting deep connections between Daoism and Christianity, however, or in pursuing a form of apologetics 'in which Christian rabbits will suddenly appear by magic out of a Taoist hat' (1965: 32, 10–11), but believed that the teachings of Zhuangzi, as well as the related teachings of Zen, were valuable in extending the spiritual horizons of Christians. His curiosity about Daoism developed relatively late in his life in a period when, following the Second Vatican Council, the Catholic Church was more ready than hitherto to learn from non-Christian traditions, and he was one of several Christian monks who sought to revivify their own contemplative tradition through contact with Eastern religions.

Merton's writings have achieved considerable popularity and have played an important role in the developing interfaith dialogue. Of equal significance is the work of the Jewish Existentialist philosopher Martin Buber, whose lifelong involvement with Daoism did not become widely known until relatively recently, and whose admission that his philosophical thinking was 'indebted a great deal' to Daoism will still come as a surprise to many (quoted in Herman 1996: 15).[3] Even more strongly than in the case of Merton, his writings demonstrate the subtle and not always fully acknowledged ways in which Daoist thinking has begun to have an impact on Western intellectual debates. His work on Daoism, though not that of a trained sinologist, was by no means superficial, and involved a translation of and commentary on a large section of the *Zhuangzi*, a partial translation and commentary on the *Daodejing*, and the editing of a collection of Chinese folk tales. For these reasons, his connection with Daoism and with the issue of mysticism is worth exploring in a little more detail.

At first sight, Buber's interest in Daoist texts and ideas, and his insistence on the need for dialogue between Eastern and Western religions, must seem a long way from his own Jewish tradition and his particular form of existentialist philosophy. The key to this interest lies in his involvement at the turn of the century with the revitalisation of the mediaeval Hasidic mystical tradition. Hasidism, a pietistic movement which sought to supplement traditional Jewish ritual observance with a more inward and personal spirituality, contained features which in Buber's mind bore striking resemblances to some central aspects of Daoism. These included elements of social protest and even of anarchism, methods of meditation, the use of tales and anecdotes as means of enhancing spiritual awareness, and above all an emphasis on some kind of mystic union with ultimate reality. The link with Daoism developed even more strongly in his later dialogical philosophy of 'I and thou', with which his name is most famously associated. In *Ich und Du*, first published in 1923, he moved decisively away from his earlier concern with the mystical union between man and God and embraced instead the notion of a dialogical encounter in which, while transcending absolute

THE WAY IS INCOMMUNICABLE

separation, the distinct identities of self and other are preserved. On this view God is the supreme Thou, relationship with whom is both the highest existential encounter and the archetype for authentic relations with other beings.

There might appear to be an unbridgeable gulf between these two stages in Buber's thinking, between the mature 'I–thou' philosophy with its emphasis on dialogue on the one hand and on the other his youthful enthusiasm for monistic mysticism which transcends all dualities. Nevertheless, there are some intriguing convergences between Daoist thinking and Buber's 'I–thou' philosophy which illuminate the transition between these two stages of Buber's thinking. In a sense, Buber's evolving appreciation of Daoism seems to have accompanied and facilitated the evolution of his own philosophy, and this can best be illustrated by reference to his understanding of the relational quality of the self. In the thinking of both Daoism and Buber, there is a rejection of the idea that the fullness of one's being can be achieved in isolation from the Other, whether as person or nature, God or *dao*. And in both cases, though the 'I' is in a way irreducible and cannot be dissolved into the Other, neither can it be conceived without relationship with that Other. The philosopher Jonathan Herman, in a detailed study, has argued that, while Buber in his early period was inclined to see the *dao* as 'a singular and ineffable cosmic principle' with which the individual soul seeks to unite, a kind of 'obliterating oneness' which seems to foreclose any possibility of dialogue, an interpretation of the *dao* which was typical of his day, there were also clear anticipations of the I–thou dialogical principle in Buber's early reading of the *Zhuangzi*, anticipations that were later to be formulated in his mature philosophy (1996: 154). The grounds for claiming this lie in Buber's insistence on the diverse and concrete manifestation of *dao* in the transformations of the world of human experience, complementing the recognition of *dao*'s ultimate all-encompassing wholeness. There is a 'dialogical tension', as Herman puts it, between the unity of the *dao* and the multiplicity of its manifestations. It is on the basis of this tension, which points to Zhuangzi's mysticism as truly 'earthy' or 'worldly' rather than unqualifiedly transcendent, and in which the One is essentially manifested in the Many, that Herman feels able to claim that the 'fundamental ingredients of the I–Thou relation...are in fact already present within Buber's [earlier] encounter with *Chuang Tzu*' (1996: 163). Zhuangzi's mystical engagement with nature was therefore seen by Buber, not as one of total absorption, a Vedānta-like dissolving of self into the All, but rather as one of symbiotic reciprocity, an interactive I–thou process in which the self is transformed and sublimated by its encounter with nature but not thereby absorbed or obliterated.

This brings us back to the general issue of mysticism, for what Herman's study seeks to demonstrate is the possibility of fertile transcultural comparisons in this field without denying the fact of significant cultural differences. There is no question in his mind of a return to the 'perennial philosophy' paradigm which simply obliterates differences in the interests of a trans-historical narrative, but on the other hand the 'particularist' school seems to close off all possibility of comparative, cross-cultural analysis. The study of Buber's own attempt at cross-cultural comparison challenges both these extremes for, while avoiding any claim to be able to leap across cultural and historical boundaries into the mind of Zhuangzi, it suggests the possibility of a dialogue with Zhuangzi as 'a valid interpretive lens for interpreting Chuang Tzu's intraworldy mysticism'. It shows that it is possible to draw fruitful comparisons between an ancient and a contemporary form of mysticism, and to show how Daoist philosophy 'can help one better to understand or realize the I–Thou relation', without reducing the one to the other. This makes it possible, Herman believes, to retain mysticism as a conceptual category with which to comprehend distinct mystical traditions without resorting to the perennialist perspective (1996: 198–9).

Some critics have questioned the validity of this kind of 'interpretive lens', arguing that thinkers such as Merton and Buber have simply transposed Daoist mysticism into their own terms and for the purposes of their own projects, and that they are guilty of the misappropriation of material across cultural boundaries. Moreover, it has been pointed out that Buber's textual exploits in this area failed to match up to the well-established norms of modern scholarship, and that he evidently lacked appropriate linguistic and scholarly skills.[4] In Herman's view, however, Buber's method represents a perfectly admissible way of approaching the *Zhuangzi*, and helps to cast light on the issue of intercultural hermeneutics. The setting up of a hermeneutical relationship between Buber's dialogical philosophy and Zhuangzi's mysticism, he argues, provides a legitimate vehicle with which to interpret the text, one which is imaginative rather than arbitrary, and which recognises the historical nature of the interpretative exercise and the inescapability of present concerns in attempts to understand an ancient text. There is of course a wide historical and cultural chasm separating the two traditions; Buber does not seek to bridge this by claiming any privileged insight into the original text 'in itself' or into the essence of Zhuangzi's thinking, but rather draws it consciously into his own sphere of contemporary interest whereby the text becomes 'real' for him and for his generation, not a 'dead tortoise' to be scientifically dissected but a living example of human experience and insight (1996: Part II *passim*).[5]

The model that Herman resorts to here is, once again, Gadamer's hermeneutics. A key notion is Gadamer's claim that 'understanding always involves something like the application of the text to be understood to the present situation of the interpreter' (Gadamer 1975: 274), a view which grants equal respect for the integrity of the text and the reader by 'locating the gist of interpretation within the interactive "conversation" or "play" between the two' (Herman 1996: 135). This point is echoed by Isabelle Robinet, who sees the relationship between text and reader/commentator as a dialogical one, and points out that Chinese scholars have traditionally interpreted a text such as the *Daodejing* in terms of their manifold and shifting concerns rather than in any timeless manner, thereby sustaining 'an active connection with the past' (1998: 140). Evidently on this Gadamerian view there can be no 'mysticism as such'. Nevertheless the creative encounter between traditions in which the work of thinkers like Buber – and Merton – have engaged points to the dialogical openness of traditions which overlap in unusual and unanticipated ways, and suggests that it is 'premature to discard a comparative study of mysticism, even within the particularist paradigm' (Herman 1996: 200). Thus, in spite of the fact that Buber's interpretation of Daoist ideas remains self-consciously tied to his own tradition and concerns, it does provide important illumination for mystical studies, for it draws attention to an important aspect of Daoist mysticism, namely its avoidance of a purely and absolutely monistic conception and its openness to the uniqueness of individual phenomena. This has some interesting implications, not least of which is the recognition of a distinctive Chinese mystical tradition, which, when loosened from ties with the language of monistic metaphysics, points to a kind of non-transcendental mysticism that can be productively compared with certain trends in contemporary Western thought.

A good example of this kind of endeavour is to be found in the work of the sinologist Livia Kohn. In her wide-ranging research in this area she has done much to substantiate the idea of a unique, indigenous Chinese mystical tradition which cannot simply be assimilated to a universalist paradigm, and which has often been underrated in the West when compared with the Indian mystical tradition.[6] While allowing that at certain levels there are comparisons to be made with Christian mysticism, in particular with regard to the stages of illumination, she insists at the same time that the Daoist mystical tradition is highly distinctive and differs in some important ways from the classical Western model. Thus, where in the latter case the emphasis has largely been on the centrality of the mystical *experience*, described by Christian mystics as an overwhelming illumination of the divine reality, 'full of knowing certainty', the Chinese tradition has concentrated on the *transformation of body and mind*.[7] The key to Daoist mysticism, therefore, 'is not whether one has had a certain experience, but to what degree one's self has already been transformed into cosmic dimensions, how sagely and non-acting one has become'. This is a divergence which clearly corresponds to significant differences in world-view. She concedes that in both traditions the ultimate aim is unity with an absolute ground – God or *dao* – but where in the Christian case this ground is identified with a transcendent divine being who is 'wholly other', and where mysticism involves a rare vision of the deity who is 'entirely out of this world', with Daoism the concern is rather with an immanent reality which resides in the here-and-now, both in the natural world and within oneself. Mystical experience for the Daoist is therefore 'not a rare instance of divine grace', but perfectly natural, the 'birthright of every human being' (1992: 10–12).[8]

This insistence on the contrast with Christian transcendentalism, emphasising the intraworldly mysticism of Daoism, its sense of transcendence-in-immanence as one might call it, is evident in a number of other writers. For Graham, the mysticism of Zhuangzi, as for Daoists in general, implies no ecstatic fireworks, no awesome experience of the *numinosum* in Rudolf Otto's term, but is a fairly ordinary, down-to-earth affair, not even like the sudden all-or-nothing illumination of Zen *satori* but more akin to the perfect grace of Cook Ding who, in Zhuangzi's story, learns to carve an ox carcass with heedless but consummate spontaneity and ease. It is a kind of *eureka* that expresses, not a revelation of truth or a moment of insight, but rather something more like the sudden acquisition of a skill which seemed hitherto unattainable (Graham 1989: 189; see also Graham 1981: 20–1; Schipper 1993: 158–9). For Lee Yearley, a specialist in religious studies, Zhuangzi's intraworldly mysticism is a distinctively Chinese contribution to this genre, one which he believes to be 'fundamentally different from more familiar mysticisms of unity and unison'. In his view, it should be firmly contrasted with the mysticism typical of both India and the West, which relies on a contrast between a fleeting and insubstantial world of experience and an eternal and unchanging world beyond. Looked at in this way, Daoist mysticism does not lead to an insight into a different world but 'aims to see the world in a new way', and thereby positively affirms it rather than denying and drawing away from it (1983; see also Yearley 1996).[9] Several other scholars agree with this approach. Benjamin Schwartz, for example, while continuing to find the generic term useful, sees in Daoism a naturalistic form of mysticism which affirms rather than negates the world, and which evinces deep appreciation of the value of 'just living' (1985: 200, 192). Maurice Friedman sees in Daoism an example of the 'mysticism of the particular' which quite plainly undermines the perennial philosophy notion that there is a single underlying essence that is shared by all forms of mysticism (1976).

The anti-transcendental interpetation of Daoist mysticism plays an important role in the writings of Joseph Needham. For him, a clear distinction must be drawn between a transcendental mysticism which directs our attention to ultimate truths that lie beyond normal experience, and mystical naturalism which focuses on the world of everyday experience. The attacks on knowledge which are an oft-quoted feature of the classical Daoist texts, and which have persuaded many Western commentators to align Daoism with the traditional Western sense of religious transcendence, are not, he believes, to be construed as anti-rational mysticism but rather as 'proto-scientific anti-scholasticism'. Daoist 'empirical mysticism', by contrast with Confucian 'ethical rationalism', actually favoured the development of science, and was indeed 'the only system of mysticism which the world has ever seen which is not fundamentally anti-scientific' (1969: 163). The element of paradox in this judgement, which Needham quotes from Fung Yu-lan, is made more palatable by the comparison between Daoist naturalism and the early development of empirical science in Europe. He points out that in its early stages the new scientific outlook in Europe had to struggle against scholastic rationalism and that, contrary to an older conception, the mystical approach associated with such figures as Paracelsus and van Helmont was much more helpful than the theoretical formulations of the followers of Aristotle. Even the reforms advocated by Francis Bacon, canonised in the Enlightenment period as the founding philosopher of the scientific method, were 'part of a mystical interpretation of the Christian tradition', and in the light of this Needham is led to the conclusion that the association between nature-mysticism and science is 'embedded in the very foundation of modern (post-Renaissance) scientific thought' (1956: 94–5).[10]

Such views have certainly not gone unchallenged. As we noted earlier, Needham's attempts to forge an alliance between Daoism and scientific naturalism in general have sometimes been seen to obscure aspects of Daoism which plainly run counter to a scientific ethos, and the overall aim of the Daoist mystical quest – union with the *dao* – is patently at odds with that of modern science which seeks a purely 'objective' understanding of the natural world, one which eschews (consciously, at any rate) both value judgements and metaphysical speculations. Some of the more other-worldly elements within Daoism (perhaps borrowed from Buddhism) are left inadequately accounted for in his and similar arguments, as are some of the more obscure passages in classical Daoist texts which strongly suggest a transcendentalist interpetation. Just as the early Jesuit missionaries sought to underplay the religious elements in Confucianism in order to render it open to Christian assimilation, so too Daoism has in recent times been demystified in the interests of its secular adoption, a process sometimes assisted by the claim that extreme mystical elements were imports from India rather than being indigenously Chinese (Douglas 1911: 191). Thus, in their desire to rehabilitate Daoism in Western eyes and to draw it into the circle of Western intellectual discourse, Needham and others have often given us a view of Daoism which is, once again, perhaps too deeply coloured by the demands of our own modern standpoint. An intraworldly 'I–thou' kind of mysticism has great appeal, and perhaps validity in its own right, but to what extent it is compatible with the *dao* remains an open question.

This sort of question arises too out of the writings of the philosopher Chad Hansen, who gives the argument for an intraworldly interpretation of

Daoist mysticism a further twist. His overriding concern is to demystify Daoism. He wants to see it not as a version of an outmoded mystical monism where it has typically been pigeonholed, but rather as concerned with common-or-garden prescriptive discourse. Typically, mysticism has been seen as a way of taking us beyond the everyday and of heightening our grasp of true Reality, but for Hansen it is more correctly to be seen as directed towards the regulation of human and social behaviour, and has therefore a performative rather than a descriptive function. The language of Daoist mysticism is not to be construed in terms of the familiar Buddhist or Western concerns with the inability of language to describe ultimate reality, nor is it a pathway to the illogical or the irrational. Rather, it is about the need to subvert the demands of language as 'a regulative social mechanism shaping our attitudes, desires, and actions' (1992: 228–9). Hansen's argument certainly represents an important and imaginative attempt to rescue Daoism from the sort of mystical oblivion that has so often proved a convenient waste disposal tip for Western critics. Nevertheless we are led to wonder whether, like Needham, he is drawing Daoism too comfortably into his own agenda, and thereby neutering the subversive otherness of Daoist thinking. Is his deployment of a modern analytical/linguistic paradigm simply substituting one Western 'ruling theory' for another, and thereby blurring important differences between Daoism and modern philosophy? Is it simply a perpetuation of the old positivist inability to find a place for mystical language within the well-guarded frontiers of meaningful discourse? Hansen's arguments will occupy us again in the next chapter in a different context, but in the meantime we will return to the Daoist concern with nature, largely avoided in Hansen's account.

## Mysticism made visible: landscape painting

The anti-transcendence bias of thinkers such as Needham and Hansen is understandable enough in an age which has been dominated by secularist and scientistic agendas, but there is an aspect of Daoist mysticism, religious at a deep level yet secular in outward form, which has a growing appeal in the West. This could be summed up as 'Daoist nature mysticism'. This aspect of Daoism, most often identified with the writings of Zhuangzi, implies a joyous sense of kinship with nature in all its beauty and diversity, a feeling for the presence of the *dao* in all things, and an aesthetic sense of our ultimate identification with the natural world which avoids the extreme monism and asceticism of other forms of Asian and Western mystical philosophy. As many commentators have pointed out, while fondness for nature is not limited to the Chinese, its people have developed an especially refined sense of reverence for mountains, rocks, streams, pools, animals, trees and flowers in which the ever-moving spirit of the *dao* is to be observed, and through association with which an elevated spiritual awareness is attained. As we indicated in Chapter 4 above, landscape for the Chinese was not just a scenic backdrop to human activities but was invested with deep religious significance, its contours reflecting cosmic influences and its meaning decipherable like a sacred text.[11] According to John Blofeld, travelling in China prior to the Communist revolution, 'A feeling for nature amounting almost to worship was apparent to the traveller in any part of the country where traditional ways had not yet been supplanted', a feeling which he found especially apparent in the Daoist monasteries which he visited (1985: 168–70).

This sense of mystical communion with the natural world was most fully expressed in the great landscape paintings created in China from the Song dynasty onwards, summed up memorably in J.C. Cooper's phrase 'mysticism made visible' (1990: 98). For the sake of economy, I shall deal almost exclusively with landscape painting and gardening in this section, but many of the principles discussed here also apply to the closely related field of poetry.[12] Of all the Chinese arts, landscape painting stands supreme and expresses most completely the Daoist vision of nature. It may be an overstatement to claim that these works 'which are the glory of Chinese painting are of Taoist origin' (Lagerwey 1987: 288), for a number of other cultural factors need to be drawn into the genealogy of this distinctively Chinese genre, including those which derive from Confucian, Buddhist and even shamanistic traditions.[13] But there is no doubt that this art form was a particularly important medium for the expression of Daoist mystical impulses, even where pursued by Confucianists. It was, as Arthur Danto rhapsodically observes, 'the Taoist spirit we admire in those pale grey landscapes of the Sung dynasty, where the individual barely punctuates the formless mists in which mountains are washed in as vague, dreamful forms' (1976: 115). According to all the standard accounts within the Chinese literary tradition, landscape painting was practised not purely as an artform in the Western sense, but primarily as a kind of spiritual exercise, as a way of attaining insight into the *dao* itself, and even as a way of participating in the creative activity of the *dao*; 'To the basically irreligious Chinese, art became religion itself, the highest expression of his mysticism...[through which] he will feel with the utmost intensity the timeless reality of artistic emotion which obliterates his ego just as effectively as many years of religious meditation' (de Riencourt 1965: 35).[14] This form of art was widely practised in monasteries – Chan Buddhist as well as Daoist – as part of the religious discipline of these foundations, and in more secular contexts the creation of such paintings, and of associated landscape gardens and miniature tray landscapes, provided the Confucian literati not only with a means of recreation and escape from their urban environment, but a form of spiritual exercise intimately related to meditation practices (Paper 1995: 174–5).[15] In the words of the Tang poet Fuzai, concerning the work of a contemporary artist:

When we contemplate Master Chang's art, it is not painting, it is the very Tao itself. Whenever he was engaged in painting, one already knew that he had left mere skill far behind. His ideas reach into the dark mystery of things, and for him, things lay not in the physical senses, but in the spiritual part of his mind.

(quoted in Sullivan 1979: 49)

The enthusiasm of such modern writers as de Riencourt should not disguise from us the fact that Chinese painting in general, and landscape painting in particular, has not always been appreciated in the West. There has been a tendency to judge this artform by narrow Western standards, and to see it as involving an immature technique which must inevitably give way to the more 'advanced' techniques developed in the West since the Renaissance. Even de Riencourt, who uses the term 'sublime' to characterise the Chinese painting tradition, felt obliged to add that 'it failed miserably in the portrayal of human forms', a failure which he put down to its lack of appreciation of light and shade and of the principles of perspective (1965: 37). This supposed deficiency was first remarked upon in the seventeenth century by Matteo Ricci. While commenting on the extraordinary natural talent displayed by Chinese artists, he excluded them from any comparison with contemporary Western artists on account of their ignorance of the use of oils and of the technique of *chiaroscuro*. For a long time thereafter, even when Chinese artworks entered circulation in Europe, it became standard practice to accuse Chinese painters of a lack of understanding of perspective. The Portuguese scholar Alvarez de Sumedo, writing in 1635 shortly after the time of Ricci, allowed that the Chinese artists, though weak in figure painting, excelled in depicting nature, but went on to lament that 'They know not how to make use either of *Oyles* or of *shadowing*', but that those who had been taught to make use of 'Oyles' by Western missionaries 'are come to make perfect pictures' (quoted in Sullivan 1979: 3; italics in the original).

All of this clearly implied the belief that Chinese painting, talented and charming though it might be, must be assigned to a relatively primitive and childlike stage of cultural development compared with the more advanced stage of development of European art, a view which has accorded well with Western paradigms of world cultural history until very recent times. Moreover, the perception of a tedious repetitiveness in Chinese painting, often seen as executed in accordance with age-old formulae and underlined by the widely accepted practice of the copying of old masters, has been reinforced by the cliché of Chinese cultural stagnation which we referred to in an earlier chapter.[16] This attitude prevailed throughout the nineteenth century, typified in Herbert Spencer's condemnation of Chinese paintings as 'grotesque in their utter disregard of the laws of appearance' (Chisolm 1963: 146). An important shift in attitude was signalled around the turn of the century, however, in the writings of Laurence Binyon and Ernest Fenollosa who sought to accord Chinese painting recognition as an important artform in its own right. In 1908 Binyon, who like Fenollosa had spent some years in East Asia studying its art in its indigenous environment, rejected the then standard view that Chinese landscape painting was inferior to the Western genre, and at the same time emphasised the deep metaphysical dimensions of the former, writing that it is an art 'without parallel in the rest of the world', and that it is 'near to us as anything contemporary in ourselves' (1935: 73, 104; see also Fenollosa 1912, vol. 2: 11; Sullivan 1990: 284–5). Nevertheless, beyond a small circle of enthusiasts there remained for many subsequent decades a tendency to see these works as inherently lightweight, conveying a vaguely poetic mood rather than a serious philosophical intent, and in spite of the mania for chinoiserie in the eighteenth century and the continued admiration for the meticulous perfection of Chinese craftsmanship, landscape painting, the artform which the Chinese themselves held to be their supreme creation, was still in the 1960s 'regarded as some sort of whimsical negation of our Western standards' (Bussagli 1969: 14).

In spite of this continuing lack of appreciation in the West, Chinese landscape painting has begun to acquire a belated recognition, and its philosophical significance in relation to Daoism is at last being revealed in ways that might lead towards a more adequate understanding of this tradition. We are beginning to realise, as the art historian Mario Bussagli puts it, that 'this form of painting can never be separated from other aspects of the spiritual life', and must be seen within the wider context both of 'the religious and philosophical ideas of the various ages', as well as its moral and political dimensions (1969: 32). This emerging rapprochement is due to a number of factors. One of these is the growth of abstract art in the West, which has rendered the somewhat conceptual, intangible and elusive qualities of Chinese landscape painting more accessible to Western taste. Furthermore, the spiritual/mystical dimension of art, which was so important to the founders of abstract painting in the West, Kandinsky and Mondrian, and which is divested of all explicit religious connotation, may also have helped to open minds to the spiritual aspects of Chinese painting.[17] There is a growing awareness too of depth of feeling and truth to nature that is present in the great landscape paintings of the Song period, albeit in a way that is not strictly representational, and which bears thought-provoking comparison with landscape artists of the Romantic period in Europe such as Turner and Friedrich. And finally, the more recent work of abstract expressionists such as Franz Kline and Jackson Pollock has made it much easier for Westerners to draw comparisons between their own and Chinese artistic traditions.[18] In the view of the Oriental art historian Michael Sullivan, it is such factors as these which have led to the beginnings of a dialogue between Western and Chinese art traditions, and it is not surprising in his view that Zen painting, deeply influenced by Daoist ideas of

naturalness and spontaneity and able to express the profoundest philosophical ideas, seems to speak to us in ways which transcend its original
historical context (Sullivan 1979: 6).[19] The paintings of Mu-ch'i (mid-
thirteenth century CE) for example, which offer an image of man-and-
nature in which everything is on the point of being dissolved in an all-
enveloping haze, make sense to us now in the light of Victorian struggles to
assimilate artists like Turner who seem to be giving expression to a similar
vision.

Another factor which has helped us to become more attuned to Chinese
landscape art undoubtedly is the growing need to integrate our conception
of human existence more intimately with nature, and to challenge the well-
established belief in man's right to dominate and control the natural world.
Chinese landscape painting is arguably ecological in spirit and presents an
almost mystical sense of the underlying interconnectedness of all things, in
particular the integration of the microcosmic human world within the
macrocosm of nature as a whole. In this form of art, no lordly place is given
to the human element, and the image of the tiny human figure and human
dwellings in the landscape teaches us, in terms which cannot adequately be
expressed in words, that it is in nature that 'man finds symbolic values and,
above all, universal harmony', and that 'nature rules over everything and
succeeds in overwhelming man's tiny existence' (Bussagli 1969: 38).
Mountains held a central place in many landscape paintings. They were seen
as symbolising closeness to untrammelled nature and as embodying a
spiritual power, a source of energy and life with which we are invited to
become identified, a view which almost certainly has roots that go back to
earlier animistic beliefs. This attitude is something with which it is possible
for us in our own age to empathise, though it is important to remember that
a positive and even a mystical attitude to mountains only emerged in the
West in fully articulated form in the Romantic period. Prior to that time, the
mountainous regions of the world were looked upon by Christian thinkers
as alien and 'horrid', and the seventeenth-century theologian Thomas
Burnet was typical in finding mountains an incomprehensible irruption on
the face of God's otherwise beautiful world, to be explained away as the
rubble heap left over from the creation![20] By contrast with European
traditions of landscape painting since the Renaissance, which have often
portrayed nature as a background to the central drama of human or
mythological activity, in these Chinese paintings the human element is not
allowed to dominate the scene but is integrated into it. It is important to
stress that this configuration is not designed to overwhelm and humble the
human world but rather to place the human and the natural in due
proportion to one another, and in the view of the philosopher Peter
Marshall this does not imply an escape into nature from the demands of the
'real' world but rather 'direct contact with reality, a state in which the
observer and observed are no longer felt as separate' (1992b: 15). It is this

quality that inspired the Thomist philosopher Jacques Maritain to comment in 1952 that the great Chinese landscape artists were primarily concerned not with the depiction of nature but with a 'sort of interpenetration between Nature and Man', a feature which gave Chinese art a uniquely spiritual quality (1955: 84, 13–14).

The language of Chinese landscape painting is one which not only evokes feelings of peace, harmony, and mystical union with nature, but generates at various levels an underlying sense of life and creativity. The landscapes themselves seem to be alive, animated by *qi*, expressing under the painter's brush the movements of animals and suggesting that the painter's art is in some sense associated with the cosmic processes of creation. Some painters expressed this by saying that when painting they actually *become* the mountain, the water, the bamboo, and in the words of the ninth-century writer, Zhang Yanyuan, 'Painting brings the finishing touches to the world of the universal creator' (Leys 1983: 15).[21] The painter was therefore expected not merely to represent the visible topography of nature, but in some sense to draw out its spiritual topography through a process of empathetic identification, and in so doing was seen to be necessarily engaged in a process of self-transformation. It was a tradition which early on led to the idea that 'the picture was not an object in a frame, to be looked at and admired for its form and colour, but rather a mysterious thing that...contained the essence of the world of nature' (Sullivan 1979: 29). According to the twentieth century writer and artist Mai-mai Sze, painting in China 'is not a profession but an extension of the art of living, for the practice of the *tao* of painting is part of the traditional *tao* of conduct and thought, of living in harmony with the laws of *Tao*' (1959: 6). Moreover, this is an art which manifests most expressively the element of creative spontaneity which is central to Daoist thinking, even the aim of life, and which bids us not to attempt to impose our wills on nature, or to struggle with the obduracy of our own limitations, but to achieve an inner freedom which transcends the narrow demands of the ego.

This psycho-spiritual feature of Chinese art is one which has increasingly attracted the attention of Western commentators in recent years, particularly in so far as it contrasts with mainstream traditional European approaches. Whereas in the West the emphasis has been largely on the art object, and, until the twentieth century at least, on its representational element, in China the main focus of interest, particularly in the Daoist context, has been more on the process of artistic creation itself, and indeed on its fundamentally religious nature. Painting was seen not just as a way of producing an aesthetic object, or even as merely an object of spiritual contemplation, but as an expressive act, more precisely as a way of achieving and manifesting and circulating the *qi*. As such, it is a form of yoga which directly parallels other forms of yoga; including that of the bedchamber (Wile 1992: 72). Painters, suitably prepared through quiet sitting and through the lifelong absorption of nature into their very being, achieve a state of emptiness out of which the painting emerges spontaneously yet with the utmost artistry, thus imitating and indeed participating in the way in which the world of nature itself emerges spontaneously yet with the utmost harmony out of the primal emptiness of the *dao*. According to Jianping Gao, landscape painting was a way of 'mutual transformation' in which the artist 'becomes the semi-Creator of the world', and in which

> [the painter] was not supposed to 'gaze' at the world with the aim of conquering its appearance, but to 'contemplate it' with an inborn love, continually identifying with it in his soul, in order to make . himself part of nature and nature part of him.
>
> (Gao 1996: 167, 157)

At one level the creative activity of the artist is therefore nothing less than the Daoist quest for recovery of the *dao*, for that emptiness which is the root of the 'thousand things', and from the Tang period onwards landscape painting became intimately related to the meditation practices of both Daoist and Chan monks. It manifested itself even more widely amongst the literati as a form of aestheticism, as the cultivation of a certain kind of refined sensibility which merges imperceptibly with what we would standardly describe as 'spiritual' or 'mystical' practices. Jordan Paper has pointed out that the meditation practices of Daoists and Buddhists that emerged during and after the period following the fall of the Han dynasty were not necessarily oriented towards mystic experiences in the full sense, but were manifested through aesthetic activities such as painting, poetry and music. Such practices displayed ecstatic elements, sometimes assisted by wine, and though in a sense ritualised (for example, in the grinding of the ink and the manipulation of the brush), they were not part of any formal religious ceremony or practice. In this way, Paper argues, there emerged at that period a unique relationship between aesthetic and religious activity in China where artistic activities became 'an alternative mode of religious behaviour for the traditional elite', particularly amongst those who had retired from office or were in exile. Moreover, for such people aesthetic activity was an effective means to express and assert individuality and the values of self-expression, and hence could be pursued as a reaction against 'the rigidly conformist and non-self-assertive nature of most of their lives and occupations' (1995: 158, 186 and ch. 6 *passim*).

On the face of it, this represents from the Western perspective a largely novel approach to the understanding of art, though there are some points at which comparisons can be drawn. For example, with the rise of psychology and the advent of expressionism, there has emerged a greater appreciation of the subjective and unconscious elements within the production of artwork, though there is little to compare with the Daoist idea of the art process as a yogic exercise or form of self-cultivation. The aestheticism of Beardsley, Pater, Wilde and others at the end of the nineteenth century has certain parallels with Chinese aestheticism, but is more dilettantish and lacks anchorage in a coherent and comprehensive attitude to life and values in general. Surrealist automatism also bears superficial resemblances to Chinese ideas and techniques, but as the art historian Harold Osborne points out, 'The Chinese painter worked spontaneously only after an elaborate preparation consisting of meditation on an idea or concentration on an object, a discipline that required training and cultivation', so that he in no sense gave expression to his own unfettered subjectivity but only to processes that resulted from concentration on attaining harmony both within and without (1968: 72). Perhaps the nearest comparison with Western aesthetic theory and practice is to be found in the Romantic period. Here, not only was the metaphysical significance of art recognised, and even given a privileged position, but the expressive factor came to be of central importance and the process of artistic creation was sometimes seen to be endowed with a spiritual, even a priestly, function.[22]

Whatever the plausibility of these historical comparisons, the religio-aesthetic tradition of the literati and the Daoist and Chan monks, with its emphasis on inner freedom and self-realisation, its simplicity and its gentle enhancement of emotion and awareness, seems able to speak to us today in ways that would have been difficult to comprehend until relatively recently. It is not that art has begun to replace religion – or morality for that matter – but rather that through the *activity* of art, in contrast to its passive contemplation or critical appreciation, many people have begun to discover an access to experiences of ecstasy and fulfilment that have in the past been almost exclusively identified with formal religions.

But before we get carried away by these seductive ideas it is necessary to become aware of a certain tendency towards idealisation in all of this, both in China and in the West, a tendency to place art and the aesthetic experience in a realm which detaches it from the real world. Typically, Chinese landscape painting, as well as the closely related arts of poetry and calligraphy, has been seen as a pursuit worthy only of the gentleman, scholar or monk, and as an activity that embodies the highest ideals of Chinese élite culture (Cooper 1990: 103). But the ideal and the reality were not always identical with each other. As with so many other aspects of our understanding of traditional Chinese culture, things are not always what they seem, and we need to be suspicious of the image of Chinese art as a realm of purely disinterested spiritual-aesthetic endeavour. The art historian James Cahill, to cite a contemporary authority, has sought to encourage a more balanced approach by emphasising the social and economic contexts of Chinese artistic production, contrary to its usual treatment in purely aesthetic terms, and has drawn our attention to the fact that Chinese painting was very often involved in commercial transaction and that many artists were professionals who painted in order to make a living, or simply for pleasure and relaxation. It is true that there were artists, whether monks or scholar-gentlemen, who painted for spiritual or aesthetic uplift, but there were also those who produced paintings for the market. The creation of the myth of a class of scholars who produced art for purely non-utilitarian purposes was, he believes, a way of 'dematerializing the art, removing it from all taint of vulgarity, commercialism, functionalism, philistine response' (1994: 9). No doubt it was, he allows, a great cultural achievement, comparable to the Western myth of romantic love and chivalry in mediæval Europe, but it has tended to distort many aspects of this great artistic tradition, and in particular to place it in an almost exclusively ideal realm that is divorced from the totality of Chinese social and economic history, a tendency which we have noted in an earlier chapter in relation to Daoist thought in general. Furthermore, he insists, this idealisation was certainly not merely a Western fantasy, even though it became stock-in-trade to generations of Western scholars, but was uncritically accepted by the Chinese themselves who sought to construct a certain mystique around this art form, identifying it with the disinterested scholar who was unconcerned with material rewards.[23]

Though the appeal of Chinese landscape painting has been slow to establish itself in the West, and will probably always remain a somewhat restricted channel for the dissemination of Daoist ideas, the impact of the Chinese landscape *garden* is much older and has had relatively wide cultural repercussions. As with landscape painting, with which landscape gardening has 'an intimate relation' (Sirén 1949: 3), we need to beware of simply identifying this artform with Daoism, for in many ways it was much more closely associated with the ways of life of the imperial court and the Confucian élite. However, the harmony between the human and the natural worlds and the close relationship between nature and architecture that is manifested in these gardens, as in the closely related genre of landscape painting, combined with the spiritual ambience of peaceful contemplation and self-cultivation, point to a Daoist inspiration behind these creations (Keswick 1986). Even in Daoist hermitages, often situated in remote and inhospitable locations, the principles of harmony with nature that underlie the private landscape garden were evident in the careful siting of the buildings and in the creation of miniature rock gardens in the hermitage courtyard (Blofeld 1985: 168–70).

Historically, the Chinese landscape garden was a typical feature of the imperial palace, traceable back into the mythic past, and was traditionally seen as a small-scale representation of the world over which the emperor ruled. It had magical significance too, in that it was thought to be a means whereby the imperial mandate could be enacted at a distance, as it were, and was also linked with the quest for immortality by virtue of its symbolic replication of the fabled islands of the Immortals in the Eastern Seas. Later, when the genre was adopted more widely, such gardens became places of refreshment and relaxation for the scholar officials, offering a means of retreat from the demands of the social and political world, a space for meditation and reflection as well as for conversation and conviviality. According to orthodox theory, they were arranged and constructed in such a way that the owner could find spiritual communion with nature and absorb the vital spirit of the earth, though in less exalted terms they were also just agreeable places in which to loaf, paint, write poetry and drink wine with friends; activities which, of course, were perfectly compatible with the Daoist outlook. The miniaturisation of nature and of the cosmos at large which these gardens represented was carried a stage further by the creation of 'tray' or 'container' landscapes (*benjing*) which also acted as conduits of the energies of nature at large, and by the collecting of rocks which were valued for 'their microcosmic mimicry of mountain landscapes' (Schafer 1961: 3). In general these gardens, at whatever scale, were evidence of the widespread Chinese reverence for mountains, rocks and water. This reverence had its roots in ancient animistic beliefs, but at the same time expressed some of the central concerns of Daoist philosophy with its aim of bringing the human world back to a more direct relationship with the creative forces of the universe and with the vital spirit that runs through the body of the earth.[24]

Traces of this Daoist spirit entered Europe in the late seventeenth century, and in the long term may even have contributed something towards that great shift of thought and sensibility known as the Romantic movement. To be sure, the ideas and traditions of Daoism were almost entirely opaque to those early travellers and writers who transmitted images of Chinese gardens to Europe, for they approached the whole experience not only with European eyes, but also through the eyes of the Confucian literati. In spite of this, however, it is possible to discern through this medium a flow of Daoist ideas, however attenuated, into Europe during the eighteenth century. Rumours about strange, irregular Chinese gardens circulated in Europe from the reports of the Jesuits, and had little impact at a time when the formal style of gardening was the norm, but with the appearance of Sir William Temple's *Upon the Gardens of Epicurus* in 1685, Europe began to take Chinese garden design seriously. Through Temple's influence, and that of a series of subsequent writings by such figures as William Chambers, Joseph Addison and Joseph Spence, certain aspects of Chinese garden design, both at the level of architectural detail and of overall shape and texture, entered into the ferment of ideas and debates about nature during that period, and had an important influence on the emergence of a new fashion which became known as the 'Anglo-Chinese' style of landscape garden design.[25] Looking beyond such popular features as pagodas and bridges, the most important characteristic of the Chinese garden to impinge on European consciousness at that time was its supposed wildness, summed up in the word *sharawadgi*. The exact origin of this term is a matter of dispute, but it was employed to refer to a certain disorderly grace, a wild harmony – an orderly chaos, perhaps – that was detected in Chinese garden aesthetic, and that was seen to contrast sharply with the restrained geometric formality of the French-dominated style of landscape garden design. As Sullivan puts it, this new style helped to 'provoke a reaction against the formal, geometrical gardens of Italy and France, and helped to bring to birth the natural gardens that were so much more in accordance with English taste' (1990: 286).

It is difficult to assess precisely the extent of the Chinese influence here. The work of Chambers, for example, was not always well received in his day, and in any case his descriptions of Chinese gardens employed a vocabulary that was embedded in European critical traditions rather than in Chinese aesthetics, and seem to have been inspired more by the romantic landscape paintings of Salvator Rosa than by any gardens he may have seen in China (Sullivan 1990: 286). Moreover, the intimacy and human scale of the Chinese originals tended to evaporate in the somewhat inflated and even grandiose 'copies' that made their appearance in England and the rest of Europe in the eighteenth century. According to one art historian, 'Europe, and England with it...by-passed the reality of Chinese gardens, and interpreted them entirely in the image of their own experience' (Keswick 1986: 24). Nevertheless the Chinese garden, albeit mediated and contorted by European categories, traditions and predilections, certainly played some kind of role not only in establishing a new and more 'natural' style of garden design, but beyond that in helping to bring about the revolution in aesthetics that came to full realisation in the Romantic movement. In this way we can see that the oft-noted affinity between Daoist and Romantic sensibilities may not be merely a coincidence (Lovejoy 1948; see also Reichwein 1925: 113ff; Sullivan 1989: 108, 113).

## Transcendence

The contemporary appeal of both Daoist 'mysticism of the particular' and the 'mysticism made visible' in Chinese landscape painting undoubtedly lies in their construction as a form of spirituality without transcendence. This is not to deny other constructions or other sources of appeal, but in contemporary Western thought and culture there is a manifest shift away from certain traditional representations of Judaeo-Christian teaching and Enlightenment values and assumptions, and the emergence of various intellectual movements engaged in a radical reformulation of our cultural inheritances. Whether in disputes about morals or human rights, about life and death issues, about politics or cosmology, appeals to some transcendent source of validation seem less and less persuasive. Where earlier generations founded their religious or moral or political standards on seemingly firm principles that transcended the contingencies of history and fashion, the late modern or postmodern age is forced to have recourse to more pragmatic considerations and must seek as a guide to life factors which arise from immediate cultural or personal experience rather than from timeless truths or unquestioned traditional authorities. In philosophical terms, this shift is evident in the increasingly sharp criticism since the time of Nietzsche of certain types of foundational concept – Platonic Forms, God, Natural Law, Reason, Will, Self, to give a few obvious examples – which have hitherto given philosophy a role as a higher court of appeal beyond the ever-shifting perspectives of common experience and common belief systems. Furthermore, the dominant trend is clearly away from appeals to transcendent criteria in the establishment of principles for the guidance of society, which must now operate 'without any transcendent standards of rationality, without any final conception of human nature, and without any progressivist or apocalyptic vision' (Hall and Ames 1998: 218). Evidently this is not only a philosophical problem, for in all sorts of fields from literature and theology to politics and science, we are witnessing an assault upon traditional notions of transcendence and a corresponding acceptance of a radical historical contingency of human understanding and valuation. In theological terms this shift is dramatised in Nietzsche's announcement of the 'Death of God' and his anticipation of the 'de-deification of nature', in socio-cosmological terms it is made memorable in Max Weber's phrase, 'the disenchantment of the world', and in contemporary philosophy it appears in various deconstructive enterprises.

In a series of three major joint investigations, David Hall and Roger Ames, who combine philosophy with expertise in Asian thought and intercultural studies, have used the issue of what might be called 'the crisis of transcendence' as a means of setting up a dialogue between Eastern and Western traditions of thought and creating a methodological bridge between them. For Hall and Ames, the West's disenchantment with transcendence need not lead to nihilism and anguish, as it is often experienced, but rather a liberating episode in Western thought which opens up the possibility of bringing certain long-ignored or long-despised strands of Chinese philosophy into a new intercultural dialogue. Mystical experience, shorn of its more orthodox transcendental and monistic assumptions, provides for them an important comparative vehicle for this project. As we saw in the preceding sections, it is precisely this kind of immanentist, intraworldly mysticism that is seen to be characteristic of the Chinese Daoist tradition, a feature which provides a critical standpoint in relation to Western traditions, and at the same time resonates with certain contemporary problematics. The loss of transcendence in the contemporary context is thus both 'a point of departure within our own tradition that we can best move to understand alternative assumptions that undergird the cultural narrative of China', and also a means for reflecting critically on that contemporary context from the standpoint of an alternative vision (1998: 218; see also Hall and Ames 1987, 1995).

In seeking to bridge the gap between the two traditions there is, as we have witnessed throughout this volume, an ever-present danger of reducing the unfamiliar to the familiar and thereby simply transposing Daoism into Western terms. One consequence of this is that, with the collapse of the concept of transcendence in the West, the common ground hitherto sought by both Chinese and Western interpreters slips away, leaving the twain without a place to meet. Hall and Ames are especially sensitive to this danger. They point out that European translations of Chinese texts have frequently employed a transcendentalist vocabulary, thereby perhaps unwittingly 'attempting to transplant Western understandings of "God" or "the absolute" into Chinese soil' (1998: 219). From this arises the question whether the idea of transcendence is, strictly speaking, applicable to Chinese thought at all, or whether it represents a cultural and intellectual tradition which, in this respect at least, differs fundamentally from the West's where such notions have been central. In the opinion of Hall and Ames, the notion of transcendence is indeed largely irrelevant to the interpretation of classical Chinese texts, and they argue that Daoist and Confucian texts and systems of thought have been profoundly misunderstood by being transposed into such terms. A serious disservice has been done by attributing to the Chinese way of thinking a language of transcendence and of foundationalism which is familiar to the Western thought, but which they believe is absent in the Chinese intellectual tradition.

As far as Daoism itself is concerned, there are a number of traps that we fall into if we insist on applying to it transcendental modes of thinking. For example, we tend to treat the *dao* as an entity of a rather special, ennobled kind rather than as a fairly ordinary modality or action or process; we represent the *dao* as something imposed from a higher reality rather than experiencing it as an immanent order that is 'site specific' like 'grained wood'; we tend to overlook the fact that in Daoism there is a general indeterminacy in the ordering of events; and we fail to appreciate that the interdependence of things requires no externally initiated cosmic source, no Leibnizian pre-established harmony but a harmony which arises spontaneously. In brief, what is being insisted on in these studies by Hall and Ames is the non-transcendent nature of the *dao*, a term which does not represent a 'Being' that lies behind or prior to or as an explanation of the myriad beings, and that does not refer to the 'One behind the Many, [the] Reality behind Appearance' (1998: 274). Neither is there a transcendent self that stands outside the world of appearances, for the 'Daoist self is a function of its relations with its world' and human presence within the world is embedded *within* the world, without the possibility of a transcendent vantage point from which to establish timeless and completely objective truths (1998: 48, 247). Moreover, the spiritual goals of Daoism, often identified in the West as representative of a universal wisdom tradition, a perennial philosophy which seeks ultimate identity with a divine transcendence, needs to be rethought in immanentist terms that avoid the sorts of dualism that have characterised the Western accounts of mystical experience. Thus, Zhuangzi's entreaty that we become 'one with all things' is not to be construed as a 'Vedanta-like call to surrender one's particularity and dissolve into a unitary and perfect whole', but rather 'a recognition that each and every phenomenon is continuous within one's field of experience', or in other words a sense of identity with the whole which avoids the subordination of 'thisness' and 'hereness' to totality.

The absence of transcendent categories in the Chinese tradition, Hall and Ames believe, does not contradict the view that there has existed a profoundly religious tradition in China. They seek to combat the old cliché, dating back to the time of Voltaire, that the Chinese are essentially a non-religious people. The spiritual quest does not need to be seen in exclusively transcendental terms, and once again we can see here how the teasing out of differences between the two traditions provides illumination for both. Whereas in the Christian spiritual–mystical quest the ultimate goal is one of union between the soul and God, thereby transcending the fallen world of material things, for the Daoist the spiritual quest is one which seeks not to go beyond the particularity of things to their ultimate source, but rather to discover unity with the *dao* within that very particularity, within the flux and flow of existence itself. It expresses an ontology which, in the words of the *Zhuangzi*, 'evens things out', and which finds the *dao* equally present in all things, even in such commonplace items as insects, weeds, smashed tiles, excrement and urine, thus allowing the sage to appreciate the *dao* 'Without leaving his door' (*Daodejing*: ch. 47). For Daoism, therefore, the spiritual quest does not lead beyond this world to the worship of the source of our being, but rather to the enfoldment within the 'thousand things' that constitute the multifarious yet unified and ever-changing whole – or rather the many wholes – that is the *dao*. This spiritual path, though inappropriately characterised by means of the Western Christian vocabulary of 'God', 'sin', 'grace', 'soul' and so on, is nevertheless a profoundly religious one, a different form of religiosity to the one we have been used to in the West, yet one which is strangely in tune with contemporary post-Christian inclinations. The great Chinese landscape paintings that we discussed in the previous section are spiritual testaments therefore, not because they point beyond the contingent world to the ultimate reality or to the true essence of things beyond appearances, but because, by locating us within the world, they hold us in a symbiotic process of self-transformation. In a word, the Chinese experience helps to teach us that the death of God is not equivalent to the death of religion.[26]

The kind of comparative enquiry carried out here inevitably brings us to the question whether, looking at the divergences between the Chinese and the Western spiritual traditions, the Chinese think and experience the world differently from Europeans. For Hall and Ames, the inclination is clearly towards difference, away from the search for underlying universal archetypes and towards an approach which emphasises the embeddedness of Chinese thinking in its historical context. But how far does their kind of 'difference' go? Does it reach all the way down to the very foundations of rational thought? From one extreme and uncompromising point of view, emphasis on difference leaves the two traditions in a state of incommensurability. For our two authors, however, while they insist on significant differences between the mystical–spiritual traditions of the two cultures, it is precisely these differences which, paradoxically, make communication possible and indeed desirable. Similar to Gadamer, they believe that differences make productive thought possible by opening up the space in which to identify alternatives to familiar modes of expression and action; one's own reality is illuminated by its very contrast with that of the 'other'. Though in their view there is, in a sense, only one global culture, one conceptual framework in which we all operate, this unity itself is not what makes creative exchange possible, a view typical of old-style universalists, but rather the fact that within that global environment there are many diverse and only imprecisely individuated cultural communities with differing yet overlapping vocabularies, perspectives and traditions at whose interface the business of self-awareness becomes most productive; indeed, to communicate at all is essentially to trade along the vague and indefinable boundaries that divide yet unite people (1995: 165–79). They conclude that the inclination on the part of Western scholars, and following them of certain modern Chinese scholars as well, to employ the language of transcendence has led, in their view, to a serious underappreciation of 'the contribution of Chinese philosophy to world culture as a real alternative to dominant Western sensibilities' (1998: 228).

Before bringing this section to a close, we need to sound a pair of cautionary notes. The first is a matter of historical judgement, amplified by a linguistic qualm. Is it true, as Hall and Ames claim, that there is an absence of transcendental categories in traditional Chinese thought? As indicated in Chapter 4 above, there are arguably traces of transcendental thinking at both the popular and intellectual levels of thinking, though the whole question of identifying such occurrences may be bedevilled by a certain indeterminacy in the concept of transcendence itself. If, for example, we construe the term 'transcendence' to mean 'surpassing' or 'going beyond', then there does seem to be a sense in which the *dao* is transcendent, for it surpasses and goes beyond our attempts to encapsulate it in language. Yet at the same time we are led to believe that *dao* is immanent, present in the most ordinary objects of ordinary experience, and is therefore not transcendent in the way that the Christian deity is traditionally seen to be. In the light of such an example, it is not clear that a decision on whether to assign *dao* to the category of transcendence could be made unequivocally.[27] A more general criticism along these lines comes from the German philosopher Heiner Roetz. While accepting that in Chinese thought there is no strong ontological sense of a world that transcends this one, he points out that for the Daoists, the *dao* is transcendent in so far as it entails a radical critique of culture and of the political and social status quo. He argues that the neopragmatist, contextualist approach of Hall and Ames fails to give credit to the post-conventional, tradition-transcending nature of Chinese philosophical speculation in the classical period, and seeks to minimise the distinction, commonly made in the West, between the supposed inner-worldliness of Chinese religions and the radical transcendence which, from Weber onwards, has been seen to be a characteristic of Jewish and Christian thought (1993: 273 and chaps 1–2 *passim*).[28]

The second note of caution is a methodological one, and will be familiar to the reader by now. As I mentioned above, Hall and Ames are careful to draw attention to the danger of transposing Chinese concepts into typical Western ones, and of viewing Daoist spirituality through the home-ground lens of transcendence. It is possible that in their enthusiasm to build a new bridge, one constructed out of the crooked timber of difference rather than the honed steel of identity, Hall and Ames have fallen into the same trap as those they have reproved. Put broadly, in the great orientalist game, each age and each special interest group has sought to draw Asian thought into the orbit of its own intellectual constellation; one thinks here of the ways in which progressively over the past century and a half there has been a sequence of attempts to think Buddhism in terms of prevailing intellectual fashions, originating from, for example, Kantian, evolutionist, existentialist, psychoanalytic, Wittgensteinian or New Age paradigms. The current intellectual fashion now is, on Hall and Ames' own terms, recognisably postmodernist, and in the light of this we have a right to question whether their own version of the game represents a better and more insightful understanding of Daoism, or is simply another inescapably contingent perspective, a postmodern interpretation fit for a postmodern age. Their undoubtedly sophisticated and well-documented rethinking of the Chinese intellectual and spiritual traditions shoehorns almost too easily into certain postmodern concerns, and leads us to ask whether in any absolute sense their story represents an advance on previous narratives. Does the theoretical approach which has emerged in the West under the banner of postmodernity lead us any closer to 'the Chinese mind' than earlier fashions of thought, or is it simply another Western game that is being played out? Hall and Ames certainly accept that philosophy is inescapably perspectival and culturally embedded, and their endorsement of the contemporary turn towards pragmatism and historicism suggests that for them, at least, the kind of intellectual performance they themselves are engaged in can never constitute the final definition or version but is always open to yet further transformations.[29] These and related matters will occupy us more fully in the next chapter.

# 8

# 'THE TWITTER OF BIRDS'

## Philosophical themes

### Thinking differences

From the standpoint of Western philosophy, Daoism seems the most unphilosophical of traditions, bent on subverting the kind of rational discourse which is the very foundation stone of philosophy as it is practised in the West. In both the *Laozi* and the *Zhuangzi*, a central theme is the ultimate inaccessibility of the world to the categories of language, and Zhuangzi has often been characterised as a great anti-rationalist who derides the claims of reason and offers us only knacks and skills of a distinctly non-intellectual kind. In this chapter I want to question the assumption, widely held until recently, that Daoism has no philosophical message to convey, and to explore some of the ways in which Daoism and Western philosophical discourse have entered into fruitful conversation in recent times.

One of the barriers to the development of philosophical understanding between China and the West has undoubtedly been the convention that philosophy is to all intents and purposes absent in China, and the belief that traditional China in general and Daoism in particular failed to produce philosophical systems parallel to and hence commensurable with those of the West (Dubs 1929). Oriental thought *tout court* has frequently been ruled out of philosophical consideration on the grounds either that it is inherently mystical or that it is a form of everyday moralising that contains no serious attempt at analysis or argument. We have for long laboured under a ruling stereotype, aptly named by Hansen as 'the right-brain-left-brain school of interpretation' of comparative East–West thought (1992: 302), which has structured a West–East dichotomy round a contrast between complementary categories such as 'reason' and 'intuition' according to which Chinese thought is characterised as a form of anti-rational mysticism. A classic example of such a construct is the distinction made by F.S.C. Northrop between 'concepts by postulation' and 'concepts by intuition, the former dominant in Western speculation, the latter inherent in much oriental culture (1946: 83).[1] The origins of this can, once again, be traced back to the time of Matteo Ricci and his followers, who became convinced that Western philosophical categories were inapplicable to Chinese ways of thinking and that the Chinese were deficient in reasoning powers (Gernet 1985: 241). This belief is often graphically underlined in histories of philosophy which have tended to focus exclusively on European traditions, and to assume that philosophy is a uniquely Greek affair (Flew 1971); as one philosopher ironically puts it: 'Philosophy speaks Greek and only Greek' (Critchley 1995: 18).[2] It has tended to be assumed, almost without question, that the Chinese, regularly cast as an essentially practical people, have had no interest in metaphysics, that there is no logic in Chinese philosophy, and that even its great thinkers such as Confucius and Laozi were not really genuine philosophers at all but moralists or poets who have nothing to contribute to philosophy as such (Moore 1968: 8–9; de Riencourt 1965: 75).

Part of the problem here is that the style and methodology employed by Chinese thinkers is patently different from that which is typical of Western philosophers, a fact which led Max Kaltenmark to comment that the *Daodejing* 'is not a philosophical treatise [for] it contains no demonstrations of any kind. It gives only conclusions' (1969: 36). Daoism, with its strange vocabulary, its partiality for equivocation and paradox, its seeming abrogation of the rules of logical probity, and most especially its perverse doubts about the possibility of saying anything at all, has proved a particularly difficult camel for Western philosophy to swallow. This attitude has been highlighted by the debate from the time of Marcel Granet onwards over whether the evident structural differences between Chinese and European languages imply a fundamental difference in ways of thinking. In 1934, Granet wrote that 'The Chinese language does not appear to be organised to denote concepts, to analyse ideas, or to expound doctrines in a discursive manner. It is entirely fashioned to communicate sentiments, to suggests ways of acting, to convince, and to convert' (1934: 82). Even prior to Granet, Ernest Fenollosa had speculated that Chinese characters, with their compressed evocativeness and their evident proclivity for poetic expression, point to a different way of thinking, a feminine *yin* as opposed to the masculine *yang* of the West (1936).[3] More recently, Hajime Nakamura has suggested that the peculiar grammatical features of Chinese are a key to the 'non-logical character of the verbal expression of Chinese thought', and the historian of science Toby Huff has pronounced the Chinese language as unsuitable for science or for dialectical disputation (1993: 299). Johannes Lohman takes the even more extreme position that, due to its peculiar grammatical features, the Chinese language represents the 'state of the primitive human language' which is close to that of the ape and the Neanderthal (Nakamura 1964: 37; Huff 1993: 215, 299; Lohman 1965: 172–3; see also Harbsmeier 1981; Lenk and Paul 1993).

This perceived incongruity between the two civilisations has persisted in Western minds until quite recently. The situation is beginning to change, however, and even several decades ago when positivism and linguistic analysis were still dominant in anglophone circles, there were philosophers like Archie Bahm and Arthur Danto who were beginning to give serious consideration to Daoist ideas (Bahm 1958; Danto 1976). Daoism can, of course, get on perfectly well without the attentions of Western philosophy. We need to be on our guard against the orientalist assumption that the exclusion of Daoism from the charmed circle of philosophy represents some kind of failing or immaturity on the former's part. Bryan Van Norden points out that, 'It is just as ethnocentric to assume that every other culture must be engaged in what we call "philosophy" as it is to assume that no other culture could do philosophy' (1996b: 225). We can imagine that Zhuangzi himself would dismiss the importunities of modern philosophy in the way that he spurned the ponderous moralisms of Confucius, and some might hope that Daoism could be left alone to happily drag its tail in the mud rather than be called to account before the court of philosophy.

Nevertheless, our charting of Daoism's Western voyage would be incomplete without some discussion of the ways in which the ideas of that ancient tradition have begun to resonate with recent philosophical thinking. One of the most vehement opponents of the belief that Chinese thinking disqualifies itself from serious philosophical consideration is Chad Hansen. As we intimated in the last chapter, he rejects the long-entrenched belief that Chinese philosophy is based exclusively on a poetic, analogical, non-rational way of thinking, one which operates in accordance with a 'special logic' radically different from Western modes, and which even 'countenances contradiction and incoherence' (1983a: 14). This is an essentially racist view, he argues, which is often supported by such specious claims as that there are no deductive arguments in Chinese philosophy. But these sorts of claims, even if true, lead neither to inferences concerning fundamental differences in thought patterns nor to the impossibility of dialogue with Western philosophy.

For Hansen, the key to this gateway into mutual understanding lies in the central concept of *dao*. This term has been typically construed by Western interpreters in dualist terms, viewed as an ineffable and transcendent *one* that lies beyond the *many* of ordinary experience, acquiring at various times the permanence of the Parmenidean One or the mystical transcendence of the Christian Logos. According to Hansen, Chinese philosophy of the classical period starts from an implicit premise which is fundamentally different from this, and should be viewed in comparison not with traditional Western metaphysics or mysticism, but with modern linguistic philosophy. Whereas in the earlier Western philosophical tradition, thought and linguistic meaning have tended to be seen as operating on the dualist model of an inner, subjective world of 'meaning' that hopefully corresponds to events in the outer or transcendent world beyond, Chinese philosophers saw them as a set of overt dispositions, like a computer program, a 'guiding discourse' whose function is primarily the performative one of prescribing and controlling conduct rather than that of representing or explaining the world. In brief, the pre-eminent role of language is a regulative rather than a descriptive one. On this functionalist or pragmatist view, therefore, the *dao* is not an alluringly elusive object of mystical awe and contemplation, but rather is to be found in the mundane realm of functioning human discourse. There are however important differences here between Daoists and Confucians, differences that, according to Hansen, are central to classical Chinese philosophical argument. For whereas Confucians adopted a conventional theory of language-as-guidance, construing the *dao* in terms of sanctified tradition and social conformity, the Daoists spoke more of the limitations of language and of the dangers of treating too seriously conventional forms of discourse; according to Zhuangzi, 'we have many different, incommensurable guiding *daos*'. Where Confucians advocated 'a social, conventional form of discourse to guide behaviour', the Daoists believed that *dao* 'guides differently when language is different', and advised that we try to 'escape the socializing effects of language' (Hansen 1992: 268, 203, 210).

Thus, while Chinese thought differs in many important respects from traditional Western philosophy – a gulf which has fuelled doubts that traditional China has produced any real philosophy – it at least shares with contemporary Western philosophy an interest in the pragmatics of knowledge and language, in how language, mind and society interact. To that extent, traditional Chinese philosophy actually anticipated some of the important developments in twentieth century philosophy, and hence the two are to that extent commensurable. What we need to do, Hansen believes, is to stop reading Daoists as if they were Parmenidean metaphysicians, characterising *dao* as the pure unchanging being behind appearances. On his alternative interpretation Zhuangzi turns out to be, not a mystic escorting us beyond reason and behind our everyday experience, but a radical philosopher of language whose aim was to subvert the restrictive practices of conventional speech and the tyranny of established ideas and prejudices, in particular those which are ritualised and beatified by the ruling Confucians (1992: chaps 1, 6 and 8).

Precisely how does this argument relate to Western philosophical thinking? For Hansen, the primary value of Daoism in the context of contemporary thought lies in its heuristic possibilities, in its potential as an example of a different way of doing philosophy one which can function as a critical foil to certain traditional Western ways of thinking. In particular it enables us to raise the crucial question, 'what would it be like to do philosophy with a *radically different* set of assumptions?' without having recourse to fictional alternatives of the sort that philosophers delight in inventing.[4] It thus opens up the possibility of re-examining the credentials of Western philosophy, of starting over again, as it were, not from an imaginary nowhere but from 'a real place that is just very different' (1992: 2).

This strategy looks promising as a way of drawing the two traditions into some kind of dialogue by virtue of their differences rather than their fundamental identity. But in the end, the alternative Daoist model as described by Hansen turns out to be rather too familiar; suggestive difference is neutralised by assimilation into a new philosophical orthodoxy. The claim to see Daoism as a 'philosophy of language', concerned with the analysis of the conventional functions of discourse, certainly contrasts in important ways with that tradition in Western philosophy which sees its task as the establishment of foundational truths about knowledge and being. As Hansen puts it, Chinese philosophy has a 'modern ring' about it because it offers a picture of language and mind which is sceptical of traditional Western philosophical assumptions in a way which is recognisable in the context of contemporary radical thinking (1989: 119). But the assumption that language performs a primarily social pragmatic rather than an essentially denotative function, and the allied rejection of the model of knowledge as some inner process that is speculatively linked to the outer world, are both ideas that would raise few eyebrows at the present time; indeed, Hansen makes no attempt to disguise his kinship with Wittgenstein, who is a crucial figure in this context. Furthermore, the substitution of a linguistic for a metaphysical model of philosophical thinking, one which matches the 'linguistic turn' of twentieth-century anglophone philosophy, could look like simply the substitution of one form of European projection for another. As one critic argues, Hansen, with his somewhat positivistic contempt for metaphysics, undermines his own thesis to the extent that he assumes the priority of a form of rationalistic thinking, namely modern linguistic philosophy, which is pre-eminently Western. Hansen's project is thus weakened by his own 'uncritical rationalism which demands compliance with analytical standards of evidence that...are only marginal in the classical Chinese world', and in this way he 'collapses the richness of sometimes divided and conflicted voices to the monotone of one right explanation' (Ames 1994: 559).[5] There are certainly questions here too about the historical plausibility of Hansen's interpretation of classical Chinese thought, and it is arguable that in his eagerness to make Chinese philosophy accessible and acceptable to Western minds he has ignored the inescapably metaphysical implications of some early Daoist writings and their links with spiritual-religious ideals of self-development and inner purification. To put the matter another way, it may be that such attempts to assimilate Daoism to contemporary philosophy encourage us to ignore the distinctiveness, even alienness, of Daoism in relation to Western thought, in spite of Hansen's claims about 'radical differences', and moreover to smooth them out in such a way that the more subversive potential of Daoism is lost.

Several thinkers have agreed with Hansen, at least to the extent of confirming the dialectical complexity and philosophical aptitude of the classical Chinese tradition. Thus both Needham and Graham have recognised in the Chinese language a tool which, though distinctive in many respects in comparison with European languages, has both technically and historically shown itself capable of engaging in systematic and clear thinking.[6] Graham's important work *Disputers of the Tao* is especially convincing in its portrayal of the philosophical sophistication of pre-Han thinking, an epoch which is certainly comparable with the concurrent flowering of philosophical debate in Greece, and he comments that recent scholarship has concluded that 'most of the ancient Chinese thinkers are very much more rational than they used to look' (1989: 7; see also Roetz 1993).

Others, though, have moved in a different direction and have tried to locate Daoism in a place which both emphasises more radically than Hansen the differences between traditional Daoism and modern Western philosophy, while at the same time viewing this difference as subversive of and hence commensurable with the Western tradition. This sort of approach has meant emphasising rather than seeking to overlook the more poetic, metaphorical and even primitivist inclinations of Daoist language, and setting this up in contrast not only with traditional Western philosophy but also with modernist discourse in general. To understand this point, we need to look briefly at the transformation taking place within Western philosophy itself, which is often nowadays seen as being in process of profound transition, even in terminal crisis.

The supposed end of Western philosophy, its death or radical transformation announced in various ways by Nietzsche, Heidegger, Ayer, Wittgenstein, Derrida and Rorty, is now familiar enough, and, even amongst those who view reports of its imminent demise as exaggerated, speculation about a significant transformation in the nature of philosophical discourse is enjoying open season.[7] New ways of thinking about or of doing philosophy typically challenge the standard hierarchy which places philosophy in a superior category in relation to other genres such as literature, and subverts its established role as a foundational discipline, a master narrative which defines and legitimises the boundaries of knowledge in its various forms through methodological and theoretical objectivity. And even in quarters where talk of the 'death' of philosophy is rejected, there is increasing recognition of the need to take more serious account of the roles of interpretation, historicity and differing cultural, ethnic and gender perspectives in the philosophical enterprise. Assumptions about the possibility of certainty based on universally agreed premises, buttressed by a privileging of Western knowledge over Asian and other alternatives, have been subject to increasingly intense questioning. According to Richard Rorty, one of the more radical propagandists for this transformation and a prophet of 'postphilosophy', the new philosophical style is one of conversing rather than convincing, its aim is to edify rather than to act as a mirror of nature or to systematise human experience, and its role is 'to help [the] reader, or society as a whole, break free from outworn vocabularies and attitudes, rather than to provide "grounding" for the intuitions and customs of the present' (1980: 12).[8] By contrast with systematic philosophers such as Plato, Descartes and Russell, who are 'constructive and offer arguments', edifying philosophers 'are reactive and offer satire, parodies, aphorisms' (1980: 369). This has meant an important transformation in Rorty's own way of doing philosophy, which has become 'much less dialectical than before, more explicitly narrativist; he argues now by telling a story' (Hall 1994: 9). The most recent impulse behind these developments has come from new fields such as neopragmatism, deconstruction, hermeneutics, feminist, and environmental philosophy, a list to which we should add orientalism as yet another critical perspective that stands beyond earlier Enlightenment-inscribed boundaries. Daoism is clearly in the frame here, and, following the links we have already noted with anarchist, feminist, and environmental thinking, we should not be surprised to learn that connections have been made with Daoism and that several of Rorty's 'edifying' philosophers have been associated in one way or another with this ancient oriental mode of thought.[9]

Heidegger is a particularly crucial link in this East–West chain, and we will need to gain some understanding of his associations with Daoist thinking in order to bring into focus an alternative strategy to the one envisaged by Hansen. Though Heidegger makes very few references to Asian thought in his published writings, it has now become clear that he was familiar with Daoism through early translations of the *Daodejing* and the *Zhuangzi*, and that he felt a close affinity with its philosophy right from the time when he was writing his most influential work, *Being and Time*, in the 1920s (May 1996; Parkes 1987). In many ways, his thinking is quintessentially European and represents a long series of meditations on Western thought and culture, but this well-established perception may now need to be placed in a wider context. His reflections on the globalising *telos* of European language and thought, and remarks such as 'we Europeans presumably inhabit a quite different house from East Asians', must be set alongside comments concerning 'our inevitable dialogue with the East Asian world' (Heidegger 1971: 5). But above all, they must be reconsidered in the light of the now inescapable fact that he drew inspiration for some of his major ideas from the East, namely from Daoist and Zen Buddhist classics. It now seems that Heidegger's work not only shows a 'deeply hidden kinship' with Daoism, but was actually 'influenced by East Asian sources to a hitherto unrecognized extent' (May 1996: 51–3), a fact which, along with its hitherto concealment, has led Graham Parkes to speculate that 'a chapter in the history of modern Western ideas may have to be rewritten' (May 1996: x).[10]

What was it about Heidegger's thinking that made such a 'hidden kinship' with Daoism possible? Certainly a number of well-known Heideggerian notions and perspectives, from both early and later periods, have a distinctly Daoist flavour: the return to the buried ground of thinking beneath the sediments of rationalising metaphysics; the sense of our ontological integration in nature as encapsulated in the idea of *Dasein* and of being-in-the-world; the overcoming of dualistic thinking; the view that *Dasein* is not a fixed entity but is always underway yet without a predetermined goal; the affirmation of the 'worldliness' of things; a non-manipulative attitude towards the world and a sense of 'releasement' or 'letting be' (*Gelassenheit*) towards entities; a way of thinking which emphasises openness to Being rather than rational judgement; a realisation of the fundamental role of care and concern in our relationship with Being; and the repeated associations between thinking and poetising. Inevitably there are divergences as well, for in spite of a shared concern with the cultivation of a way of being-in-the-world which could be summarised with the word 'authenticity', there is in Daoism no sense of the revealing of human freedom in the face of death, nor any awareness of being 'thrown' into the world. Nevertheless, there are points of convergence which go to the very heart of both ways of thought. Significantly the fate of Being is curiously reminiscent in some respects of the fate of *dao*, for while in Heidegger's thinking the history of Being begins with its 'fall' in the speculations of Platonic metaphysics, for Daoists the history of *dao* begins with its decline with the emergence of language and the social practices of civilisation.

Heidegger was indeed particularly drawn to the concept of the *dao*, and in his book *On the Way to Language*, he spoke of *dao* as not just 'the key word in the poetic thinking of Laotse', but as 'the way that gives all ways, the very source of our power to think...Perhaps the mystery of mysteries of thoughtful Saying conceals itself in the word "way", *Tao*' (1971: 92).[11] As Reinhard May points out in his detailed study of Heidegger's affinities with Daoism, the concept of way (*Weg*) was central in his thinking, and he offers some telling suggestions as to how Heidegger's use of this term carries coded Daoist affinities, for example in his connection between 'way' and 'saying' which is precisely parallel with a similar connection in the use of *dao* in the *Daodejing* (1996: 35–43). An interesting reflection on this is to be found in Heidegger's work entitled *Holzwege* (Woodpaths), where the idea of a path cut by woodcutters through a forest, a path which does not lead anywhere but is merely a by-product of the woodcutter's activity, indicates the way in which human thinking can be envisaged as a kind of questioning whose outcome cannot be determined in advance and which has no specifiable goal

(Stambaugh 1987: 80); in the words of the *Zhuangzi*, 'The Way comes about as we walk it'. It is a path which provides no universal, prescriptive way for others to follow, and hence, to quote the *Zhuangzi* again, 'The greatest Way is not cited as an authority, the greatest discrimination is unspoken' (Graham 1981: 53, 57).

Heidegger's concern with the *dao* as a way of rethinking Being gave rise to a significant, though not widely known, episode in his career. In 1946, at a time when his professional and personal life were in crisis, he embarked on a project to translate the *Daodejing* into German. He had the help of a Chinese scholar, Paul Shih-yi Hsiao, and though in spite of prolonged effort he succeeded in completing only a small portion of the text, it clearly had a transformative influence on him. According to his student Otto Pöggeler, it enabled him 'to confront the beginnings of Western thinking with the beginnings of one of the great East Asian traditions', an experience which 'transformed Heidegger's language in a critical situation and gave his thinking a new orientation'. It was, insists Pöggeler, 'an important step on the way along which his thinking was proceeding', a path which guided him in his turning away from the philosophical thinking of *Being and Time* towards a more primordial form of thinking associated with art and poetry (1987: 52, 65). Paul Shih-yi Hsiao also confirms that the experience of translating the *Daodejing* 'exercised a significant influence on Heidegger', and according to Parkes, too, it 'exerted a decisive effect on the form and direction of his later thinking' (Hsiao 1987: 98; Parkes 1987: 8).[12]

One of the crucial components of this later thinking was Heidegger's ambition to subvert the Western metaphysical or logocentric tradition and to challenge the domination of the sort of calculative thinking which first arose with the metaphysical philosophy of Plato, a tradition which has more recently become associated with the rise of scientific and technological rationalism. His proposal to rethink Being involved nothing less than an 'overcoming' of two thousand years of Western metaphysics and, according to Pöggeler, by shifting from an analytical to a meditative mode of thinking it opened up a pathway which 'made possible a new encounter between Eastern and Western thought' (1987: 48).[13] As we have seen, there is strong evidence that a major impetus for this 'new beginning' (as he himself called it), and for 'the trajectory of a path of thinking that is to lead be-yond...Western metaphysics' came from Asian sources (May 1996: x).

It is indeed questionable whether Laozi, like Heraclitus, was anything more than a construct with which to elaborate his own position (Pöggeler 1987: 66), and his public silence on his debt to Daoism may simply be a recognition that a true dialogue between East and West is not possible in a world still subject to what he described as 'the complete Europeanization of the Earth and of Man' (Heidegger 1971: 15). It may also be true that, as possibly was the case with Leibniz, his encounter with Daoism was more confirmative than seminal, and that the parallels found by May are more coincidental than causal.

Nevertheless, in the light of Heidegger's 'new beginning' and his gesturing beyond traditional Western philosophy with its Platonic pedigree towards a more poetic mode of thinking, we can discern another way, different from Hansen's, in which Daoism can be brought into dialogue with Western thought without obliterating its radical difference. From this alternative perspective Daoism might appear, not as some esoteric oddity deviating wildly from universal norms of rationality, an example perhaps of China's supposed inability to think philosophically, but rather as an alternative way of thinking and knowing which is both well-founded and effective in its own terms, and at the same time is able to provide an important challenge to traditional Western attitudes towards knowledge in general and philosophy in particular. It may represent a way, not so much of denial of the possibility of philosophical knowledge as such, but rather of letting go of a traditional Western way of thinking in order to reveal an altogether different mode. This is underlined by the way in which the crisis in Western philosophy, to which Heidegger's thinking has significantly contributed, has signalled amongst other things a move towards a more *praxis*-oriented approach to philosophy. Heidegger's own thinking was strongly motivated by a desire to place philosophy back into the stream of life rather than to perpetuate its role as a detached seeker of objective, foundational truth. So too is the neo-pragmatism of Rorty, who was deeply influenced by Heidegger and for whom philosophy came to be seen as grounded in social practice, in communication and conversation, rather than in the search for foundational truths and objectively warrantable methods. As Bernstein puts it, this has meant 'turning away from the obsession to "get things right" and turning our attention to coping with the contingencies of human life' (1983: 203). What becomes important here, then, is not that Daoist philosophy constructs the world differently from its Western counterparts – for example, in terms of evanescent process rather than of eternal substance – but rather that it represents an alternative way of doing philosophy, one that is 'self-transformative' and 'orientative' rather than truth-seeking or certainty-seeking (Lao 1989: 277, 290–1).

## Scepticism, relativism and irrationalism

This sort of challenge to philosophy as a foundational, truth-seeking discipline leads inevitably to the question of scepticism and relativism. For if philosophy can no longer legitimise the rational quest for knowledge but is concerned solely with self-transformation, or free-floating conversation or poetic thinking, or simply 'coping with the contingencies of human life', then truth has no champion and 'anything goes'. And if a number of competing or alternative philosophical traditions appear equally legitimate, and there are no available means of reducing their differences to singularity, then we may be led to conclude that none has any final command on our allegiance. 'Scepticism' and 'relativism', though closely related, are indeed not equivalent terms and there are various versions of each in the philosophical literature, but it will be useful for the sake of the present discussion to take scepticism to mean rejection of or doubt about the possibility of attaining truth about the world or about values, and relativism to mean that in the absence of the possibility of objective truth, all knowledge is perspectival and depends on the point of view of the individual or the group. 'Anti-rationalist', a term used frequently in this context, can be taken for present purposes to be close in meaning to 'scepticism' in that it denotes the playing down or denial of the validity, and even the usefulness, of standard canons of rationality and logic. All these terms have been applied at one time or another in relation to Daoist thought, and in this section we will consider how they have entered into Western philosophical encounters with Daoism.

Let us start with relativism. As an issue this has been a factor – albeit often only implicit – in European orientalism as far back as the Enlightenment period when ideas from the East were seized upon as a rival to orthodoxy, and a newly self-confident Europe found itself confronted with civilisations in the East which, while fundamentally different in certain cultural respects, appeared to be as advanced and as sophisticated as Europe. Indeed the point can be generalised, for the issue of relativism is largely unavoidable in any inquiry into the thought and language of other cultures, and as Zhang Longxi notes, the issue of relativism has become a major factor in contemporary Asian studies, sometimes even putting into question the very possibility of cross-cultural understanding (1998: 8–9).[14] Facing up to a plurality of world-views, in particular ones which in spite of their historical and cultural remoteness seem plausible and attractive to a growing number of people, represents an inevitable challenge to the sturdy confidence in the exclusive veracity of one's own indigenous belief systems. The very rationalism which was so characteristic of the Enlightenment period, an instrument which promised to sweep away all ancient superstitions and to establish universal norms of right thinking, helped to create a climate in which Asian traditions could not only become objects of scholarly investigation but also help to create an intellectual counterpoint which would eventually be used to challenge the authority of Enlightenment rationality itself. This epistemological 'threat' from the East has hovered on the borders of Western consciousness for several centuries, one response being its relegation to the status of the primitive or the pre-rational. Nevertheless, the greatly augmented level of interaction in recent years between Western and Asian cultures has helped to pose an increasingly powerful challenge to Enlightenment views about the universality of its underlying assumptions. Current philosophical concerns about incommensurability, pluralism, realism, representation, and the universality of truth-claims are in effect only the late manifestations of a long history of a mood of intellectual insecurity, arising in part from confrontation with a variety of alternative perspectives from both within and beyond Europe's borders. Orientalist concerns have recently entered these debates from several directions, for example from Christian theology which has had to face up to the issue of the uniqueness and exclusiveness of its own doctrinal assumptions (Swidler *et al.* 1990), and in the field of philosophy where the issue of relativism has been the subject of renewed interest of late, and where Eastern paradigms have often taken over from the 'primitive societies' of an earlier generation of philosophers as exemplars of alternative rationalities or value systems (Winch 1970; MacIntyre 1991).

It is hardly surprising that Daoism has been drawn into contemporary debates on such issues. The label of 'relativist' has frequently been attached to Daoism, and its philosophical teachings have standardly been portrayed as representing a radically anti-rational or logophobic, even irrationalist, point of view, by contrast not only with Western philosophy but also with Confucianism. There is in Daoism, so it is argued, a pervasive relativistic outlook which emphasises the irreducible multiplicity of perspectives with regard to both language and values. It has become commonplace to point to the *Daodejing* as supporting a relativist position, in particular concerning the possibility of saying anything fixed and unvarying about the true nature of *dao*. Max Kaltenmark writes that according to this classic work, 'our language cannot express anything other than relative truths', and Mark Berkson maintains that the text 'advocates abandoning language altogether and returning to the ancient practice of knotting rope in order to communicate' (Kaltenmark 1969: 35; Berkson 1996: 102).

It is the *Zhuangzi*, however, which is most commonly identified with a relativistic outlook and which has given rise to the most extensive commentary in this connection. Though often viewed as a work of entertaining fables and allegories, this classic text is now being treated more and more as a work of philosophical importance, its literary qualities inseparable from its serious message. In a number of passages, Zhuangzi appears to be asserting the arbitrariness of judgements and the relativity of the distinctions we make by means of language. For example:

> What is It is also Other, what is Other is also It. There they say 'That's it, that's not' from one point of view, here we say 'That's it, that's not' from another point of view. Are they really It and Other?

Saying is not blowing breath, saying says something; the only trouble is that what it says is never fixed. Do we really say something? Or have we never said anything? If you think it different from the twitter of birds, is there proof of the distinction?

(Graham 1981: 53, 52)

An increasing number of studies in recent years has read passages such as these as a powerful challenge to our ability to interpret the world correctly or to make assured value judgements about it. Peerenboom, to take but one example, argues that the relativist/perspectivist implications of this work represent an attack on all foundational epistemologies which claim to be able to discover objective truth, and that from the *Zhuangzi*'s point of view there is no escape from any given perspective in order to verify one's theories or beliefs, no access to any transcendent realm of values with which to underpin one's actions (1993: 200–3).[15] In epistemological terms, this means that Zhuangzi's approach 'manifests a powerful incapacity to understand, a nurtured inability to understand what seems so evidently true to most people', and continually questions 'cherished beliefs about the seemingly obvious', such as the distinction between waking and dreaming and between knowledge and ignorance (Yearley 1996: 157). In linguistic terms, it implies that there are no ultimate or permanent means for validating the discriminations and categorisations we make in language, for there is no perspective-free way of carrying out such tasks, no independent or trans-historical standpoint from which to judge. Where dispute occurs there can be no final resolution since 'words mean what the debaters choose to make them mean', and their points of view are in effect incommensurable in the sense that there is no independent, objective or transcendent viewpoint from which to judge the relative merits of different uses of language (Graham 1983: 5).[16]

What is being claimed, then, is that at the heart of the *Zhuangzi* there is a form of epistemological pluralism, the belief that there are many possible perspectives on the world, that there is no rational means of discriminating between these perspectives, and hence that there is no way of identifying the one correct way of conceptualising reality. Human conventions are historically contingent in a radical sense; they differ from one place and person to another, and offer no way of reconciling their differences. Thus Zhuangzi's scepticism 'arises from the fact that many different discourses are possible and that what is good inside one discourse, from one perspective, may be bad inside another discourse, from another perspective' (Yearley 1983: 126). Furthermore, the linguistic process of discriminating and conceptualising is itself seen as in some way inadequate and even degenerate. It is not just that there are many possible linguistic distinctions or categorisations that can be made, but that this process in itself represents a regrettable departure from the ultimately unnameable *dao*, a kind of

Heideggerian 'fall' from an original condition in which it was not necessary or desirable to make or worry about such distinctions. This pluralist viewpoint is itself supported, appropriately enough in Zhuangzi's case, not by systematic argument but by what can best be described as a rhetorical method, by the deployment of a variety of styles, voices and expressive devices, by a pot-pourri of vivid stories, anecdotes and colourful aphorisms, as well as by the use of wit, irony and paradox, techniques which jolt rather than argue us out of our ingrained preconceptions and convictions. Here are some examples: 'When the human sleeps in the damp, his waist hurts, and he gets stiff in the joints. Is that so of the loach?'; 'Nothing in the world is bigger than the tip of an autumn hair, and Mount T'ai is small'. Perhaps the most famous, though, is the butterfly dream, quoted on page 1, in which Zhuangzi dreamed he was a butterfly, and when he awoke he could not be sure 'whether he is Chou [Zhuangzi] who dreams he is a butterfly or a butterfly who dreams he is Chou' (Graham 1981: 58, 56, 61).[17]

The seemingly capricious prolixity of this kind of writing, along with its fragmentariness, has as we noted earlier inevitably given rise to a plurality of interpretations of Zhuangzi by modern Western scholars and to differing opinions as to the extent of his supposed anti-rationalism, scepticism or relativism. The very method adopted, like that of Nietzsche in a later age, is calculated – if that is not too contrived a notion – to subvert our more conventional hermeneutical strategies. There are those like Graham who speak of Zhuangzi's 'uncompromising moral relativism', and portray him as the 'great anti-rationalist' who rejects logic, despises disputation and 'derides all claims that reason can give us certainty', or Hansen, who sees in the *Zhuangzi* 'a skeptical, relativistic reaction to the philosophy of the Neo-Mohists', and a belief that 'all ways are equally valid – none has any special status or warrant from the point of view of the universe' (Graham 1981: 4, 9, 11; Hansen 1983b: 27, 35; see also Graham 1989: 176–83). Robert Allinson, in an attempt to sort out the various interpretations of the *Zhuangzi*, calls this view 'hard relativism', a category which embraces Creel and Kohn as well as Graham and Hansen (1989a: 112). On the other hand, there are those for whom Zhuangzi is not strictly a relativist, or at least only a 'soft' one. Thinkers like David Wong, for example, argue that Zhuangzi is indeed a relativist with regard to language in that he encourages us to be sceptical about the universal validity of conventional linguistic distinctions, but at the same time Wong sees him as expounding a distinctive moral wisdom which founds the virtues of compassion and toleration precisely on a relativistic foundation (1984). And then there are those who deny that he is a relativist altogether. Amongst these are Allinson himself, who sees Zhuangzi's relativistic statements as being of only a provisional nature, the means towards the further and more important non-relativistic goal of self-transformation. For Allinson, Zhuangzi's aim is to disengage the conceptual or analytical functions of the mind, not as a purely epistemological ploy but in order to encourage the development of the more intuitive functions of the mind. In a similar vein, Philip Ivanhoe rejects the view that for Zhuangzi all ethical claims are equally valid, and interprets him instead as offering a 'pluralistic ethic of self-flourishing', and Peerenboom, while allowing that Zhuangzi is a 'fallibilist', denies that his perspectivism commits him to an 'anything-goes relativism' (Ivanhoe 1996b: 211; Peerenboom 1993: 202–3, 212; see also Ivanhoe 1993b).[18]

The importance of these differences and distinctions, leaving aside the aspiration simply to understand Zhuangzi, is that they reflect much of the current anxiety about relativism and the complexities of the arguments surrounding it, while at the same time establishing a standpoint beyond the Western tradition. In the first place, there is the perennial issue of the supposedly self-refuting implication of the relativist position. As Russell Goodman, amongst others, points out, there is in Zhuangzi a pervasive difficulty in reconciling 'his lively interest in the world's operations with his mocking and skeptical flights' (1985: 231–2). How can Zhuangzi sweep away all standards of rational discourse, yet advocate the desirability of certain forms of behaviour, without impaling himself on the horns of self-contradiction? Considerable ingenuity has been deployed in recent years to extract Zhuangzi from this dilemma, and while the details of this should not detain us here, we need to indicate some of the ways in which this interest has contributed to the wider contemporary debate on relativism.

One of the ways in which this contribution can be observed concerns the manner in which Zhuangzi's scepticism has been seen to be *different* in certain crucial respects from its Western counterparts. It is true, as Paul Kjellberg points out, that the ancient Graeco-Roman scepticism of Pyrrho and Sextus Empiricus bears some striking similarities to the arguments of Zhuangzi, for both exploit the diversity of opinions in order to call into question the reliability of our claims to knowledge. Others have seen a connection with the Pyrrhonist idea of *ataraxia*, namely, peace of mind attained through the suspension of judgement, and have used similarities between Zhuangzi and ancient Greek philosophy to argue against the long-standing tendency to mark out sharp differences between the two traditions (Kjellberg 1996: 9; Nivison 1991: 136; Raphals 1996).[19] But differences emerge again when consideration is given to the fundamental impulses behind the two traditions. Where in the case of Greek philosophy in general, and the school of Sceptics in particular, we find a radical distinction between reality and appearance and doubts about the possibility of transcending the limitations of the latter, in Daoism the sceptical arguments, though making use of uncertainties about the representational proficiency of language, are concerned more with the question of how to live skilfully and naturally.[20] There is certainly in the latter no outright rejection of sense perception such as that notoriously advocated by Parmenides, nor any strong inclination towards solipsism or the notion that the world might be an illusion. This may well point to a fundamental divergence of assumptions about the nature of knowledge itself, for, as Lee Yearly points out, where Western epistemologies have tended to see knowledge in terms of the representation of reality, the matching of thought with object, for the Chinese classical thinkers 'to know is to follow out a learned system of meaning and evaluating, to be guided by a learned process of construing that we are taught when we learn a language' (1983: 126). The contrast is also sharply drawn by Hansen who, as we saw above, contrasts the Western philosophical tradition's concentration on truth, knowledge and common meaning with the concern of classical Chinese philosophers with a pragmatic rather than a semantic model of knowledge, and concludes that the critical thrust of Daoist scepticism is not directed against the idea of an external world which, tragically, we cannot reach, but against the notion that the social conventions and prescriptions embodied in language have universal validity; in brief, it is a linguistic rather than an epistemological scepticism (1981, 1989).[21]

This in turn may point to another important difference in what, in William James's phrase, might be called the 'metaphysical pathos' of scepticism. Though for the Pyrrhonists the sceptical attitude was expected to lead not to anguished disenchantment but to tranquil peace of mind, the historic career of these teachings in the West has evinced a more tragic demeanour. From the sixteenth century, when the rediscovery and redeployment of Pyrrhonist arguments helped to beget what the philosopher Richard Bernstein has called the 'Cartesian anxiety', namely the fear that the security of certainty in knowledge is unattainable, scepticism has been viewed as a serious threat, not only to orthodox belief but even to the very moral fabric of civilisation (Bernstein 1983: 16–25). Few philosophers since Descartes have managed to free themselves from the urgent demand of the question how to establish knowledge on a firm foundation, or have been able to avoid the fear that without the assurance of such a foundation there are no rational constraints to what we believe or how we act. Hume despaired of solving the problem and escaped into the distractions of the games saloon. Kant sought to refute Hume's scepticism, but only at the cost of drastically reducing reason's scope. And the best that Bertrand Russell could offer in the middle years of the twentieth century in the face of the tragic collapse of epistemic certitude was a teeth-gritting stoicism.

A significant exception to the rule is of course Nietzsche, for whom the advent of scepticism and nihilism held out the possibility of the reign of free spirits who would be liberated from the thrall of traditional notions of good and evil, though even he was daunted by the prospect of an epoch of dizzying uncertainty and disquieting loss of moral anchorage. The recent preoccupation with sceptical and relativist ideas, whether in philosophical or in wider circles, has triggered a similar kind of anxiety, giving rise to 'an uneasiness that has spread throughout intellectual and cultural life', and which Henry Rosemont laments as 'a rather frightful state of affairs', a harbinger of a new Babel which threatens to render intercultural studies futile (Bernstein 1983: 1; Rosemont 1996: 155). The sense that even our most cherished beliefs and values are only contingent, historically determined linguistic customs, and that there is no intelligible order behind the flux of ever-changing appearances, tends to cause deep anxiety in a culture which has been founded and nurtured on the ideals of Truth, Objectivity and Certainty. The contemporary vocabulary with which this scepticism is expressed is often dark and foreboding, with talk of the 'death' or the 'end' of reassuring traditions and beliefs whipped along by tropes of 'fragmentation' and 'disruption' of familiar conceptual landmarks, all of which helps to reinforce a sense of disillusionment and pessimism that, in many people's minds, has become a characteristic mark of our postmodern age.

In this context, it has come as something of a revelation to experience Daoist relativism in a completely different way, not as a denial of some life-enhancing gift, but as a blessed relief and as a way to enlightenment. Indeed, as Zhang Longxi points out, in the Chinese intellectual tradition as a whole, where in his view there is a greater open-minded acceptance of different readings and interpretations than in the West, 'relativism does not seem to be the bugbear that every [Western] critic holds in absolute abhorrence' (1992: 196–7). More positive in intent than the Pyrrhonists' *ataraxia*, and more optimistic in vision than most modern Western sceptics, Zhuangzi's relativism appears to many commentators as a teaching which, far from being angst-ridden, offers therapy and liberation; in Zhuangzi's own cryptic comment, 'Why be bothered by doubts?' (Graham 1981: 63), and in the *Daodejing* the loss of the ability to know is not to be dreaded, for if learning is banished 'there will no longer be worries' (ch. 20). By contrast with the standard perception of scepticism within Western thought, Zhuangzi is seen as moving on from the negative position of denying the capacity of thought or language to represent reality objectively to the more positive goal of living naturally and spontaneously in the world. Graham is only one of a number of critics who, while espousing a relativist and even an anti-rationalist interpretation of Zhuangzi's thinking, discovers in his writings no sense of angst or perturbation, no 'vertigo of doubt', as he puts it, but rather a sense of joy and release by loosening the grip of mental habits and obsessions (1983: 7; 1989: 235). A similar view is offered by Schipper, who sees the 'relativity of all established ideas and judgements of value', in the *Daodejing* as much as in the *Zhuangzi*, as 'the first step in the search for freedom', and by Hansen, who contrasts the existentialist fear of the abyss of nothingness that yawns beneath our feet with Zhuangzi's blissful 'floating free' of the constraints of traditional authority (Schipper 1993: 201; Hansen 1992: 285; see also Cheng 1977). Some have compared this Daoist approach favourably with what is perceived as the nihilism of much contemporary thought of a postmodern hue. Berkson, for example, compares Derrida's strategy, which he sees as lacking in any soteriological intent and which 'leaves us playing in a sea of signifiers', with that of Zhuangzi, who offers us 'therapy for better living' and whose aim is to 'undermine rational modes of thought in order to allow one to reach a state of *skillful* living' (1996: 120–2). Berkson may have exaggerated the negative quality of Derrida's writings, which often have a political thrust and display an emancipatory and liberating intent. Nevertheless, the disintegration in recent years of so much that has seemed reassuringly stable does not appear to most commentators as a joyful release, and the postmodern world is one which creates in most people's minds an atmosphere of spiritual vacuity and aimlessness.

On this sort of interpretation, Zhuangzi's butterfly dream is far from being a purely theoretical exercise in scepticism concerning the validity of human experience in a manner familiar to historians of Western philosophy. No doubt it is almost inevitable that Western interpreters should view it in the light of Descartes' famous dream argument, even as dallying with solipsism, but Zhuangzi's dream can be seen as part of a quite different agenda, clearly intended to open up the way towards a happy awakening from delusory fixations rather than towards a confirmation of troubled doubts about our knowledge of external reality; in Wu Kuang-ming's words it represents an insight, a form of knowledge, which 'releases the dreamer (ourselves) from the tyranny of obsession with objective realism', or indeed from worrying whether we are dreaming or awake (1986: 379). Descartes, of course, aimed at liberating us from the anxieties of epistemic uncertainty by solving the problem posed by his original doubt, but in the case of Zhuangzi the problem is not so much solved as *dis*solved: we are cured rather than convinced.[22]

The reader will have noticed already that the language of therapy is often used in this context, and Zhuangzi's method of curing us of obsessive attachment to linguistic conventions has almost inevitably been compared with Wittgenstein's view of philosophy as a method of release from the 'mental cramp' induced by a misguided view of language; Wittgenstein's notorious contempt for academic philosophy and philosophical theorising, and his aim 'to show the fly the way out of the fly bottle', certainly displays something of the spirit of Zhuangzi, and reminds us of the latter's remark that 'You can't discuss the Way with a cramped scholar – he's shackled by his doctrines' (Watson 1968: 97).[23] To conclude, then, according to this interpretation Zhuangzi's scepticism is not theoretical but therapeutic, and shares with Wittgenstein the aim of 'searching for something which may be described as peace, freedom, contentment, and acceptance' (Goodman 1976: 152).[24] The objective of this way of thinking is not to establish an invulnerable philosophical position in the traditional Western sense, but to bring about a change of attitude and sensibility, 'a therapy to free us from the confines of our cramped and narrow perspective', and to engender 'a kind of open-mindedness that consists in putting less faith than is standard in one's own and others' beliefs' (Ivanhoe 1996b: 210; Schwitzgebel 1996: 91; see also Burneko 1986).

## Postmodernism

The difference that makes a difference here, and which makes an East–West perspective on the debate concerning scepticism and relativism rewarding for us, is that Daoism seems to be taking its departure from a different set of assumptions from those that have traditionally been foundational to Western philosophical discourse, perhaps in a more radical sense than that envisaged by Hansen. What has begun to emerge in the previous sections is that Zhuangzi's view of knowledge differs in important respects from the Western tradition. The outcome of a number of recent studies suggests that he is not rejecting knowledge as such and hence falling into a self-refuting relativism, but rather he is calling into question the kind of knowledge that aspires to an objectively and impersonally accurate representation of the world, and thereby opening up a space for a different approach to knowledge, seeing it as more a kind of skill or knack, one which is acquired naturally or intuitively rather than through the exercise of analytical reason. It is more a matter of 'knowing how' than 'knowing that', to use Ryle's distinction, or in Lisa Raphals's terminology, it is a distinctive form of 'metic intelligence', the kind of practical knowledge with which she claims the Chinese intellectual tradition is primarily concerned, an approach which she compares with the key Buddhist notion of 'skillful means' (*upāya*) (1992).[25] In similar vein, Graham notes that the crucial question for classical Chinese philosophers 'is not the Western philosopher's "What is the truth?" but "Where is the Way"' (1989: 3).[26]

This is not necessarily to deny the role of theoretical or representational knowledge in the Chinese context, nor to make some totalising claim about the essentially practical nature of the Chinese mind, but to underline its typically secondary role in relation to practical knowledge. As Robert Eno puts it, Zhuangzi 'identifies two types of knowing – practical or skill knowing and theoretical or fact knowing', and goes on to argue that he 'celebrates practical knowing, which he associates with the Dao and with learned skills of actions, but asserts that its value and power are, in principle, vitiated by the development of theoretical knowledge' (1996: 127).[27] It is pointed out that, however many examples he offers of the inadequacy of language to mirror nature, he offers an equal number of illustrations of the way in which we – and animals – are able to acquire knowledge of how to operate successfully and intelligently in the world. In illustrating this point, many commentators draw attention to Zhuangzi's tale of a certain cook, Ding, whose skill in carving an ox carcass derives, not from theoretical knowledge about the animal's anatomy, but from a kind of unspecifiable know-how which is unteachable in linguistic terms (Graham 1981: ch. 3). Such anecdotes remind us 'of the limitations of the language [Taoists] use to guide us towards [an] altered perspective on the world and [the] knack of living' (Graham 1989: 199). On this view, the self-confessed scepticism of both the *Daodejing* and the *Zhuangzi* concerning the possibility of communicating the *dao*, or indeed anything at all, often the butt of ridicule as much in ancient China as in the modern West, points not so much to the failure of language as to the failure of a perennially seductive *theory* of language to account for Cook Ding's skill. In much the same way, for Wittgenstein the problem lies not with the ordinary use of language but with the theories that philosophers have constructed thereon.

This alternative, pragmatic epistemology, as we might call it, can be compared with certain trends within contemporary postmodern thinking. Like the latter, it calls into question the apparent coherence and self-consistency of certain types of familiar discursive practices, and, through a combination of paradox and irony, forces us to place philosophical thinking back into the stream of life out of which it has been lifted, preferring the life-world of *praxis* to the Platonic abstractions of *theoria*. And like Daoism, it has often been accused of undermining our ideas of rationality and truth, and even of civilised life itself. Postmodernism, as in the case of the relativism with which it is often associated, is of course a contested term, and indeed one might say that contention is at its heart, for in its mistrustful embrace we find ourselves preferring questioning to answering, enjoying perpetual conceptual motion rather than secure anchorage in timeless truths, and even promoting chaos over order. In its more widely promoted usage – an overly-grand narration for some tastes – this term is usually taken to indicate such things as a lack of sympathy for grounding, universalising, totalising, and essentialising, preferring in their stead a fragmented and unterminable type of thinking, a philosophising in terms of transient becoming rather than of permanent being, and – from our point of view most significantly – a partiality for the language of plurality, difference and otherness. It is usually seen as a reaction against the Enlightenment project, against logocentrism and against the hypostatisation of the self as an originating centre of rational thought and action, a strategy which holds out the promise of release from all kinds of linguistic imbroglios and their accompanying political entrapments.[28]

Much of this undoubtedly has a Daoist flavour to it, and in spite of the wide cultural and historical chasm that separates Daoism and postmodern-ism, recent years have witnessed a number of efforts to draw Daoism into postmodernist discourse and even to postulate some sort of underlying affinity between them, in particular with Jacques Derrida, whose decon-struction is often seen as a key strategy within postmodern discourse. Thus according to the Chinese philosopher Chi-hui Chien, 'Between Jacques

185

Derrida...and Chuang Tzu...there exist striking affinities', and even more bluntly, Michelle Yeh affirms that, 'Chuang Tzu and Derrida make essentially the same statement'. David Hall goes so far as to suggest that Chinese classical thought *tout court* 'is in a very real sense postmodern', seeing in Daoism itself a radical perspectivism that is grounded in the notions of particularity, difference and chaos (Chien 1990: 32; Yeh 1983: 116; Hall 1991: 59, 62).[29]

This alliance is not seen just in terms of Daoism's well-known preference for disturbing paradox or in its penchant for roguish wordplay, though in this regard there are indeed some interesting stylistic affinities between Zhuangzi and Derrida, for in both cases there is a teasing play of different voices and an unsettling spirit of fracture and incompleteness. Nor is it merely a matter of the refreshingly anti-conventional and anti-traditional characteristics that people have found in both Daoism and Derrida. Beyond these factors, some critics are beginning to see Daoism in the revealing light afforded by such notions as anti-foundationalism, difference, and decentering, and in the minds of a number of contemporary thinkers it is being explicitly associated with issues surrounding such notions as incommensurability, perspectivism, pluralism, and pragmatism. Burneko, for example, notes the appositeness of the playful style of the *Zhuangzi* to postmodern experience, and reads it 'as a caveat concerning any and all cognitive attempts at reality formation' (1986: 393–4). And to quote Chien again, 'Chuang Tzu's ironic style is just as deconstructive as that of Derrida, exposing blind spots in a supposedly unified structure, and then showing its self-transgression and undecidability' (1990: 32).

The central issue here is obviously the question of language. Right from the opening lines of the *Daodejing* – 'The way that can be told is not the constant way' – there can be found a series of assaults on the traditional fortress of language as a possible bearer of unambiguous and literal meaning, as a true mirroring of the world, and along with this a series of tropes and figurations whose aim seems to be to destabilise the structures of convention and of standard communication. This assault is evident in the *Zhuangzi* as well, where words are seen as having no permanent or definitive referential status but perform their functions in ever-shifting contexts: 'What is It is also Other, what is Other is also It...The Way has never had borders, saying has never had norms. It is by a "That's it" which deems that a boundary is marked' (Graham 1981: 53–7).

The crucial term here is Derrida's *différance*, a neologism which conflates the ideas of 'difference' and 'deferring'. By contrast with the 'philosophy of presence', which according to Derrida has characterised Western metaphysics since Plato and which implies an essential congruence between language and reality whereby reality is directly given to the subject, *différance* points to the indefinite differing and deferring of meaning that typifies all thought and speech. It is a 'decentering' which rejects the idea that a sign can refer to an absolute self-identifying reality such as 'God' or 'substance' or 'self', concepts which have been central to Western metaphysics. According to Chung-ying Cheng, classical Daoist thinking, with its emphasis on change and transformation, stands alongside Derridean deconstruction in contrast to Western metaphysics, and passes beyond the Parmenidean and Platonic insistence on the quest for Being as the permanent object of philosophical inquiry and hence its inability to think non-being – that which is never present (1989: 203–4).[30] As Hall observes, the truth of Daoism represents a 'mildly ironic send-up' of Parmenides' famous maxim that only Being is, not-being is not; for the ever-transmuting *dao*, which eludes our attempts to constitute it as a stable presence or as transcendental signified, stands in marked contrast to the eternal permanence of Parmenidean Being. It is this sort of reflection which has led a number of critics to identify the central Daoist notion of *wu-wei* with Derridean *différance*, and to see the idea of *wu-wei* as marking out the possibilities of openness and self-transformation that are implied in Derridean thinking (Owens 1993). On this view, the paradoxical process of saying in language what cannot be said, evident notoriously in the *Daodejing*, is not sheer mystical mischief-making, nor just a matter of linguistic idiosyncrasy, but in Derrida's terms is the corollary of *différance*, the inevitable consequence of the non-presence, and hence the unnameability, of the transcendental signified.[31]

The deconstructive strategy of Derrida depends crucially on undermining binary opposites which not only characterise language as a whole but which have proved instrumental, so it is argued, in the fabrication of Western metaphysics. Here too we find material which has proved useful for bridge-building between ancient and postmodern thinking. The notion that the world is divided into naturally discriminable pairs of opposites, and that fundamental principles of meaning and metaphysics are determined by the mutual exclusion of such opposites and the privileging of one over the other – being/non-being, reality/appearance, mind/body, nature/culture are typical examples – is challenged by Derrida, who attempts to show how they collapse into each other, thereby undermining the metaphysical tradition which rested upon them. Daoism has, of course, always been associated with the idea of the complementarity of opposites, archetypally evident in the pair *yin* and *yang*. The *Daodejing* contains a number of passages in which typical pairs of opposites, such as good and evil, and beautiful and ugly, are destabilised by revealing their mutual dependence and by undermining the standard priority of the first over the second. In the *Zhuangzi*, too, we find an insistence on the relative and perspectival nature of standardly opposed pairs of terms, for 'dividing is formation', and even the distinction between 'life' and 'death' is dissolved for 'simultaneously with dying one is alive' (Graham 1981: 52–3). Moreover, as Berkson points out, there is a political agenda underlying the deconstruction of binary opposites, 'for such pairs are often typical of ideologies that want to elevate one side at the expense of another: central/marginal, white/black, male/female, a point which reflects back on our earlier discussion of the radical political potential within Daoism (1996: 107).

The subversive nature of this process for both Daoism and Derrida is given special emphasis by Graham. He sees a close affinity between the conceptual reversals of the *Daodejing* and the deconstructive strategies of Derrida. In the case of the former, accepted descriptions are overturned by 'the reversal of priorities in chains of oppositions' such as male/female/, big/small, strong/weak, active/passive. In parallel with this, according to Graham, Derrida pursues the objective of 'deconstructing the chains of oppositions underlying the logocentric tradition of the West' (1989: 223, 227). Derrida's undermining of the privileging of speech over writing and of reality over appearance thus runs parallel with the Daoist rethinking of the standard elevation of strength over weakness and of activity over passivity; 'both use reversal to deconstruct chains in which A is traditionally preferred to B' (1989: 223, 227). Nevertheless there are, he argues, some important differences here. Whereas in Derrida's thinking there is a move towards 'elevating writing above speech' and 'abolish[ing] A in revenge against the traditional effort to abolish B', for Laozi, by contrast, the reversal is not strictly speaking a switch from preferring A to preferring B but rather 'a balancing of A and B'. Thus, in preferring to be submissive rather than intractable the sage does not seek to demote strength in favour of weakness but to achieve a measure of the former through the latter.[32] As we noted in an earlier chapter, Daoist ethics does not prescribe weakness as a virtue *per se*, but rather as a means towards the end of harmony and accommodation. Similarly, the reversal of the standard evaluation of activity over passivity, a preference which supports the elevation of human purposive activity over nature's 'blindness', implies not inaction or idleness, but an activity that is attuned to rather than in conflict with the natural harmony of things. On the cosmological level, all things are seen in Daoist eyes as interdependent, without benefit of foundational, transcendent principles which can explain or justify the priority of one pole over another, or which can support claims to precedence or ultimate origins. Moreover, the grounding of Chinese thought in conceptual polarities, in which neither pole is privileged over the other, has had the effect, not only of precluding the language of transcendence but also of discouraging the emergence of dualistic thinking and of any idea of *creatio ex nihilo* (Hall and Ames 1987: 17–21).

This discussion inevitably raises the question of whether the Chinese philosophical tradition is logocentric. This is hinted at by Derrida himself, who identified China as a non-logocentric civilisation, thereby bringing more sharply into focus the logocentricity of the Western philosophical tradition (1976: 90–2).[33] For Derrida, 'logocentrism' represents the key assumption behind Western metaphysics, namely the idea that 'Truth' can be attained through language and that speech can provide an immediate intuitive access to meaning, an assumption which, significantly in the context of our present discussion, is portrayed by Derrida as a form of ethnocentrism which 'is related to the history of the West'. By contrast, the non-phonetic writing of the Chinese, where there is no isomorphic link between writing and speech, provides 'the testimony of a powerful movement of civilisation developing outside of all logocentrism' (1976: 79, 90). If the answer is in the negative, this adds support to the supposition, not indeed that the Chinese 'think differently' or have a 'different logic', but that the classical Chinese tradition represents an alternative way of doing philosophy. This is not an issue that can be dealt with adequately here, but it is worth noting that in Graham's view the answer is indeed in the negative, for in his view there is no aspiration on the part of Daoist thinkers to attain to the full presence of the transcendental signified but, quite to the contrary, an already deconstructed acceptance that the *dao* is only, for us, a trace which leads to yet another trace, and so forth. In Graham's words, 'Perhaps *Lao-tzu's* Way is how the Trace will look to us when we are no longer haunted by the ghost of that transcendent Reality the death of which Derrida proclaims' (1989: 228; see also Berkson 1996: 121).[34] This view is supported by Zhang Longxi, who points to Chinese non-phonetic writing as offering a way 'that may overturn the metaphysical hierarchy more easily and efficiently than Western phonetic writing does'. He surmises that Chinese writing is not traditionally conceived as a mere recording of oral speech, but tends to carry within it the quality of trace, and thus reveals better than phonetic writing, 'language as a system of differential terms'; indeed, he goes on to claim that *dao* was already deconstructed by the Chinese two millennia ago (1992: 30–33; see also Zhang 1985, 1998).[35]

The conjectured links with Derridean deconstruction are matched by some interesting comparisons with Richard Rorty's own particular form of neo-pragmatist, post-epistemological thinking, ones already hinted at in our discussion of Heidegger.[36] The common ground here is that of pluralism and perspectivism, but a particular feature of Rorty's thinking that has drawn the attention of comparativists is his critique of the Western idea of philosophy as a foundational discipline that stands in marked contrast to, and possesses authority over, other fields of discourse such as history, literature, myth, and poetry. Long before Rorty, of course, philosophers had begun to cast doubt on the possibility of a philosophical language purified of all traces of myth and metaphor, and on the existence of what Hilary Putnam has called a 'ready-made world' to which our language aspires to correspond, the most famous example being Nietzsche's view of truth as 'a mobile army of metaphors'. With Rorty, as indeed with Nietzsche, this issue is central to the fate of philosophy itself. Metaphor, on Rorty's view, must no longer be seen as some superficial embellishment to, or even distraction or lapse from, the serious task of truth-telling, for as Nietzsche had earlier insisted, it is in the very ground of metaphorical uses of language that Western philosophy has ever been firmly planted. For Rorty, the endemic metaphoricity of language in general is evident specifically in philosophical discourse as well, a conclusion which inevitably calls into question the distinction, drawn first by Plato, between philosophical and poetic thinking and the prioritising of the former over the latter. The hermeneutical approach to philosophy which Rorty favours has tended to give a more central place to literary-style discourse, to tropes, metaphors, and narrative structures and devices, rejecting the primacy of the literal over the metaphorical and calling into question the traditionally hallowed virtues of systematic argumentation and scientific objectivity in the context of philosophical discourse.

Rorty nevertheless rejects altogether the pursuit of the ideal of a distinct and unique philosophical methodology, and calls instead for a 'postphilosophy' which would be characterised by a proliferation of new and competing forms of discourse, new vocabularies and fresh ways of thinking. This has revolutionary implications for Rorty, for the deployment of metaphors and the creation therewith of new narratives enables philosophy to undermine entrenched styles of thinking and to weave new patterns of beliefs and desires. Moreover, the withdrawal from the idealised and dehumanised detachment of much traditional Western philosophical writing has led to an emphasis on the communal and communicative nature of philosophical thinking which is better conceived on the model of a dialogue or conversation rather than of a process of logical deduction; indeed, for Rorty, conversation is 'the ultimate context within which knowledge is to be understood' (1980: 369).

In the light of all this, it is not difficult to see how modern commentators might find in the richly and self-consciously figurative style of the *Zhuangzi* an ancient anticipation of this sort of view. To quote Zhang once again, 'Zhuangzi's highly figurative text shows clearly how the play of metaphor blurs the usual distinction between philosophy and literature', and Rorty's account of the history of language as the history of metaphor is seen by the philosopher Kwang-sae Lee as a way of recovering the philosophical seriousness of Zhuangzi in whose writings metaphor is a way of loosening old rigidities of thought and opening up new existential possibilities (Zhang 1992: 40; Lee 1996: 182).[37] For Hall and Ames, it is this postmodern ambition to 'unmask the metaphorical character of our putatively rational discourse', and the consequent rehabilitation of 'the constitutive role of analogical and metaphorical language...[that] has provided a context within which to approach the task of intercultural conversation'. Recognising the contingency of any given mode of cultural or philosophical expression will, therefore, prevent us from assuming that classical Chinese thought 'must be evaluated by appeal to the idiosyncrasies of our own cultural paradigm' (1995: 106, 108).

This loosening of rigidities and the opening up of a plurality of possibilities, by contrast with the search for hidden essences or for new and more secure foundations, is closely tied to the quest for a new philosophical language. The challenge in recent philosophy to the long-established opposition of 'logic/poetry', and of the prioritising – for philosophical purposes, at any rate – of the former over the latter, of literal over figurative uses of language, is a project sometimes seen as linking Zhuangzi with both Derrida and Rorty. This transformation is not just an abstract theoretical matter but, as we have seen, has led to a disturbing yet refreshing deployment of play, irony and humour in philosophical *praxis*. The difficulty for the Western reader in approaching the *Zhuangzi* as a philosophical text has typically been not so much its apparent mystical obscurity, as in the case of the *Daodejing*, but rather its manifest lack of gravity, in its tricksterish addiction to amusing vignettes, satirical mockeries, and paradoxical wordplay. As we noted in an earlier chapter, the multivocity of the *Zhuangzi* – a veritable 'linguistic and literary *hun-tun* [primal chaos]' (Burneko 1986: 393) – has given rise to a bewildering assortment of labels – mystic, satirist, nihilist, sage, mythologist or plain story-teller – and led to the ascription of a variety of philosophical positions ranging from relativism to metaphysical absolutism.[38] The text certainly represents a curious way of doing philosophy judged by traditional Western models, but in the view of the philosopher Kuang-ming Wu, this must not be seen simply as a rejection of rationality or as a lapse into other-worldly mysticism, but rather as a different way of philosophising altogether. For Wu, the 'overflow of ironies and metaphors, frivolity and seriousness' is an effective way of forcing us out of our standard ways of thinking which presuppose that life presents us with problems that can be 'solved' (1982: 34). Irony is a particularly powerful tool for this purpose, for, with its 'collage of disrelations of things [which] defies the existing order…[it] shakes us out of our fixed way of combining things', and even 'smashes our pride in logic and knowledge' (Wu 1990: 374–5). Zhuangzi's idiosyncratic style too is not, for Wu, something that adorns or gets in the way of his philosophy, but springs from the very nature of his philosophical thinking. The *Zhuangzi* is poetic, 'not because its wording conforms to the canons of poetic style, but because its thought has poetic thrust [which] is part and parcel of his thought' (1990: 26). The writings of Derrida and Rorty, which in both cases have often involved the use of playfulness and irony as a way of subverting the logocentric assumptions of Western philosophical language, help to confirm and amplify this interpretation. The ultimate aim – if one can speak in these terms – is the undermining of the very notion of some kind of universal, rational objectivity as the principal aim of philosophical thinking, and its replacement with a discourse which, through the deployment of a variety of literary and methodological strategies, opens up different possibilities of thought and action. In Rorty's words, it is 'a matter of conversation and social practice, rather than...an attempt to mirror nature...to keep conversation going rather than to find objective truth' (1980: 171). Furthermore, as Derrida himself insists, the task of subverting logocentrism and its philosophical justification can hardly be accomplished by the traditional methods of philosophy, for to attempt to do so would be to employ the very methodological assumptions that are under question; the disruption of these assumptions can only be undertaken by the deployment of a quite different language and the use of a different kind of writing.

What is common to Daoism and postmodernism in this context, therefore, is that they are both concerned, not with establishing a new and more legitimate way of conceptualising the world, but rather with subverting the very possibility of doing so, at any rate in the manner that traditional Western philosophy has prescribed. On this view, the *Zhuangzi* can be characterised as a kind of 'counterdiscourse', and its author a 'profound and brilliant jester', quintessentially a *homo ludens* on a par with Erasmus, the author of *In Praise of Folly*, whose aim is to 'stand in a perpetually antithetical relationship to all fixed categories' and whose strategy is 'to jar the reader out of his mundane complacencies and waken him to the possibility of another realm of experience' (Mair 1983a: 86, xi). Its droll style is in effect a 'deconstructive humour', as Joel Kupperman puts it, a way of conveying the emptiness that results from trying to say what cannot be said (1989).

This unsettling quality of Daoist discourse which seems to put it into curious resonance with certain postmodern writings should also warn against falling back into the comforting view that the Daoists are, in a sense, 'talking our language', and that Zhuangzi is 'one of us' after all. From one point of view, it may be that the assimilation of Daoist ideas into contemporary postmodernist problematics helps to bring to an end ages of mutual misunderstanding so that we can now rest assured that in this postmodern age, we and they think alike. Mair puts this attractive but questionable sentiment in the following way: 'Regardless of his significance for the past, Zhuangzi still speaks to us today with the authentic voice of intelligence and good sense [and] adumbrates an intellectual attitude that is both engaging and compelling' (1983a: xv). Certainly the recently discovered philosophical rapport that we have been speaking of in this chapter has a number of attractive benefits. For example, on the one hand it has helped to bring about an unprecedented appreciation by philosophers of Daoist thinking, or at the very least the opening up of fresh hermeneutical possibilities, and a corresponding enrichment of our understanding of the potentialities of human thought and inquiry. And on the other hand it has helped to locate post-Nietzschean philosophy in a wider, global space, one that can help us to recognise the historical contingency of our own local vocabularies and perspectives.

At the same time, however, we need to remind ourselves that these putative benefits are not the consequence of credal solidarity, and certainly not of a revamped confidence in universalism or in a new Western-inspired perennial philosophy. The benefits lie more in the tensions and differences that prevail and which continue to place Daoism and contemporary philosophical thinking in a creative counterpoint with each other rather than in comforting unison. Delicate balance is needed here, for there is an all-too-easy passage from fruitful difference to hostile incommensurability, from conversation to conflict, from liberating otherness into repressive toleration. In moving away from old-style universalism which sees all the world's major philosophical systems as expressions of a single underlying metaphysical Truth, with all its attendant Eurocentric implications, we risk gravitating to a view which patronises Daoist thinkers as merely convenient sparring partners in a contemporary philosophical game, one which helps to confirm our current thinking and to beatify our favoured cultural narratives. There is a danger here that, as with our earlier criticism of Hansen, once again we integrate the unsettling foreignness of an oriental way of thinking by assimilating it neatly into our own language game, even if that game – whether it be postmodernism, neopragmatism, or hermeneutics – happens itself to be an unsettling counter-discourse. As the contemporary philosopher Hongchu Fu insists, it might simply be misleading to stress certain similarities between the two and to ignore the fact of 'disparate cultural traditions which set deconstruction and Taoism apart' (Fu 1992: 319). Both ways lead us into labyrinths of self-questioning, but while Daoist probing was part of a spiritual-religious quest, with its lighthearted irony tied to a serious soteriological enterprise, postmodernism is a theoretical discourse, a product of academic disputation rather than a pathway towards wisdom or to the enhancement of life and compassion. Deconstructive postmodernism, in spite of its rejection of some central tenets of Enlightenment modernity, its much publicised quarrels with science and its emancipatory instincts, still tends to portray the (constructed) world as inherently banal and aimless, and therefore to exude a kind of scepticism that leads to cynicism and even despair rather than to wisdom or spiritual growth.[39]

# 9

# 'JOURNEY TO THE WEST'

## By way of concluding

### Beyond orientalism

The unsettling contrariness of Daoism noted at the end of the previous chapter is nicely illustrated by the great sixteenth-century Chinese novel *Journey to the West* (the *Xiyou ji*). It tells the story of a motley group of pilgrims, including a mischievous 'Monkey King' Sun Wukong, who undertake a long and arduous journey to India in search of Mahayana scriptures. The novel recounts many years of adventure and vicissitude, of ludicrous mishaps, and of wisdom and folly, but when finally the pilgrims reach their destination they discover that the scriptures that they have so painfully struggled to acquire are completely blank. The story, which is loosely based on the epic pilgrimage of the seventh-century Buddhist monk Xuan Zang, has usually been interpreted as a serious spiritual allegory of Buddhist enlightenment, the blank scriptures being a metaphor for Buddhist 'emptiness'. On the other hand, it has sometimes been construed as a book of profound nonsense in which the Monkey King, a trickster figure, leads the pilgrims on a crazy journey only to find that the effort has been entirely wasted. On this view, the blank scriptures epitomise the absurdity of the quest and warn us to return home and, as Jung advises, 'build on our own ground with our own methods' (Waley 1977: 5; Jung 1995: 203).[1]

This cautionary tale might serve to raise some fundamental questions about Daoism's own 'Journey to the West'. Is Daoism, with its deconstructive humour and irreverent scepticism, anything more than a glorious hoax, the product perhaps not so much of philosophical ironists as of philosophical pranksters? Have we taken with sufficiently serious levity Laozi's admonition: 'Those who know do not speak; those who speak do not know' (*Daodejing*: ch. 56). Zhuangzi's own brand of insouciant scepticism, with his inclination to embrace 'uselessness', his frequent refrains of 'let be' and 'let alone', 'forgetting one's mind', his 'going rambling without a destination', his elevation of unlearning over learning, and his advocacy of silence and cultivation of a state of forgetfulness and ignorance, all this must seem alien to modern Western minds. Who nowadays would take seriously Laozi's admonition to 'discard knowledge...human kindness...morality', or be guided by a man who says 'Mine is indeed the mind of an idiot' (*Daodejing*: chaps 19–20)? The image of the Monkey King might serve to remind us that the Daoist sage was often portrayed as a simpleton, and that infants, fools and blockheads are probably 'closest in spirit to the primordial Tao' (Strickmann 1994: 51).

This is not quite the picture of Daoism that most Western seekers after Eastern wisdom have hoped to find. Many of the pilgrims we have met on this book's journey have seen Daoism, not as foolish or empty but as a wise teaching which has much to offer the modern world, possibly even, as Needham proclaimed, a philosophy for the future. There was speculation early in this century that Daoism might become the basis of a new world religion, and at the beginning of a new century Daoism still offers for some a Way for the West, a path which might guide us in our current search for enlightenment – or at least teach us how to forgo this doubtful spiritual luxury with equanimity. For pilgrims such as these, the emptiness of the sacred scripture may well be indicative of a profound philosophy beyond all words, one in which we may hope to discover some much-needed truth about ourselves and our world. Others see this path as leading towards a new syncretism, a 'Eurotaoism', as Peter Sloterdijk calls it, in which threads of Eastern wisdom are re-spun into useful modern – or postmodern – garments (1989). For yet others, it may be a palimpsest on which we are tempted to inscribe our own 'profound nonsense', or simply condemned as another form of orientalism, feeding the insatiable fantasies of Western consumerism, a product of cultural domination, even a new wave of postmodern colonialism.

Our journey has indeed revealed a wide range of interests and motivations in undertaking the pilgrimage along the Daoist way. Throughout this book we have encountered many ways in which Daoism has been drawn into Western interests, debates, schools of thought, disciplines and assumptions, exploited and transformed in pursuit of a whole range of home-grown projects. It has been allied with theosophy, with the *philosophia perennis*, with Jungian synchronicity theory, and with organicist metaphysics. Some have seen it through the lens of modern science, Marxism, analytical philosophy, or positivism. Links have been traced with thinkers as seemingly diverse as Heraclitus, Plotinus, Blake, and Nietzsche. It has been drawn into recent environmentalist debates, into Deep Ecology, feminism, New Age thinking, and the explorations of post-Christian spirituality. Modern concerns with sexual fulfilment, health, and fitness have adapted it for their own ends.

Much of the flood of new literature in these areas can easily be dismissed as 'rubbish of the most extraordinary sort' (Palmer 1991: 110), and it is not difficult to sneer at titles such as *The Tao of Baseball* or at the commercial chic of some of the many new *feng-shui* publications. Yet we cannot easily ignore the fact that Daoism is emerging as a reticent yet increasingly visible player in contemporary culture, and has become a site of cultural transformation and spiritual creativity that is beginning to operate globally at many levels. I have tended to emphasise the ambitious and wide-ranging speculations of certain scholars and philosophers, but we need to remember that in more modest ways, works such as Ray Grigg's *The Tao of Relationships*, or Raymond Smullyan's *The Tao is Silent*, or Peter Marshall's *Riding the Wind*, while claiming no special scholarly authority, have succeeded in transposing ancient Daoist ideas into contemporary frames of reference in remarkably original ways. Even *The Tao of Pooh*, through the stutterings of a 'bear of little brain', may have insights into the wisdom of Daoist teachings that are obscured in 'the lifeless writings of humorless Academic Morticians' (Hoff 1994: 34). These are but a few examples of the many new and creative ways in which ancient Daoism and modern thought are beginning to encounter one another along the old Silk Road between China and the West.

But is it truly an encounter, a dialogue, or are we simply projecting our own preoccupations onto a blank manuscript? In the final analysis, is Daoism simply a myth residing in the heads of Westerners, 'a mere stage prop for our own fantasies' (Bokenkamp 1997: xv)? The dialogue between Daoism and the West is, of course, part of a much older meeting between the cultures of Europe and Asia, and carries with it all the time-worn ambivalences towards the East. As we have indicated in earlier chapters, Daoism has clearly joined with Buddhism and Hinduism as an object of sometimes unbounded admiration, not just as an object of exotic romancing or of cultural tourism, but as a source of ancient wisdom that promises both spiritual renewal for Europe's jaded soul and an intellectual counterpoint to questionable home-grown orthodoxies. But it has also drawn upon itself the usual deposit of orientalist fantasies and stereotypes, still often dismissed as unfathomable and obscurantist, an easily scorned foil to the progressive outlook of the West. Our own historical narrative in this book has revealed not simply a growing awareness of a remote and exotic religious/ philosophical culture, but a dialectical interplay in which Daoist ideas have been drawn into, transformed and reconstructed by the conflicting and often myopic demands of peculiarly Western discursive traditions.

Some aspects of this transformative process have set up disturbing vibrations. In particular, Daoism's deployment as a critique of modernity may seem to cast a shadow over its otherwise sunny visage. Certain postmodernist positions, including those of Derrida and Rorty, have themselves often appeared to critics such as Jürgen Habermas and Roy Bhaskar as quietistic, conservative, anti-democratic, even fatalistic, 'beyond good and evil' and therefore incapable of articulating a language of justice, rights, or social responsibility. These are the sorts of criticism which are sometimes levelled against Daoism itself, and even where it has been seen as an attractive and life-enhancing philosophy, its apparent heedlessness of the enormous fact of evil is a worry to some critics (Küng and Ching 1989: 183; Sardar 1998: 173–4). Moreover, the nostalgic utopianism of Daoism – if we take its primitivism literally – which appears to favour a distant mythical past over the present, combined with a certain irrationalist and messianic mysticism, carries more sinister connotations. We have already drawn attention to the possibility that Daoism implies a form of amoralism, an apparent elevation of self-realisation above social solidarity and moral responsibility, which is open to exploitation for all sorts of undesirable ends, and that its supposed relativism can lead to moral indifferentism. At the level of the individual this attitude, especially evident in the cultivation of an inner spontaneity, may have unfortunate consequences; at the political level in the hands of a ruler who sees himself as above right and wrong, beyond good and evil, or as a species of romantic national self-realisation, the consequences could be catastrophic. We must inevitably ask, therefore, whether Daoism in the modern context could offer a subtle and seductive pathway towards the sort of irrationalist politics which fears critical thinking and seeks to return to an organic unity wherein the individual is lost to the demands of the whole or to the visions of a charismatic leader. The liaison, albeit brief, between Daoism and Legalism in the period of Warring States gives some historical substance to this fear. This seemingly unlikely conjunction might be seen as a portentous foreshadowing of certain forms of twentieth-century fascism in its identification of the sage ruler's vision with the natural order of things, the eternal ground which transcends the contingent needs and desires of individuals, a General Will which is validated by Nature itself.

Also troubling is the notion that the Daoist world 'is above all the world of nature rather than that of society' (Robinet 1998: 20), and that, despite its involvement in the wider political and cultural life of China, its concern with human life is submerged in a preoccupation with a larger, all-encompassing whole. As with certain criticisms levelled by feminists at Deep Ecology, Daoism might be seen as advocating a somewhat abstract, even esoteric love of nature while discounting the importance of the love that is cultivated through personal relationships, and as obliterating the value of the individual in favour of a greater cosmic totality (Plumwood 1993).

These anti-modernist, anti-democratic fears are enhanced by the interest shown in Daoism by a philosopher such as Heidegger. His criticism of the modern world led him to reject many of the key assumptions that are associated with the European Enlightenment, and for a while at least he came to identify the 'disclosure of Being' with the aims of the Nazi revolution. Such an association hardly amounts to a condemnation of Daoism, and indeed its robust individualism, its anarchist radicalism and its decentralist, anti-statist tendencies may prove liberating in ways that we

197

have already indicated. But, as with the support given by Zen Buddhism (itself a part-product of Daoism) to militaristic nationalism in Japan in the 1930s and 1940s, it warns us against the seductive assumption that Eastern wisdom is entirely unproblematic from a contemporary political and moral point of view (Heisig and Maraldo 1994). Political philosophies in the West with irrationalist and organicist tendencies have often proved to have powerful reactionary and oppressive implications, and we need to remain alert to the possible misuse of Daoism in a contemporary Western environment where democratic ideals can no longer be taken for granted.

These worries, it must be added, are not directed towards Daoist ways of life in their traditional setting which, leaving aside the brief association with Legalism, have not displayed any of these fascist or collectivist tendencies, but rather against their possible misuse in their Western re-embodiment. Looking at things in a wider context in the West, orientalism has at various times during the last hundred or so years become implicated in certain unsavoury social and political movements in the West, but this is an issue concerning European, not Asian, pathology (Clarke 1997: ch. 11). The need for reflexive vigilance within the discourse of orientalism has indeed become the object of close critical attention in recent years. The uncovering by critics such as Edward Said of the suppressed historical origins and the hidden ideological agendas of the West's understanding of Eastern cultures has contributed to a profound rethinking of the West's relationship to the cultures of Asia over which it has exercised various forms of power and exploitation, a rethinking which reflects a much more pervasive geopolitical re-orientation. In our own studies of Daoism's 'Journey to the West', we have drawn on this orientalist criticism and sought to go beyond the rather bland idealist, textual approach which sees the historical relationship between Daoism and the West as a polite scholarly exchange of ideas or as pure spiritual serendipity. From the time of the Jesuit missionaries of the Counter-Reformation onwards, we have seen how Daoist thinking has been constructed and reconstructed within the relentless machinery of Western intellectual discourse which, in its turn, has often been geared to wider cultural and political objectives. The 'fusion of horizons' accomplished through civilised dialogue which Gadamer speaks of may prove to be illusory, even oppressive, for it is an engagement in which the West still remains the dominant voice, dictating the terms of the exchange. At one level, globalisation represents a postmodernist transcendence of the old binarism of the 'West versus the rest', the orientalist discourse in which the world was constructed in terms of and within institutional frameworks marked out by Western imperialism. At yet another level, it can be seen as simply a late modern extension of European cultural hegemony. Western scholarship and intellectual endeavour still to a large extent dictate the vocabulary in which the East–West conversation is couched, and hence the ways in which the non-Western 'other' is conceptualised and theorised; this book is itself inevitably an example of this process.

As we have seen, Daoist ideas have certainly proved a powerful antidote to a variety of Western ideas and traditions, yet there are problematic side-effects. There has been a strong inclination on the part of many writers – including myself – to 'demythologise' Daoism in order to adapt it to modern purposes, to extricate it from discredited metaphysical and mythological entanglements in order to render it suitable for Western use. One result of this may have been to tame and domesticate its wild, anarchistic spirit, to moderate and make respectable its childlike vision, and to play down its more extravagant occultist tendencies. In welcoming it into the Western intellectual establishment as 'one of us', we risk blunting its ironic barbs and neutering its subversive force. Paradoxically, therefore, such strategies of normalisation, where the dangerous Other is comfortably absorbed into myself, might have the effect of *diminishing* its value to the modern world.

This sort of consideration has led some critics to see the Western appropriation of Daoism as yet another form of exploitation, a continuation of colonial habits of mind long after the lowering of the flags of empire. Even its association with postmodernism, however subversive the latter appears, might represent simply 'a new wave of domination riding on the crest of colonialism and modernity', one in which 'the westernisation of the globe is suffocating non-western cultures' (Sardar 1998: 13, 20). The notion of Daoism as a kind of 'conceptual resource' has, as we noted in an earlier chapter, been criticised for perpetuating an endemic Western attitude towards the East, one which reinforces the hegemonic myth of the West's right to expropriate the world's assets for its own use (Larson 1987: 153–4). For some critics the faddish Western adoption of Daoism is an example of a new imperialist expansion, the *imperium Americanum* as it is sometimes called, which views past and alien traditions as ripe for conquest, and which, in Steve Bradbury's view (1992), is driven by a strange mixture of aggressive market capitalism and liberal Protestantism. Or, like other exotic imports from the Orient, it may be simply a fetishised commodity, an object of desire, an alluring means of escape into a pleasurable world of fantasy, a place of idealised promise, release, and idyllic pleasure and enchantment. In a postmodern context, the cultural and religious traditions of the Orient almost inevitably become consumer items whereby, in the view of some critics, Eastern values become subject to a new form of colonial expropriation (Sardar 1998: 138–40). Suren Lalvani sees the new orientalism, not so much in terms of colonialism in any literal sense, but as part of the West's 'therapeutic ethos', a form of exploitation by marketing and advertising interests, with Daoist ideas of spontaneity, energy and self-cultivation constituting yet another set of bland, usefully marketable items (1995). Murray Bookchin had something similar in mind when he concluded that traditional Daoism has simply been recycled into 'vulgar Californian spiritualism' (1995: 100). As Jean Baudrillard surmises, we now consume signs rather than objects, and Daoism, in some of its manifestations, can already be observed alongside other intellectual and religious products as a fashion icon, the current vogue for *feng-shui* and the popularity of the *taiji* symbol providing obvious examples of this phenomenon.

There is, though, another side to all this. We need to bear in mind that this 'appropriation' or 'exploitation' has not merely served to satisfy Western appetites, or even the more sober desire to understand a foreign religious tradition. It has often been seriously counter-cultural in intent as well, a challenge to endemic cultural narcissism and a catalyst for cultural transformation. Said's orientalist thesis, though relevant here as a critique of a certain stage in the development of colonialism, is itself in the process of being transformed. Said tended to see orientalism through the lens of post-colonial criticism (he was indeed one of the chief lens-grinders), and that perspective has proved immensely valuable in relation to certain historical and cultural contexts. But it is an approach which, in spite of our demurrers above, does not do justice to the role that orientalism has sometimes played, and plays with increasing effectiveness, as an agent of subversion and transformation within the West itself, as a method used by Western thinkers to reconstruct their own world rather than to buttress the West's essential supremacy. Nor does it take adequate account of the ways in which in a post-colonial epoch, the balance of power and cultural influence between East and West has shifted significantly. In the chapters above, we have seen many examples of the polemical use of Daoist ideas, above all as a critical tool for the reappraisal of modernity and as a contributor to the postmodern revisioning of Enlightenment ways of thinking. This has often involved a steady and painful process of unlearning, a retreat from the safe bastion of privileged knowledge, but it has also led to the unfolding of new creative thinking and perspectives which have global implications.

At one stage in this retreat from Eurocentric orthodoxy, orientalists, while taking Asian systems of thought seriously, often took refuge in the idea that the apparently distinct cultures of East and West shared underlying similarities, even seeing Daoism along with Hinduism and Buddhism as a manifestation of a universal or perennial philosophy. This was a strategy which effectively minimised the threat of a radical epistemological break which non-European systems of thought posed, but at the cost of denying the distinctiveness of Eastern intellectual traditions. At another stage, the differences between East and West were ascribed to the evolutionary disparity between the cultures of Asia and Europe, the West having passed irreversibly beyond the childlike stage in which the East was frozen. This strategy allowed the West to approach Asian thought from a position of claimed absolute difference and intellectual superiority, and to construct a model of its oriental Other in ways best suited to the purposes of domination. The emphasis in recent times has been once again on difference, not that of condescending superiority but rather a dialectical difference which, through the fusion of horizons, betokens the possibility of a creative engagement between equals. It is a difference which is increasingly seen not as one of absolute incommensurability where all intercultural communication is effectively precluded, but as one in which, as Gadamer has argued, difference is a precondition of communication. This commitment to a 'hermeneutics of difference' cannot simply cancel out earlier asymmetries and injustices, which are deeply ingrained in our history, but it does represent a concerted aspiration towards genuine dialogue, one in which the creation of a reflexive distance between cultures can facilitate mutual understanding as well as 'a significant transvaluation of [our] categories of thinking, acting, and feeling' (Hall and Ames 1998: 21; see also Kögler 1996: 266–7).[2]

Moreover, this new approach also recognises the potential of orientalism for conserving and honouring traditional patterns of thought and evaluation. It is true that in the past traditional cultural formations have often been marginalised and even obliterated in the course of colonial expansion, a process which was impelled by *realpolitik* and justified by belief in the superiority and historical inevitability of Western-style progress. Taking up the 'White Man's Burden' was indeed seen as a noble duty. We have seen some of the ways in which Daoism itself has been subjected to an oppressive discourse of this kind, characterised as backward and obscurantist within an ideological framework which gave to Western thought a vanguard place in the historical march of Reason. We saw too that Chinese intellectuals have themselves sometimes been persuaded by this kind of rhetoric to denigrate their own cultural traditions. And in broad geopolitical terms, it may be the case that the forces of modern liberal universalism and global capitalism inevitably dismantle traditional cultures, in spite of the growing resistance of certain hitherto marginalised groups.

But at the same time, we must not be blind to the fact that orientalist scholarship has often aided in the conservation of traditions, albeit often as little more than historical relics; it has the power not only to kill the thing it loves but also to save it, not only to silence but to amplify Daoism's voice. The work of Needham, for example, though shaped as we have seen by his own personally and culturally determined agendas, has helped to reveal the extraordinary richness of the Chinese scientific and technological traditions, and has in many ways contributed towards the liberation of China from Western intellectual thrall. The writings of Graham, too, though less ideologically driven, have enabled us to see more clearly the great scope and depth of philosophical argument that prevailed in ancient China. The wide-ranging research of the French school of sinologists has done much to bring to light the unique indigenous Chinese spiritual/mystical tradition. These are but three examples of the contribution that Western scholars have made in recent years to the rediscovery, conservation, and revitalisation of intellectual and cultural traditions. It might still be argued that this process has been carried out on a selective basis dictated by Western predilections, but this view ignores, first, that Chinese (and Japanese and Korean) scholars have themselves increasingly in the past century been participants in this activity, and second that, far from helping to obliterate ancient traditions, the use of modern scholarly techniques and philosophical language may help to preserve them. This attitude has certainly been assisted by a sea-change in Western culture in recent years, where there is evidence of increasing scepticism towards deeply entrenched Eurocentric attitudes, and the espousal of a more pluralist and decentered approach to human cultures, evident for example in the burgeoning fields of postcolonial and subaltern studies. In opposition to the universalism of modernist discourse, there has been a marked shift in recent years towards the valorisation of indigenous cultural forms and vernacular idioms, an affirmation of the importance of hitherto undervalued and marginalised practices and beliefs. Moreover, taking a view from a broader perspective, it is increasingly recognised by critics in this field that the whole orientalist phenomenon, hitherto often seen as a monolithic process of oppression carried out by the West at the expense of the East, has been a highly complex process in which currents of power and influence have operated in both directions (Young 1990: 148ff; King 1999: ch. 9).

There is of course a blurred boundary between exploitation on the one hand and creative transformation on the other. However, the issue of cultural conservation, with its inescapable ambivalences, should not obscure the growing importance of Daoism in the world beyond its ancestral homeland, nor deter us from celebrating and amplifying its global impact at the present time. As we have emphasised throughout this book, Daoism has no single, unitary essence but enjoys a polychromatic richness that has been subject to constant renewal, reinterpretation and proliferation throughout its long history in China. Its relationship with Confucianism and Buddhism, for example, has not been one of mutual exclusion but rather of dynamic interaction, a long hermeneutical engagement in which Daoism has been a stimulant to and a beneficiary of these rival teachings, shaping its own thinking and practice in relation to them, sometimes co-operating, sometimes competing, sometimes in open conflict. And contrary to the stereotype of a hermetically sealed civilisation, defensively refusing contact with all that is foreign, China as a whole is itself now recognised as having been in fairly constant interaction with other civilisations, intellectually and culturally as well as commercially and politically (Waley-Cohen 1999).

Thus the study of Daoism can help us to see that traditions are not monolithic and timeless phenomena, closed off and lacking in the capacity for critical reflection, but systems in interactive play, multiple and competing narratives that transform and reinvent themselves through dialogue or struggle with rival traditions as well as with their own traditions and through their own inner dynamics and tensions. As Kohn points out, 'Cultural traditions need change to keep alive. Intellectual heritage is valuable only as long as it remains relevant to the people of ever new ages'. This observation is especially relevant in the case of Daoism which, she goes on to point out, has flourished not by hanging on to ancient teachings and preserving them 'like a fossil' to be 'put into a museum and admired', but by progressively transforming, re-defining and reinterpreting its ancient texts, 'mixing in the visions and practices of other traditions' with little regard to 'original intentions' (1991a: 225–6).[3] We might recall as well that in ancient times Japan assimilated various doctrines from Chinese sources, including Daoism itself, and while venerating these doctrines and honouring their originators, adapted them to fit native perspectives and indigenous traditions. The rejection of the myth of a stagnant, hermetically sealed culture incapable of reflecting critically on itself or of relating to alien traditions, and thus incapable of transforming itself, must lead us to rethink not only the historical reality of Daoism but its role in contemporary intellectual and cultural discourse.

This is the spirit in which I believe we need to approach Daoism at the present time: respectful of its traditions and anxious to honour and help preserve them, to study and interpret them in their original context, while at the same time appreciating these traditions as, 'Relevant to ever new ways of thought and going along with continuously changing times' (Kohn 1991a: 226). William de Bary is surely right when he insists that 'no tradition…can survive untransformed in the crucible of global struggle' (1988: 138), and we need to accept that Daoism has gained a new, and inevitably different, life of its own in the modern world. It is a life in which Daoism will no doubt interact creatively with non-Chinese traditions of thought in ways similar to those which have characterised its earlier productive relationships with the other ancient traditions of China, India and Japan, and which will progressively involve scholars, writers and practitioners of all kinds from both Asia and the West. The 'New Confucianism' that has been mooted in China for over a century and is increasingly debated nowadays (Berthrong 1998: 185–200) is already being mirrored by the emergence of a 'New Daoism', a cultural development which, as we have seen throughout this book, is a hybrid of texts, thinkers and ideas that derives from both East and West and which increasingly transgresses the confines of this very distinction.

## Beyond Daoism

In the light of all of this, precisely what kind of role can we see Daoism playing in the intellectual and cultural life of the postmodern, postorientalist world? It is not difficult to sympathise with Arthur Danto's remark that 'The fantastic architectures of Oriental thought...are open to our study and certainly our admiration, but they are not open for us to inhabit', or with William Halbfass's view that in the final analysis 'we cannot escape into foreign traditions and ways of orientation' (Danto 1976: 9; Halbfass 1988: 441). In the current postmodernist climate there are few who would imagine that Daoism could become a fully-fledged religious movement reconstructed in the West in anything like its original indigenous form, let alone acquire the status of a new grand narrative or cultural orthodoxy to replace those we are busily discrediting. Daoism's journey to the West has certainly brought with it more than just blank scriptures, but these scriptures do not provide us with a complete groundplan for our future dwelling. It is true that certain explicitly or implicitly Daoist movements have emerged in the West which seek to perpetuate ancient Chinese traditions; the recently formed 'British Taoist Association' and the 'Orthodox Daoism in America' movement are examples of this, and a number of traditional Daoist temples have been opened in North America in recent years which are attempting to reach out beyond local Chinese communities. Furthermore, many Daoist masters are active in the West, instructing pupils from all ethnic groups in *taiji* and *qigong* within the framework of traditional Daoist teachings, and a wide-circulation Daoist journal, *The Empty Vessel*, is now in its eighth year of publication.

In the final analysis, though, Daoism as a comprehensive cultural package is not yet a real option for the West, and indeed the very notion of importing a whole way of life makes little sense, for even in the cases just mentioned Daoism has inevitably been decontextualised and adapted to suit its new environment. After all, Daoism was a product of a closed agrarian society, very different from the industrial commercial society of today, and we could hardly expect the values of the former to match precisely the problems arising from the latter. To be sure, Daoism continues to flourish in Taiwan where the Celestial Masters sect is now based and where, in addition to the maintenance of ancient public rites and festivals, there has developed in recent years a lively intellectual discourse concerning Daoism. And at one level, Daoism remains deeply rooted in Chinese life, and continues to thrive, albeit often *sans la lettre*, in the cultural inheritance of Chinese people everywhere. But even in mainland China, where it has enjoyed something of a revival in recent years, and where the government of the People's Republic has given it a certain measure of protection and patronage, Daoism is not likely to be restored to its former ubiquitous cultural role in the foreseeable future.[4]

A comparison with the Western path of Buddhism is instructive here. It is not simply that the latter has enjoyed a longer history in the West than Daoism, and has firmly established itself, both philosophically and institutionally in the West well in advance of Daoism, but rather that its

Western expansion has been impelled by factors which are largely absent in the case of Daoism. The powerful impact on the West of Zen and Tibetan Buddhism, to take two obvious examples, has been the product not just of Western-inspired enthusiasms but of wider political and social factors, in particular the American occupation of Japan and the Chinese occupation of Tibet, respectively, which in both cases has fortuitously opened up facilitative pathways to the West. These are of a kind which is unlikely to be matched by Daoism. It is true that a small handful of Daoist monks have recently visited the West – though under strict surveillance by Beijing – and a number of ethnic Chinese Daoist-educated masters teach Daoist-related practices in the West, but this cannot compare with the extensive East–West links that have been established in the case of Buddhism, nor with the active dissemination of the Dharma by Asian teachers. As we indicated earlier, the Daoist message has come to the West in largely textual form, mediated by scholars and travellers who have selectively conveyed fleeting glimpses of texts, beliefs and practices, rather than an image of a whole way of life or a model of a whole living tradition. As Knut Walf points out, the Daoist presence in the West has had, appropriately enough, a distinctly individual-ist, even anarchist quality and, unlike Buddhist and Hindu movements in Europe and America, lacks for the most part the institutional underpinning of social groups and organised communities (1997: 29–30). There is no Daoist Sangha, no Daoist monastic or ritual tradition in the West from which we might gain inspiration, no equivalent of the robed Buddhist monk or of the seated Buddha has entered the Western imagination, and until recently the Daoist tradition has barely rated in the Western mind as a religion of world stature or been seen to be worthy of systematic study in our schools and universities.

One inevitable result of these factors is that the Daoist future in the West is likely to take a different, albeit related, path from that of Buddhism. It is likely that the direction of this pathway will lie in its potential as an attitude of mind, rather than as a complete philosophy. It will probably appeal as a set of loosely related insights and practices which will be subject to considerable variation and transformation as they become absorbed into Western ways of thinking and into modern global preoccupations, and remain largely a matter of personal choice and lifestyle rather than aspire to being a mass religious movement. In brief, we are likely to be inheritors of a disassembled, plural Daoism that will touch increasingly on different aspects of our lives without necessarily providing us with a single, clear and alternative philosophy or with a focus for collective action. It is a prospect which is surely appropriate for a 'way that cannot be told', which 'stands on the edge of chaos' and which 'gives rise to the ten thousand things'.[5]

Following the discussions in this book, we can already begin to discern the vague and disjointed outlines of this Way for the West, a West which is increasingly having to come to terms with its place within a global culture, and in which the boundaries between East and West are going the way of the Berlin Wall. Marx once observed that it is only in quite special conditions that a society is able to adopt a critical attitude towards itself, but it seems that today the whole of our civilisation is being propelled into a veritable fever or self-analysis and self-re-evaluation, from the levels of abstract philosophy and science to those of day-to-day living and survival. Even at the margins Daoism has begun to play a role in this restless self-appraisal, offering as we have already suggested not only a means of throwing into relief and challenging our cherished orthodoxies – as such, it might be seen as merely fanning the flames of nihilism – but also of suggesting imaginative new ways of thinking about our predicament, offering a new vocabulary and a radically different set of assumptions, and suggesting new insights and paradigms. It is, as with other alternative movements such as Gnosticism, Romanticism and anarchism, a counter-point and source of resistance to prevailing orthodoxies, an antidote to the one-sidedness and singleness of vision associated with the still dominant role of Eurocentric attitudes, a way of dislodging the still-privileged position of Western culture within an emerging postcolonial discourse, and a defence against the standardisation of modern life associated with global capitalism. It is a challenge to the West's over-valuation of Enlightenment-style rationalism, to its dependence on technology, to a certain philosophical over-simplification which leads to either/or-ness, and to a kind of monotheism of the imagination which ties thought to a single methodological viewpoint or a single model of historical evolution. Daoists could in future be like Harold Bloom's 'strong poets', who seek to go beyond the status quo by means of all kinds of tricks and subterfuges, by re-reading and re-contextualising ideas that have become settled, or like Said's ideal intellectuals who raise embarrassing questions and confront orthodoxy and dogma. And far from being an adjunct to consumerism, as Lalvani suggests, it may represent a subversive influence on capitalism with its 'perpetual quest for meaning through consumption' and its hidden disciplines of control and manipulation (Sardar 1998: 40). Daoist primitivism may in this perspective be seen not as a utopian, backward-looking irrelevance, but as a challenge to ingrained habit and unthinking conformity, provoking us into rethinking our lives in the present.

The growing popularity of Daoism in the West, then, is not just about nostalgia or romantic retreat, but speaks directly to our contemporary condition. But neither is it just a gadfly, stinging us into irritable self-scrutiny. Its attraction for the present age lies in various affirmative and productive ways of thinking, many of which we have discussed in the course of this book. They tend to cluster around several related factors which, without simply repeating the substance of earlier chapters, can briefly be reiterated here.

The first of these factors is the desire to discover an alternative or transformed spirituality or religiosity without credal commitment or doctrinal
validation, a sense of meaning without transcendence or teleology, a non-
theistic spirituality which is contained within our finite existence, is
concerned with how to make the best of our life in this world, and gives us a
secure and life-giving anchorage in the natural world. The philosopher Ray
Billington is one of a number of thinkers who have emphasised the appeal of
Daoism's naturalness, its this-worldliness. Where other Eastern philosophies
speak of the unsatisfactoriness of the world about us, its suffering and even
its illusoriness, Daoism affirms our desire for being at-home-in-the-world, of
our ultimate oneness with nature, and of the value of our present condition
and experience. In this sort of view, increasingly attractive nowadays,
Daoism represents a timely balance between the extremes of traditional
Christian otherworldliness and scientific materialism, a 'balance of Yang
and Yin [which] can make for a rich and comprehensive existence', and
permits us a sense of religious awe without religious doctrines, of the secular
as sacred (Billington 1990: 191–201, 281). This can be linked with the need,
expressed in many quarters, for a spirituality which reconnects us with the
earth and with the living world, an ecological attitude of mind which does
not merely value the earth for utilitarian reasons but places it at the heart of
our struggle for a broadened sense of self-realisation, an ideal which
substitutes the old individualistic sense of this phrase with a broadened
spiritual development that, as in Arne Naess's Deep Ecology, encompasses
the human and the natural orders.

This ecological spirituality certainly has a focus which is distinct from
that of traditional Christianity, but increasingly there are Christian thinkers
and practitioners too who, while remaining loyal to that tradition, have
drawn elements of Oriental philosophy, including Daoism, into their
thinking. For example, the attraction of Daoism to the Cistercian monk
Thomas Merton lay not only in its cultivation of the contemplative and
interior life but also in its 'Franciscan simplicity and connaturality with all
living creatures' (1965: 27). And Joseph Needham, an Anglican and an
active member of the Teilhard de Chardin Association, was quite explicit
about the need for an '*aggiornamento*' between Christianity and Daoism, a
'widening of spiritual horizons' in which Daoist symbols might play a
significant counterbalancing role to the traditional Christian image of God,
not only as male but as a 'ruthless Caesar' and as a military 'Lord of Hosts'
(1979: 7, 25–6).

Closely related to this is, second, a need which revolves round a holistic
attitude of mind and which seeks fulfilment through the overcoming of the
dualism of body and spirit. It is a part of what Thomas Luckman has called
the 'invisible religion of self-realisation', which approaches the ancient
religious quest for meaning and purpose without feeling the need to sacrifice
the body, the senses and our sense of self-worth. Its quality is neatly

summed up in the title of Lin Yutang's delightful book *The Importance of Living*. The precise techniques of inner alchemy may seem remote and even alien to us, but its underlying principles and many of its methods remain alive for us today, and find a ready acceptance in an age tuned into a holistic sense of personal growth and fulfilment. Alan Watts was one of the first to spot this therapeutic quality of Daoism, and for him it appealed to the modern need for liberation, not so much from political chains but rather from those 'mind-forged manacles', in Blake's phrase, which constrain us from achieving our desire for self-fulfilment (1973: ch. 3). It is an attitude which is most clearly manifested in the extraordinary proliferation of various Daoist-inspired practices brought to the West by Chinese masters, and which have proved a key for many to mental and physical health, and to paths of self-realisation.[6]

It is, finally, a need which can be viewed within the wider context of intellectual currents that had begun to flow strongly a century ago. In the first half of the twentieth century, where the influence of positivism meant that traditional religious systems from remote parts of the globe could conveniently be ignored, Daoism had little place. But in recent years the pendulum has swung in the opposite direction, and our times are marked by a retreat from the certainties sought by positivists, and a compensating emphasis in science, philosophy and literature on unpredictability, disorder, incommensurability and a suspicion of the truth-telling power of language. In the previous chapters, we have noted in various ways not only the importance of Chinese ideas in the emerging ecumenism of philosophical hermeneutics, but the relevance of this intercultural discourse to contemporary philosophical interest in issues concerning self, truth and gender identity, and of course in general to postmodern critiques of the Western Enlightenment project. The impact of Asian thought has long been felt, if only marginally, in the West's struggle with the nihilistic mood that arose both out of and in reaction to modernism. Earlier, it was Hinduism and Buddhism that entered into this dialectic. Now it is the turn of Daoism, with its robust sense of finitude and its romantic healing of our relationship with the natural and the ordinary, to help find a way beyond nihilism without having recourse to narratives of transcendence. In this sense, the discovery of blank scriptures may not be a tragedy for our pilgrimage but the important revelation that the journey has been the end, not the means to an end. By way of comparison, we can also discern this kind of therapeutic response to nihilism in the work of a number of contemporary philosophers; for example, Stanley Cavell, who writes of 'the task of bringing the world back, as to life…a return to the ordinary…a new creation of our habitat' (1988: 52–3), and Simon Critchley, who speaks not of a renewed quest for meaning as a response to nihilism, for the world is already 'too easily stuffed with meaning', but of 'meaninglessness as an achievement', a task which avoids the manic desire to overcome nihilism and redeems us from the desire for redemption itself (1997: 27).

Lying behind these speculations is the ongoing work of scholars. The 'open sea' of which Nietzsche spoke still lies before them. The huge corpus of the *Daozang*, the canon of traditional Daoist writings, remains largely untranslated. The various Daoist sects and movements, with their proliferation of teachings and complex liturgies, is still to be fully explored. The ancient origins of Daoism still remain obscure. With further research into these and related areas, someone may yet dare to embark on the writing of a definitive history of Daoism.

What else can we expect in the future? Are we about to enter an 'Asian Century', as some prophesy? Will the future belong to Daoism as Needham predicted (1956: 152)? Whatever we may think of these forecasts, there has been enough said in this book to indicate a growing role in the future for Daoist ideas. In the light of the recent economic crisis in Asia, not to mention the emphasis on discontinuities and ruptures in contemporary historiography and the protean quality of Daoist writings that we have emphasised throughout this book, it is risky to make predictions. Nevertheless, it is safe to say that in one shape or another the nations and peoples of Asia are going to make an increasingly important contribution in the next century, not only to the world's economy but to its intellectual, cultural and geopolitical dimensions. Globalisation will take care of that, and indeed is almost another word for it, for the encounter between the civilisations of Asia and Europe will become increasingly intrinsic and pervasive; for this reason alone, it is important not to underestimate the potential role of Daoism, as of other Eastern systems of thought, in the emerging global civilisation.

A question which inevitably arises here is: will this new East–West encounter amount to a violent 'clash of civilisations' or to a productive dialogue? If thinkers like Samuel Huntington are right, it will be the former. Huntington sees China as an essentialised other, and the hostile confrontation between mutually alien civilisational blocks as inevitable (1996). I maintain, on the contrary, that the world is changing, in both geopolitical and intellectual terms, in ways that render this scenario improbable. China and the West are slowly coming to terms with each other, politically, culturally and intellectually; a mark of the latter is the extraordinary proliferation of writings about China in recent years, a small representative sample of which is cited in this book. There are issues such as those of human rights and democracy which are still far from being resolved, but from our present perspective, talk seems more likely than war, accommodation than confrontation. More and more people are coming to recognise that the hope of global survival and prosperity depend on our willingness to engage in dialogue, to listen and learn from each other. This does not mean the transcendence of cultural diversity, or the assimilation of differences into the melting pot of a higher universal synthesis, but willingness to engage in agonistic dialogue where even liberal values such as these are subject to continual reappraisal.

To conclude, the task that we now face as a global civilisation is to create a framework of ideas and values, not in order to arrive at universal consensus or a new global narrative, but in order to facilitate the harmonious co-existence of different beliefs and to encourage the flourishing of divergent ways of thinking and being. I have already indicated doubts that Daoism can provide us with any overarching framework, but in its pursuit we can learn from Daoism to back away from confrontation and to prefer accommodation and mutual harmony over self-assertiveness and aggressive contentiousness. The co-existence of the Three Teachings in China, which, at its best, emphasised the complementarity of different approaches to life, offers an attractive alternative model to the discredited Western universalism with its unrelenting pursuit of a single Truth. The Chinese way holds out the prospect of a pluralism which offers not just a grudging toleration of difference but the possibility of an enriching mutual influence between diverse cultures and ways of life. At a more personal level, Daoism may become in the years ahead what Buddhism has already become, a serious option for the spiritually disenchanted and spiritually seeking, or at least an inspiration towards the emergence of a new pluralistic syncretism, a new form of spirituality which draws together elements of Daoism and other Asian religions to bring them, not only into dialogue, but also into active symbiosis with indigenous Western traditions and thinkers. This symbiosis is likely to have a strong affinity with green thinking, with the concern not just for a personal way of salvation but for the future of the planet, a counter to excessive consumption, materialism, environmental degradation, and, in a word, a new way of thinking about our relationship with the natural world. This implies a non-exploitative relationship with the earth and with non-human creatures, and the development of technologies which go with rather than against nature. The Graeco-Christian conception of human dignity, for all its historically emancipatory impulse, has arguably not only cut us off from nature and from animals, but has also tended to place women in a lower place than men, earth than heaven, body than spirit.

A philosophy such as Daoism, which has the potential to heal these fractures, will surely find a congenial home in the culture of the twenty-first century. So too will a philosophy which values and swims with the ever-changing currents of the natural order, even recognising the spiritual power of chaos and disorder, and which ceases to long for an eternal and unchanging realm whose inevitable elusiveness threatens to plunge us into nihilism. The acceptance of this Heracleitan flux is not necessarily a harbinger of angst and forlorn longing for a more stable world of ultimate order but, in Daoist thinking, a sense of sufficiency and simplicity which contrasts with the kinetic restlessness of Western civilisation, a therapeutic philosophy which is an essential counterbalance to the frenzied, self-destructive 'being-towards-movement', which is overtaking modern life (Sloterdijk 1989). In J.C. Cooper's words, it offers 'a practical way for the alleviation and cure of the tensions and pressures of life today and for taming the "monkey mind" with its restless and purposeless leaping about', an image of inner harmony through recollection and simplicity of life (1990: 129). This is clearly a long way from the 'unyielding despair' with which Bertrand Russell confronted the ultimate burial of human achievement 'beneath the debris of a universe in ruins' (1953: 51). It is nearer to what Martin Heidegger called 'releasement', a letting go of things rather than always seeking to transform them and to impose intellectual conformity on nature, or lapsing into despair if this proves impossible. A 'being towards stillness' that embraces and celebrates rather than evades the world: this may be the wisest lesson that we can learn from Daoism's *Journey to the West*.

# APPENDIX I
## Chinese dynastic chronology

| | |
|---|---|
| *Xia* (legendary) | 1953–1576 BCE |
| *Shang* | 1576–1046 |
| *Zhou* | 1046–221 |
| Warring States period | 479–221 |
| *Qin* | 221–207 |
| *Han* | 206 BCE–220 CE |
| *Weijin* period | 220–420 |
| Six Dynasties | 420–589 |
| *Sui* | 589–618 |
| *Tang* | 618–906 |
| Five Dynasties | 907–960 |
| *Song* | 960–1279 |
| *Yuan* (Mongol) | 1279–1368 |
| *Ming* | 1368–1644 |
| *Qing* (Manchu) | 1644–1911 |
| Republic of China | 1911–1949 |
| People's Republic of China | 1949– |

# APPENDIX II

## Wade–Giles/Pinyin conversion table

| | |
|---|---|
| Ch'i | Qi |
| Chi-gung | Qigong |
| Chin | Qin |
| Ching | Qing |
| Chou | Zhou |
| Chuang Tzu | Zhuangzi |
| Chu Hsi | Zhuxi |
| Hsia | Xia |
| Hsün Tzu | Xunxi |
| Huai Nan Tzu | Huainanzi |
| I Ching | Yijing |
| Lao Tzu | Laozi |
| Lieh Tzu | Liezi |
| Mencius | Mengzi |
| Nei-tan | Neidan |
| San-chiao | Sanjiao |
| Ssu-ma Ch'ien | Simaqian |
| Ssu-ma T'an | Simadan |
| Sung | Song |
| Tai-chi-ch'uan | Taijiquan |
| Tao | Dao |
| Tao Te Ching | Daodejing |
| Tao-tsang | Daozang |
| Tzu-jan | Ziran |
| Wang Pi | Wangbi |
| Wei-tan | Weidan |
| Yang Chu | Yangzhu |

# NOTES

## 1 'THE WAY THAT CAN BE TOLD'

1 For historical and critical studies of Western images of China see Dawson (1967), Mackerras (1989), Spence (1998) and Zhang (1988, 1998).
2 On the dominance of Confucianism in the Western perception of China, see Jensen (1997).
3 The term 'sinologist' has fallen out of favour of late, largely due to the necessarily multi-disciplinary tendency of much recent study of Chinese thought and culture, and to the emergence of 'area studies', but I shall use it in order to distinguish between those who approach Daoism from the foundation of a primary professional study of classical Chinese language and literature, and those who approach Chinese studies from a religious, historical or philosophical viewpoint. Needless to say, the distinction is not always very precise in practice.
4 Said's analysis was directed specifically towards European colonial relationships with the Middle East, but his arguments are frequently extrapolated to include the whole of Asia. The orientalist debate has moved on and proliferated since this classic statement. for summaries of post-Saidian arguments, see King (1999), MacKenzie (1995), Prakash (1995) and Turner (1994). See also Said's 'Afterword' to the 1995 Penguin edition of *Orientalism*.
5 I have discussed them in more detail in Clarke (1997).
6 Kögler's book is an important attempt to construct a 'middle way' between Gadamer's hermeneutics, which has sometimes been criticised for being blind to underlying layers of political interest and the ideological manipulation of ideas, and the discourse analysis of Foucault which has been seen as rejecting too ruthlessly the role of subjective consciousness and freedom of action. See also Dallmayr (1996: ch. 2) for a useful discussion of Gadamer's more recent thinking on this matter.

## 2 'THE MEANING IS NOT THE MEANING'

1 The profusion of viewpoints is summarised in Kohn (1993: 1), and discussed at length in Kirkland (1997a) which also offers a classificatory and chronological framework for understanding Daoism.
2 The distinction goes back to the commentaries of Wangbi (226–249 CE) (Schipper 1993: 192–6; Chan 1991: 5, 11, 178).
3 See Thompson (1993) which provides a summary of this debate, and also Girardot (1972), Robinet (1997), and Sivin (1978). Paper (1995) argues for a

more integrative approach to Chinese religions by contrast with certain in-grained Western assumptions.

4 This 'degenerescence thesis', as Steve Bradbury calls it (1992: 33), is typical of orientalism which has tended to privilege ancient over more recent forms of Eastern religions and philosophies. It is worth recalling that ideas of cultural and even biological degeneration have at various times been favoured notions in purely European contexts, arising in part from the theological concept of the 'fall', but evident too in secular writings such as those of Nordau and Spengler.

5 For a useful summary of this debate, see Bell (1983). John Blofeld, who met many Daoist sages prior to the Communist revolution, is insistent that Daoist recluses in the first half of this century were 'keen exponents of the teachings of Lao Tzu and Chuang Tzu' (1973: 152).

6 The theme of unity-in-diversity is elaborated in Girardot (1983: 276–81).

7 On the convergence of Daoism and Confucianism in the Song dynasty, see Berling (1979), and on the Linzhaoen sect and the historical and philosophical background of syncretism, see Berling (1980). For a summary of the movements towards synthesis of Confucianism, Daoism and Buddhism from the Song dynasty onwards, see Wong (1997b: ch. 6). Julia Ching notes that a new sect registered in 1982 publicly venerates Jesus and Muhammad as well as Confucius, Laozi and the Buddha (Ching 1993: 217–8). Schipper stresses the role of Daoists in the formation of Neo-Confucianism (1993: 14).

8 It is interesting to compare the successful mutual accommodation between Buddhism and Daoism both with the doomed attempts of the Jesuits in a later age to accommodate Christianity with Confucianism, and more recent attempts to accommodate Buddhism with Christianity.

9 This work was written much earlier but was prevented from publication by the author's tragic fate at the hands of the Nazis. It is worth recalling here the common belief amongst the Chinese that the Buddha was a pupil of the exiled Laozi, a clever way of domesticating the former's otherwise foreign teachings. On the historical and philosophical relationship between Daoism and Buddhism, see Campany (1993), Demiéville (1970), Inada (1988), Saso and Chappell (1977), Wu (1985) and Zürcher (1980). Brook (1993) offers a conceptual as well as an historical analysis of syncretism, indicating the varieties of meanings of this somewhat protean term, and pointing as well to anti-syncretistic elements in China which sought doctrinal purity. For a Japanese parallel to Chinese religious syncretism, see Robertson (1992: 93–4).

10 See Creel (1987) for an elaboration of Bodde's argument with respect to China's legal system, its commercial and business traditions and its bureaucratic prac-tices, all of which, Creel believes, betray a strong accommodationist tendency.

11 It is important that in concentrating on the Three Teachings we should not ignore popular religious traditions in China which, though linked to them, should not be subsumed under any of these three official categories. The folk traditions performed important ritual functions within the day-to-day communal and domestic lives of ordinary Chinese people, such as conducting funerals, exorcising ghosts, paying respects to ancestors and consulting spirit mediums; see for example Lopez (1996), Paper (1995), and Welch and Seidel (1979). It is beyond the scope of our present study to give more than passing attention to these popular religious traditions.

12 Langlois and Sun (1983) examine the syncretistic policies of the founder of the Ming dynasty, Mingdaizi, following the Mongol rule.

13 Robinet emphasises the regimented, bureaucratic and hierarchical aspect of Daoism, by contrast with the more informal and uncontrolled practices of the popular priests. On the relationship between Daoism and popular or folk cults,

see also Seidel (1989–90: 283–93), which points out that, while at local level there was much interaction and even identification between the two, Daoism was often seen as antithetical to and in competition with popular indigenous religious practices. Lagerwey draws attention to a parallel between the Daoist relation to popular religious cults and to the transformation and absorption by Mediaeval Christianity of pagan cults (1987: 253–4). Kleeman (1994) and Paper (1995) both try to avoid the typical demotion of popular cults in favour of the more literate and organised traditions of Taoism. Stein (1979) emphasises the way in which Daoism was at pains to distinguish itself from folk religion, a view disputed by Bernard Faure who sees the two as 'hopelessly intertwined' (1991: 87). The contrast is also underlined by Strickmann, thereby emphasising the status of Daoism as a 'higher religion' (1978: 1045).

14 This work provides one of the most comprehensive studies of philosophical argument in ancient China; see also Henderson (1984: chaps 6–8), Kroll (1987) and Strickmann (1978: 1053). Gernet (1985) documents sophisticated debates that took place between the early Jesuit missionaries and the Chinese literati.

15 See also Graham (1981), whose introduction emphasises the dialectical tradition in which the *Zhuangzi* must be located; also Cua (1985) and Hall and Ames (1998: 128–35) on the relationship between rational argument and social values in China.

16 Like 'Neo-Confucian', 'Neo-Daoist' is a Western coinage, and for some scholarly tastes its denotation is too diffuse to be useful; see for example Strickmann (1980: 207).

17 See Berling (1997) on the dynamic intellectual climate that often prevailed in China prior to the Ching period when suppression of unorthodox thinking became common, and Yü (1985) on philosophical debate in the Weijin period.

18 This work contains a detailed account of these debates. The question of whether the Chinese tradition produced logically sound types of argument, and the extent to which they were aware of related methodological issues, has been subject to some discussion in recent years; see for example Graham (1978), Hansen (1989) and Harbsmeier (1989).

19 In the Tang dynasty royal princes were permitted to choose whatever faith they desired, and private visions were at least tolerated and often encouraged and celebrated, an attitude which would be difficult to conceive in the Mediaeval period in Europe (Benn 1991: 104–5).

20 Nevertheless the Jesuits saw this credal debility as playing into their hands since it appeared to render the Chinese more susceptible to the attractions of Christian doctrinal certitude. Gernet points out that certain currents of thought in China in the seventeenth century looked upon Christian beliefs as opening up the possibility of a new synthesis: the Four Teachings!

21 Schipper notes that official dynastic annals, though exact and abundant on other matters, are virtually silent on the subject of Daoism, a factor which has helped to disguise the importance of Daoism in Chinese cultural life.

22 These factors may help to explain why no comprehensive history of Daoism has yet been written. For prolegomenas to such a history see Baldrian (1987), Kaltenmark (1969), Liu (1993), Robinet (1991, 1997), Seidel (1990), Strickmann (1978) and Welch (1957). Accessible histories are also to be found in Ching (1993), Fung (1966), Palmer (1991) and Wong (1997b).

23 Daoists, however, did not accept the idea of possession by 'external' spirits, a common feature of shamanism. It should not be imagined that shamanism, any more than Daoism, represents a single, simple cultural entity or tradition.

24 For the philosophical debates of the period of Warring States, see Graham (1989); on Yangzhu, see pp. 53–64. On the historicity of and legends surrounding Laozi himself, see Graham (1990).

25 On the development of Chinese cosmological thinking, see Graham (1989), Henderson (1984), Needham (1956) and Schwartz (1985).

26 Michael Saso draws attention to the way in which right up to the present time Daoist priests were making use of Daoist religious texts and manuals that were based explicitly on the teachings of the *Laozi* (1990: 59–65). Martin Palmer notes the resemblance between the Daoist liturgies of Cosmic Renewal and those of the Australian Aborigines and the Greek Orthodox Church (1991: 126).

27 For fuller treatment of these 'mystical' schools see Kohn (1992), Robinet (1997), Strickmann (1981) and Wong (1997b). We will return to many of these ideas below.

28 As we noted above, Strickmann rejects the very idea of a distinct Neo-Daoist school, seeing it more as a diverse literary tradition. On the role of the 'Seven Sages', see Maspero (1981: 301–8) and Balazs (1964: 236–42).

29 On Daoism in the Tang and Song period, see Barrett (1996) and Ebrey and Gregory (1993).

30 This latter conjecture is supported by the fate of the Falun Gong, a new syncretistic movement which combines elements from both Buddhism and Daoism, which has been subject to fierce repression in response to mass rallies by its members. There is a 'Taoist Restoration Society' in the USA which is dedicated to the rehabilitation and rebirth of China's Daoist tradition (and explicitly *not* to its Westernisation), and which helps in the restoration of Daoist temples in China. It has a website which can be contacted on http://www.taorestore.org. This is a useful place to begin exploring the many websites devoted to Daoism.

## 3 'CRAMPED SCHOLARS'

1 As noted earlier, Jensen sees 'Confucius' and 'Confucianism' as essentially interpretative constructs rather than representations of historical realities, manufactured in the first place by the Jesuit missionaries for their own ideological purposes out of material from the long history of narrative embellishment surrounding the name of Confucius/Kongzi created within China itself.

2 On this whole episode, see also Gernet (1985), Mackerras (1989), Paper (1995), Ronan and Oh (1988) and Young (1983).

3 An important work in propagating Jesuit opinions concerning China, especially among the *philosophes*, was Halde (1736).

4 This viewpoint had earlier been suggested by English deists such as Matthew Tindal, and according to David Hume the Chinese were 'the only regular body of Deists in the universe' (1898: 149). On the relationship between deism and orientalism see Halbfass (1988: ch. 4) and Leites (1968).

5 Leibiniz's concern was more with the Neo-Confucian synthesis than with classical Confucianism.

6 Later, though, Mungello insisted on the importance of the comparison in encouraging Leibniz to be confident of the correctness of his theory (Lee 1991: 117). Cook and Rosemont argue that Leibniz found Chinese thought merely 'consonant' with his own (1994: 2–3). See also Ching and Oxtoby (1992).

7 This attitude is also evident in the fifteen volume work of the Jesuit, Henri Doré, entitled significantly *Recherches sur les superstitions en Chine*.

8 There is an even earlier discussion of Daoism in Clarke 1871. See also the Jesuit Leo Wieger's work of 1911, which is in many ways a fair and scholarly account

but which goes out of its way to allot Daoism an inferior moral status in relation to both Christianity and Confucianism, and to portray it as a religion of 'Systematic idleness. Absolute amorality. The following of natural instincts' (1976: 53). On nineteenth-century interpretations of classical Chinese texts, see Girardot (1999).

9 See also Giles (1906b), Ular (1902) and Wilhelm (1921a) as further examples of translations in that period.

10 Tolstoy's plan to translate the *Daodejing* was little more than a fond hope, but Heidegger actually embarked on the project with help from a Chinese colleague (May 1996). We will return to Heidegger's 'translation' in Chapter 8.

11 On the first Daoist international conference, see Welch (1969–70), and for a summary of the significance and achievements of the first three international conferences see Sivin (1979). On the 1993 Euro-Sinica Symposium in Montreal on the reception of Daoism in East and West see Hsia 1994. For summaries of the history of Daoist scholarship in the West since Maspero, see Seidel (1989–90) and Verellen (1995). For bibliographical sources of Western writings on Daoism, see Barrett (1987), Cordier (1968), Kardos (1998), Pas (1998), Thompson (1985) and Walf (1992). I have concentrated in this work on the *West's* interest in Daoism, but mention must also be made of the considerable scholarly interest shown in Daoism in Japan over the past hundred years; on the history of this endeavour, see Fumimasa (1995).

12 Ling's work on the history of religions (1968), for example, almost completely ignores Daoism. The concept of 'world religions' has itself become problematised in recent years in the light of retreat from globalised, highly abstract and universal conceptions of religious experience; see King (1999: 94).

13 For a survey of the grass-roots spiritual penetration of the West by Asian religions in recent years, see Rawlinson (1997).

14 Though it has now become apparent that such emissaries were themselves not representing pure Asian traditions but conveyed teachings that in part reflected back European assumptions and expectations (King 1999). Moreover an earlier generation of Chinese scholars, including Wing-tsit Chan and Fung Yu-lan, who were important disseminators of Daoist ideas in the West, tended to reinforce a textualist view of Daoism, and were at the same time members of the Western academy.

15 Schwartz examines the relationship between the élite culture fed on classic texts and mentalities embedded in popular culture. The 'sacred' nature of Daoist texts is discussed in Robinet (1997: 125–8).

16 For an historical account of the *Daozang*, see Ōfuchi (1979), which points to the inspiration of the Buddhist canon in the formulation of the Daoist version. See also Schipper (1975), Seidel (1989–90: 231–5) and Boltz (1987a, 1987b).

17 It is interesting to compare this with the process by which Buddhist texts were initially translated into Chinese through, in part, the medium of a Daoist vocabulary, *nirvana*, for example, being translated in some instances as *wu-wei*; see Ch'en (1964: 68–9), Fung (1966: 242) and Maspero (1981: 406).

18 Creel censured the Christian bias in James Legge's translations of Daoist texts, though he went on to point out that 'The translator must to some extent be an interpreter' (1929: 3). Legge believed that the Chinese were descendants of Noah and sought to harmonise Chinese history with the *Book of Genesis*.

19 See Bokenkamp (1997: xiv–xv) which highlights the problems of the translator of Daoist texts. Welch (1957: ch. 1) discusses at some length the perils and difficulties encountered in translating classical Chinese texts. Hansen (1992: 7–10) attacks the view that translation precedes interpetation. See also Duyvendak (1953) for an early discussion of these issues.

20  Merton, a Cistercian monk who embarked on a dialogue between Christian and Eastern monasticism, admits that he knew only a few Chinese characters, offering his version as a 'personal and spiritual interpretation' based on an 'intuitive approach', and disclaiming any intention of producing 'a new apologetic...in which Christian rabbits will suddenly appear by magic out of a Taoist hat' (1965: 9–10). See the comments on this edition in Bradbury (1992: 36–7).

21  For a useful summary of the different methodological approaches, see Herman (1996: 188–92). Herman speaks of the need for 'moving a fragmented academy one step closer toward a comprehensive discourse' (191), though I find it difficult to imagine what such a discourse would look like, and wonder if it would even be desirable.

22  The work was also translated by Lionel Giles in 1912, and by Richard Wilhelm in 1921. For a recent edition, see Wong (1995); Wong comments that as a child in Hong Kong, she became familiar with the stories of the *Liezi* long before she had even heard of the *Daodejing*. See also Morgan (1933) for a translation of the second century BCE Daoist text *Huainanzi*, which is representative of attempts at syncretism in the early Han, and Legge's collection of Daoist texts published in 1891. For some more recent sources of other less well-known Daoist texts see Bokenkamp (1997), Chan (1963a), Cleary (1987, 1991), de Bary *et al.* (1960), Kohn (1991a, 1993) and Wong (1992, 1997a, 1998).

23  See Needham (1956: 163 fn.b), where he refers to the intriguing suggestion that William Blake had access to one of these translations which had been presented to the Royal Society in 1788; the translators stated that their intention was to show that the Christian mysteries were 'anciently known to the Chinese nation' (Legge 1891, vol. 1: xiii).

24  Bradbury comments that 'Even today, the vast majority of all English translations of the *Tao te ching*, even by professional sinologists, Western and Chinese alike, are the products of some kind of ecumenical and liberal humanist commitment, often allied with an apocalyptic environmentalism' (p. 40, n. 8). See also Kraft (1981). Bynner, who was primarily a poet, also played an important role in familiarising Western readers with Chinese poetry, for example in his anthology *The Jade Mountain*.

25  For a close study of two such commentaries see Chan (1991), for a study of commentaries during the early centuries see Robinet (1977), and for an example of such a commentary see Bokenkamp (1997: ch. 2). See also Kohn (1992: ch. 3).

26  This is brought out well in Wong (1997a). Allinson believes that this multi-layered quality of classic Chinese texts has provided us in the West with an excuse not to take these works seriously from a philosophical point of view, allowing us to treat them as mystical curiosities or as poetry (1989a: 10–13).

27  Welch's view, that the author is likely to be a single individual in view of the coherence of the text's thinking, is now very much in the minority (1957: 3 & Appendix I). According to Victor Mair the *Daodejing* is 'a selection of proverbial wisdom' (1990: 119). Hansen sees it as drawing on 'popular political maxims, practical aphorisms, and other familiar wise sayings' (1996: 186–7). LaFargue sees it as 'probably an anthology of once independent chapter-collages' (1992: 199). For an authoritative discussion of the dating of the text, see Graham (1990).

28  The so-called *Mawangdui* manuscripts were discovered in 1973 in an early Han tomb. For a comparative study of three relatively recent translations of the *Daodejing*, bringing out differences in methodological approaches, see Wu (1993).

29  On issues concerning the multiplicity of translations, see Wu (1993).

30 Schwartz prefers to give prominence to the mystical aspect of the work. Graham refers to Brecht's reading of the work as 'the little man's strategy of survival' (1989: 234).

31 Mair talks of 'different voices' speaking out of the text: the mystic, the political strategist, the utopian architect, the clairvoyant poet, and the meditative yogin (1990: xv).

32 See Csikszentmihalyi and Ivanhoe (1999), and Kohn and LaFargue (1998) for useful collections of writings on the history and issues surrounding *Daodejing* translation and interpretation; Hardy (1998), included in the latter volume, provides an especially useful summary of Western interpretations of the *Daode-jing*, as well as of Daoism in general.

33 The variety of ways of reading the *Zhuangzi* is also emphasised in Mair (1983b).

34 See also Levering (1984) which offers a critical summary of different readings to date of the *Zhuangzi*, and suggests the need to combine divergent readings in order to obtain a balanced and well-rounded interpretation (p. 229).

35 On the history of the text in China, see Rand (1983).

36 Both of these works have been pre-eminent in their contribution to the new scholarship on the *Zhuangzi*, though Liu (1994) puts forward some important alternative views on the text.

37 *The Speaker*, 8 February 1890.

38 For a review of Wu's interpretation, see Kjellberg (1993). For an extension of this debate, see Herman (1996: 129–37), which draws on the hermeneutical thinking of Gadamer and Paul Ricoeur and argues that the gist of interpretation must lie in the 'play' between text and reader rather than purely in some detached insight into authorial intent.

39 Thomas Cleary reads the *Yijing* as an instrument of spiritual alchemy for the Daoists, and as a key to living in harmony with nature (1986: 25, 8–9).

40 This is a pioneering work long hidden from the West which offers a useful study of the interpretative history of the *Yijing* up to the beginning of the First World War.

41 The Régis translation was later published in Germany in 1834 and 1839. See also Jackson (1981: 129–34).

42 Shchutskii believed that Wilhelm had a deep understanding of the work and that his translation was 'the best that has ever been done in Europe' (1979: 45). For Karcher, Wilhelm's translation, though essentially a Confucian reading, was 'a landmark...readable and useful. It took the book seriously as a spiritual document and a psychological tool' (1999: 7). The English translation of Wilhelm's version carried out by Cary F. Baynes was clearly influenced by the latter's Jungian predispositions (Wilhelm 1989: xli).

43 See for example Blofeld (1965), Cleary (1986), Ritsema and Karcher (1994), Shaughnessy (1996) and Shchutskii (1979). Wu Jung-nuan's translation (1991) is critical of the Legge and Wilhelm translations as products of a Neo-Confucian interpretation of the text, and seeks to offer a more Daoist rendering. Ritsema and Karcher, whose edition includes a concordance, seek to go beyond the text's Confucianised surface to its oracular core, and Shaughnessy's translation, based on the recently discovered *Mawangdui* text, emphasises the Daoist tone of the Appended Statements. Blofeld's version is explicitly designed for oracular consultation.

## 4 'THE GREAT CLOD'

1 See Jantsch (1980), a work which outlined an early model of self-organising systems based on Prigogine's theory of dissipative structures, though now largely

outdated due to the development of the new mathematics of complexity.

2 This term was coined by Humberto Maturana and Francisco Varela (Capra 1997: 97–9).

3 Strictly speaking, chaos theory rests ultimately on deterministic assumptions, and the emptiness of the quantum vacuum is usually viewed not as nothing in an absolute sense, but as the absence of anything determinate.

4 I am using the term 'cosmology' here to embrace the notion of cosmogony, the study of the origins of the universe. The cosmological concepts and theories discussed below were to a large extent common to Chinese culture as a whole, but Daoist thinking was associated with them in important ways. The *Zhuangzi* sometimes suggests, however, that raising the question of origins merely leads us into paradox (Graham 1981: 105).

5 For an example of this way of thinking in the *Liezi*, see Graham (1960: 18–19).

6 Hall and Ames speak of the Daoist conception as a form of *acosmic* thinking (1998: 61, 125). The second century BCE syncretist/Daoist text, the *Huainanzi*, offers a cyclical cosmology of creation, loss and return (Girardot 1983: ch. 5); Daoist thinking could in this respect be compared with the emanationist cosmology of Plotinus. Some recent cosmological thinking represents the universe in evolutionary terms, as cyclical and self-reproducing, with new universes arising out of the death of old ones, for example in the work of Andrei Linde and Lee Smolin.

7 *Wu* is sometimes translated as 'non-being', 'non-existence' or 'void'. It was Neo-Daoists such as Wangbi and Xiangguo who, under the influence of Buddhist philosophy, made explicit the identification of *dao* with emptiness.

8 For examples of 'evolutionary' thinking in the *Liezi*, see Graham (1960: 21–2); the boundlessness of the universe and the infinite variety of natural phenomena are also emphasised in Graham (1960: ch. 5).

9 Whitehead himself noted the closeness of his process philosophy to Chinese cosmological thinking (1978: 7).

10 In the *Liezi*, for example (Graham 1960: 97, 100).

11 At this stage in his thinking (perhaps influenced by the ascendancy of positivistic thinking at that time), Graham was inclined to see the mythological side of Daoist writings as 'parables' and hence not to be read literally (1960: 16–17).

12 The mythic dimension of early Daoist thinking is emphasised in Girardot (1983: 6–7); see also Schwartz (1985: 226–9).

13 The idea of correlative thinking first appeared as such in Granet (1934), where it was portrayed as a characteristic of the 'Chinese mind'. It was later elaborated in Needham 1956 as the foundation of Chinese cosmology (and compared with pre-modern Western cosmological thinking), and is dealt with extensively in Graham (1989), Henderson (1984) and Schwartz (1985). This cosmological model, of ancient origin but systematised in the Han period, is fundamental to Chinese thinking as a whole, and while Daoists made use of it, they by no means enjoyed exclusive ownership; indeed the *Yin/Yang* (or Cosmological) school was quite separate from the Daoists in Simadan's classification, and, with their taste for chaos, they were often sceptical about the possibility of specifying a single cosmic order.

14 Arguments directed against Lévy-Bruhl's claim that Chinese correlative thinking was 'pre-logical' are elaborated in Henderson (1984: 35), and Needham (1956: 284–7).

15 Graham adds that correlative thinking, for long under siege in the West, has been reaffirmed by such thinkers as Ryle, Wittgenstein and Derrida as deeply inscribed in language itself. It has also reappeared in Jung's notion of 'synchronicity'. The first serious attempt to find parallels between Chinese

cosmological thinking and that of other civilisations is to be found in Forke (1925).

16 More to Neo-Confucianists such as Zhuxi than directly to the Daoists, but the latter contributed to the synthesis associated with the former (see Needham 1956: 291–2, 496–505). Mungello sees the influence as 'more corroborative than germinal' (1977: 15), a view supported in Cook and Rosemont (1981).

17 *Wuxing* has been variously translated as five 'phases', 'agents', 'powers', 'actions' and 'movements'.

18 We should remember, though, that for the Greeks the stuff of the natural world – *physis* – was also considered to be alive in some sense.

19 It is worth noting, however, that the Moists did sketch an atomic theory.

20 See Wile (1992: 61–9) for a survey of more popular expressions of this viewpoint. The role of the language of the feminine in Daoist cosmology is discussed in Schwartz (1985: 200), where it is associated with *wu-wei*, the idea of spontaneity and receptivity which is at once passive and yet powerful. On the role of female spirits in Chinese religion, see Paper (1995: ch. 8) in which the author seeks to rebut earlier Eurocentric preconceptions by emphasising the equal importance and power of male and female spirits in Chinese religion. For studies of specific Chinese female deities, see Boltz (1986), Cahill (1993) and Paul (1985).

21 There are some interesting parallels here with the drawing of Buddhism into Western discourse about science in the nineteenth century (Almond 1988: ch. 4).

22 For an earlier version of Capra's thesis, see Siu (1957).

23 For a criticism of the use made of Daoist ideas in New Age thinking, see Palmer (1991: 127–8).

24 There has been a number of critical reviews and studies of Capra's ideas, for example Clifton and Regehr (1989), Esbenshade (1982) and Scerri (1989), the latter providing a useful summary of published criticisms of Capra's work.

25 In the 1930s Needham came under the influence of Russian Marxist thinkers such as Aleksandr Bogdanov and Boris Hessen, and the American sociologist Robert Merton, and was associated with a group of British scientists including J.B.S. Haldane and J.D. Bernal, who sought to draw the natural sciences into a much closer association with social developments and who pioneered a more 'externalist' approach to the historiography of science which emphasises factors such as social and political conditions in explaining the emergence and evolution of scientific thinking. His 'Marxism' was hardly orthodox, and was paired with strong liberal and humanistic values which are evident in his persistent rebuttal of Western racist attitudes towards China. His organicist leanings, which are explicitly anti-Newtonian, appear to have been inspired by A.N. Whitehead. To make matters even more complicated, he was also a High Anglican! (See Needham 1969: 214–5; Gare 1995b; Nakayama and Sivin 1973).

26 On the links between Daoism and modern biological science, see Barnett (1986), who argues that the similarities between the two are 'nothing short of remarkable', and indicate 'a fundamental continuity of mental processes within the human mind' (p. 315).

27 For a discussion of this question see Bodde (1991: 354–5), who argues that modern science could only have emerged from mechanistic assumptions; see also Hall and Ames (1995), Hansen (1992: 29) and Sivin (1990). Needham's line of thinking is supported in broad terms by Gaston Bachelard and Georges Canguilhem, who pioneered the argument that natural science does not necessarily evolve in accordance with a universal logical pattern.

28 For a critical comparison between Needham and Weber, see Nelson (1974).

29 This question was actually first raised by J. de Groot in 1897; his answer was that China was trapped in an unbounded reverence for everything ancient (1892–1910, vol. 3: 1050).

30 Needham's explanation also takes into account intellectual factors such as the absence of the idea of laws of nature in Chinese thought (1969: ch. 8).

31 See also Graham (1973), and the extended critique in Sivin (1995a).

32 Nevertheless, Gare then proceeds to defend Needham against this charge by construing his work as an elaboration of a new synthesis which transcends both Western and Eastern thought, and as contributing towards the liberation of China from Western cultural domination. In a different context, though, it must be pointed out that Needham was insistent that earlier attempts to measure Chinese 'stagnation' against Western concepts of its own progressive dynamism were crucially misplaced, for they not only failed to give credit to the continuous cultural changes that had in fact taken place in China since the earliest times, but also overlooked the 'cybernetic' factor in China's history, a kind of cultural homeostatic mechanism which, in his view, had enabled it to cope with periodic convulsions without succumbing to them (1969: 118–21, 284).

33 There is a much closer attention to natural phenomena in the *Zhuangzi* and the *Liezi*, however.

34 See John Lagerwey's critique of this view (1987: 255), and also Graham (1960: 16).

35 See also Schwartz (1985: 201–5), who discerns in Laozi no inclination to engage in disinterested observation of nature or any desire to know the causes of things, and Sivin (1971), who maintains that, by blurring the distinction between science and technology, Needham has tended to overestimate the extent of Chinese scientific achievement; see also Sivin (1978).

36 See also Hall and Ames (1998: 35–7) and Schwartz (1985: 416–8), where the term 'holistic' is preferred to 'organismic'.

37 The ideals of frugality and simplicity of living were common to almost all schools of classical Chinese thought, including the Confucian which disapproved of trade and foreign travel as conducive to unnecessary affluence.

38 This brings to mind a parallel conundrum in Christian theology where God is both infinitely perfect yet creates a world in which evil arises.

39 This contains a discussion of different Daoist-inspired views about what is 'natural'. See Rolston (1979) which also urges a similarly relaxed interpretation of the injunction to 'follow nature'. Ames (1986) argues that Daoism does not provide us with a metaphysical system but rather with an 'ars contextualis' which is based on an 'aesthetic' rather than a logically coherent understanding of nature.

40 For a fuller discussion of this, see the epilogue to Callicott and Ames (1989), and also Tuan (1968) who argues that environmental destruction in China was related to social attitudes and beliefs that were inconsistent with, but more powerful politically than, those of Daoism.

41 Arguably, the 'primitivist' passages in Daoist writings were in any case not intended to be taken entirely literally but rather as enjoining a more natural life within the prevailing civilisational context.

## 5 'GOING RAMBLING WITHOUT DESTINATION'

1 For the sake of simplicity, and following a growing tendency, I shall use the terms 'moral' and 'ethical' interchangeably here.

2 On the criticism of quietism in ancient China, see Waley (1977: 43). For a rethinking of Zhuangzi on this point, see Wu (1982: 6–8), which rejects the idea

that he was a nihilist or a selfish hedonist. On Yangzhu's 'selfishness', see Graham (1989: 59–64) and Smullyan (1977: 124–7). For the 'Yangzhu' passages in the *Zhuangzi*, see Graham (1981: 221–53). Yangzhu's thinking appears to avoid any of the mysticism associated with Daoist philosophy, and is concerned only with the question 'What are my true interests?'. For the text of Zhuangzi's famous refusal of office, see Graham (1981: 122).

3 This brief summary does not do justice to the sophistication of the thinking of the Seven Sages, who certainly cannot be identified with simplistic egocentric individualism or hedonism. On the 'wild man' and 'holy fool' themes, see Girardot (1983: 271–4, 300–01) and Strickmann (1994).

4 See Koestler (1960) which is concerned with Japanese Zen, a tradition which has drawn on certain aspects of Daoist thinking.

5 In the Confucian tradition, *li* is linked closely with the ideas of *ren*, the cultivation of human-heartedness and of care for one's fellows, with *yi*, righteousness, and with *ming*, names correctly used.

6 Daoist and Confucian ideals are much closer in spirit than he allows in this passage. See also Peerenboom (1993: 191) and Schwartz (1985: 209–10) which emphasise the Daoist animus against predetermined rules and prescriptions.

7 Ames (1985), Chan (1963a), Ivanhoe (1993a), Nivison (1991) and Tu (1985) all emphasise the centrality of the ideal of self-cultivation (*xiu sheng*) in Confucian thought. Tu points to this ideal as the syncretistic junction between Confucianism and Daoism that took place in the Ching dynasty.

8 See also Taylor (1992), where links are also drawn with Nietzsche and with Romantics such as Herder and Schiller. Contrary to typical criticisms of authenticity as an expression of a selfish 'me-generation', Taylor argues that 'My own identity crucially depends on my dialogical relations with others' (p. 48), and links self-cultivation with the sense of solidarity with nature as, for example, in the poetry of Wordsworth (p. 88).

9 For a general discussion of the issue of self-cultivation as a central moral concept, see for example Chapman and Galston (1992), Schneewind (1990) and Yearley (1990). In relation to Daoism, see Allinson (1989a), Hansen (1996), Ivanhoe (1996b), LaFargue (1992), Thompson (1990) and Tominaga (1994).

10 Kuo (1996) draws links between Daoism and Abraham Maslow's self-actualisation theory. Coward argues that Jung was influenced by Daoist ideas in the formation of his notion of individuation and his belief that the self is the goal of psychic development (1996: 483–91). See Lahar (1996) on the contribution of Daoism to the new field of philosophical counselling.

11 The idea of bringing the self to maturity as a moral task is evident in Rousseau's *Émile*, and also much earlier in Stoic philosophy with its advocacy of the practice of self-discipline (*ascesis*). Compare also Gadamer's notion of *Bildung*, deployed earlier by Romantic thinkers such as Wilhelm von Humboldt, and meaning 'self-education as an unfolding of innate potential'. The ethical ideal of self-creation also finds a central role in the thinking of Isaiah Berlin and Jean-Paul Sartre, though in neither case as an unfolding of a pre-formed human essence.

12 Daoist understanding of the role of physiological processes in self-cultivation will be dealt with more fully in the next chapter.

13 Quoted from a Six Dynasties source in Schipper (1993: 127).

14 For the Heidegger connection, see Chang (1977: 412), which speaks of Daoist philosophy as leading towards 'the freedom of man towards things'. We will return to this in Chapter 8.

15 Graham argues that the question of free-will was not an issue as such for Daoists, but he concludes that there was an assumption of freedom of choice amongst Chinese thinkers in general, even if this facility was seen as severely

NOTES

circumscribed by the rule of heaven or fate (Graham 1960: 118–21). Peterson (1988) claims that there were indeed arguments for and against the ideas of fate and pre-determination in the fourth to second centuries BCE.

16 For a Derrida-inspired deconstructive analysis of 'spontaneity', see Fu (1992: 312).

17 Compare the idea of self-realisation in the Deep Ecology of Arne Naess, who likewise sees it as a means of dimming down rather than amplifying individualistic and selfish tendencies.

18 Bokenkamp (1997: 49–50) provides a lengthy list of ethical precepts quoted from an early commentary on the *Daodejing*; the author of the commentary criticises the Confucian ethic for being superficial and insincere (p. 53).

19 Blofeld (1973) and Goullart (1961) provide firsthand accounts of life in Daoist monasteries prior to the Communist revolution, and testify to the continuing vitality of these institutions well into the twentieth century.

20 On the more radical side of Confucianism, see Peerenboom (1993: 205) and Bloom and Fogel (1997). W.T. de Bary disputes the oft-repeated belief that Confucianism encourages a despotic style of politics (1988: 115).

21 On the role of the Daoist sage as counsellor to emperors, see Seidel (1989–90: 273–78) and Verellen (1995: 326–7). On Daoism as a state philosophy in the Tang dynasty, see Benn (1987).

22 The role of Daoist thinking in political debate in China is brought out in Graham (1989) and Kohn (1995).

23 Once again, it is important not to over-emphasise the contrast with Confucianism which was opposed to the excessive imposition of law and punishment, and taught that education and ritual were preferable to compulsion or intimidation. For examples of primitivist utopian passages in classic Daoist texts, see *Daodejing* (ch. 80) and Graham (1960: 102–3; 1981: 171–5).

24 On Zhuangzi as a social thinker, see Wu (1982).

25 Needham draws a parallel with the religious/political dissenters of seventeenth-century England, and with Renaissance utopian movements (1956: 89–98). Schipper sees early Daoist communes as having 'a democracy in some ways comparable to that of ancient Greece' (1993: 9).

26 Muramatsu (1960) emphasises the role of Daoism in inspiring mass rebellion in the eighteenth and nineteenth centuries. Though the Taiping Rebellion in the mid-nineteenth century is primarily associated with a Christian-inspired ideology, Daoist writings and practices also had some influence (Franke 1970: 33). For a different view, see Sivin (1978), who argues that Daoist sects played no active role in rebellions after the Han period, and Strickmann (1980) who refers to the 'lingering myth of the subversive Taoists' (p. 211). Some interesting links between Daoism and Mao's political thinking are drawn in Ching (1990: 91).

27 Ames explicitly aligns Daoism with the anarchist theories of Proudhon and Colin Ward (1983a: 113–14).

28 For a critique of the interpretation as a form of libertarianism, see Bradbury (1992: 34).

29 It must be noted that, while an individualist spirit pervades much anarchist thinking, particularly in the case of Stirner, there is a strong communitarian/collectivist tendency in the thinking of Bakunin and Kropotkin, for example, which runs counter to the individualism of classical liberal thinking, and organicist metaphors perform an important role in Kropotkin's writing. Furthermore, there has been a significant reaction against individualist/libertarian assumptions in recent anarchist writings, such as those of Murray Bookchin.

30 It should be noted that different kinds of authority are identified by anarchist writers.

225

NOTES

31 On the link with Legalism, see Graham (1989: 285–92), Vandermeersch (1965: 241–70) and Vervoon (1981). Amoury de Riencourt likens Laozi to Rousseau, both of whom, with their contempt for civilisational structures, unwittingly paved the way for dictatorships (1965: 33–4). For a general historical account of Daoism and anarchism in China, see Zarrow (1990). See also Dirlik (1991) and Gasster (1969), both of whom argue that anarchist theory in general, and Daoist ideas in particular, played a crucial if largely unacknowledged role in the shaping of twentieth-century political thought in China.
32 Graham suggests that in these terms, even Confucius could be regarded as an anarchist.
33 The positive role of chaos in social thinking is emphasised in Hall and Ames (1995: 9–10).
34 Julia Ching comments on the danger in such beliefs of a lapse into 'political authoritarianism' (1993: 90), and Thomas Merton sees Daoist anarchist tenden-cies as playing into the hands of the extreme right (1961: 50), though for Schip-per the Celestial Masters movement encouraged a decentralised, almost democratic, form of local government (1993: 195).
35 According to Girardot, this does not mean a literal demolition of civilised life but a rediscovery of primitive impulses in a life irreversibly shaped by civilisa-tion. See also Graham (1989: 306–11), where Zhuangzi's 'primitivism' is seen as a reaction to state repression and to the useless moralism of the Confucian sages.
36 This principle was generally shared by the Confucians who, as we noted above, opposed the Legalist-inspired imposition of harsh punishments, believing that education and ritual were better means to social order than legal coercion.
37 Pacifism has of course also played its part in Western anarchist thinking, for example in that of Tolstoy, who was influenced by Daoist ideas (Bodde 1950). Tolstoy rejected the title 'anarchist' because of its association with terrorist violence.
38 It is worth noting that women are prominent in terms of numbers and eminence in the field of Daoist scholarship.
39 From the *Classic of Su Nü*, quoted in Wile (1992: 11).
40 See also Chen (1969), which links the feminine creative principle with the Daoist concept *wu* – emptiness – and which speculates that matriarchy predominated in early China.
41 Despeux (1990) offer an historical survey of the place and image of women in Daoism.
42 A similar argument is put forward in Black (1986), who also points out that the image of the sage ruler in Daoist writings remains obdurately male.
43 A view similar to this is advocated in Kleinjaus (1990). Paper is critical of any one-sided view, whether masculinist or feminist, and favours a polytheistic position which tends towards an equality between female and male divinities and avoids baneful dualities between good and evil, heaven and earth and so on (1995: 239–43).

6 'THE TRANSFORMATION OF THINGS'

1 Though see Hans Küng's discussion of Daoism in Küng and Ching (1989). This represents one of the few attempts at an extended Daoist-Christian dialogue.
2 Needham believes that the two views are compatible since the alchemical processes were deemed to be perfectly natural (1974: 83); see also Bodde (1976), Graham (1989: 202–4) and Girardot (1983: 84).

3 The phrase is that of Arthur Waley quoted in Welch (1957: 93). For the famous passage by Zhuangzi on the death of his wife, see Graham (1981: 123–4).
4 For this sort of reason, Bokenkamp prefers the term 'longevity' to 'immortality'.
5 For Girardot, the 'return to the undifferentiated ground' of Boehmer is understood as a return to the original state of chaos. Girardot (1983: ch. 9) offers some interesting reflections on the relationship between Chinese and European alchemy.
6 Cinnabar is a red crystalline form of mercuric sulphide. The usual Chinese term for alchemy is *jin-dan*, literally 'gold-cinnabar'.
7 The intertwining of literal and metaphorical meaning in alchemical recipes is emphasised in Bokenkamp (1997: 292–5). Compare Jung's view that European alchemists 'were talking in symbols' (1983: 230). For comprehensive studies of Chinese alchemy see Needham (1976) and Sivin (1968).
8 Accounts of the origins of internal alchemy can be found in Boehmer (1977), Kirkland (1997b), Kohn (1989), Maspero (1981), Needham (1983), Robinet (1995, 1997), Roth (1991a) and Wong (1997b). It is interesting to compare Needham's concentration on the scientific aspects of internal alchemy with the more spiritual approach of Kohn, Maspero and Robinet. Techniques for controlling the breath are referred to in the *Zhuangzi* (Graham 1981: 68, 84, 97).
9 For useful summaries see Blofeld (1985: ch. 8), Kohn (1989), Lu (1964), Maspero (1981), Robinet (1997) and Wong (1997b: ch. 12).
10 On the stages of inner alchemical transformation see Robinet (1997: 245–8). See also Roth (1997: 311), where it is argued that meditation techniques similar to those of the Daoists 'are found cross-culturally and throughout human history'.
11 See also Kohn (1989), Robinet (1993) and Schipper (1995) for detailed discussion of Daoist visualisation techniques, and Maspero (1981) for a detailed account of the indwelling of spirits.
12 On the history of the study and use of mental images and visualisation in modern psychology, see Watkins (1986).
13 For accounts of Daoist visualisation techniques see Kohn (1989, 1992) and Robinet (1993). See Robinet (1997: 138–48) for discussion of mental travelling and ecstatic journeying.
14 Similar techniques to those developed by Jung are incorporated into the psychosynthesis method of Assagioli (Hardy: 1987).
15 Livia Kohn examines some of these Daoist 'journeys' in detail, and sees them as symbolising and illustrating 'the transformation of a human into a cosmic being' (1992: 95, and chaps. 4 and 5).
16 For a fuller discussion of these issues in relation to Jung, see Clarke (1994: ch. 9), and Gómez (1995). See also some comments on Jung and Chinese alchemy in Bertschinger (1994).
17 According to Maspero, the Buddhists condemned such practices as 'pestilential impropriety' (1981: 386). Robinet argues that the sexual rites were in fact strictly controlled and that the reputation for orgies was purely a consequence of Buddhist denunciations which were aimed at discrediting the Daoists (1997: 60).
18 See Wile 1992 for a more detailed analysis of the history and variety of these practices and ideas, along with relevant primary texts. Wile also discusses the relationship between Daoism and the wider Chinese culture with regard to these matters.
19 See Needham's postscript in Chang (1995).
20 See the critique of Schipper's views, as well as those of Gulik and Needham, in Wile (1992: 57–61).
21 Robert van Gulik also noted the parallels between the ideas of the ancient Chinese and modern Western sexologists (1961: 156).

22 Though Bokenkamp has compared the sublimated versions of Daoist sexual practice which are manifested in visionary and meditational experience with Christian mystics such as St Teresa and St Bernard, whose ecstatic visions have sometimes been interpreted in sexual terms (1996: 168).

23 This volume contains translations of works specifically on women's 'solo' inner alchemical practices, and as Schipper points out, 'Chinese sex manuals are the only ancient books in the world on this subject that do not present sexuality solely from the male point of view' (1993: 126). According to Kaltenmark, the kind of 'vampirism' which makes use of uninitiated women to increase vitality at the partner's expense was condemned as unorthodox (1969: 126).

24 For an introduction to the history and methods of *taijiquan* see Wong (1996). *Quigong* is a meditation practice which combines breathing with physical movements. On its history and its relation to Daoism, see Miura (1989).

25 For an introduction to the history and theory of traditional Chinese medicine, see Porkert (1990), which advocates a cooperative rather than a competitive approach to the medical traditions of Europe and Asia. Unschild's 'history of ideas' approach to Chinese medicine includes criticism of both Porkert and Needham for emphasising those aspects of Chinese medicine which fit with their own Western assumptions (1985: 2). For a discussion of Chinese medicine in relation to Western paradigms of health and sickness, see Capra (1982: ch. 10). On the connections between Chinese medicine and Daoist sexual alchemy, see Wile (1992: ch. 3). See also Sivin (1990).

26 The role of shamanism in the formation of the internal alchemy tradition is discussed in Kohn (1992: ch. 4).

## 7 'THE WAY IS INCOMMUNICABLE'

1 For an influential statement of the latter viewpoint, see Katz (1978). For general discussion of this issue, see Forman (1990) and King (1999).

2 A link with the mystical teaching of Plotinus, the founder of Neoplatonism, is made in Welch (1957: 57–8); see also Kohn (1987: 58). Cooper (1990) brings a strong element of the perennial philosophy of Fritjof Schuon, as well as Neoplatonism, to her study of Daoist mysticism. Parallels with Western mystical traditions are also drawn in Seidel (1978: 1043).

3 Herman's book offers the most extensive study of Buber's encounter with Zhuangzi, and includes Buber's translation of the *Zhuangzi* and his commentary on it. See also Friedman (1976), which claims that Buber's translation of the *Zhuangzi* 'had a great impact on the German Youth Movement' (p. 415), and Eber (1994), which investigates the ways in which Daoist ideas became retranslated into Buber's own philosophical discourse, and the impact his translation had on writers such as Hermann Hesse.

4 See Eber (1994). Buber's work of 'translation' was, as he himself readily admitted, in effect a creative transformation of the renderings of Giles and Legge, with help from Wang Chingdao, a visiting lecturer from China at the Berlin Seminar for Oriental Languages from 1907 to 1911. A similar procedure was adopted by Thomas Merton and Witter Bynner.

5 In his review of Herman's book, Allinson points to the tenuousness of the link between Buber's personalist philosophy, with its strong sense of concern for the other person, and the naturalistic/holistic world-view of Daoism. He nevertheless agrees with Herman that any reading of the *Zhuangzi* must inevitably be personal and transformative (1998: 531).

6 The idea of 'mystic Hinduism' is itself a Western construct according to Richard King (1999: ch. 6).

7  Richard King criticises the skewing of contemporary discussions of mysticism in largely private, experiential terms to the neglect of its wider social, ethical, and political dimensions (1999: ch. 8).

8  Though it should be added that the concept of divine immanence can also be found in the case of Christian mystics, for example in the Quaker, gnostic and Eastern Orthodox traditions, in Eckhart and Teilhard de Chardin, and also in Spinoza and a number of thinkers from the Romantic period. A similar point to Kohn's is made in Welch (1957: 60, 77), and is reiterated in Hall and Ames (1998: 66), which rejects the interpretation of the *dao* as the ultimate unity of all things, and insists that 'the "mystical" experience of the Daoist sage, rather than that of Oneness with all things, is closer to an experience of the particularity of all things'. See also Hall and Ames (1995: 233–4) and Tominaga (1982), which examines the issue of transcendence and immanence in comparing Eastern and Western mysticism, in the latter case with particular reference to Wittgenstein.

9  Archie Bahm rejects the comparison between Daoism and Hindu or Christian mysticism, and sees the so-called mysticism of the former in purely naturalistic terms: 'no mystery exists for those accepting nature's way' (1958: 106).

10  This interpretation of the scientific revolution, which Needham rests on the authority of Walter Pagel, has been amplified in the work of Frances Yates, amongst others.

11  For an overview of recent investigations into the 'sacred geography' of China see Holzman (1996).

12  On the relationship between Daoism and nature poetry, see Frodsham (1960–1).

13  On the importance of Confucianism in the inspiration of Chinese painting, see Cahill (1960). On the Daoist influence on Chinese landscape painting and aesthetics, see Delahaye (1981), Parker (1997) and Shaw (1988).

14  See also Shaw (1988) for a detailed discussion of the link between Chinese landscape painting and spiritual cultivation.

15  For a study of the history of miniature gardens in China, see Stein (1990), in which emphasis is placed in the micro–macrocosmic relationship.

16  The variety of styles and dynamic historical development of Chinese landscape art is emphasised in Sullivan (1979: 17; 1990: 275–7) and in Sze (1959: 4).

17  Kandinsky and Mondrian were both influenced by oriental ideas via the Theosophical Society, though not specifically by Daoist philosophy or Chinese painting (Clarke 1997: 103).

18  Neither of these artists has acknowledged any oriental influence on his work, in spite of conjectures by some critics.

19  The art historian Ananda Coomaraswamy played an important role in mediating Asian art in general and Chinese painting in particular to the West (1977: 11–12).

20  The spiritual significance of mountains in Chinese religious culture in general is brought out in Schafer (1989). Hay (1985) also discusses the importance of the Chinese concern with mountains and rocks, and draws comparisons with Western attitudes.

21  The creative aspect of Chinese painting and its link with Daoism is also emphasised in Chang (1975a) and Danto (1976).

22  See for example Wackenroder's *Effusions from the Heart of an Art-Loving Monk* and Shelley's *A Defence of Poetry*. Coleridge believed that art is not an imitation of *natura naturata* (nature formed) but participates in *natura naturans* (nature creating). For Blake, the artist has a privileged insight into spiritual reality through the power of imagination. Other possible comparisons are the tradition of sacred icon painting in the Eastern Orthodox churches, and the arts and crafts

movement that flourished in Britain and the USA in the late nineteenth and early twentieth centuries.

23 See also Bush (1971) who, while recognising the character and psychology of the artist as being at the core of painting from the Song period onwards, is nevertheless wary of the tendency, encouraged by the Chinese literati themselves, to over-idealise this by portraying the tradition in mystical terms (pp. 64–6). The element of idealisation is also noted by Paper, who tells us that 'idealized attitudes towards aesthetics' were common in Chinese biographies (1995: 186).

24 Amongst the earliest modern Western attempts to appreciate the philosophical significance of the Chinese landscape garden are Reichwein (1925) and Sirén (1949).

25 A useful source here is Hunt and Willis (1975). Chambers, who journeyed to China, published *A Dissertation on Oriental Gardening* in 1772. Spencer's *A Particular Account of the Emperor of China's Gardens* of 1752 was a translation of a work by the French Jesuit Fr Attiret.

26 Hall and Ames point out that there is also a strong immanentist religious tradition in the West, and argue that mystical *experience*, by contrast with the theoretical expressions thereof, is fundamentally non-transcendent (1998: 204, 244).

27 Difficulties over the definition of 'transcendence' are examined in Hall and Ames (1998: 189–93). Another candidate for transcendence-hood is the idea of 'Heaven's Mandate' (Tang 1991).

28 Hall and Ames might riposte that Roetz's adoption of a method of 'reconstruction of Chinese axial age ethics as the ethics of an epoch of enlightenment' (1993: 23) is a projection of European modernist historicism.

29 Their 'interpretive pluralism' is outlined in Hall and Ames (1995: 142–6).

## 8 'THE TWITTER OF BIRDS'

1 In the hands of Northrop, this distinction is indeed more than just a thoughtless stereotype but the basis of a sophisticated framework for the development of comparative philosophy. For an appreciation of Northrop, see Inada (1992).

2 See Halbfass (1988: ch. 9) for an overview of the place of Asian traditions of thought in Western histories of philosophy. The irrationalist presumption in orientalist discourse is examined in Goody (1996).

3 Published some years after his death in 1908.

4 Presumably Hansen has in mind here Wittgenstein's widely emulated habit of inventing fictional worlds and language games as a way of confronting us with the peculiarities of our standard ways of thinking in philosophy.

5 This criticism comes from an otherwise largely appreciative review of Hansen's project. For another critique of Hansen, see Alt (1996).

6 On the issue of abstraction and the Chinese language, see Graham (1989: 398–401).

7 On the supposed crisis of the Western philosophical tradition, see the collection of essays in Baynes *et al.* (1987). It is also discussed in Hall and Ames (1987: 35–40). Needless to say, there are many who deny that philosophy is in a state of crisis, let alone dead.

8 Rorty is referring especially to the later writings of Wittgenstein and to Heidegger and Dewey. This work is in some senses a 'foundational' text in this debate. Habermas has speculated about the transformation of philosophy into a form of social inquiry, MacIntyre into a form of historiography.

9 In spite of his enthusiasm for the idea of 'the conversation of mankind', and his advocacy of diversity of vocabularies, Rorty's writings are surprisingly Eurocentric.

10 The proceedings of a symposium on 'Heidegger and Eastern Thought' are published in Volume 20(3) (1970) of *Philosophy East and West*.

11 See also Chang (1975b x–xi), which drew close affinities between Daoism and Heidegger well before the actual historical links were uncovered.

12 The text of the truncated translation has not been discovered. See also chapters in Parkes (1987) by Joan Stambaugh, Graham Parkes and Hua Yol Jung, and Owens (1990). Volume 11(4) (1984) of the *Journal of Chinese Philosophy* is devoted to comparisons between Daoism and Heidegger, some of the articles there being reprinted in Parkes (1987).

13 The point is also made in Heim (1984). A similar view, though more in relation to Indian philosophy, is put forward in Mehta (1990). According to Graham Parkes, Heidegger is '*the* modern philosopher who is most read and discussed throughout Asia' (May 1996: x).

14 Hall and Ames argue that the increased encounter in recent years with the cultures of China, Japan and Korea, which have values and understandings which are distinct from those embedded in Enlightenment rationality, has helped to encourage a spirit of relativism (1995: 114). On the relativising effect of orientalism see Clarke (1997: 28–34).

15 For a comparison between the scepticism of Zhuangzi and Nagarjuna, see Loy (1996).

16 For examples of the *Zhuangzi*'s linguistic relativism, see Graham (1981: 52, 57), and see also Chapter 33 of the *Liezi*.

17 The ironic character of Zhuangzi's writing is emphasised in Wu (1990: 373–77 and *passim*).

18 For a fuller discussion of varieties of views concerning Zhuangzi's supposed relativism, see Allinson (1989a: ch. 8), Kjellberg and Ivanhoe (1996), Smith (1991) and Wong (1984). See Norden (1990) for a review of Allinson's arguments on this subject, and Norden (1996a) for a discussion of the competing interpretations of the *Zhuangzi*. The charges of 'sceptic' and 'relativist' are both rejected in Wu (1982). On the comparison between Nietzsche and Daoism on the question of relativism and scepticism, see Parkes (1983, 1989).

19 As Kjellberg reminds us, Pyrrho, who lived between 360 and 275 BCE, travelled to India with Alexander's expedition and was fascinated by the remarkable peace of mind displayed by the *gymnosophists* or 'naked philosophers' whom he met there (1996: 2).

20 A hint of the issue of solipsism and other minds is to be found in the *Zhuangzi* (Graham 1981: 123).

21 Hansen points out that the quasi-idealist philosophy of the Buddhist Yogacara school did not catch on in China (1981: 323), though Graham argues that the idea that life might be a kind of dream was indeed introduced into China by the Buddhists (1989: 194).

22 See also Allinson (1989a: 131) where the butterfly dream is interpreted, not as an illustration of methodological scepticism in the style of Descartes, but as an analogue for philosophical awakening.

23 On Wittgenstein and Daoism see Goodman (1976), Tang and Schwartz (1988) and Tominaga (1982, 1983).

24 Compare: 'Philosophy is the battle against the bewitchment of our intelligence by means of language'. 'A philosophical problem has the form "I don't know my way about"'. 'Don't think! Look!' (Wittgenstein 1953: 47, 49, 31).

25 Here and in Raphals (1996), comparisons are drawn between classical Greek and Chinese thought.

26 This point is developed in Hall and Ames (1998: ch. 5). See also Gadamer's use of Aristotle's concept of *phronesis*, and his talk of moral knowledge as akin to the skill of the craftsman (1975: 281). For examples of Zhuangzi's knack-thinking, see Graham (1981: 63–4, 135–42).

27 Raphals is more uncompromising in her claim that the *Laozi* 'denies the value of conventional, textual, and discursive knowledge...[and] presents an entirely negative and critical account of...Mohist and Confucian "knowledge" (1992: 85).

28 'Postmodernism' is clearly a protean term, and here I shall associate it mainly with the deconstructive philosophy of Derrida and the neo-pragmatism of Rorty, both of which have been the chief recipients of comparative comment in relation to Daoism.

29 One of the earliest comparisons between Derrida's deconstruction and Daoism is in Yeh (1983). Volume 17(1) (1990) of the *Journal of Chinese Philosophy* is devoted to the comparative study of Daoism and deconstruction.

30 See also Nietzsche (1968: 35) for a parallel attack on Western philosophers' Parmenidean 'hatred of even the idea of becoming, their Egyptianism'.

31 This latter point is elaborated in Nuyen (1995), which also draws links with Derrida's device of *sous rature* in which the limits of what is literally sayable are denoted by crossing through the problematic word. The identification of *dao* with *différance* is also argued for in Owens (1993), which points to the existential implications of these views.

32 Graham's argument is not altogether clear since he goes on to say that 'for Derrida reversal is *not* a switch from preferring A to preferring B' (1989: 228; his italics). This latter interpretation is in my view closer to Derrida for whom the original opposition does not give place to a reverse hierarchy but undercuts it altogether.

33 This move is criticised by Jensen as a form of orientalism, or 'exoticism', which elevates China as a civilisation on the basis of the absence of the endemic logo-centrism of the West, and which serves to perpetuate the stereotype of the Chinese language as lacking the potential for critical rationality (1997: 273–4).

34 The view that classical Chinese lacks a distinction between Being and beings, and that classical Chinese philosophy is for the most part 'already deconstructed', is argued in Hall and Ames (1995: 227–30); see also Hall (1994: 225–6).

35 For a critique of Zhang's argument – all too briefly summarised here – see Fu (1992), which questions attempts to emphasise similarities between Daoism and Derrida's deconstruction.

36 On the comparison between Rorty and Zhuangzi, see Lee (1996). Though the names of Rorty and Derrida are often uttered in the same breath, there are significant differences between their thinking; see Hall (1994: 221–30) and Mouffe (1996).

37 Lee's views are inspired by Wu (1990), which brings out most eloquently the playful and story-telling aspect of the *Zhuangzi*.

38 See Norden (1996a) on the competing interpretations of the Inner Chapters.

39 The possibility of a more constructive form of postmodernism has been put forward in a number of recent writings, including Gare (1995a), Griffin (1988) and Zimmerman (1994).

## 9 'JOURNEY TO THE WEST'

1 For analyses of *Journey to the West*, see Plaks (1987), Raphals (1992) and Yu (1977). Yu stresses the alchemical symbolism of the text, and Oldstone-Moore

notes that a number of traditional commentaries considered Daoism the proper lens through which to focus the work (1998: 51).

2 For a discussion of the 'hermeneutics of difference' in relation to the East–West dialogue, see Dallmayr (1996). An approach similar to Gadamer's is adopted in Zhang (1998), which sees dialogue as a model for inter-cultural understanding.

3 Similar ideas in relation to modern reappropriations of Confucianism are explored in Berthrong (1998: ch. 7) and Jensen (1997: Epilogue).

4 On the continuing influence of Daoism in China post-1949, see Dean (1993), Li Yuhang (1994) and Saso (1995). Wing-tsit Chan was a little premature in his judgement that 'Taoism is approaching extinction', though at the same time he acknowledged that its philosophical, artistic and literary influence would persist (1953: 146). Doubts about the survival of Daoism in China were also expressed at the first international Daoist conference in 1968, i.e. at the height of the Cultural Revolution (Welch 1969–70: 129).

5 Marshall (1998) represents an interesting recent attempt to incorporate Daoist principles alongside Western-originating ideas at the heart of a 'philosophy for a new era'.

6 For surveys of Daoist teachers now working in the West, see Rawlinson (1997) and Towler (1996).

# BIBLIOGRAPHY

Abegg, L. (1952) *The Mind of East Asia*, London: Thames & Hudson.
Adams, W.H. (1991) *Nature Perfected: Gardens Throughout History*, New York: Abbeville Press.
Alexander, G.G. (1895) *Lâo-Tsze the Great Thinker*, London: Kegan, Trench, Trübner & Co.
Allinson, R.E. (1986) 'Having your Cake and Eating it, Too: Evaluation and Trans-Evaluation in Chuang Tzu and Nietzsche', *Journal of Chinese Philosophy*, 13(4).
—— (1989a) *Chuang-Tzu for Spiritual Transformation*, Albany: State University of New York Press.
—— (ed.) (1989b) *Understanding the Chinese Mind: The Philosophical Roots*, Hong Kong: Oxford University Press.
—— (1998) Review of Herman (1996), *Philosophy East and West*, 48(3).
Almond, P.C. (1988) *The British Discovery of Buddhism*, Cambridge: Cambridge University Press.
Alt, W. (1996) 'Philosophical Sense and Classical Chinese Thought', a review of Hansen (1992), *Asian Philosophy*, 6(2).
Ames, R.T. (1981) 'Taoism and the Androgynous Ideal', *Historical Reflections*, 8(3).
—— (1983a) *The Art of Rulership: A Study in Ancient Chinese Political Thought*, Honolulu, HA: University of Hawaii Press.
—— (1983b) 'Is Political Taoism Anarchism?', *Journal of Chinese Philosophy*, 10(2).
—— (1985) 'The Common Ground of Self-Cultivation in Classical Taoism and Confucianism', *Qing Hua Journal of Chinese Studies*, 17(1–2).
—— (1986) 'Taoism and the Nature of Nature', *Environmental Ethics*, 8(4).
—— (1991a) 'Meaning as Imagining: Prolegomena to a Confucian Epistemology', in Deutsch (1991).
—— (1991b) 'Nietzsche's "Will to Power" and Chinese "Virtuality" (*De*): A Comparative Study', in Parkes (1991).
—— (1994) Review of Hansen (1992), *Harvard Journal of Asiatic Studies*, 54(2).
—— (1995) 'Translating Chinese Philosophy', in Chan and Pollard (1995).
Arnold, E. (1998 [1879]) *The Light of Asia: The Life and Teaching of Gautama Prince of India and Founder of Buddhism*, Twickenham: Tiger Books International.
Bahm, A. (1958) *Tao Teh King: Interpreted as Nature and Intelligence*, New York: Ungar.

Balazs, E. (1964) *Chinese Civilization and Bureaucracy: Variations on a Theme*, New Haven, Yale University Press.

Baldrian, F. (1987) 'Taoism: An Overview', *Encyclopedia of Religions*, vol. 14, New York: Macmillan.

Balfour, F.H. (1881) *Taoist Texts: Ethical, Political, and Speculative*, London and Shanghai: Trübner.

Barbour, I.G. (ed.) (1972) *Earth Might be Fair: Reflections on Ethics, Religion, and Ecology*, Englewood Cliffs, NJ: Prentice-Hall.

Barnett, R. (1986), 'Taoism and Biological Science', *Zygon*, 21(3).

Barrett, T.H. (1987) 'Taoism: History of Study', *Encyclopedia of Religions*, Vol. 14, New York: Macmillan.

—— (1990) 'Religious Traditions in Chinese Civilization: Buddhism and Taoism', in Ropp (1990).

—— (1996) *Taoism under the T'ang: Religion and Empire during the Golden Age of Chinese History*, London: Wellsweep.

Baynes, K., Bohman, J. and McCarthy, T. (eds) (1987) *After Philosophy: End or Transformation?*, Cambridge, MA: MIT Press.

Bell, C. (1983) 'In Search of the Tao in Taoism: New Questions of Unity and Multiplicity', *History of Religions*, 33(2).

Bender, F.L. (1983) 'Taoism and Western Anarchism', *Journal of Chinese Philosophy*, 10(1).

Benn, C.D. (1987) 'Religious Aspects of Emperor Hsüan-tsung's Taoist Ideology', in Chappell (1987).

—— (1991) *The Cavern Mystery Transmission: A Taoist Ordination Rite of A.D. 711*, Honolulu, HA: University of Hawaii Press.

Benton, R.P. (1962) 'Tennyson and Lao Tzu', *Philosophy East and West*, 12(3).

Berkson, M. (1996) 'Language: The Guest of Reality – Zhuangzi and Derrida on Language, Reality, and Skillfulness', in Kjellberg and Ivanhoe (1996).

Berling, J.A. (1979) 'Paths of Convergence: Interactions of Inner Alchemy, Taoism and Neo-Confucianism', *Journal of Chinese Philosophy*, 6(2).

—— (1980) *The Syncretic Religion of Lin Chao-en*, New York: Columbia University Press.

—— (1997) 'When They go their Separate Ways: The Collapse of the Unitary Vision of Chinese Religions in the Early Ching', in Bloom and Fogel (1997).

Bernstein, R. (1983) *Beyond Objectivism and Relativism: Science, Hermeneutics, and Praxis*, Oxford: Blackwell.

—— (1991) 'Incommensurability and Otherness Revisited', in Deutsch (1991).

Berthrong, J.H. (1998) *Transformations of the Confucian Way*, Boulder, CO: Westview.

Bertschinger, R. (1994) *The Search for Everlasing Life*, Shaftesbury: Element.

Billington, R. (1990) *East of Existentialism: The Tao of the West*, London: Unwin Hyman.

Binyon, L. (1908) *Paintings in the Far East: An Introduction to the History of Pictorial Art in Asia, Especially China and Japan*, London: Arnold.

—— (1935) *The Spirit of Man in Asian Art*, Cambridge: Harvard University Press.

Black, H. (1986) 'Gender and Cosmology in Chinese Correlative Thinking', in Bynum, Harrell and Richman (1986).

Blofeld, J. (trans.) (1965) *The Book of Change*, London: Allen & Unwin.

—— (1973) *The Sacred and the Sublime: Taoist Mysteries and Magic*, London: Allen & Unwin.

—— (1985) *Taoism: The Road to Immortality*, Boston: Shambhala.

Bloom, I. and Fogel, J.A. (eds) (1997) *Meeting of Minds: Intellectual and Religious Interaction in East Asian Traditions of Thought*, New York: Columbia University Press.

Bodde, D. (1950) *Tolstoy and China*, Princeton, NJ: Princeton University Press.

—— (1953) 'Harmony and Conflict in Chinese Philosophy', in Wright (1953).

—— (1976) Review of Needham, *Science and Civilization in China, Vol.5, Part 2, Journal of Asian Studies*, 35(3).

—— (1979) 'Chinese "Laws of Nature", a Reconsideration', *Harvard Journal of Asiatic Studies*, 39(1).

—— (1991) *Chinese Thought, Science and Society: The Intellectual and Social Background of Science and Technology in Pre-modern China*, Honolulu, HA: University of Hawaii Press.

Boehmer, T. (1977) 'Taoist Alchemy: A Sympathetic Approach through Symbols', in Saso and Chappell (1977).

Bokenkamp, S.R. (1994) 'Time after Time: Taoist Apocalyptic History and the Founding of the T'ang Dynasty', *Asia Major*, 7(1).

—— (1996) '*Declarations of the Perfected*', in Lopez (1996).

—— (1997) *Early Daoist Scriptures*, Berkeley, CA: University of California Press.

Boltz, J. (1986) 'In Homage to T'ien-fei', *Journal of the American Oriental Society*, 106(1).

—— (1987a) 'Taoist Literature' *Encyclopedia of Religions* Vol. 14, New York: Macmillan.

—— (1987b) *A Survey of Taoist Literature: Tenth to Seventeenth Centuries*, Berkeley, CA: University of California Press

Bookchin, M. (1989) *Remaking Society*, Montreal: Black Rose.

—— (1995) *Re-enchanting Humanity*, London: Cassell.

Bradbury, S. (1992) 'The American Conquest of Philosophical Taoism', in Moore and Lower (1992).

Brook, T. (1993) 'Rethinking Syncretism: The Unity of the Three Teachings and their Joint Worship in late Imperial China', *Journal of Chinese Religions*, 21.

Buber, M. (1910) *Reden und Gleichnisse des Tschuang-tse*, Leipzig: Insel-Verlag.

—— (1956) *The Tales of Rabbi Nachman*, New York: Horizon.

Burneko, G.C. (1986) 'Chuang Tzu's Existential Hermeneutics', *Journal of Chinese Philosophy*, 13(4).

Bush, S. (1971) *The Chinese Literati on Painting: Su Shih (1037–1101) to Tung Ch'i-ch'ang (1555–1636)*, Cambridge, MA: Harvard University Press.

Bussagli, M. (1969) *Chinese Painting*, London: Paul Hamlyn.

Bynner, W. (1978) *The Chinese Translations*, ed. James Kraft, New York: Farrar, Straus, Giroux.

Bynum, C., Harrell, S. and Richman, P. (eds) (1986) *Gender and Religion: On the Complexity of Symbols*, Boston: Beacon.

Cahill, J. (1960) 'Confucian Elements in the Theory of Painting', in Wright (1960a).

—— (1994) *The Painter's Practice: How Artists Lived and Worked in Traditional China*, New York: Columbia University Press.

—— (1996) *The Lyric Journey: Poetry and Painting in China and Japan*, Cambridge, MA: Harvard University Press.

Cahill, S. (1986) 'Performance and Female Daoist Adepts: Hsi Wang Mu as the Patron Deity of Women in Medieval China', *Journal of the American Oriental Society*, 106(1).

—— (1990) 'Practice makes Perfect: Paths to Transcendence for Women in Medieval China', *Taoist Resources*, 2(2).

—— (1993) *Transcendence and Divine Passion: The Queen Mother of the West in Medieval China*, Stanford, CA: Stanford University Press.

Callicott, J.B. (1994) *Earth's Insights: A Multicultural Survey of Ecological Ethics*, Berkeley, CA: University of California Press.

Callicott, J.B. and Ames, R.T. (eds) (1989) *Nature in Asian Traditions of Thought: Essays in Environmental Philosophy*, Albany, NY: State University of New York Press. ·

Campany, R.F. (1993) 'Buddhist Revolution and Taoist Translation in Early Mediaeval China', *Taoist Resources*, 4(1).

Capra, F. (1976) *The Tao of Physics: An Exploration of the Parallels between Modern Physics and Eastern Mysticism*, Oxford: Fontana/Collins.

—— (1982) *The Turning Point*, London: Wildwood.

—— (1997) *The Web of Life: A New Synthesis of Mind and Matter*, London: HarperCollins.

Carman, J. and Juegensmayer, M. (eds) (1991) *A Bibliographic Guide to the Comparative Study of Ethics*, Cambridge: Cambridge University Press.

Carrithers, M., Collins, S. and Lukes, S. (eds) (1985) *The Category of the Person: Anthropology, Philosophy, History*, Cambridge: Cambridge University Press.

Carus, P. (1907) *Chinese Thought: An Exposition of the Main Chracteristic Features of the Chinese World-Conception*. Chicago: Open Court.

—— (trans.) (1913) *The Canon of Reason and Virtue: Lao-Tze's Tao Teh King*, Chicago: Open Court.

Cavell, S. (1988) *In Quest of the Ordinary*, Chicago: University of Chicago Press.

Chalmers, J. (1868) *The Speculations on Metaphysics, Polity, and Morality of 'The Old Philosopher' Lau-Tsze*, London: Trübner & Co.

Chan, A.K.L. (1991) *Two Visions of the Way: A Study of the Wang Pi and the Ho-shang Kung Commentaries on the Lao-Tzu*, Albany, NY: State University of New York Press.

Chan, Sin-wai and Pollard, D.E. (1995) *An Encyclopedia of Chinese Translation: Chinese-English/English-Chinese*, Hong Kong: The Chinese University Press.

Chan, Wing-tsit (1953) *Religious Trends in Modern China*, New York: Columbia University Press.

—— (1963a) *A Source Book in Chinese Philosophy*, Princeton, NJ: Princeton University Press.

—— (1963b) *The Way of Lao Tzu*, New York: Bobbs-Merill.

Chang Chung-yuan (1975a) *Creativity and Taoism*, London: Wildwood House.

—— (1975b) *Tao: A New Way of Thinking*, New York: Harper & Row.

—— (1977) 'The Philosophy of Taoism According to Chuang Tzu', *Philosophy East and West*, 27(4).

Chang, Jolan (1995) *The Tao of Love and Sex: The Ancient Chinese Way to Ecstasy*, Aldershot: Gower.

Chang, S. (1986) *The Tao of Sexology*, San Francisco: Tao Publishing.

Chapman, J.W. and Galston, W.A. (eds) (1992) *Virtue*, New York: New York University Press.

Chappell, D.W. (ed.) (1987) *Buddhist and Taoist Practice in Medieval Chinese Society*, Honolulu, HA: University of Hawaii Press.

Chavannes, E. (1895–1915) *Les mémoires historiques de Se-ma Ts'ien*, 5 vols, Paris: Leroux.

Chen, E.M. (1969) 'Nothingness and the Mother Principle in Early Chinese Taoism', *International Philosophical Quarterly*, 9(4).

Chen Guying (1991) 'Zhuang Zi and Nietzsche: Plays of Perspectives', in Parkes (1991).

Ch'en, K. (1964) *Buddhism in China: A Historical Survey*, Princeton, NJ: Princeton University Press.

Cheng Chung-ying (1977) 'The Nature and Function of Skepticism in Chinese Philosophy', *Philosophy East and West*, 27(2).

—— (1986) 'On the Environmental Ethics of the *Tao* and the *Ch'i*', *Environmental Ethics*, 8(4).

—— (1989) 'Chinese Metaphysics as Non-metaphysics: Confucian and Taoist Insights into the Nature of Reality', in Allinson (1989b).

Chia, Mantak (1984) *Taoist Secrets of Love: Cultivating Male Sexual Energy*, New York: Aurora.

Chien, Chi-hui (1990) "Theft's Way: A Comparative Study of Chuang Tzu's Tao and Derridean Trace', *Journal of Chinese Philosophy*, 17(1).

Ching, J. (1990) *Probing China's Soul:Religion, Politics, and Protest in the People's Republic*, San Francisco: Harper & Row.

—— (1993) *Chinese Religions*, London: Macmillan.

—— (1997) 'Chu Hsi and Taoism', in Bloom and Fogel (1997).

Ching, J. and Oxtoby, W.G. (1992) *Moral Enlightenment: Leibniz and Wolff on China*, Nettetal: Steyler Verlag.

Chisolm, L.W. (1963) *Fenollosa: The Far East and American Culture*, New Haven, CT: Yale University Press.

Clark, J.P. (1978) 'What is Anarchism?', *Nomos* 19.

—— (1983) 'On Taoism and Politics', *Journal of Chinese Philosophy*, 10(1).

Clarke, J.F. (1871) *Ten Great Religions*, Boston: Osgood.

Clarke, J.J. (1994) *Jung and Eastern Thought: A Dialogue with the Orient*, London: Routledge.

—— (1997) *Oriental Enlightenment: The Encounter between Asian and Western Thought*, London: Routledge.

Cleary, T. (trans.) (1986) *The Taoist I Ching*, Boston: Shambhala.

—— (trans.) (1987) *Understanding Reality: A Taoist Alchemical Classic by Chang Po-tuan*, Honolulu, HA: University of Hawaii Press.

—— (trans.) (1991) *The Secret of the Golden Flower*, San Francisco: Harper & Row.

Clifton, R.K. and Regehr, M.G. (1989) 'Capra on Eastern Mysticism and Modern Physics: A Critique', *Science and Christian Belief*, 1(1).

Cook, D. and Rosemont, H. (1981) 'The Pre-established Harmony Between Leibniz and Chinese Thought', *Journal of the History of Ideas*, 42(3).

—— (eds) (1994) *G.W. Leibniz: Writings on China*, La Salle, IL: Open Court.

Coomaraswamy, A.K. (1977) *On the Traditional Doctrine of Art*, Ipswich: Golgonooza Press.

Cooper, J.C. (1990) *Taoism: The Way of the Mystic*, London: HarperCollins.

Cordier, H. (1968[1904]) *Biblioteca sinica: dictionnaire bibliographique des ouvrages relatifs à l'empire chinois* 6 vols, New York: Burt Franklin.

Coward, H. (1996) 'Taoism and Jung: Synchronicity and the Self', *Philosophy East and West*, 46(4).

Creel, H.G. (1929) *Sinism: A Study of the Evolution of the Chinese World-View*, Chicago: Open Court.

—— (1954) *Chinese Thought from Confucius to Mao Tse-tung*, London: Eyre & Spottiswood.

—— (1970) *What is Taoism, and Other Studies in Chinese Cultural History*, Chicago: University of Chicago Press.

—— (1987) 'The Role of Compromise in Chinese Culture', in Le Blanc and Blader (1987).

Critchley, S. (1995) 'Black Socrates? Questioning the Philosophical Tradition', *Radical Philosophy*, 69.

—— (1997) *Very Little...Almost Nothing: Death, Philosophy, Literature*, London: Routledge.

Crowley, A. (trans.) (1976) *Tao Teh Ching*, ed S. Skinner, London: Askin.

Csikszentmihalyi, M. and Ivanhoe, P.J. (eds) (1999) *Religious and Philosophical Aspects of the Laozi*, Albany, NY: State University of New York Press.

Cua, A.S. (1977) 'Forgetting Morality: Reflections on a Theme in *Chuang Tzu*', *Journal of Chinese Philosophy*, 4(4).

—— (1985) *Ethical Argumentation: A Study in Hsün Tzu's Moral Epistemology*, Honolulu, HA: University of Hawaii Press.

—— (1989) 'The Concept of *Li* in Confucian Moral Theory', in Allinson (1989b).

—— (1996) *Beyond Orientalism: Essays on Cross-Cultural Encounter*, Albany, NY: State University of New York Press.

Dallmayr, F. (1996) *Beyond Orientalism: Essays on Cross-Cultural Encounter*, Albany, NY: State University of New York Press.

Danto, A. (1976) *Mysticism and Morality: Oriental Thought and Moral Philosophy*, Harmondsworth: Penguin.

Dawson, R. (1967) *The Chinese Chameleon: An Analysis of European Conceptions of Chinese Civilization*, Oxford: Oxford University Press.

Dean, K. (1993) *Taoist Ritual and Popular Cults of South-East Asia*, Princeton, NJ: Princeton University Press.

de Bary, W.T., Wing-tsit Chan and Watson, B. (eds) (1960) *Sources of Chinese Tradition*, 2 vols, New York: Columbia University Press.

—— (1988) *East Asian Civilization: A Dialogue in Five Stages*, Cambridge, MA: Harvard University Press.

Delahaye, H. (1981) *Les premières peintures de paysage en Chine: aspects religieux*, Paris: École Française d'Extrême-Orient.

Demiéville, P. (1970) 'Le Buddhisme chinois', *Encyclopédie de le Pleiade*, Vol. 1, Paris; Gallimard.

Derrida, J. (1976) *Of Grammatology*, Baltimore, MD: Johns Hopkins University Press.

—— (1988) *Limited Inc*, Evanston, IL: Northwestern University Press.

Despeux, C. (1976) *Ta'i-ki k'uan: technique de longue vie, technique de combat*, Paris: Presses Universitaires de France.

—— (1989) 'Gymnastics: The Ancient Tradition', in Kohn (1989).

—— (1990) *Immortelles de la Chine ancienne: Taoïsme et alchimie féminine*, Paris: Pardès.

Deutsch, E. (ed.) (1991) *Culture and Modernity: East-West Philosophic Perspectives*, Honolulu, HA: University of Hawaii Press.

Dirlik, A. (1991) *Anarchism in the Chinese Revolution*, Berkeley, CA: University of California Press.

Doré, H. (1911–38) *Recherches sur les superstitions en Chine*, 18 vols, Shanghai.

Douglas, R.K. (1911) *Confucianism and Tauism*, London: Society for Promoting Christian Knowledge.

Dubs, H.H. (1929) 'The Failure of Chinese Philosophy to Produce Philosophical Systems', *T'oung Pao*, 26.

Durant, W. (1942) *The Story of Civilization: Vol.1. Our Oriental Heritage*, New York: Simon & Schuster.

Durkheim, E. and Mauss, M. (1963) *Primitive Classification*, Chicago: University of Chicago Press.

Duyvendak, J.J.L. (1947) 'The Philosophy of Wu Wei', *Asiatische Studien*, 1(1).

—— (trans.) (1953) *Tao To King: Le Livre de la voie et la vertu*, Paris: Maisonneuve.

Eber, I. (1994) 'Martin Buber and Taoism', *Monumenta Serica*, 42(4).

Ebrey, P.B. and Gregory, P.N. (eds) (1993) *Religion and Society in T'ang and Sung China*, Honolulu, HA: University of Hawaii Press.

Edkins, J. (1855) 'Tauism', *Pamphlets of Chinese Missionaries*, conference held at The School of Oriental and African Studies, London.

—— (1893[1859]) *Religion in China, containing A Brief Account of the Three Religions of the Chinese, with Observations on the Prospects of Christian Conversion amongst that People*, London: Kegan Paul, Trench, Trübner.

—— (1889) *Ancient Symbolism*, London: Trübner.

Eitel, E. (1984[1873]) *Feng-shui: The Science of Sacred Landscape in Old China*, with commentary by John Mitchell, Bonsall, CA: Synergetic Press.

Eno, R. (1996) 'Cook Ding's Dao and the Limits of Philosophy', in Kjellberg and Ivanhoe (1996).

Esbenshade, D.H. (1982) 'Relating Mystical Concepts to those of Physics: Some Concerns', *American Journal of Physics*, 50(3).

Eskildsen, S. (1998) *Asceticism in Early Taoist Religion*, Albany, NY: State University of New York Press.

Fang, T. (1981) *Chinese Philosophy: Its Spirit and Development*, Taipei: LinKing.

Faure, B. (1991) *The Rhetoric of Immediacy: A Cultural Critique of Chan/Zen Buddhism*, New York: Columbia University Press.

Fenollosa, E. (1912) *Epochs of China and Japanese Art*, 2 vols, London: Heinemann.

—— (1936) *The Chinese Character as a Medium for Poetry*, London: Stanley Nott.

Feuchtwang, S.D. (1974) *An Anthropological Analysis of Chinese Geomancy*, Laos: Vithagna.

Fleming, J. (1998) 'On Translation of Taoist Philosophical Texts: Preservation of Ambiguity and Contradition', *Journal of Chinese Philosophy*, 25(1).

Flew, A. (1971) *An Introduction to Western Philosophy*, London: Thames & Hudson.

Forke, A. (1925) *The World-Conception of the Chinese: Their Astronomical, Cosmological, Physico-Philosophical Speculations*, London: Probsthain.

Forman, R.K.C. (ed.) (1990) *The Problem of Pure Consciousness: Mysticism and Philosophy*, Oxford: Oxford University Press.

Franke, W. (1970) *A Century of Chinese Revolution*, Oxford: Blackwell.

Friedman, M. (1976) 'Martin Buber and Asia', *Philosophy East and West*, 26(4).

Frodsham, J. (1960–1) 'On the Origins of Chinese Nature Poetry', *Asia Major*, 8(1).

Fu, Hongchu (1992) 'Deconstruction and Taoism: Comparisons Reconsidered', *Comparative Literature Studies*, 29(3).

Fumimasa, F. (1995) 'The History of Taoist Studies in Japan, and Some Related Issues', *Acta Asiatica*, 68.

Fung Yu-lan (1966[1948]) *A Short History of Chinese Philosophy*, ed. D. Bodde, New York: The Free Press.

—— (1952–3) *A History of Chinese Philosophy*, 2 vols, Princeton, NJ: Princeton University Press.

Furrow, D. (1995) *Against Theory: Continental and Analytic Challenges in Moral Philosophy*, London: Routledge.

Gadamer, H.-G. (1975) *Truth and Method*, London: Sheed & Ward.

Gao, Jianping (1996) *The Expressive Act in Chinese Art: From Calligraphy to Painting*, Stockholm: Almqvist Wiksell International.

Gare, A.E. (1995a) *Postmodernism and the Environmental Crisis*, Routledge: London.

—— (1995b) 'Understanding Oriental Cultures', *Philosophy East and West*, 45(3).

Gasster, M. (1969) *Chinese Intellectuals in the Revolution of 1911*, Seattle, WA: University of Washington Press.

Gernet, J. (1985) *China and the Christian Impact: A Conflict of Cultures*, Cambridge: Cambridge University Press.

Giles, H.A. (1886) 'The Wisdom of Lao Tzu', *The China Review*, 16.

—— (1889) *Chuang Tzu: Mystic, Moralist, and Social Reformer*, London: Quaritch.

—— (1915) *Confucianism and its Rivals*, London: William & Newgate.

Giles, L. (trans.) (1906a) *Musings of a Chinese Mystic: Selections from the Philosophy of Chuang Tzu*, London: John Murray.

—— (trans.) (1906b) *The Sayings of Lao Tzu*, London: John Murray.

—— (trans.) (1912) *Taoist Teachings from the Book of 'Lieh Tzu'*, London: John Murray.

Gilligan, C. (1982) *In a Different Voice: Psychological Theory and Women's Development*, Cambridge, MA: Harvard University Press.

Girardot, N.J. (1972) 'Part of the Way: Four Studies in Taoism', *History of Religions*, 11(3).

—— (1983) *Myth and Meaning in Early Taoism: The Theme of Chaos (hun-tun)*, Berkeley, CA: University of California Press.

—— (1987) 'Chinese Religion: History of Study', *Encylopedia of Religions* Vol. 3, New York: Macmillan.

—— (1992) 'The Course of Sinological Discourse: James Legge (1815–97) and the Nineteenth Century Invention of Taoism', in Luk (1992).

—— (1999) *The Victorian Translation of China*, Berkeley, CA: University of California Press.

Glasenapp, H. von (1954) *Kant und die Religionen des Osten*, Kitzingen-Main: Holzner Verlag.

Gómez, L.O. (1995) 'Oriental Wisdom and the Cure of Souls: Jung and the Indian East', in Lopez (1995).

Goodman, R.B. (1976) 'Style, Dialectics, and the Aims of Philosophy in Wittgenstein and the Taoists', *Journal of Chinese Philosophy*, 3(2).

—— (1980) 'Taoism and Ecology', *Environmental Ethics*, 2(1).

—— (1985) 'Skepticism and Realism in the *Chuang-Tzu*', *Philosophy East and West*, 35(3).

Goody, J. (1996) *The East in the West*, Cambridge: Cambridge University Press.

Goullart, P. (1961) *The Monastery of the Jade Mountain*, London: John Murray.

Graham, A.C. (trans.) (1960) *The Book of Lieh Tzu*, London: John Murray.

—— (1973) 'China, Europe, and the Origins of Modern Science: Needham's Grand Titration', in Nakayama and Sivin (1973).

—— (1978) *Later Mohist Logic, Ethics and Science*, Hong Kong: Chinese University Press.

—— (1979) 'How much of *Chuang-tzu* did Chuang-tzu Write?', *Journal of the American Academy of Religions*, 47(3).

—— (trans) (1981) *Chuang-Tzu: The Inner Chapters*, London: HarperCollins.

—— (1983) 'Taoist Spontaneity and the Dichotomy of "is" and "ought"', in Mair (1983a).

—— (1989) *Disputers of the Tao: Philosophical Argument in Ancient China*, La Salle, IL: Open Court.

—— (1990) *Studies in Chinese Philosophy and Philosophical Literature*, Albany, NY: State University of New York Press.

Granet, M. (1975[1924]) *The Religion of the Chinese People*, Oxford: Blackwell.

—— (1934) *La pensée chinoise*, Paris: Albin Michel.

Gray, J. (1995) *Enlightenment's Wake: Politics and Culture at the Close of the Modern Age*, London: Routledge.

Griffin, D.R. (ed.) (1988) *The Reenchantment of Science: Postmodern Proposals*, New York: State University of New York Press.

Griffin, S. (1978) *Women and Nature*, New York: Harper & Row.

Grigg, R. (1989) *The Tao of Relationships: A Balancing of Man and Woman*, Aldershot: Wildwood.

Groot, J.J.M. de (1892–1910) *The Religious System of China*, 6 vols, Leiden: Brill.

Gross, R.M. (1993) *Buddhism after Patriarchy: A Feminist History, Analysis, and Reconstruction of Buddhism*, Albany: State University of New York Press.

Gulik, R.H. van (1961) *Sexual Life in Ancient China: A Preliminary Survey of Chinese Sex and Society from ca.1500 till 1644 AD*, Leiden: Brill.

Hackmann, H. (1927) *Chinesische Philosophie*, Munich: Reinhardt.

Halbfass, W. (1988) *India and Europe: An Essay in Understanding*, Albany, NY: State University of New York Press.

Halde, J.B. du (1736) *Description géographique, historique, chronologique, politique, et physique de l'empire de la Chine et de la Tartarie chinoise*, 4 vols, The Hague: Henri Scheurleer.

Hall, D.L. (1978) 'Process and Anarchy: A Taoist Vision of Creativity', *Philosophy East and West*, 28(3).

—— (1982a) *The Uncertain Phoenix: Adventures Toward a Post-Cultural Sensibility*, New York: Fordham University Press.

—— (1982b) *Eros and Irony: A Prelude to Philosophical Anarchism*, Albany, NY: State University of New York Press.

—— (1983) 'The Metaphysics of Anarchism', *Journal of Chinese Philosophy* 10(2).

—— (1984) 'Nietzsche and Chuang Tzu: Resources for the Transcendence of Culture', *Journal of Chinese Philosophy*, 11(2).

—— (1987) 'On Seeking a Change of Environment: A Quasi-Taoist Proposal', *Philosophy East and West*, 37(2).

—— (1991) 'Modern China and the Postmodern West', in Deutsch (1991).

—— (1994) *Richard Rorty: Prophet and Poet of the New Pragmatism*, Albany, NY: State University of New York Press.

Hall, D.L. and Ames, R.T. (1987) *Thinking Through Confucius*, Albany, NY: State University of New York Press.

—— (1995) *Anticipating China: Thinking through the Narratives of Chinese and Western Cultures*, Albany, NY: State University of New York Press.

—— (1998) *Thinking from the Han: Self, Truth, and Transcendence in Chinese and Western Culture*, Albany, NY: State University of New York Press.

Hansen, C. (1981) 'Linguistic Skepticism in the *Lao Tzu*', *Philosophy East & West*, 31(3).

—— (1983a) *Language and Logic in Ancient China*, Ann Arbor, MI: University of Michigan Press.

—— (1983b) 'A Tao of Tao in Chuang-Tzu', in Mair (1983a).

—— (1989) 'Language in the Heart-mind', in Allinson (1989b).

—— (1992) *A Daoist Theory of Chinese Thought*, New York: Oxford University Press.

—— (1996) 'Duty and Virtue', in Ivanhoe (1996a).

Harbsmeier, C. (1981) *Aspects of Classical Chinese Syntax*, London: Curzon Press.

—— (1989) 'Marginalia Sino-logica', in Allinson (1989b).

Hardy, J. (1987) *A Psychology with a Soul: Psychosynthesis in Evolutionary Context*, London: Routledge.

Hardy, J.M. (1998) 'Influential Western Interpretations of the *Tao-te-ching*', in Kohn and LaFargue (1998).

Harlez, C. de (trans.) (1889) *Le Yih-King*, Brussels: Hayez.

Harper, D. (1987) 'The Sexual Arts of Ancient China as Described in a Manuscript of the Second Century B.C.', *Harvard Journal of Asiatic Studies*, 34(2).

Hartshorne, C. (1979) 'Process Themes in Chinese Thought', *Journal of Chinese Philosophy*, 6(4).

Hay, J. (1985) *Kernels of Energy, Bones of Earth: The Rock in Chinese Art*, New York: China Institute of America.

Hegel, G.W.F. (1944) *The Philosophy of History*, New York: Wiley.

—— (1987) *Lectures on the Philosophy of Religion* Vol. 2, Berkeley, CA: University of California Press.

—— (1995) *Lectures on the History of Philosophy* Vol. 1, Lincoln, NB: University of Nebraska Press.

Heidegger, M. (1971) *On the Way to Language*, New York: Harper & Row.

Heim, M. (1984) 'A Philosophy of Comparison: Heidegger and Lao Tzu', *Journal of Chinese Philosophy*, 11(4).

Heisig, J. and Maraldo, J. (eds) (1994) *Rude Awakenings: Zen, the Kyoto School, & the Question of Nationalism*, Honolulu, HA: University of Hawaii Press.

Henderson, J.B. (1984) *The Development and Decline of Chinese Cosmology*, New York: Columbia University Press.

Henricks, R.G. (1979) 'Examining the Ma-wang-tui Silk Texts of the *Lao-tzu*', *T'oung Pao*, 65(4–5).

—— (trans.) (1983) *Philosophy and Argumentation in Third Century China: The Essays of Hsi K'ang*, Princeton, NJ: Princeton University Press.

—— (trans.) (1990) *Lao-tzu: Te-tao Ching*, London: Bodley Head.

Herman, J.R. (1996) *I and Tao: Martin Buber's Encounter with Chuang Tzu*, Albany, NY: State University of New York Press.

Heyndrickz, J. (ed.) (1990) *Philippe Couplet, S.J. (1623–93): The Man Who Brought China to Europe*, Nettetal: Steyler Verlag.

Heysinger, I.W. (trans.) (1903) *The Light of China: The Tâo Teh King of Lâo Tsze, 604–504 B.C.*, Philadelphia: Research Publications Limited.

Hoff, B. (1994) *The Tao of Pooh and The Te of Piglet*, London: Methuen.

Holzman, D. (1996) *Landscape Appreciation in Ancient and Early Medieval China: The Birth of Landscape Poetry*, Taipei: National Tsing Hua University Press.

Hoornbeck, J. (1669) *De Conversione Indorum & Gentilium*, Amsterdam: Jansson.

Hoster, B. and Waedow, G. (1995) 'Internationale Konferenz in Xi'an: Laozi – Interpretation und Wirkung', *China Heute*, 14(6).

Hsia, A. (ed.) (1994) *Tao: Reception in East and West*, Bern: Peter Lang.

Hsiao, K.S. (1979) *A History of Chinese Political Thought*, Vol. 1, Princeton, NJ: Princeton University Press.

Hsiao, Shih-yi, P. (1987) 'Heidegger and Our Translation of the *Tao Te Ching*', in Parkes (1987).

Huang Chun-Chieh and Zürcher, E. (eds) (1995) *Time and Space in Chinese Culture*, Leiden: Brill.

Huff, T. (1993) *The Rise of Modern Science: Islam, China, and the West*, Cambridge: Cambridge University Press.

Hulin, M. (1979) *Hegel et l'Orient*, Paris: Vrin.

Hume, D. (1898) *Essays Moral, Political and Literary*, London: John Murray.

Hunt, J.D. and Willis, P. (eds) (1975) *The Genius of the Place: The English Landscape Garden 1620–1820*, London: Elek.

Huntington, S. (1996) *The Clash of Civilizations and the Remaking of World Order*, New York: Simon & Schuster.

Inada, K. (1988) 'Zen and Taoism: Common and Uncommon Grounds of Dissonance', *Journal of Chinese Philosophy*, 15(1).

—— (1992) 'Northropian Categories of Experience Revisited', *Journal of Chinese Philosophy*, 19(1).

—— (1994) 'The Challenge of Buddho-Taoist Metaphysics of Experience', *Journal of Chinese Philosophy*, 21(1).

Ip, Po-keung, (1983) 'Taoism and the Foundations of Environmental Ethics', *Environmental Ethics*, 5(4).

Ivanhoe, P.J. (1993a) *Confucian Moral Self-Cultivation*, New York: Peter Lang.

—— (1993b) 'Zhuangzi on Skepticism, Skill, and the Ineffable *Dao*', *Journal of the American Academy of Religion*, 61(4).

—— (ed.) (1996a) *Chinese Language, Thought, and Culture*, Chicago and La Salle, IL: Open Court.

—— (1996b) 'Was Zhuangzi a Relativist?', in Kjellberg and Ivanhoe (1996).

Jackson, C.T. (1981) *The Oriental Religions and American Thought*, Westport, CT: Greenwood.

Jan Yü-hua (1977) 'The Silk Manuscripts on Taoism', *T'oung Pao*, 63.

Jantsch, E. (1980) *The Self-Organizing Universe*, New York: Pergamon.

Jensen, L.M. (1997) *Manufacturing Confucianism: Chinese Traditions and Universal Civilization*, Durham, NC: Duke University Press.

Johnson, S. (1877) *Oriental Religions and their Relation to Universal Religion: China*, Boston: Mifflin.

Jones, R.H. (1979) 'Jung and Eastern Religious Traditions', *Religion*, 9(2).

Julien, S. (1841) *Lao Tseu: Tao Te-king: le livre de la voie et la vertu*, Paris: Imprimerie Royale.

Jung, C.G. (1983) *Memories, Dreams, Reflections*, London: Fontana.

—— (1985) *Synchronicity: An Acausal Connecting Principle*, London: Routledge.

—— (1995) *Jung on the East*, ed. J.J. Clarke, London: Routledge.

Kaltenmark, M. (1969) *Lao Tzu and Taoism*, Stanford, CA: Stanford University Press.

—— (1979) 'The Ideology of the T'ai-p'ing Ching', in Welch and Seidel (1979).

Karcher, S. (1999) 'Journey to the West', *Oracle: The Journal of Yijing Studies*, 2(9).

—— (2000) *Ta Chuan: The Great Treatise*, New York: St Martin's Press.

Kardos, M. (1998) 'Western Language Publications on Religions in China, 1990–94', *Journal of Chinese Religions*, 26.

Katz, S.T. (ed.) (1978) *Mysticism and Philosophical Analysis*, New York: Oxford University Press.

Kauffman, S. (1995) *At Home in the Universe: The Search for the Laws of Self-Organization and Complexity*, Harmondsworth: Penguin.

Keswick, M. (1986) *The Chinese Garden: History, Art and Architecture*, London: Academy Editions.

Kim, Young Kun (1978) 'Hegel's Criticism of Chinese Philosophy', *Philosophy East and West*, 28(2).

Kimura, E. (1974) 'Taoism and Chinese Thought' in *Acta Asiatica: Bulletin of the Institute of Eastern Culture*, 27.

King, R. (1999) *Orientalism and Religion: Postcolonial Theory, India and the 'Mystic East'*, London: Routledge.

Kircher, A. (1667) *China Illustrata*, Amsterdam: Jansson.

Kirkland, R. (1992) 'Person and Culture in the Taoist Tradition', *Journal of Chinese Religions*, 20.

—— (1997a) 'The Historical Contours of Taoism in China: Thoughts on Issues of Classification and Terminology', *Journal of Chinese Religions*, 25.

—— (1997b) 'Varieties of Taoism: A Preliminary Comparison of Themes in the *Nei Yeh* and other Taoist Classics', *Taoist Resources* 7(2).

Kjellberg, P. (1993) 'The Butterfly as Companion', *Philosophy East and West*, 43(1).

—— (1996) 'Sextus Empiricus, Zhuangzi, and Xunzi on 'Why be Skeptical?'', in Kjellberg and Ivanhoe (1996).

Kjellberg, P. and Ivanhoe, P.J. (eds) (1996) *Essays on Skepticism, Relativism, and Ethics in the Zhuangzi*, Albany, NY: State University of New York Press.

Kleeman, T. (1991) 'Taoist Ethics', in Carman and Juegensmayer (1991).

—— (1994) *A God's Own Tale: The 'Book of Transformations' of Wenchang, the Divine Lord of Zitong*, Albany, NY: State University of New York Press.

Kleinjaus, E. (1990) 'The Tao of Women and Men: Chinese Philosophy and the Women's Movement', *Journal of Chinese Philosophy*, 17(1).

Koestler, A. (1960) *The Lotus and the Robot*, London: Hutchinson.

Kögler, H.H. (1996) *The Power of Dialogue: Critical Hermeneutics after Gadamer and Foucault*, Cambridge, MA: MIT Press.

Kohn, L. (1987) *Seven Steps to the Tao: Sima Chengzhan's 'Zuowanglun'*, Nettetal: Steyler Verlag.

—— (ed.) (1989) *Taoist Meditation and Longevity Techniques*, Ann Arbor, MI: University of Michigan Press.

—— (1991a) *Taoist Mystical Philosophy: The Scripture of Western Ascension*, Albany, NY: State University of New York Press.

—— (1991b) 'Taoist Visions of the Body', *Journal of Chinese Philosophy*, 18(2).

—— (1992) *Early Chinese Mysticism: Philosophy and Soteriology in the Taoist Tradition*, Princeton, NJ: Princeton University Press.

—— (ed.) (1993) *The Taoist Experience: An Anthology*, Albany, NY: State University of New York Press.

—— (1995) *Laughing at the Tao: Debates amongst Buddhists and Taoists in Ancient China*, Princeton, NJ: Princeton University Press.

—— (1996) Review of *Dokyo Bunka E No Tembo* (New Perspectives on Chinese Culture), Tokyo 1994, *Journal of Chinese Religions*, 24.

—— (1998) 'The *Tao-te-ching* in Ritual', in Kohn and LaFargue (1998).

Kohn, L. and LaFargue, M. (eds) (1998) *Lao-tzu and Tao-te-ching*, Albany, NY: State University of New York Press.

Kraft, J. (ed.) (1981) *The Works of Witter Bynner*, New York: Farrar, Straus, Giroux.

Kroll, J.L. (1987) 'Disputation in Ancient Chinese Culture', *Early China*, 11–12.

Kroll, P.W. (1996) 'Body Gods and Inner Vision: The Scripture of the Yellow Court', in Lopez (1996).

Küng, H. and Ching, J. (1989) *Christianity and Chinese Religions*, New York: Doubleday.

Kuo You-yuh (1996) 'Taoist Psychology of Creativity', *Journal of Creative Behaviour*, 30(3).

Kupperman, J. (1989) 'Not so Many Words: Chuang Tzu's Strategies of Communication', *Philosophy East and West*, 39(3).

—— (1996) 'Spontaneity and Education of the Emotions in the *Zhuangzi*', in Kjellberg and Ivanhoe (1996).

LaFargue, M. (1992) *The Tao of the Tao Te Ching: Translation and Commentary*, Albany, NY: State University of New York Press.

—— (1994) *Tao and Method: A Reasoned Approach to the Tao-te-ching*, Albany, NY: State University of New York Press.

—— (1998) 'Recovering the *Tao-te-ching*'s Orginal Meaning: Some Remarks on Historical Hermeneutics', in Kohn and LaFargue (1998).

LaFargue, M. and Pas, J. (1998) 'On Translating the *Tao-te-ching*', in Kohn and LaFargue (1998).

Lagerwey, J. (1987) *Taoist Ritual in Chinese Society and History*, New York: Macmillan.

Lahar, R. (1996) 'Philosophical Counselling and Taoism', *Journal of Chinese Philosophy*, 23(3).

Lalvani, S. (1995) 'Consuming the Exotic Other', *Critical Studies in Mass Communication*, 12(3).

Langlois, J.D. and Sun K'o-Kuan (1983) 'Three Teachings Syncretism of the Thought of Ming T'ai-tsu', *Harvard Journal of Asiatic Studies*, 43(1).

Lao Sze-kwang (Lao Yung-wei) (1989) 'Understanding Chinese Philosophy: An Inquiry and a Proposal', in Allinson (1989b).

Larson, G.J. (1987) '"Conceptual Resources" in South Asia for "Environmental Ethics", or The Fly is still Alive and Well and in the Bottle', *Philosophy East and West*, 37(2).

Larson, G.J. and Deutsch (eds) (1988) *Interpreting Across Boundaries: New Essays in Comparative Philosophy*, Princeton, NJ: Princeton University Press.

Lau, D.C. (trans.) (1963) *Lao Tzu: Tao Te Ching*, Harmondsworth: Penguin.

Le Blanc, C. (1985) *Huai-nantzu: Philosophical Synthesis in Early Han Thought*, Hong Kong: Hong Kong University Press.

—— (1985–6) 'A Re-Examination of the Myth of Huang-ti', *Journal of Chinese Religions*, 13–14.

Le Blanc, C. and Blader, S. (eds) (1987) *Chinese Ideas about Nature and Society: Studies in Honour of Derk Bodde*, Hong Kong: Hong Kong University Press.

Lee, Kwang-sae (1996) 'Rorty and Chuang Tzu: Anti-Representationalism', *Journal of Chinese Philosophy*, 23(2).

Lee, P.K.H. (ed.) (1991) *Contemporary Confucian-Christian Encounters in Historical and Contemporary Perspective*, Hewiston: Edwin Mellen.

Legge, J. (1881) *The Religions of China*, New York: Charles Scribner's Sons.

—— (1883) 'The Tao Teh King', *British Quarterly Review*, 78.

—— (trans) (1891) *Sacred Books of the East: The Texts of Taoism*, 2 vols, Oxford: Clarendon Press.

le Gobien, C. (1698) *Histoire de l'édit de l'Empereur de la Chine en faveur de la Religion Chrestienne*, Paris: Anisson.

Leites, E. (1968) ' Confucianism in Eighteenth Century England: Natural Morality and Social Reform', *Philosophy East and West*, 18(2).

Lenk, H and Paul, G. (eds) (1993) *Epistemological Issues in Classical Chinese Philosophy*, Albany, NY: State University of New York Press.

Levering, M. (1984) 'Reading Chuang-Tzu: One Way or Many?', *Religious Studies Review*, 10(3).

Leys, S. (1983) *The Burning Forest: Essays on Chinese Culture and Politics*, New York: Holt, Rinehart & Winston.

Li Yangzheng (1994) 'Daoism versus Buddhism in China', *Social Sciences in China*, 15(4).

Li Yuhang (1994) 'Taoism', *Chinese Sociology and Anthropology*, 26(3).

Lin Tongqi, Rosemont, H. and Ames, R.T. (1995) 'Chinese Philosophy: A Philosophical Essay on the "State of the Art"', *The Journal of Asian Studies*, 54(3).

Lin Yutang (1938) *The Importance of Living*, London: Heinemann.

—— (1939) *My Country and My People*, London: Heinemann.

—— (ed. and trans.) (1963) *The Wisdom of China*, London: Four Square.

Ling, T. (1968) *A History of Religion East and West*, London: Macmillan.

Liu, Da (1979) *The Tao in Chinese Culture*, New York: Schocken.

Liu, Ming-wood (1982) 'The Harmonious Universe of Fa-tsang and Leibniz: A Comparative Study', *Philosophy East and West*, 32(1).

Liu Xiaogan (1993) 'Taoism', in Sharma (1993).

—— (1994) *Classifying the Zhuangzi Chapters*, Ann Arbor, MI: University of Michigan Press.

Lohman, J. (1965) *Philosophie und Sprachwissenschaft*, Berlin: Duncker & Humboldt.

Lopez, D.S. (ed.) (1995) *Curators of the Buddha: The Study of Buddhism under Colonialism*, Chicago: University of Chicago Press.

—— (ed.) (1996) *Religions of China in Practice*, Princeton, NJ: Princeton University Press.

Lovejoy, A.O. (1948) *Essays in the History of Ideas*, Baltimore, MD: Johns Hopkins University Press.

Loy, D. (1987) 'On the Meaning of the *I Ching*', *Journal of Chinese Philosophy*, 14(1).

—— (1996) 'Zhuangzi and Nagarjuna on the Truth of No Truth', in Kjellberg and Ivanhoe (1996).

Lu Kuan Yu (1964) *The Secrets of Chinese Meditation*, New York: Weiser.

Luk, B. H-K. (ed.) (1992) *Contacts between Cultures* Vol. 4, Lewiston, NY: Edwin Mellen.

MacIntyre, A. (1981) *After Virtue: A Study in Moral Theory*, London: Duckworth.

—— (1988) *Whose Justice? Which Rationality?*, Notre Dame: University of Notre Dame Press.

—— (1991) 'Incommensurability, Truth, and the Conversation between Confucians and Aristotelians about the Virtues', in Deutsch (1991).

MacKenzie, J.M. (1995) *Orientalism: History, Theory and the Arts*, Manchester: Manchester University Press.

Mackerras, C. (1989) *Western Images of China*, Oxford: Oxford University Press.

Mair, V.H. (ed.) (1983a) *Experimental Essays on Chuang-tzu*, Honolulu, HA: University of Hawaii Press.

—— (1983b) 'Wandering in and through the Chuang-tzu', *Journal of Chinese Religions*, 11.

—— (trans.) (1990) *The Tao Te Ching: The Classic Book of Integrity and the Way*, New York: Bantam.

Mann, S. (1997) *Precious Records: Women in China's Long Eighteenth Century*, Stanford, CA: Stanford University Press.

Maritain, J. (1955) *Creative Intuition in Art and Poetry*, New York: The World Publishing Company.

Marshall, P. (1992a) *Demanding the Impossible: A History of Anarchism*, London: HarperCollins.

—— (1992b) *Nature's Web: An Exploration of Ecological Thinking*, London: Simon & Schuster.

—— (1998) *Riding the Wind: A New Philosophy for a New Era*, London: Cassell.

Maspero, H. (1965[1927]) *La Chine antique*, Paris: Presses Universitaires de France.

—— (1937) 'Les Procédés de "nourir le principe vital" dans la religion taoiste ancienne', *Journal Asiatique*, 228.

—— (1971[1950]) *Le Taoïsme et les religions chinoises*, Paris: Musée Guimet.

—— (1981) *Taoism and Chinese Religion* (trans. of Maspero 1971), Amherst: University of Massachusetts Press.

Mather, R.B. (1969–70) 'The Controversy over Conformity and Naturalness during the Six Dynasties', *History of Religions*, 9(2).

May, R. (1996) *Heidegger's Hidden Sources: Asian Influences on his Work*, translated with a complementary essay by Graham Parkes, London: Routledge.

Mehta, J.L. (1990) *Philosophy and Religion: Essays in Interpretation*, New Delhi: M. Manoharlal.

Merton, T. (1961) *Mystics and Zen Masters*, New York: Delta.

—— (1965) *The Way of Chuang Tzu*, London: Burns & Oates.

Miura, K. (1989) 'The Revival of *Qi*: Qigong in Contemporary China', in Kohn (1989).

Mollier, C. (1990) *Une apocalypse taoïste du Ve siècle*, Paris: Mémoires de l'Institut des Hautes Études Chinoises.

Moore, C.A. (ed.) (1951) *Essays in East-West Philosophy*, Honolulu, HA: University of Hawaii Press.

—— (ed.) (1968) *The Chinese Mind: Essentials of Chinese Philosophy and Culture*, Honolulu, HA: University of Hawaii Press.

Moore, N. and Lower, L. (eds) (1992) *Translation East and West: A Cross-Cultural Approach*, Honolulu, HA: University of Hawaii Press.

Morgan, E. (trans.) (1933) *Tao the Great Luminant: Essays from Huai Nan Tzu*, London: Kegan Paul, Trench, Trübner & Co.

Mouffe, C. (1996) *Pragmatism and Deconstruction*, London: Routledge.

Mungello, D.E. (1977) *Leibniz and Confucianism: The Search for Accord*, Honolulu, HA: The University of Hawaii Press.

—— (1989) *Curious Land: Jesuit Accommodations and the Origins of Sinology*, Honolulu, HA: University of Hawaii Press.

Munro, D.J. (ed.) (1985) *Individualism and Holism: Studies in Confucian and Taoist Values*, Ann Arbor, MI: Centre for Chinese Studies, University of Michigan.

Muramatsu, Y. (1960) 'Some Themes in Chinese Rebel Ideologies', in Wright (1960a).

Nakamura, H. (1964) *Ways of Thinking of Eastern Peoples*, Honolulu, HA: University of Hawaii Press.

Nakayama, S. and Sivin, N. (1973) *Chinese Science: Explorations of an Ancient Tradition*, Cambridge, MA: MIT Press.

Nash, F. (1967) *Wilderness and the American Ideal*, New Haven, CT: Yale University Press.

Needham, J. (1954) *Science and Civilisation in China*, Vol. 1, Cambridge: Cambridge University Press.

—— (1956) *Science and Civilisation in China*, Vol. 2, Cambridge: Cambridge University Press.

—— (1969) *The Grand Titration: Science and Society in East and West*, London: George Allen & Unwin.

—— (1974) *Science and Civilisation in China*, Vol. 5, Part 2, Cambridge: Cambridge University Press.

—— (1976) *Science and Civilisation in China*, Vol. 5, Part 3, Cambridge: Cambridge University Press.

—— (1979) *Three Masks of Tao: A Chinese Corrective for Maleness, Monarchy, and Militarism in Theology*, London: The Teilhard Centre for the Future of Man.

—— (1983) *Science and Civilisation in China*, Vol. 5, Part 5, Cambridge: Cambridge University Press.

Nelson, B. (1974) 'Sciences and Civilizations, East and West: Joseph Needham and Max Weber', *Boston Studies in Philosophy and Science*, 11(4).

Neville, R.C. (1989) 'The Chinese Case in a Philosophy of World Religions', in Allinson (1989b).

Nickerson, P. (1996) 'Abridged Codes of Master Lu for the Daoist Community', in Lopez (1996).

Nietzsche, F. (1956) *A Genealogy of Morals*, Harmondsworth: Penguin.

—— (1968) *Twilight of the Idols*, Harmondsworth: Penguin.

—— (1974) *The Gay Science*, New York: Vintage.

Nivison, D.S. (1991) 'Hsün Tzu and Chuang Tzu', in Rosemont (1991).

Norden, B.W. van (1990) Review of Allinson (1989a), *The Journal of Asian Studies*, 49(2).

—— (1996a) 'Competing Interpretations of the Inner Chapters of the *Zhuangzi*', *Philosophy East and West*, 46(2).

—— (1996b) 'What Should Western Philosophy Learn from Chinese Philosophy?', in Ivanhoe (1996a).

Northrop, F.S.C. (1946) *The Meeting of East and West: An Inquiry concerning Human Understanding*, New York: Macmillan.

Nuyen, A.T. (1995) 'Naming the Unnamable: The Being of the *Tao*', *Journal of Chinese Philosophy*, 22(4).

Nylan, M. and Sivin, N. (1987) 'The First Neo-Confucians: An Introduction to Yang Hsiung's "Canon of Supreme Mystery"', in Le Blanc and Blader (1987).

Ōfuchi, N. (1979) 'The Formation of the Taoist Canon', in Welch and Seidel (1979).

Olds, L. (1991) 'Chinese Metaphors of Interrelatedness: Re-Imaging Body, Nature, and the Feminine', *Contemporary Philosophy*, 13(8).

Oldstone-Moore, J. (1998) 'Alchemy and *Journey to the West*: The Cart-Slow Kingdom Episode', *Journal of Chinese Religions*, 26.

Osborne, H. (1968) *Aesthetics and Art Theory: An Historical Introduction*, London: Longmans.

Olson, C. (ed.) (1985) *The Book of the Goddess, Past and Present*, New York: Crossroad.

Owens, W.D. (1990) 'Radical Concrete Particularity: Heidegger, Lao Tzu, and Chuang Tzu', *Journal of Chinese Philosophy*, 17(2).

—— (1993) 'Tao and Différance: The Existential Implications', *Journal of Chinese Philosophy*, 20(3).

—— (1997) *A Select Bibliography of Taoism*, Saskatoon, Sask.: China Pavilion.

Palmer, M. (1991) *The Elements of Taoism*, Shaftesbury: Element Books.

—— (1996) *Travels Through Sacred China*, London: Thorsons.

Paper, J. (1995) *The Spirits are Drunk: Comparative Approaches to Chinese Religion*, Albany, NY: State University of New York Press.

Parker, E. (1905) *China and Religion*, London: John Murray.

Parker, J.D. (1997) 'Attaining Landscapes in the Mind', *Monumenta Nipponica*, 52(2).

Parkes, G. (1983) 'The Wandering Dance: Chuang Tzu and Zarathustra', *Philosophy East and West*, 33(3).

—— (ed.) (1987) *Heidegger and Asian Thought*, Honolulu, HA: University of Hawaii Press.

—— (1989) 'Human/Nature in Nietzsche and Taoism', in Callicott and Ames (1989).

—— (ed.) (1991) *Nietzsche and Asian Thought*, Chicago: University of Chicago Press.

Pas, J.F. (ed.) (1989) *The Turning of the Tide: Religion in China Today*, Hong Kong: University of Hong Kong Press.

—— (1998) *Historical Dictionary of Taoism*, Lanham, MD: Scarecrow.

Paul, D. (1985) 'Kuanyin: Savior and Savioress in Chinese Pure Land Buddhism', in Olson (1985).

Peerenboom, R.P. (1990a) 'Cosmogony, the Taoist Way', *Journal of Chinese Philosophy*, 17(2).

—— (1990b) 'Natural Law in the *Huang-Lao Boshu*', *Philosophy East and West*, 40(3).

—— (1991) 'Beyond Naturalism: A Reconstruction of Daoist Environmental Ethics', *Environmental Ethics*, 13(1).

—— (1993) *Law and Morality in Ancient China: The Silk Manuscripts of Huang-Lao*, Albany, NY: State University of New York Press.

Pennick, N. (1979) *The Ancient Science of Geomancy*, London: Thames & Hudson.

Peterson, W.J. (1982) 'Making Connections: 'Commentary on the Attached Verbalizations' of the *Book of Change*', *Harvard Journal of Asiatic Studies*, 42(1).

—— (1988) 'Some Connective Concepts in China in the Fourth to Second Centuries B.C.E.', *Eranos Jahrbuch*, 57.

Plaks, A.H. (1987) *The Four Masterworks of the Ming Novel*, Cambridge, MA: Harvard University Press.

Plumwood, V. (1993) *Feminism and the Mastery of Nature*, London: Routledge.

Pöggeler, O. (1987) 'West-East Dialogue: Heidegger and Lao-tzu', in Parkes (1987).

Porkert, M., with Ullmann, C. (1990) *Chinese Medicine*, New York: Henry Holt.

Prakash, G. (1995) 'Orientalism Now', *History and Theory*, 34(3).

Prigogine, I. and Stengers, I. (1984) *Order out of Chaos*, New York: Bantam.

Rand, C.C. (1983) 'Chuang Tzu: Text and Substance', *Journal of Chinese Religions*, 11.

Raphals, L. (1992) *Knowing Words: Wisdom and Cunning in the Classical Traditions of China and Greece*, Ithaca, NY: Cornell University Press.

—— (1996) 'Skeptical Strategies in the *Zhuangzi* and *Theaetetus*', in Kjellberg and Ivanhoe (1996).

Rawlinson, A. (1997) *The Book of Enlightened Masters: Western Teachers of Eastern Traditions*, Chicago: Open Court.

Rawson, P. and Legeza, L. (1973) *Tao: The Eastern Philosophy of Time and Change*, New York: Avon.

Reichwein, A. (1925) *China and Europe: Intellectual and Artistic Contacts in the Eighteenth Century*, London: Kegan Paul, Trench, Trübner & Co.

BIBLIOGRAPHY

Reid, D. (1989) *The Tao of Health, Sex, and Longevity: A Modern Practical Approach to the Ancient Way*, London: Simon & Schuster.

—— (1998) *Harnessing the Power of the Universe*, London: Simon & Schuster.

Riencourt, A. de (1965) *The Soul of China: An Interpretation of Chinese History*, New York: Harper & Row.

Ritsema, R. and Karcher, S. (trans.) (1994) *I Ching: The Classic Chinese Oracle of Change* (with concordance), Shaftesbury: Element.

Robertson, R. (1992) *Globalization: Social Theory and Global Culture*, London: Sage.

Robinet, I. (1977) *Les commentaires du Tao Te King jusqu'au VIIe siècle*, Paris: Institut des Hautes Études Chinoises.

—— (1989) 'Original Contributions of *Neidan* to Taoism and Chinese Thought', in Kohn (1989).

—— (1991) *Histoire du Taoisme des origines au XIVe siècle*, Paris: Cerf.

—— (1993) *Taoist Meditation: The Mao-shan Tradition of Great Purity*, Albany, NY: State University of New York Press.

—— (1994) 'Primus movens et création récurrente', *Taoist Researches*, 5(2).

—— (1995) *Introduction à l'alchimie intérieure taoïste de l'unité et de la multiplicité*, Paris: Cerf.

—— (1997) *Taoism: Growth of a Religion*, Stanford, CA: University of Stanford Press, a translation and adaptation by Phyllis Brooks of Robinet (1991).

—— (1998) 'Later Commentaries: Textual Polysemy and Syncretistic Interpretations', in Kohn and LaFargue (1998).

Roetz, H. (1993) *Confucian Ethics of the Axial Age: A Reconstruction under the Aspect of the Breakthrough Toward Postconventional Thinking*, Albany, NY: State University of New York Press.

Rolston, H., III (1979) 'Can and Ought we to Follow Nature', *Environmental Ethics*, 1(1).

—— (1987) 'Can the East Help the West to Value Nature', *Philosophy East and West*, 37(2).

Ronan, C.E. and Oh, B.B. (eds) (1988) *East Meets West: The Jesuits in China (1582–1773)*, Chicago: Loyola University Press.

Ropp, P.S. (ed.) (1990) *Heritage of China: Contemporary Perspectives on Chinese Civilization*, Berkeley, CA: University of California Press.

Rorty, R. (1980) *Philosophy and the Mirror of Nature*, Oxford: Blackwell.

Rosemont, H. (ed.) (1991) *Chinese Texts and Philosophical Contexts: Essays Dedicated to Angus Graham*, La Salle, IL: Open Court.

—— (1996) 'Beyond Post-Modernism', in Ivanhoe (1996a).

Roth, H.D. (1991a) 'Psychology and Self-Cultivation in Early Taoist Thought', *Harvard Journal of Asiatic Studies*, 51(2).

—— (1991b) 'Who Compiled the *Chuang Tzu*?', in Rosemont (1991).

—— (1997) 'Evidence for Stages of Meditation in Early Taoism', *Bulletin of the School of Oriental and African Studies*, 60(2).

Rousselle, E. (1962) *Zur Seelischen Führung im Taoismus*, Darmstadt: Wissenschaftliche Buchgesellschaft.

Russell, B. (1953) *Mysticism and Logic*, London: Penguin.

Said, E. (1985) *Orientalism*, Harmondsworth: Penguin.

—— (1989) 'Representing the Colonized: Anthropology's Interlocutors', *Critical Inquiry*, 15(2).

Sangren, P.S. (1983) 'Female Gender in Chinese Religious Symbols: Kuan Yin, Ma Tsu, and the 'Eternal Mother'', *Signs*, 9.

Sardar, Z. (1998) *Postmodernism and the Other: The New Imperialism of Western Culture*, London: Pluto.

Saso, M. (1978) *The Teachings of Master Chuang*, New Haven, CT: Yale University Press.

—— (1983) 'The *Chuang-tzu nei-p'ien*', in Mair (1983a).

—— (1990) *Taoism and the Rite of Cosmic Renewal*, Pullman, WA: Washington State University Press.

—— (1995) *The Golden Pavilion: Taoist Ways to Peace, Healing, and Long Life*, Boston: Tuttle.

Saso, M. and Chappell, D.W. (eds) (1977) *Buddhist and Taoist Studies I*, Honolulu, HA: University of Hawaii Press.

Scerri, E.R. (1989) 'Eastern Mysticism and the Alleged Parallels with Physics', *American Journal of Physics*, 57(8).

Schafer, E.H. (1961) *Tu Wan's Stone Catalogue of Cloudy Forest*, Berkeley, CA: University of California Press.

—— (1973) *The Divine Woman, Dragon Ladies, and Rain Maidens*, Berkeley, CA: University of California Press.

—— (1989) *Mao Shan in T'ang Times*, Boulder, CO: Society for the Study of Chinese Religions.

Scharfstein, B.-A., Alon, I. Biderman, S., Daor, D. and Hoffmann, Y. (1978) *Philosophy East/Philosophy West: A Critical Comparison of Indian, Chinese, Islamic, and European Philosophy*, Oxford: Blackwell.

Schipper, K. (1975) *Concordance du Tao Tsang: Titres des ouvrages*, Paris: Publications de l'École Française d'Extrême-Orient.

—— (1993) *The Taoist Body*, Berkeley, CA: University of California Press.

—— (1995) 'The Inner World of the *Lao-Tzu Chung-Ching*', in Huang and Zürcher (1995).

Schneewind, J. (1990) 'The Misfortunes of Virtue', *Ethics*, 101(1).

Schwartz, B.I. (1985) *The World of Thought in Ancient China*, Cambridge, MA: Harvard University Press.

Schwitzgebel, E. (1996) 'Zhuangzi's Attitude toward Language and his Skepticism', in Kjellberg and Ivanhoe (1996).

Seager, R.H. (ed.) (1995) *The World's Parliament of Religions: The East/West Encounter, Chicago, 1893*, Bloomington, IN: Indiana University Press.

Seidel, A.K. (1969a) *La divinisation de Lao-tseu sous le Han*, Paris: École Française d'Extrême-Orient.

—— (1969b) 'The Image of the Perfect Ruler in Early Taoist Messianism: Lao-tzu and Li-hung', *History of Religions*, 9(2).

—— (1978) 'Taoism', *Encyclopaedia Britannica*, Vol. 17, 15th Edition, Chicago: Encyclopaedia Britannica Inc.

—— (1989–90) 'Chronicle of Taoist Studies in the West 1950–1990', *Cahier d'Extrême Asie*, 5.

—— (1990) *Taoismus: Die inoffizielle Hochreligion Chinas*, Tokyo: Deutsche Gesellschaft für Natur- und Völkerkunde Ostasiens.

Sharma, A. (ed.) (1993) *Our Religions*, San Francisco: HarperCollins.

Shaughnessy, E. (trans) (1996) *I Ching: The Classic of Changes*, New York: Ballantine.

Shaw, M. (1988) 'Buddhist and Taoist Influences on Chinese Landscape Painting', *Journal of the History of Ideas*, 49(2).

Shchutskii, I.K. (1979) *Researches on the I Ching*, Princeton, NJ: Princeton University Press.

Shu Yunzhong (1987) 'Gary Snyder and Taoism', *Tamkang Review*, 17(3).

Sirén, O. (1949) *China and the Gardens of Europe in the Eighteenth Century*, New York: Ronald Press.

Siu, R.G.H. (1957) *The Tao of Science: An Essay on Western Knowledge and Eastern Wisdom*, London: Chapman & Hall.

Sivin, N. (1968) *Chinese Alchemy: Preliminary Studies*, Cambridge, MA: Harvard University Press.

—— (1971) Review of Needham 1969, *Journal of Asian Philosophy*, 30(4).

—— (1978) 'On the Word "Taoist" as a Source of Perplexity, With Special Reference to the Relationship between Science and Religion', *History of Religions*, 17(3).

—— (1979) 'Report on the Third International Conference on Taoist Studies', *Bulletin of the Society for the Study of Chinese Religions*, 7.

—— (1990) 'Science and Medicine in Chinese History', in Ropp (1990).

—— (1995a) *Science in Ancient China: Researches and Reflections*, Aldershot: Valiorum.

—— (1995b) 'State, Cosmos, and Body in the Last Three Centuries B.C.', *Harvard Journal of Asian Studies*, 55(1).

Sloterdijk, P. (1989) *Eurotaoismus: Zur Kritik der politischen Kinetik*, Frankfurt: Suhrkamp Verlag.

Smil, V. (1977) *The Bad Earth: Environmental Degradation in China*, Armonk, NY: Sharpe.

Smith, H. (1991[1958]) *The World's Religions: Our Great Wisdom Traditions*, San Francisco: Harper & Row.

—— (1972) 'Tao Now: An Ecological Testament', in Barbour (1972).

Smith, K. (ed.) (1991) *Chuang-tzu: Rationality: Interpretation*, Brunswick, NJ: Breckinridge Public Affairs Center.

Smullyan, R. (1977) *The Tao is Silent*, New York: HarperCollins.

Soothill, W.E. (1913) *The Three Religions of China*, London: Hodder & Stoughton.

Spence, J.D. (1990) 'Western Perceptions of China from the late Sixteenth Century to the Present', in Ropp (1990).

—— (1998) *The Chan's Great Continent: China in Western Minds*, New York: Norton.

Stambaugh, J. (1987) 'Heidegger, Taoism, and the Question of Metaphysics', in Parkes (1987).

Stein, R.A. (1942) 'Jardins en miniature de l'Extrême-Orient: Le Monde en Petit', *Bulletin de l'École Française d'Extrême-Orient*, 42(1).

—— (1979) 'Religious Taoism and Popular Religion from the Second to the Seventh Centuries', in Welch and Seidel (1979).

—— (1990) *The World in Miniature: Container Gardens and Dwellings in Far Eastern Religious Thought*, Stanford, CA: Stanford University Press.

Strauss, V.F. von (1870) *Laò-Tsè's Taò Te King*, Leipzig: Fleischer.

Strickmann, M. (1978) 'Taoism, History of', *Encyclopaedia Britannica*, Vol. 17, 15th Edition, Chicago: Encyclopaedia Britannica Inc.

—— (1979) 'On the Alchemy of the T'ao Hung-ching', in Welch and Seidel (1979).

—— (1980) 'History, Anthropology, and Chinese Religions', review article on Saso (1978), *Harvard Journal of Asiatic Studies*, 40(1).

—— (1981) *Le taoïsme du Mao Shan, chronique d'une révélation*, Paris: Collège de France.

—— (1994) 'Saintly Fools and Chinese Masters', *Asia Major*, 7(1).

Sullivan, M. (1979) *Symbols of Eternity: The Art of Landscape Painting in China*, Oxford: Clarendon Press.

—— (1989) *The Meeting of Eastern and Western Art*, Berkeley, CA: University of California Press.

—— (1990) 'Chinese Art and its Impact on the West', in Ropp (1990).

Swidler, L., Cobb, J.B., Knitter, P.F. and Hellwig, M.K. (1990) *Death or Dialogue: From the Age of Monologue to the Age of Dialogue*, London: SCM.

Sylvan, R. and Bennett, D. (1988) 'Taoism and Deep Ecology', *The Ecologist*, 18 (4–5).

Sze, Mai-mai (1959) *The Way of Chinese Painting: Its Ideas and Technique*, New York: Random House.

Tang, P.C.L. and Schwartz, R.D. (1988) 'The Limits of Language: Wittgenstein's *Tractatus Logico Philosophicus* and Lao Tzu's *Tao Te Ching*', *Journal of Chinese Philosophy*, 15(1).

Tang Yijie (1991) 'Transcendence and Immanence in Confucian Philosophy', in Lee (1991).

Taylor, C. (1989) *Sources of the Self: The Making of Modern Identity*, Cambridge: Cambridge University Press.

—— (1992) *The Ethics of Authenticity*, London: Harvard University Press.

Taylor, R.L. (1997) 'Chu Hsi and Meditation', in Bloom and Fogel (1997).

Teiser, S.F. (1996) 'The Spirits of Chinese Philosophy', in Lopez (1996).

Thompson, K.O. (1990) 'Taoist Cultural Reality: The Harmony of Aesthetic Order', *Journal of Chinese Philosophy*, 17(2).

Thompson, L.G. (1985) *Chinese Religions in Western Languages: A Comprehensive and Classified Bibiliography of Publications in English, French, and German through 1980*, Tucson, AZ: University of Arizona Press.

—— (1993) 'What is Taoism? (With Apologies to H.G. Creel)' *Taoist Resources*, 4(2).

Tominaga, T.T. (1982) 'Taoist and Wittgensteinian Mysticism', *Journal of Chinese Philosophy*, 9(3).

—— (1983) 'Ch'an, Taoism and Wittgenstein', *Journal of Chinese Philosophy*, 10(1).

—— (1994) 'Possibility of a Taoist-Like Wittgensteinian Environmental Ethics', *Journal of Chinese Philosophy*, 21(2).

Towler, S. (1996) *A Gathering of Cranes: Bringing the Tao to the West*, Eugene, OR: The Abode of the Eternal Tao.

Tu Wei-ming (1985) *Confucian Thought: Selfhood as Creative Transformation*, Albany, NY: State University of New York Press.

Tuan, Yi-fu (1968) 'Discrepancies between Environmental Attitude and Behaviour: Examples from Europe and China', *The Canadian Geographer*, 12(2).

Tucker M.E. and Grim, J.A. (eds) (1994) *Worldviews and Ecology: Religion, Philosophy, and the Environment*, Maryknoll, NY: Orbis.

Turner, B.S. (1994) *Orientalism, Postmodernism and Globalism*, London: Routledge.

Turner, K. (1990) 'Sage Kings and Laws in Chinese and Greek Traditions', in Ropp (1990).

Ular, A. (trans) (1902) *Le livre de la voie et la ligne-droite de Lao-Tsé*, Paris: Éditions de la Review Blanche.

Unschild, P.U. (1985) *Medicine in China: A History of Ideas*, Berkeley, CA: University of California Press.

Vandermeersch, S. (1965) *La formation du Légisme*, Paris: Publication de l'EFEO.

Verellen, F. (1995) 'Taoism', *Journal of Asian Studies* 54(2).

Vervoon, A. (1981) 'Taoism, Legalism, and the Quest for Order in Warring States China', *Journal of Chinese Philosophy* 8(3).

Waldrop, M. (1993) *Complexity: The Emerging Science at the Edge of Order and Chaos*, London: Viking.

Waley, A. (1977[1934]) *The Way and its Power: The Tao Te Ching and its Place in Chinese Thought*, London: Unwin.

Waley-Cohen, J. (1999) *The Sextants of Beijing: Global Currents in Chinese History*, New York: Norton.

Walf, K. (1992) *Westliche Taoismus: Bibliographie*, Essen: Die Blaue Eule.

—— (1997) *Tao für den Westen: Weisheit, die uns nottut*, München: Kösel.

Walters, D. (1989) *Chinese Geomancy*, Shaftesbury: Element (excerpted from de Groot 1892–1910).

Wang Gungwu (1991) *The Chineseness of China*, Hong Kong: Oxford University Press.

Watkins, M. (1986) *Waking Dreams*, Dallas: Spring Publications.

Watson, B. (1968) *The Complete Works of Chuang Tzu*, New York: Columbia University Press.

Watts, A. (1957) *The Way of Zen*, Harmondsworth: Penguin.

—— (1973) *Psychotherapy East and West*, Harmondsworth: Penguin.

—— (1979) *Tao: The Watercourse Way*, London: Arkana.

Weber, M. (1951[1916]) *The Religion of China: Confucianism and Taoism*, New York: The Free Press.

Welch, H. (1957) *Taoism: The Parting of the Way*, Boston: Beacon Press.

—— (1969–70) 'The Bellagio Conference on Taoist Studies', *History of Religions*, 9(2).

Welch, H. and Seidel, A. (eds) (1979) *Facets of Taoism*, New Haven, CT: Yale University Press.

Whitehead, A.N. (1925) *Science and the Modern World*, Cambridge: Cambridge University Press.

—— (1978) *Process and Reality*, London: Collier Macmillan.

Wieger, L. (1976[1911]) *Taoism: The Philosophy of China*, Burbank, CA: Chara.

Wile, D. (1992) *Art of the Bedchamber: The Chinese Sexual Yoga Classics Including Women's Solo Meditation Texts*, Albany, NY: State University of New York Press.

Wilhelm, R. (trans.) (1921a) *Laotse: Tao Te King: das Buch des alten vom Sinn und Leben*, Jena: Diederichs.

—— (trans.) (1921b) *Liä Dsi; das Wahre Buch vom Quellenden Urgrund*, Jena: Diederichs.

—— (trans.) (1924) *'I Ging'; Das Buch der Wandlungen*, 2 vols, Jena: Diederichs; English trans. C.F. Baynes (1950), New York: Pantheon.

—— (trans.) (1989[1924]) *I Ching or Book of Changes*, foreword by C.G. Jung, London: Arkana.

—— (1931) *Confucius and Confucianism*, London: Kegan Paul, Trench, Trübner & Co.

Wilson, B. (ed.) (1970) *Rationality*, Oxford: Blackwell.

Winch, P. (1970) 'Understanding a Primitive Society', in Wilson (1970).

Wittgenstein, L. (1953) *Philosophical Investigations*, Oxford: Blackwell.

Wong, D. (1984) *Moral Relativity*, Berkeley, CA: University of California Press.

Wong, E. (trans.) (1992) *Cultivating Stillness: A Taoist Manual for Transforming Body and Mind*, Boston: Shambhala.

—— (trans.) (1995) *Lieh-tzu: A Taoist Guide to Practical Living*, Boston: Shambhala.

—— (1996) *Feng-Sui: The Ancient Wisdom of Harmonious Living for Modern Times*, Boston: Shambhala.

—— (trans.) (1997a) *Harmonizing Yin and Yang: The Dragon-Tiger Classic*, Boston: Shambhala.

—— (1997b) *The Shambhala Guide to Taoism*, Boston: Shambhala.

—— (trans.) (1998) *Cultivating the Energy of Life, by Liu Hua-Yang*, Boston: Shambhala.

Wong Kiew Kit (1996) *The Complete Book of Tai Chi Chuan: A Comprehensive Guide to the Principles and Practice*, Shaftesbury: Element.

Wright, A. (ed.) (1953) *Studies in Chinese Thought*, Chicago: Chicago University Press.

—— (ed.) (1960a) *The Confucian Persuasion*, Stanford, CA: Stanford University Press.

—— (1960b) 'The Study of Chinese Civilization', *Journal of the History of Ideas*, 21(3).

Wu Jung-nuan (trans) (1991) *Yi Jing*, Washington, DC: The Taoist Centre.

Wu Kuang-ming (1982) *Chuang Tzu: World Philosopher at Play*, New York: Scholars Press.

—— (1986) 'Dream in Nietzsche and Chuang Tzu', *Journal of Chinese Philosophy*, 13(4).

—— (1990) *The Butterfly as Companion: Meditations on the First Three Chapters of the Chuang Tzu*, Albany, NY: State University of New York Press.

—— (1993) 'On Reading the *Tao Te Ching*: Mair, LaFargue, Chan', *Philosophy East and West*, 43(4).

Wu Yi (1985) 'On Chinese Ch'an in Relation to Taoism', *Journal of Chinese Philosophy*, 12(2).

Yan Shoucheng (1994) 'The Parting of the Tao: On the Similarities and Differences between Early Confucianism and Early Taoism', *Journal of Chinese Philosophy*, 21(2).

Yang, C.K. (1961) *Religion in Chinese Society*, Berkeley, CA: University of California Press.

Yearley, L.H. (1980) 'Hsün Tzu on the Mind: His Attempted Synthesis of Confucianism and Taoism', *Journal of Asian Studies*, 39(3).
—— (1983) 'The Perfected Person in the Radical Chuang-tzu', in Mair (1983).
—— (1990) 'Recent Work on Virtue', *Religious Studies Review*, 16(1).
—— (1996) 'Zhuangzi's Understanding of Skillfulness and the Ultimate Spiritual State', in Kjellberg and Ivanhoe (1996).
Yeh, M. (1983) 'The Deconstructive Way: A Comparative Study of Derrida and Chuang Tzu', *Journal of Chinese Philosophy*, 10(2).
Young, J.D. (1983) *Confucianism and Christianity: The First Encounter*, Hong Kong: Hong Kong University Press.
Young, R. (1990) *White Mythologies: Writing History and the West*, London: Routledge.
Yu, A.C. (trans.) (1977) *The Journey to the West*, 4 vols, Chicago: University of Chicago Press.
Yu, D.C. (1981) 'The Creation Myth and its Symbolism in Classical Taoism', *Philosophy East and West*, 31(4).
Yü, Ying-shih (1985) 'Individualism and the Neo-Taoist Movement in Wei-Chin China', in Munro (1985).
Yukawa, H. (1983) 'The Happy Fish', in Mair (1983a).
Zarrow, P. (1990) *Anarchism in Chinese Political Culture*, New York: Columbia University Press.
Zhang Longxi (1985) 'The Tao and the Logos', *Critical Inquiry*, 11.
—— (1988) 'The Myth of the Other: China in the Eyes of the West', *Critical Inquiry*, 15.
—— (1992) *The Tao and the Logos: Literary Hermeneutics, East and West*, Durham, NC: Duke University Press.
—— (1998) *Mighty Opposites: From Dichotomies to Differences in the Comparative Study of China*, Stanford, CA: Stanford University Press.
Zimmerman, M. (1994) *Contesting the Earth's Future: Radical Ecology and Postmodernity*, Berkeley, CA: University of California Press.
Zürcher, E. (1980) 'Buddhist Influences on Early Taoism: a Survey of Scriptural Evidence', *T'oung Pao*, 46(1–3).

# NAME INDEX

Chisolm, L.W. 151
Chuang Tzu *see Zhuangzi*, the
Clark, J.P. 106, 107, 108
Clarke, J.J. 15, 61, 198
Claudel, P. 47
Cleary, T. 59, 122
Coleridge, S. 70, 73
Confucius xi, 167, 168
Cook, D. 60
Cooper, J.C. 95, 110, 150, 156, 211
Creel, H.G. 48, 59, 82, 119, 141, 179;
    moral explorations 94, 101, 107, 115;
    nature of Daoism 18, 19, 21
Critchley, S. 167, 208–9
Crowley, A. 54
Cua, A.S. 27, 94

Dallmayr, F. 14–15
Danto, A. 91, 150, 168, 204
Darwin, C. 64, 78
Dean, K. 36
Defoe, D. 97
Derrida, J. 171, 183, 185–6, 187, 188–9,
    191–2, 196
Descartes, R. 67, 71, 76, 98, 172, 181,
    183
Despeux, C. 138
Douglas, R.K. 44, 50, 148
Dubs, H.H. 166
Durant, W. 101
Durkheim, E. 69
Duyvendak, J.J.L. 53, 55, 113

Edkins, J. 45, 57
Einstein, A. 77, 78
Eitel, E. 83
Eliade, M. 49, 121
Emerson, R.W. 45, 54
Empedocles 71
Engels, F. 77
Eno, R. 94, 184
Erasmus, D. 192
Eskildsen, S. 124

Faber, E. 54, 61
Fang, T. 28
Fenollosa, E. 152, 167
Feuchtwang, S.D. 82
Fleming, J. 52
Flew, A. 167
Forke, A. 48, 74
Foucault, M. 6
Freud, S. 121

Friedman, M. 147
Friedrich, C.D. 152
Fung Yu-lan 19, 27, 48, 66, 86, 119, 148
Furrow, D. 96
Fuzai 150

Gadamer, H.-G. 10, 11, 14, 145–6, 163,
    198, 201
Galileo 76, 78
Gao, Jianping 155
Gare, A.E. 65, 79
Gellner, E. 91
Gernet, J. 23, 24, 28, 65, 167
Giles, H.A. 20, 55, 58
Giles, L. 46, 141
Gilligan, C. 96
Girardot, N.J. 2, 33, 44, 45, 55, 120,
    121, 122–3; moral explorations 99–
    100, 104, 109, 110, 111; natural
    philosophy of Daoism 64, 65, 66, 68
Glasenapp, H. von 41
Gobien, C. le 39
Goethe, J.W. von 73
Gómez, L.O. 128
Goodman, R.B. 84, 180, 183
Graham, A.C. 1, 12–13, 14, 52–3, 54,
    56, 58, 59, 201; moral explorations 92,
    94, 98, 101, 102, 104, 106, 107–8;
    natural philosophy of Daoism 66, 68,
    70, 72, 74–5, 79, 84, 86; nature of
    Daoism 16, 17, 18, 19, 25, 26, 27, 32;
    philosophical themes 177–8, 179, 182,
    185, 186, 187, 188–9
Granet, M. 3, 48, 55, 81, 167
Griffin, D.R. 65
Griffin, S. 112
Grigg, R. 196
Grim, J.A. 84, 112
Groot, J.J.M. de 43, 48, 50, 74, 82
Gross, R.M. 111
Gulik, R.H. van 113, 131, 132

Habermas, J. 26, 196
Halbfass, W. 42, 204
Hall, D.L. 4, 24, 28, 52, 201; moral
    explorations 99, 106, 110, 113, 116;
    natural philosophy of Daoism 64, 65,
    66, 80, 81; philosophical themes 172,
    186, 188, 190; transcendence 160, 161,
    162, 163, 164
Hansen, C. 4, 19, 57, 59, 103, 148–9;
    philosophical themes 166, 168–72,
    175, 179, 181, 182, 184, 193

261

# SUBJECT INDEX

grammar, Chinese 52, 168
Great Chain of Being 69–70
Great Peace *see Taiping*
Greeks/Greece 27, 63, 167, 171, 180,
    210; *see also* Ancient Greeks/
    Greece

Han dynasty 18, 24–5, 27, 31–3, 56, 58,
    60, 67, 69, 105; anarchism 110;
    immortality 119; inner cultivation
    124; landscape painting 155;
    mysticism 141
Hasidism 143
health 3, 18, 136–9, 195, 208
Heaven 118, 135
hermeneutics 9–12, 51, 52, 145, 172, 190,
    193, 201, 208
Hermetic tradition 63
Hinduism x, 3, 4, 7, 196, 200, 205, 208;
    inner cultivation 125; science 75;
    Western interpretations 43, 45, 46
historical origins of Daoism 28–36
'Holding to the One' 124
holism/holistic 65, 72–3, 76, 81, 207
*Huanglao* school 32
*hun-dun* (primal chaos) 66, 191

I–thou philosophy 143–5, 148
ideological factors 52
immortality 2, 16, 21, 30, 32, 34, 87,
    117–22, 131, 134, 157; *see also*
    longevity
imperialism 9
India 7, 41, 45, 147, 148, 194, 203
individualism 102
'Inner Chapters' 58
inner cultivation 122–8
'Inner Vision' (visualisation) 125–7
internal alchemy *see neidan*
irrationalism 175–84
Islam/Moslems 29, 117, 142

Japan 6, 8, 30, 48, 50, 198, 202, 203, 205
*jen* (benevolence) 93
Jesuit missionaries 23, 28, 67, 70, 198;
    landscape painting 158; mysticism
    140, 148; Western interpretations of
    Daoism 37–8, 39, 40, 44, 49, 51, 54,
    58, 60; women and gender 114
Jewish Kabbala 63
Jin dynasty 32
*jing* (sexual essence) 109, 119, 130, 131
Judaism 29, 100, 117, 128; mysticism

142, 143; sexuality 135; transcendence
    159, 164

*Kama Sutra* 129
Korea 6, 8, 202

landscape painting 58, 149–59
language 51–2, 166–75; Chinese 52, 167,
    171
*Lao-tzu see Laozi*, the
Lao-Zhuang tradition 35
*Laoism* 19, 56
*Laozi*, the 17, 45, 47, 53, 100, 104, 110,
    115, 166
laws of nature 81
Legalist school *see Fajia*
*li* 52, 91
*Liezi*, the 53–4, 118
logic/poetry 191
logocentrism 174, 185, 188–92
*Logos* (Reason) 64, 168
longevity 17, 18, 29, 32, 34, 39, 99, 117,
    119, 123, 128, 137; *see also*
    immortality

Mahayana 194
Malaysia 24
male/female 188
Manchus 105
Mandate of Heaven 105
Manichaean ideas 131
*Maoshan* (or *Shangqing*) school 34
Marxism 76, 108, 195
mechanist/materialist paradigm 73
mediaeval cosmology 69
mediaeval philosophy 63
meditation 123–4, 125
metal 31, 69
metaphors 189–90
Middle East 45
mind/body 187
Mohism 27, 179
monad theory 70
monasticism 34
Mongols 105
moral explorations 13, 90–116;
    anarchism 103–11; moral vision
    90–5; self-cultivation, ethics of
    95–103; women and gender
    111–16
Mother of the Bushell 114
mountain 154
mystical Daoism 17, 34, 50

267

SUBJECT INDEX

mysticism 2, 18, 140–9, 166, 168–9; landscape painting 149–59
'mysticism made visible' 149–50

Natural Law 160
natural philosophy in Daoism 63–89; chaos theory 63–8; cosmology 69–73; environmentalism 81–9; science 74–81
Nature 197
nature (*xing*) 119, 120
nature of Daoism 16–36; Confucianism and Buddhism 22–8; definition of Daoism 16–22; historical origins 28–36
Nature of Things 84–5
*neidan* (internal alchemy) 122–3, 128, 130, 131
*Neijing*, the 136
Neo-Confucianism 23, 24, 36, 40, 98
Neo-Daoism 27, 34–5, 98
Neo-Mohists 179
neopragmatism 172
New Age thinking 49, 76, 164, 195
new paradigm thinking 76
North America 204
not-doing *see wu-wei*
nothingness/emptiness (*wu*) 35

Objectivity 182
organic/organicism 70–1, 80–1
Other 11, 144, 186, 199, 201

pacifism 109
painting 149–59
Parmenidean One 168
particularists 141
perspectivists 178
*philosophia perennis see* philosophy, perennial
philosophical Daoism 19, 20, 28, 30, 35, 41, 48, 51, 52
philosophy 3–4, 10, 166–93; Chinese 41, 43, 166–75; histories 167; inter-cultural 5, 11, 13; linguistic 168, 170; natural 63–89; moral 92; perennial 40, 47, 55, 193, 195; postmodernism 184–93; scepticism, relativism 175–84
Pinyin system xi
Platonists 41
pluralism 27, 28
poetry 58
polarity 73

postmodernism 184–93, 195, 198, 199; deconstructive 193
Pre-Socratic philosophy 41
primal chaos (*hun-dun*) 61, 191
Protestantism 42, 44, 199
proto-Daoism 27
Pure Talk movement *see qingdan*
Puritanism 32, 42
purposive Daoism 18
Pyrrhonists 181, 182

*qi* (energy) 31, 51, 66, 75, 101, 119, 125, 137, 154
*qigong* (working the energy) 136, 137, 139, 204
Qin dynasty 118
*qingdan* (Pure Talk) 27, 35
Queen Mother of the West 114
quiet sitting 124

reading Daoism 50–62
reality/appearance 187
Reason 64, 160, 168, 201
Reichians 134
relativism 11, 175–84, 185, 197
religion 2–3, 37–49, 50, 52; Chinese 39, 42–3; comparative 4, 48; popular 26
religious Daoism 18, 19, 20, 21, 28, 30, 33, 34, 35, 43, 48, 51, 52; *see also Daojiao*
*ren* 51
Renaissance 63, 68, 69, 79
revelation 33
romantic myth 23, 25–6
Romanticism 41–2, 63, 97, 206; landscape painting 152–3, 156, 158, 159
*ru* (scholar-bureaucrat) 38
Russia 43

*Sacred Books of the East* 61
*san chiao* (three teachings) 23
scepticism 175–84
science 13, 17, 74–81
*Scripture of Salvation* 104
*Secret of the Golden Flower, The* 48, 121–2, 126, 127
sectarianism 33
Self 160
self-actualisation 96
self-cultivation 31, 199; ethics 95–103
self-massage 137

268